TYRANNY

THROUGH

PUBLIC EDUCATION

William F. Cox, Jr.

Allegiance Press

The Right Answers for America

Tyranny – Arbitrary or despotic exercise of power; the exercise of power over subjects and others with a rigor not authorized by law or justice, or not requisite for the purposes of government. (Webster's, 1828).

The Setting

Once upon a time in a far-off land, people were told by their leaders what and how to believe. They had no choice in the matter; but this was a good thing, they were told, not only for the welfare of the state, but also for their own temporal and eternal happiness.

Objections to this order simply were not tolerated. Physical oppression was the primary vehicle used by the ruling elite to extract submission and compliance. The extreme amount of pain and the loss of limb and life was of such magnitude to be hardly fathomable by the human mind. Even so, belief orthodoxy was never achieved because the mind can still be free although the body is shackled and broken.

With the opportunity to begin anew in a different land, those formerly oppressed now exuberantly promoted what they so long had been prohibited from practicing. This new orthodoxy interestingly was also good for the country as well as the citizens' own temporal and eternal happiness. Freshly mindful of being persecuted in the old country for objecting to the mandated beliefs, these new leaders, for the most part, eventually saw the error of similarly persecuting their detractors. So a great experiment was launched to reciprocate to others, for the first time ever, the liberty of belief they so fervently desired for themselves.

But since this precious new experiment was so right and so good for humanity, the leaders dared not blindly entrust it to the unenlightened general public. This time, now truly in possession of "real truth," the leaders felt an obligation to ensure that the newly granted liberty of the people was properly safeguarded. Even in granting this liberty they, by being able to grant it, still held the ultimate responsibility. So initially, parents were allowed to properly equip their children, but the leaders, hungry for control and believing that only they could do it correctly, reclaimed control of the educational process. Curriculum and teachers were certified, after being duly trained, and children were forced by law to submit to the government's education system.

And, oh, what truth these new leaders discovered! They found that the mind could be controlled directly rather than, as in the old country, by way of conquering the body. Soon, the people were so enamored with the allowed possibility by their leaders that the leaders knew best for them and their country, they willingly agreed to pay for this forced indoctrination process. The indoctrination process of the government was so efficient that the majority of recipient-taxpayers saw no problem with giving up their liberty and educating their own children to do the same. Objections to this indoctrination process and poor achievements were viewed as reasons for strengthening and extending the system, not for questioning it. Since the government had supposedly succeeded with the masses, even the recalcitrant could assumedly be made to think correctly if the government was just given even more control and more money. The indoctrination was so effective that even when revealed they were becoming more and more illiterate, citizens took little offense. The occurrence of illiteracy and loss of liberty (even when made obvious) was easily offset by confirmation of the high standard of living most people enjoyed and by the unwavering, fully indoctrinated belief that government control of education was essential to this country's success.

THE END (We hope not!!)

Opening Quotes

"So long as the State undertakes to force upon the children of any class of parents a system of education which they cannot accept without a violation of conscience and of Nature's laws, it is nothing less than the most cruel tyranny on the part of the State to make such a system compulsory" (Montgomery, 1889/1972, p. 55).

"But if a man is taxed to support a school, where religious doctrines are inculcated which he believes to be false, and which he believes that God condemns, then he is excluded from the school by the Divine law, at the same time he is compelled to support it by the human law. This is a double wrong. It is politically wrong, because, if such a man educates his children at all, he must educate them elsewhere, and thus pay two taxes... and it is religiously wrong, because he is constrained, by human power, to promote what he believes the Divine Power forbids. The principle involved in such a course is pregnant with all tyrannical consequences" (Horace Mann's Twelfth Annual Report, 1849).

"That to compel a man to furnish contributions of money for the propagation of opinions which he disbelieves *and abhors*, is sinful and tyrannical; that even the forcing him to support this or that teacher of his own religious persuasion, is depriving him of the comfortable liberty...." (Thomas Jefferson's Bill for Establishing Religious Freedom).

Example Injustices

1. Professor Paul Vitz's systematic examination in 1983, of ninety widely used public school texts and readers revealed that "[r]eligion, family values, and certain political and economic positions have been systematically omitted from these books.... In a total of 670 stories from grades three through six readers not one reference to representative Protestant religious life was found.... Aggressive feminist themes were prominent in many of the texts. None of the social studies books on modern American social life mentioned the words 'marriage,' 'wedding,' 'husband,' or 'wife....'"[1]

2. In response to a father's 1994 inquiry about the film containing nudity and lesbianism that was shown to his daughter in a California school, the teacher allegedly responded, "he would rather watch two women embrace than people being killed. He told the class that they needed to learn things from a different perspective... He also said that 'just because you're raised to think one way, it doesn't mean that another way is wrong.'" In a meeting that finally occurred after months of trying the parent concluded, "This accomplished nothing. In fact, during the meeting, the teacher had the gall to say that he feels part of his job is parenting. The assistant superintendent of instruction never did give an opinion on

the movie. Two and one-half months later the movie still has not been reviewed by the board."[2]

3. On March 19, 1996, 59 sixth-grade girls were given gynecological exams at an Intermediate School in East Stroudsburg, PA without permission of the parents and against the objections of these 11 and 12-year old girls.[3]

4. Results of the 1999 National Assessment of Educational Progress (NAEP) in writing indicated that "the average, or typical, American student is not a proficient writer." Of the 60,000 students in 35 states who took the writing test, three-fourths did not perform at levels considered proficient for their grade level. In fact, the longer in school the worse the writing abilities. Only one percent was counted as showing advanced proficiency.[4]

5. In March 2001, officials at a high school in Fairfax County, Virginia, "corralled 41 students in the cafeteria and asked them to forge their parents' signatures on a federal form." The principal claimed "that students were never bullied or threatened." He did understand however "that they might feel intimidated by being pulled out of class and sent to a room full of security officials."[5]

6. When the parents wanted to take their seven-year-old son off Ritalin for two weeks to see if that would relieve his unusual symptoms, they got a call and then a visit from a Child Protective Services worker based on a call from the child's school guidance counselor. The Albany Times Union reports in May 7, 2000 that the family name is now on a statewide list of alleged child abusers for "medical neglect." The Albany paper claims that this is not so unusual: "Public schools are increasingly accusing parents of child abuse and neglect if they balk at giving their children medication such as Ritalin, a stimulant being prescribed to more and more students."[6]

7. In 1985, the U.S. Supreme Court refused to remove a book from the required curriculum that was religiously offensive to a child and parent in that it said, among other things, "poor white trash God" and "Jesus Christ, the long-legged white s__ of a b____." (Grove v. Mead School District).[7]

8. A 1999 Los Angeles Times story reports that "Tens of thousands of students in California's special education system have been placed there not because of a serious mental or emotional handicap, but because they were never taught to read properly... There they are failed a second time, by a badly flawed system designed to be their safety net."[8]

9. One year after the 1999 Columbine shootings, a national poll by the Discovery Channel and TIME magazine reports that over one-third of both teenagers (35%) and parents (39%) say that youth violence has increased. (In 1998, students ages 12-18 were victims of more than 2.7 million non-fatal crimes.)[9] Nearly a third of the teens say they have witnessed a violent situation in school; over half say they have been verbally insulted or threatened in the past year, and nearly 4 in 10 have heard a student threaten to kill another.[10]

10. California schools, whether public or private, that receive direct or indirect government financial assistance, can no longer refuse to hire or admit transsexuals and transvestites even if for religious reasons. The state's Title 5 regulations against sexual discrimination have redefined gender so that it no longer means male or female but however the person perceives him or herself to be. As of June 2000, 18 other school districts and states have added self-determined gender definitions to their codes.[11]

As the Example Injustices demonstrate, there has been a "long Train of Abuses and Usurpations" (quoting from U.S. Declaration of Independence) in education sufficient to be labeled as an "absolute Tyranny." In addressing this matter, the author full well knows, as Read[12] says, "The myth of government education, in our country today, is an article of general faith. To question the myth is to tamper with the faith, a business that few will read about or listen to or calmly tolerate." Even so, the felt obligation, the duty, "to take alarm at the first experiment on our liberties" which was "one of the noblest characteristics of the late Revolution" according to James Madison (*Memorial and Remonstrance*, 1785) is long overdue in education.

References

1. Vitz, Paul C. (1986). *Censorship: Evidence of bias in our children's textbooks*, Ann Arbor, MI: Servant Books, back cover.
2. Duffy, Cathy (1995) *Government nannies*, Gresham, OR: Noble Publishing Associates, pp. 119-120.
3. Exams violated girls' civil rights. *Pocono Record Writer*, July 28, 1999.
4. Klicka, Christopher (2000). *Home schooling: The right choice,* Sisters, OR: Loyal Publishing, p. 29.
5. Student newspaper exposes Fairfax school's misbehavior, *Washington Post*, April 5, 2000, p. B01.
6. *The Albany Times Union*, May 7, 2000.
7. *Grove* v. *Mead School District*; 753 F. 2nd, 1540 (9th Cir. 1985). Cert. Denied, 474, U.S. 826.
8. Twice failed: California's lost students. *Los Angeles Times*, December 12, 1999, Part A, p. 1.
9. National Center for Educational Statistics, Indicators of School Crime and Safety, 2000.
10. National Campaign Against Youth Violence www..noviolence.net/cgi-bin/press.cgi?recid=63843752 and TIME.com, April 24, 2000, vol. 155.16, The Perception Gap: School Violence.
11. Bending Gender, *World*, June 16, 2001, p. 45.
12. Read, Leonard E. (1964). *Anything that's peaceful*. Irvington-on-Hudson, NY: The Foundation for Economic Education, Inc.

Acknowledgements

Thanks are due to the many students who helped bring the ideas to shape and who helped with the information search and compilation. Regent University has been most kind in its granting of time for writing the manuscript. A summer institute at Harvard University and a research conference with the Foundation for American Christian Education contributed to shaping my thoughts on the matter. Trish Tarpley, Lydia Wade, Jenny Kenner, Gloria Ross and most significantly Sue Boysen faithfully typed and retyped. And to Brian, Kristin, and Kerri go my love for their faith, patience, and encouragement.

Table of Contents

Chapter 1

Equality

It is an axiom in my mind that our liberty can never be safe but in the hands of the people themselves, and that too of the people with a certain degree of instruction. This it is the business of the state to effect, and on a general plan. (Thomas Jefferson quoted in Lee, 1961, p. 19)

A general state education is a mere contrivance for molding people to be exactly like one another; and as the mold in which it cases them is that which pleases the predominant power in the government—whether this be a monarch, a priesthood, an aristocracy, or the majority of the existing generation—in proportion as it is efficient and successful, it establishes a despotism over the mind, leading by natural tendency to one over the body. (John Stuart Mill quoted in Rapaport, 1978, p. 105)

For the highly prized ideal in this country of enabling its citizens to live in the fullest liberty and freedom possible, Thomas Jefferson (author of the Declaration of Independence and third U.S. President) believed that the state should supply and maintain a "system of general instruction, which shall reach every description of our citizens, from the richest to the poorest." However, John Stuart Mill (British philosopher and economist), whose ideas are probably most referred to in discussions on the nature of liberty, thought otherwise. How do we resolve this conflict that arises out of the paradox of educating citizens for liberty without, in the process, taking away their liberty?

As representative spokesmen on the nature of the problem, Jefferson speaks the mind of our culture in recognizing the need for an educated and literate people for maintaining liberty, yet Mill cogently pinpoints the ironic loss of liberty that results for any portion of the population when management of its affairs is freely possessed by others, no matter how well-intentioned.

The route to resolving this conflictful paradox regarding the deprivation of liberty to give liberty starts with the recognition of some very basic facts about the equality of all humans and the kind of liberties to which all humans are entitled. If it can be agreed that all people are equal as people and thus are entitled to equal liberties, then the groundwork for resolution is laid. Absent this agreement, it is doubtful that true and equal liberty will ever exist. Since these preliminaries are in fact central to the foundations of our country, lack of agreement on these points also signals some very basic misunderstandings about our country as well as our status as human beings.

The major purpose of this chapter is to establish some very basic principles regarding equality and liberty from which to address our education dilemma. These principles or tenets, summarized in advance, include:

1. All people are created equal as people.
2. Equality, by definition, prohibits the deprivation of the equal rights of others.
3. Equality of personhood guarantees certain equality of liberties to include freedom of conscience and freedom of belief.
4. Equality implies a standard to be equal to and liberty allows development toward that standard.
5. The need for human dignity impels individuals toward the exercise of their liberties, and, in turn, the right use of these

liberties fosters human dignity.
6. Violation of human equality and liberty deprives the violated and the violator as well of essential human dignity.

As we will see in this chapter, the use of force over people to prepare them for liberty destroys the very basis of that liberty. The basis of liberty, of course, is equality: "it is because men are equal that they are free" (Carlyle, 1968, p. 33). By its very nature, that kind of force, especially when institutionally legitimated, rests on the prior assumption of inequality through granting to some the right of force over others. It also rests on two other assumptions. The first assumption is that people inherently do not have the equal right of choice (i.e., liberty) regarding whether to submit to that force. The second assumption is that the liberty for which the people are forced to prepare themselves can be defined primarily by those with the original right of force. By its very nature, that right of force must therefore constantly reinforce itself. Otherwise, to prepare and grant people full liberty in equality will, by definition, allow them the right to abolish that original contradictory grant of inequality, which is the superiority of some over others. This in turn means that to perpetuate this inequality, people will perpetually be taught (i.e., "educated") to believe in a personally limiting view of themselves and a constrained view of the liberty to which they are entitled.

All of this is to say that to properly educate people for liberty, educational policy must be based in the full equality of each individual person. Legitimized coercion of the citizenry via educational policy is a sham. Based on the right of force via inequality, our current education policy contradicts the very principle of liberty for which people are to be educated.

Foundations

The orientation of this chapter emanates from a variety of sources and viewpoints. Ultimately, however, the streams of these various viewpoints converge on that foundation upon which everyone in this country can uniquely but uniformly rest their case—the U.S. Constitution. This document provides a common reference point from which to adjudicate the appropriateness of our civil responsibilities toward one another. Certainly, as other sources were used to develop this document, they can and will be looked to for further clarification, but it is this foundational document that the inhabitants of this great nation unanimously hold as their common bond or point of agreement. Residence in the United States of America automatically carries with it the tacit agreement to abide by the tenets of the U.S. Constitution.

Basis for Liberty

Accordingly, to begin our discussion on the chapter-opening paradoxical moral dilemma wherein liberty is apparently deprived (a la Mill) in order to guarantee liberty (a la Jefferson), we see that one of the expressed purposes for drafting the U.S. Constitution was "to ... secure the Blessing of Liberty..." To better understand this liberty that is secured by the Constitution, it is necessary to refer to one of the Constitution's prerequisite documents, the Declaration of Independence. In consulting the Declaration, we hope to use it for the purpose Abraham Lincoln outlined: "Its authors meant it to be—as, thank God, it is now proving itself—a stumbling block to all those who in after times might seek to turn a free people back into the hateful paths of despotism" (Wills, 1978, p. xviii). Believed to contain the moral sentiment made practical first in the Articles of Confederation and later in the Constitution, the Declaration is so worded that acknowledgment of the nature of human liberty calls for the prior acknowledgment of human equality. As stated in the Declaration, "All men are created equal, that they are endowed by their Creator with certain unalienable Rights, that among these are ... Liberty...." Abraham Lincoln (Wills, 1978, p. xvi) thought that the concept of equality unites all our foundational documents. Equality, according to political scientist Charles M. Redenius, "is the bedrock of American political philosophy" (1981, p. 147). And according to French chronicler of 19th century American life Alexis de Tocqueville, equality was the foremost fundamental idea in the United States (Wills, 1978, p. 323).

It is neither an accident nor merely a matter of linguistic

convenience that the word equality appears prior to the word liberty in the Declaration of Independence. The concept of liberty necessarily rests on the concept of equality. Most philosophers, for instance, base their thoughts about human liberties on the prior condition of the equality of all mankind. John Locke, the philosopher whose ideas greatly influenced the Declaration of Independence, claimed (Macpherson, 1980) that all men are born equal (p. 31) and that such equality influences the use of liberty (p. 9). The constitutional philosopher and legal scholar Ronald Dworkin likewise said that "the right to distinct liberties does not conflict with any supposed competing right to equality, but on the contrary follows from a conception of equality conceded to be more fundamental" (1977, p. 274).

Most importantly, the primary author of the Declaration of Independence, Thomas Jefferson, saw equality as the determining consideration regarding the needs of the republic. In fact, he believed that without equality, liberty could not properly exist (Redenius, 1981, p. 19). Later in history, Abraham Lincoln interpreted the Declaration to mean that liberty was an inalienable right that all men held equally (Redenius, 1981, p. 67). Evidence that equality formed the basis of liberty in our founding documents is also supported by the expressed intent of the Revolutionary Committee, of which James Madison, principal architect of the Constitution, was a member. That intent was to "prepare a Declaration of Rights ... [to] secure substantial and *equal* [emphasis added] liberty to the people" (Alley, 1985, p. 159).

Another major influence that helped form the philosophy of the Declaration and ultimately the Constitution was the strong biblical mindset of the time (see Alley, 1985, p. 109; Rushdoony, 1978, pp. 5 & 49). The liberty the founding fathers claimed in the very first sentence of the Declaration that allowed them "to dissolve the Political Bands" they had with the mother country is likewise based in the prior notion of their "equal station" in life as granted by "Nature's God." Their equality with the king nullified his divine right claim to deprive them of their God-given inalienable right to liberty. Then again, in the second sentence of the Declaration, the self-evident truth that all men are created equal by a Creator is likewise a solid biblical concept: "All men are created equal, that they are endowed by their Creator...." Looking specifically at this source of ideas, the Bible indicates that it is because of our equal accountability to God (Romans 14:10b-12) that we derive our liberty (Romans 14:19a & 13): "Men are free, but also they are equal: indeed it is because they are equal that they are free. If the doctrine of individual liberty is important, the doctrine of human equality is all the more so, and it is the doctrine both of the New Testament and of the Christian tradition" (Carlyle, 1968, pp. 33-34).

History in general, as another influence on the ideas contained in the Declaration, likewise points to liberty owing its existence to the notion of equality. Frederic Bastiat, a 19th century French statesman, sums up this great lesson of history in his critique of the socialistic degeneracy in France during the 1840s: "It must be admitted that the tendency of the human race toward liberty is largely thwarted ... greatly due to a fatal desire—learned from the teachings of antiquity—that our writers on public affairs have in common: They desire to set themselves above mankind in order to arrange, organize, and regulate it according to their fancy" (1950, pp. 51-52). Whenever some men see themselves as more equal than others, liberties are inevitably disproportionately allocated.

Since to understand liberty, we have to understand equality, a more complete look at the notion of equality follows. We start first with a general working definition or characterization of equality. From there, a brief history of man's search for equality is discussed, and we conclude with what seems to be some very important attributes or qualities of equality.

Definition of Equality

By way of definition, the equality of all mankind rests on the recognition that all are intrinsically equal as persons. As W. T. Stace, former Emeritus Professor of Philosophy at Princeton University, (Abernethy, 1959, p. 255) says,

"every I is intrinsically equal to every other I, ... that is I == I."

All humans possess the same type of body—skeleton, organs, and physiological functions—and the same basic mechanism. All experience pain, pleasure, fear, love, hate, empathy, joy, and despair. All are moral beings capable of making plans, anticipating the future, and selecting options. Each is born, each grows and experiences the dilemmas of life, and each is destined to die. All are created in the image of God and are brothers and sisters in the common ancestry of Adam and Eve. Each becomes concretely more aware of this mutual equality in nature through the sharing of similar experiences. The sharing of emotions like sorrow, distress, joy, exhilaration, hunger, dignity, love, compassion, and other matters of the heart reveal the uniqueness of all humanity and help to uncover the hidden marvel that all are equal while unlike any other form of life.

The intrinsic equality of all mankind stands as a truth in spite of extrinsic, external differences. Each individual is different in terms of type of personality, degree of hunger, need for recognition, power, and so on, but each is equal in their common possession of these attributes. It is not that they possess the same attributes in equal degree, but that they each equally possess the same attributes in one degree or another (Abernethy, 1959, p. 273).

History of Equality

The following cursory review of writings on equality indicate how basic a concept it is and how fervently man seeks after it, even from the beginning of time.

The Bible indicates that at the time of creation, man and woman were both created equal in God's sight: "And God said, 'Let us make man in our image, after likeness...' So God created man in his own image, in the image of God created he him; male and female created he them" (Gen. 1:26-27). The equality of all mankind exists in the common heritage in Adam and Eve as the parents of all humans (Gen. 3:20), in their common inheritance of the sin nature (Roman 5:12), and in their common need for the Savior (John 8:24).

The Greeks. To the early Greeks, equality was a basic theme of concern. Herodotus (484-425 B.C.) recorded one of the earliest accounts of a monarch being overthrown in favor of equality of all people before the law. Thucydides (460-400 B.C.) expressed the ideals of the Athenian culture claiming that their laws "afford equal justice to all in their private differences" and "extends also to our ordinary life" (Abernethy, 1959, p. 38). Isocrates (436-338 B.C.) recognized that what contributed most to good government were two kinds of equality: "that which makes the same award to all alike and that which gives to each man his due" (Abernethy, 1959, p. 40). During this same relative time period, Aristotle and Plato argued for only limited equality from the belief that men are not created equal. They basically believed in proportionate equality to each, according to his virtue. Some, being slaves of nature, were considered by Plato and Aristotle as unfit to participate in various aspects of political life. The bulk of the teachings during this time, however, seem to favor the notion that no distinction should be made between freemen and slaves.

With the disintegration of the Greek city-states, the Stoic school of philosophy gained predominance. By identifying God with reason, which all men were capable of, all human beings were considered equal. Thus it would be a fragmentation of divinity to deny the equality of each human being. Differences that exist between human beings were, to these Stoics, far less important than their resemblances. From these beliefs, the Romans interpreted and developed their own political philosophy.

The Roman philosopher Cicero (106-43 B.C.) relied on what he called "sufficient proof that there is no difference in kind between man and man" (Abernethy, 1959, p. 53). The inequality that was a result of circumstances was only superficial in nature compared to the reality that all men are created equal. Cicero maintained that all have the capability to learn, to attain virtue, and to reason, and that all find the same virtues pleasing and the same vices detestable (Carlyle, 1968). True, there are differences among men but not in terms of their creation as beings. For instance, while men may differ in terms of what they have learned, they are all equal in the capacity for learning. "There is no one thing so like or so equal to one another as all of us are to one another," Cicero explained (Corwin, 1978, p. 19).

The Romans. The Roman philosopher Seneca (4 B.C. - 65 A.D.) extended the concept of individual equality to the matter of slavery. Even where fortune has made one a slave and the other a master, they are both intrinsically equal because virtue and other enduring qualities can be attained by both. At no time is the master able to bring into bondage the mind of the slave (Abernethy, 1959, p. 56). Slavery is, after all, only external. While the body may belong to the master, the mind is its own and cannot be taken in slavery. The body may be enslaved, but the soul is free. He and other Roman jurists argued for the fair and equal treatment of foreigners and slaves from a belief in the equality and unity of mankind (Abernethy, 1959, p. 187). From the renewed notion of equality of all humans, early Roman jurists argued that the slave was not under the absolute power of a human master (Carlyle, 1968).

Christianity. The early Christian church during these times made the clearest distinction between social and moral superiority in its conception of equality. Regardless of social and personal differences that existed in the eyes of humans, all stood equal before God in His examination of their souls. Regardless of material and social status, each person stands before God with a sinful nature. Each person is in need of the salvation of Jesus Christ. Even while bearing the image of God, each person stands equally in need of salvation, and each is equally capable of receiving the salvation of Christ. All have sinned and come short of the glory of God (Romans 3:23).

From a biblical position, all men are equal before God. All are capable of living a moral and spiritual life—a life in communion with God: "For whosoever shall call upon the name of the Lord shall be saved" (Romans 10:13). As the Apostle Paul indicates, all are children of God through faith in Jesus Christ. In God's eyes, there is no inequality in men because of things like ethnic or sexual differences or slave versus master status in this life (Galatians 3:26-28). The phrase 'God is no respecter of persons" (Deuteronomy 10:17; Romans 2:11) indicates that He treats all equally; that each is loved and cherished by him. So great is this love to each individual that He would have sent His son to die if there was just one person to receive this vicarious gift of salvation. Even so, all can partake of it.

The early Christian church likewise contributed much to

understanding the inequality of slavery. Paul, in sending back the slave Onesimus, exhorts his master Philemon to see Onesimus as a brother both in Christ and in the flesh (Philemon 16). As fellow bondservants to the Lord, Philemon is urged to receive and treat Onesimus just as he would Paul.

In discussing the question of slavery as a context for equality, early Christian writers bid masters to remember that their lordship does not extend over the soul; only God has that privilege. One of the greatest practical administrators in the history of the Western Church, Pope St. Gregory the Great, gives us this classic phrase: "... by nature we are all equal—nature brought forth all man equal: Omnes namque natura aequales sumus" (cited in Carlyle, 1968, p. 43).

A careful reading of the Scriptures indicates that slavery is not to be construed as ownership of one person over another. It is a biblical truth that all men are sold into the slavery of sin by our first earthly parents. Yet we are still equal in this condition which should never used as a justification by some to keep others in bondage. The Epistle of Paul to Philemon is very clear evidence that we are all equal in God's eyes. Certainly the freedom afforded us by Jesus indicates we are not to be held in bondage, neither physical, mental, nor spiritual (John 8:31-32,36; Galatians 5:1).

Middle Ages. In the period of the foundations of modern culture, much was written regarding the equality of mankind. St. Thomas Aquinas, a theologian, philosopher, and Dominican monk (1225-1274), addresses the equality of man by appealing to the divine law of God to love one another as God individually loves each person (Carlyle, 1968, p. 73). As early as the 13th century, the Italian political theorist Marsiluis developed the position that the power of the state is based on the equality of the people. Only when men are willing to observe the law are they apt to do so. And they are apt to follow the law only when they have a voice in making the law. Thus, the equality of men serves as the foundation of a long-enduring political philosophy, even to our present Constitution. Interestingly enough, this philosophy is based on the writings of Aristotle, who had only a limited view of the equality of all mankind.

Early Modern. In the 15th century, German Cardinal Nicholas of Cusa defends leadership by those endowed with clear reason, wisdom, and foresight by appealing to the equality of all men: "For if by nature men are equally powerful and equally free, the valid and ordained authority of one man naturally equal in power with the others cannot be established except by the choice and consent of the others" (Abernethy, 1959, p. 82). Thus, through the equality of all men, some by virtue of individual abilities can be permitted by the others to represent them. Leadership from other than equality leads to despotism. Hobbes (1588-1670), the great English philosopher and theorist, also argued that

"Nature hath made men so equall, in the faculties of body, and mind; as that though there bee found one man sometimes manifestly stronger in body, or of quicker mind than another, yet when all is reckoned together, the difference between man and man is not so considerable, as that one man can thereupon claim to himselfe any benefit, to which another may not pretend as well as he" (Abernethy, 1959, p. 123).

The philosopher whose ideas most influenced the content of the U.S. Declaration ofIndependence and the U.S. Constitution may well have been the Englishman John Locke (1632-1704). Many times over, and particularly in the *Second Treatise of Government* (Macpherson, 1980), he reaffirmed the natural equality of all mankind even in the face of individual differences:

"Though I have said above that all men by nature are equal, I cannot be supposed to understand all sorts of equality. Age or virtue may give men a just precedency. Excellency of parts and merit may place others above the common level. Birth may subject some, and alliance or benefits others, to pay an observance to those to whom nature, gratitude, or other respects may have made it due. And yet all this consists with the equality which all men are in...." (Abernethy, 1959, p. 134).

At the same time that these seminal ideas about equality were being laid to form the foundations of our civil government, they were also being applied to church government. The American Congregationalist clergyman John Wise (1652-1725) argued against central governance of New England churches on the grounds that all men are created equal in God's eyes and owe "homage to none but God himself" (Abernethy, 1959, p. 139). He continued,

The third capital immunity belonging to man's nature is an equality amongst men ... and since no one can live a sociable life with another that does not own or respect him as a man, it follows as a command of the law of nature that every man esteem and treat another as one who is naturally his equal, or who is a man as well as he. There are many popular or plausible reasons that greatly illustrate this equality: viz., that we all derive our being from one stock, the same common father of human race. (Abernethy, 1959, p. 143)

The governing principle on this matter in the United States is voiced very clearly in the U.S. Declaration of Independence and repeated again in the U.S. Constitution. The Declaration begins by declaring that any one group of people are equal to another: "When in the course of human events, it becomes necessary for one people to dissolve the political bands which have connected them with another, and to assume among the powers of the earth, the separate and equal station..." (Abernethy, 1959, p. 147). From here, the concept of equality is further refined to apply to each individual person: "We hold these truths to be self-evident, that all men are created equal..." (Abernethy, 1959, p. 147).

The preamble to the French Constitution of 1791 likewise affirms the equality of all men: "Men are born, and always continue, free and equal in respect of their rights" (Abernethy, 1959, p. 156). Reflecting on the revolution in France leading up to the development of their own Constitution, John Adams, signer of the Declaration of Independence and second U.S. President, writes, "That all men have one common nature, is a principle which will now universally prevail, and equal rights and equal duties will in a just sense, I hope, be inferred from it... Equal laws are all that ever can be derived from human equality..." (Abernethy, 1959, p. 159). Writing in defense of the French Revolution, Thomas Paine (1737-1809) bases his argument on the equality of man: "Every history of the creation ... all agree in establishing one point, the *unity of man*; by which I mean that men are all of *one degree*, and consequently that all men are born equal..." (Abernethy, 1959, p. 161). He continued, "the Mosaic account of creation, whether taken as divine authority or merely historical, is full to this point, *the unity or equality of man...* If this be not divine authority, it is at least historical authority, and shows that the equality of man, so far from being a modern doctrine, is the oldest upon record" (Abernethy, 1959, p. 161).

The German philosopher Hegel (1770-1831) also appeals to the biblical record to affirm man's equality among man: "Equality was a principle with the early Christians; the slave was the brother of the owner; humility, the principle of not elevating one's self above anyone else, the sense of one's own unworthiness, was the first law of a Christian; men were to be valued not by honors or dignity, not by talents or other brilliant qualities, but by the strength of their faith" (Abernethy, 1959, p. 164). Interestingly, Hegel's philosophy ultimately stood in opposition to biblical teachings even while affirming its teaching on human equalities. This practice of appealing to the biblical truth of men's equality to ultimately deny biblical teachings is not an uncommon tactic. The Unitarian minister William Channing (1780-1842), in calling for more humane behavior of man toward man, also bases his position on the biblical teaching of equality among men even while not considered orthodox in biblical interpretation

I observe that there is one principle of the soul which makes all men essentially equal... I refer to the sense of duty, to the power of discerning and doing right, to the moral and religious principle, to the inward monitor which speaks in the name of God, to the capacity of virtue or excellence... It is this moral power which makes all men equal, which annihilates all the distinctions of this world. (p. 175)

With the concept of equality firmly embodied in both the Declaration of Independence and the U.S. Constitution, a definite reference point was established for social and political action thereafter. For instance, John Dewey (1958-1952), the American educator and philosopher, stated, "Belief in equality is an element of the democratic credo" (Abernethy, 1959, p. 254).

Important Qualities of Equality

There are four important attributes or qualities inherent in the truism that "all men are created equal." First, equality among all people implies a reciprocal granting to others of that equality. Second, individual differences among people are to be uniquely developed and, in fact, are laden with life-purpose for each person. Third, inherent in the equality of all humanity is an external standard or idealized model that serves as the goal for accompanying motivational forces. Fourth, recognition of the equality ideal in each individual as well as provision for individual development toward that ideal brings the dignity for which each person was created. These four qualities importantly relate to liberty and to the larger question of the deprivation of liberty in education, as we shall see later in this chapter.

<u>Reciprocity of Equality</u>

Being equal to others prohibits us from acting without any consideration of them. The claim to equality often gets perverted into the so-called license to do whatever is wanted via the assumption that, since on equal standing, no one has the right to forbid the actions of others. Doing whatever we individually want, however, quickly runs the danger of depriving someone else of their equal rights. The individual so deprived would correctly claim a loss of equality in relation to the antagonist who now is in position of so-called greater equality. This destruction of equality by way of the antagonist operating outside the legitimacy of equality thereby invalidates the initial action that was supposedly based on equality. The First Priority Rule in Liberty for contemporary philosopher John Rawls is that "Each person is to have an equal right to the most extensive total system of equal basic liberties compatible for a similar system of liberty for all..." (Pelczynski & Gray, 1984, p. 388).

Personal responsibility of equality therefore goes beyond claiming equality with others. Instead, personal equality carries with it the inherent responsibility not only to acknowledge the equality of others but to actually work to safeguard their equality. We as a people are only as great as we treat the least of us. Philosophers have long recognized that to demean others is to demean oneself. To treat any person unfairly, being equally a member of the human race, is to place oneself at that same demeaned level since each person is equally human. No wonder Jesus taught us to love our enemies (Matthew 5:43). It is therefore in the natural interest of each person to protect or guard the equality of all people to ensure the viability of personal equality.

Attempts to defend inhumane actions through some limited view of equality inevitably violate a crucial test of equality, that of equality of reciprocity. That is, the loss of human dignity experienced by applying the inhumane action in reverse is tacit admission by the perpetrator that the principle of equality has been violated. This violation of dignity is also an indication that there is a standard of equality appropriate to being human—a topic to be discussed later in this chapter.

The inherent requirement in the concept of equality that calls for the safeguarding of equality for others leads to the paradox that we can only enjoy equality and freedom to the extent that we restrain from participating in unlimited and unrestrained freedom and privilege. Mill (Rapaport, 1978) recognizes that equality limits a very liberal use of freedom and liberty that he would otherwise promote. He justifies the use of power over any member of society to prevent harm to others (p. 9), claiming that each member of society is "bound to observe a certain line of conduct toward the rest" (p. 73). This obligation to others as equals is so important for Mill that he justifies social intervention whenever legal obligations to others are violated (p. 97). He thus calls for proactive safeguards for maintaining equality as opposed to restrictive limits to prohibit harm.

The influential philosopher John Locke provides a theological rationale for the same position. He maintains (1690) that

"being all equal and independent, no one ought to harm another in his life, health, liberty or possessions. For men being all the workmanship of one omnipotent and infinitely wise maker—all the servants of one sovereign Master, sent into the world by his order, and about his business—they are his property, whose workmanship they are, made to last during his and not another's pleasure... Every one, as he is bound to preserve himself, and not to quit his station willfully, so, by the like reason, when his own preservation comes not in competition, ought be, as much as he can, to preserve the rest of mankind, and not, unless it be to do justice on an offender, take away or impair the life, or what tends to the preservation of the life, the liberty, health, limb, or goods of another (Macpherson, 1980, p. 9).

Even in the area of governance and authority, the reciprocity principle of equality applies. We have no more inherent right to rule over another than the other has to rule over us. As Mill (Rapaport, 1978, p. 103) says, no one is totally free to do as he or she likes in acting for another. Bastiat, as cited earlier (1850/1950), indicates that the absence of a belief in equality results in the loss of liberty. Those who legislate from other than a position of equality assume a degree of infallibility (e.g., "greater" equality) in comparison to the fallible nature that they project onto the rest of the masses. Said differently, equality of persons locates governance of any individual within that individual and not in someone else instead. Most writers ultimately locate the seat of self-governance in the conscience, as we shall see. As a hint though, we quote Jefferson on reciprocity and conscience: "... we lay it down as a fundamental, that laws, to be just, must give a reciprocation of right: that without this, they are mere arbitrary rules of conduct, founded in force and not in conscience..." (Jefferson, 1984, p. 269).

Rights of authority are, however, legitimately transferred by consent from the individual to governing authorities. This legitimate transfer typically occurs for two basic reasons: economy or efficiency of operation and as a check against the inability of individuals to be consistently moral (see Macpherson, 1980, p. xiv). Such transfer is not thought to be absolute, however.

Consistent with the reciprocal nature of equality, those who govern do so only with the consent of the governed. Locke claims that society never gives over to government arbitrary or absolute powers but limited powers only (Macpherson, 1980, p. xv). Further, Locke maintains that even these limited powers are revocable where the authority leads society against the will of God for that society.

As both a case in point and reiteration of the status of the reciprocity of equality in the United States, consider some historical perspectives that influenced the wording of the Declaration of Independence. As early as the 6th century, St. Isidore of Seville clarified the distinction between a true king and a tyrant. The king holds his title when he does so rightly and loses it (as a tyrant) when he transgresses against right (Carlyle, 1968, pp. 61-62). St. Ambrose further clarifies that the ruler is God's minister when he uses authority well (Carlyle, 1968, p. 61).

Locke's position was that the power which God has created in society and which may be entrusted to government has a reciprocal nature. Such power is forfeited and reverts back to the people when there are miscarriages by those in authority (Macpherson, 1980, p. 124). Breach of trust by those in authority makes them the rebels. Those (i.e., society) who subsequently and legitimately attempt to restore government back to its founding principles are not rebels at all. The resultant conflict between the rebellious ruler who is in breach of trust and the people as a force of resistance is between equals, with right on the side of those defending the law (Parry, 1978, p. 142). Given this position, the so-called Revolutionary War leading up to the U.S. Declaration of Independence is more aptly entitled the Resistance War or War of Independence.

Thomas Jefferson, primary author of the Declaration, reflects Locke's position in his defense of the rights of "British America." He saw the King of England as equal and in fact answerable to the people of "British America" in that "he is no more than the chief officer of the people, appointed by the laws, and circumscribed with definite powers, to assist in working the great machine of government erected for their use, and consequently subject to their superintendence" (Lee, 1961, p. 16). Jefferson, like Locke, also appealed to a theological rationale to maintain liberty through revolution: "Rebellion to tyrants is obedience to God" (Lee, 1961, p. 13). The ideology of Jefferson regarding equality, reciprocity, and rightful resistance is revealed in the Declaration as follows:

"When ... it becomes necessary for one People to dissolve the Political Bands which have connected them with another, and to assume among the Powers of the Earth, the separate and equal Station to which the Laws of Nature and of Nature's God entitle them ... that all Men are created equal ... that ... Governments are instituted among men, deriving their just Powers from the Consent of the Governed, that whenever any Form of Government becomes destructive of these Ends, it is the Right of the People to alter or to abolish it..."

To conclude, the reciprocal property of equality obligates, or better, privileges individuals to protect the equal rights of others.

Society's Golden Rule, "Do unto others as you would have them do unto you," and Jesus's words, "Therefore all things whatsoever ye would that men should do to you, do ye even so to them: for this is the law and the prophets" (Matthew 7:12), embody precisely the spirit of reciprocity of equality. Further, the reason for establishing the U.S. as a nation equal among nations emanated from the violation of this reciprocity of equality between a ruler and his people. This ruler-citizen relationship is specifically purposed to guarantee certain inalienable rights of equality for citizens. According to Locke (Macpherson, 1980, p. 8), "All men are naturally in ... a *state* also of *equality*, wherein all the power and jurisdiction is reciprocal, no one having more than another..."

<u>Individuality in Equality</u>

The age-old concept of equality is not the concept of clone as characterized by that popular term of the day. It is not the case, as the English political philosopher Thomas Hobbes would have us believe, that all men are created equal in both rights and abilities (Mace, 1979, p. 33). While equally in possession of certain basic rights, people very obviously differ in natural abilities and in other aspects of life.. As Lock (Macpherson, 1980, p. 31) said,

"Though I have said above, Chap. II, that all men by nature are equal, I cannot be supposed to understand all sorts of equality: age or virtue may give men a just precedency: excellency of parts and merit may place others above the common level: birth may subject some, and alliance or benefits others, to pay an observance to those to whom nature, gratitude, or other respects, may have made it due."

The wide range of differences in human capabilities and potentialities bestows on each individual a uniqueness among all other individuals. The effects of nurture, or environmental circumstances, and the person's genetic inheritance interact in such a way to make each newborn child an unknown quantity in terms of potentiality. On reflection, it should be obvious that individual differences are not without specific purpose. The uniqueness of individuals, especially in terms of their individual strengths and talents, specifically equip and prepare the person for his or her life's work. It is these talents, gifts, interests, abilities, etc. that actually direct the person toward occupations and professional activities and so, in that sense, could be called guides along life's pathways.

This diversity among humans is at the same time both a blessing and a problem. On the one hand, the richness of culture, tradition, and viewpoint are directly a function of human individuality. On the other hand, diversity calls for sacrifice, toleration, forgiveness, and compromise when relating to others. A dilemma inherent in this diversity is such that if everyone is treated equally, the result is inequality of outcome; but, conversely, to treat everyone unequally still is no guarantee of equality of outcome, even for systematic and needs-based treatments.

These two elements of equality and individuality do not, thankfully, stand on the same level. Individuality is based in equality and not vice versa. No matter how different, gifted, or privileged one individual is over another, each is due the same respect as humans. Both come into the world, both live in the world, and both leave the world equally human. Furthermore, one person cannot deprive another of any basic inalienable rights no matter how discrepant their abilities, stations in life. etc. Actually, individuals are freely able, in an unthreatened way, to exercise their uniqueness precisely because all such diversity is based in, rather than opposed to, human equality. The recognition of individual differences outside of equality gives license to oppression and nullifies the concept of equality. The equal standing of individuality and equality results in undesirable competition; but the grounding of individual uniqueness in equality fosters optimal development of all and not just some. According to educator and philosopher John Dewey (Abernethy, 1959, p. 254). "The democratic faith in equality is the faith that each individual shall have the chance and opportunity to contribute whatever he is capable of contributing and that the value of his contribution be decided by its place and function in the organized total of similar contributions, not on the basis of prior status of any kind whatever."

Because of the equal standing of uniquely different individuals, each is free, within the bounds of decency and morality, to develop their individuality. In fact, without the cultivation of diversity, human culture becomes stagnant and lifeless. Life, both personally and socially, is enriched and abundant with potential where individual talents are encouraged toward maturity.

Historically, individuality was not always cherished. Primitive societies, primarily for reasons of survival, favored group solidarity as opposed to individual autonomy. In early Greek culture, individuality was subjugated to the needs of the state as determined by the state. Old Testament writings typically emphasize group or nation status (e.g., Israelites, Canaanites) over individual or personal relationship with God.

With the coming of Christ, the individual was recognized as a moral entity without reference to group membership. No force more than Christianity perpetuated the concept that each individual was responsible to his own conscience (and thus to God). Christianity likewise authored the principle that each individual person is immeasurably valuable above all the rest of creation (Carlyle, 1968, pp. 14-29) yet always within the context that God loves all individuals equally. More recently, even the concept of capitalism allows that each individual has a right to enjoy the fruits of his labor and his mind. In opposition, Marxism subverts individuality to the needs of the state and existentialism tends to raise each individual above the plane of equality of all other individuals.

Where we finally come back to rest on this matter is with the Declaration of Independence. Because of their very equality as humans with the King of England and because of his failure to honor such equality, the colonists declared their right to national individuality: "When ... it becomes necessary to dissolve the Political Bands ... and to assume ... the separate and equal Station." Further, each individual colonist was recognized as an equal creation of God and deserving of "Life, Liberty, and the Pursuit of Happiness." It was the Declaration of Independence that Abraham Lincoln referenced to defend the equal rights of black people both as individuals and as a race of people:

I think the authors of the notable instrument intended to include all men, but they did not intend to declare all men equal in all respects. They did not mean to say all were equal in color, size, intellect, moral developments or social capacity. They defined with tolerable distinctness, in what respects they did consider all men created equal—equal in 'certain inalienable rights, among which are life, liberty, and the pursuit of happiness'. This they said and this they meant (Abernethy, 1959, p. 185)

Purposefully Motivated

Recognition of the equal rights of individuals to pursue their individuality, as important as this may be, constitutes an incomplete understanding of the topic of individuality. Also needed is an understanding of what we will call the purposeful motivational force of individuality. Again, even this concept is rooted in the more basic concept of equality.

The notion of being equal as creations of God is not a description of some abstract statement of human relationships; instead, this notion carries with it the idea of some standard upon which to ground the equality of mankind. Such a standard provides a definition of the nature of man and his natural rights and describes an internal motivational force for achieving such a standard. Lincoln described the intent of the signers of the Declaration of Independence as follows:

They defined with tolerable distinctness in what respects they did consider all men created equal... They meant to set up a standard maxim for free society, which should be familiar to all, and revered by all; constantly looked to, constantly labored for, and even though never perfectly attained, constantly approximated, and thereby constantly spreading and deepening its influence and augmenting the happiness and value of life to all people of all colors everywhere. (Abernethy, 1959, p. 185)

The same orientation is revealed in the words of Martin Luther as he took a stand against the early church fathers over matters of basic doctrine: "Here I stand; I can do no otherwise" (Peterson, 1978, p. 26). Luther knew he had both the right to speak what he perceived as the truth and, additionally, an internally felt urge that would allow him to do no other.

Simply put, people are equal as people, not as dogs or rocks or any other thing, and they area created to act accordingly. To be equal as humans and not as dogs or rocks means that there is an image, ideal, or standard from which to evaluate the appropriateness of the manifestations of equality.

To have only the standard without some accompanying driving force makes the standard meaningless. Merely explaining the existence of a standard contributes nothing to understanding mankind's urge toward achieving that standard. To understand this phenomenon we start with the basic premise that God created a very orderly world and populated it with a myriad of beings each uniquely but appropriately fitted into God's perfect plan. Each species, but more, each individual being within that species is differentiated to perform an intended role. For instance, more acute hearing in man would likely prohibit rest and be heard as an unmanageable cacophony whereas much less hearing ability would prohibit necessary auditory sensitivity. Further, the very existence of a created universe implies a purpose for it and all it contains. To meet this purpose, the roles all created beings are to play is "written" inside of them. In the very act of being, as God intended, each person naturally fits into his or her rightful place in the ongoing manifestation of the plan. In other words, man, in behaving as God intends, is obeying the laws of nature as internally written.

The ability to act in a way conformable to the laws of nature is what Thomas Aquinas, Italian theologian of the middle ages, calls natural liberty (Pelczynski & Gray, 1984, p. 62). This natural liberty ultimately means that each person is free or at liberty when acting according to the way and for the purpose that God intends. The laws of nature are actually guidelines for a moral purpose. To operate any other way would not be liberty but the misuse of some innate capability that God has built into each and every person. Rather than seeing the laws of nature as regulating or restraining freedom, Locke believes (Macpherson, 1980, p. 32) that such laws "preserve and enlarge freedom." This freedom he says is not for "every man to do as he lists ... but a liberty to [do] within the allowance of those laws under which he is..." According to Paul de Lagrande, "He is not free who can do what he wills, but rather he who can become what he should" (qtd. in Thielicke, 1963, p. 10). The words of Henrick Steffins are also insightful: "We call free that which is itself in inner harmony with its nature" (quoted in Thielicke, 1963, p. 13).

Critics who claim that such a definition of liberty actually inhibits rather than fosters individuality, at root, mistakenly perceive the nature of God himself. God actually created mankind with the abilities needed to be perfectly compatible with God-ordained roles and purposes. Misuse of these capabilities is not freedom or liberty but a denigration of self and a delusion regarding one's role in life. Liberty outside of the will of God actually, as 20th century philosopher Jean Paul Sartre says, "condemns" one to freedom because without moral purpose, liberty turns man against self, both personally and collectively, and eventually leads to despair.

The fact that humans, as with all creatures, are created to do God's will reveals that there is a motivational force within all creatures for enabling the accomplishment of the law of nature. Locke (Wills, 1978, p. 241) conceives of this driving force as the uneasiness one feels at the absence of something good. In his book *Essay on Understanding*, Locke describes this uneasiness in the positive terms of "a constant determination to a pursuit of happiness." This pursuit is thought by Locke to be like a gravitational pull toward some determining object. The very purpose for our God-given liberty, he says, is for "infinite perfection and happiness" (Pelczynski & Gray, 1984, p. 70). God has "by an inseparable connection, joined virtue and public happiness together" (Parry, 1978, p. 33).

Modern psychologists speak of similar drives to fulfillment such as the need for achievement (McClelland), competency motivation (White), attainment of higher levels of moral reasoning (Kohlberg), and a need for self-actualization (Maslow). Some even suggest that a major motivation in the life of all humans is to bring their image of actual self as close as possible to their image of the ideal self. German writer Johann Goethe calls this image of the ideal self the "minted form" that resides within and that which we measure ourselves against (Thielicke, 1963, p. 32).

Whatever the specific label for this driving force, because it is from God and is for His purposes, it becomes part of what we know as an obligation or duty to God. It is a duty to which man was made and from which he achieves the greatest good for his life. But most importantly, it is a duty because God is the all-perfect determiner of it. Further it is a duty in the healthiest sense and not at all a burden.

Thomas Jefferson believed that mankind's natural liberties were granted by God in order that God's purposes, as man's duty, would be achieved (Lee, 1961, p. 14). The U.S. Declaration of Independence echoes these same thoughts by appealing to the "laws of nature and of nature's God" as a basis for the colonist's independence and the fact that it was "their duty to throw off such Government" in order to secure the God-given rights of "Life, Liberty, and the Pursuit of Happiness" of which they were being deprived.

To summarize, the concept of equality is the basis from which the concept of individuality is developed. From their basis in equality, individuals have the liberty to develop and to be guided by their unique talents and abilities. In fact, we can conceive of individual differences as motivators toward some ideal based in these differences that ultimately reflect God's purpose for that individual.

Dignity

The practice of reciprocal equality, as discussed earlier, even if perfectly practiced, would not satisfy a deep inner urging that the total concept of equality implies. Even if equality with individuality, as also just discussed, were practiced, there would still not be the total satisfaction longed for through equality. That is, man could be treated equally as rocks or ants and even as an equal yet individually different and unique rock or ant and the longing still would not be satisfied.

The fullest meaning of equality is that each person must be treated as individually equal to the dignity consistent with that due the highest form of life in the universe—as one who is made in the very image of God Himself. In fact, in the physical realm alone humans cannot claim any distinct dignity. Invariably some animal somewhere surpasses some aspect of man's ability. For instance, ants run the corporate state better than any totalitarian regime or democratic government, lions are stronger, turtles are more patient, and elephants supposedly have better memories than humans. While man may even caricaturize himself as some form of animal (e.g., a member of the "rat race" of humanity) and may even behave as an animal, all of mankind deeply resents being treated like animals. Mankind even resents being told by those like psychologist/philosopher B. F. Skinner in his book *Beyond Freedom and Dignity* (1971) that we must give up the search for dignity and recognize that each person is just "a repertoire of behavior appropriate to a given set of contingencies" (p. 189). Even Skinner, in trying to do away with the typical conception of dignity, is nonetheless, looking for it by claiming that the typical conception "stands in the way of further human achievements" (p. 55) and thus, by implication, the attainment of human dignity.

Beyond Skinner, the literature of the ages is consistent in acknowledging that mankind is engaged in the transcendent quest for dignity. Theologian R. C. Sproul (1983) claims that man has an aching void or pain of indignity that cries to be silenced. He cites St. Augustine as saying that we each have a vacuum desirous to be filled to stave off the rape of insignificance. Just as basic as the need for food and air is the need for dignity and self-esteem. It seems to be the driving force that results in what we know by various labels as the need for success, recognition, and achievement. Even our founding fathers acknowledged it as being sought after through the pursuit of happiness and claimed it was a right so basic as not to be deprived.

The Bible ascribes to each person the dignity of being made in the image of God. Mankind was the only species of God's creation that received life directly from His breath. In the Old Testament, dignity is rooted in the concept of glory. Glory can be thought of as the nobility, honor, and majesty that each part of creation has, with humanity at the highest point. In Hebrew, the word for glory is *kab* or *kaved*, meaning "weighted down," as Abraham was weighted down with riches. In New Testament terms, man is considered by God as significant beyond measure, such that He sent his only Son to die to gain each person's redemption back into the family of God (John 3:16).

Man separates himself from the animals in his likeness to God through the exercise of characteristics like reason, free will, and a moral obligation to seek the truth and to live up to this truth. Where people are blocked from exercising these abilities, they are deprived of the dignity that comes from properly exercising such characteristics. Whereas there is in animals and plants an automatism for carrying out the appointed destiny, each person is consciously equipped to carry out his or her destiny (Thielicke, 1963, p. 15). Even when deprived of such opportunity, the desire for dignity still motivates in certain albeit perverted ways. For instance, self-esteem may degeneration to pride, success to covetousness, and love to lust. Alcohol and drug addictions dull the pain of bruised dignity; rebellion in criminals and juvenile delinquents is a way of saying, "If you won't respect me, at least you will have reason to fear me."

The quest for dignity in all people is easily seen in the growth needs of individuals and particularly children. Whether a toddler or a teenager, the individual is moving toward more and more freedom for individual expression and development. When learning to walk or when learning to reason as an adult, the individual is naturally motivated toward such self-expression. As long as the person can exercise these urges in normal, healthy ways, dignity for the person invariably results. However, when the natural expression and development of distinctly human attributes like free will and reason are coerced or blocked, dignity cannot be realized.

As God's image bearers, individuals receive the dignity they are due when they are treated accordingly. Each person needs to be able to exercise those distinctly human traits like free will, freedom of conscience, freedom of worship, exercise of rightful authority and responsibility, the right for gainful employment, and so on. Furthermore, each person must also be free, within the healthy restrictions of reciprocal equality, to develop their own uniqueness and to achieve their purpose or calling in life. Coercion and other forms of dignity inhibitors will be resisted either actively and/or passively since the abused (as well as perpetrating) individual will not be able to receive the glory or dignity intended.

Ultimately, the dignity of each human demands that one should be able to act in truth from his or her own conscience. Man in this way is able to move to his highest good. This principle of liberty for dignity is the basis for most civilized societies. It allows each person to develop to his or her highest potential, enjoy the fruits or profits of their efforts, and contribute to the same opportunity for others. As Mill (Rapaport, 1978) indicates, mankind is better through suffering each other "to live as seems good to themselves than by compelling each to live as seems good to the rest" (p. 12).

While neither the U.S. Declaration of Independence nor the U.S. Constitution use the word dignity, the concept of dignity is very clearly present. Where the writers of the Declaration appeal to the "Laws of Nature and of Nature's God" as entitling them to assume an "equal Station" among "the Powers of the Earth," they are addressing the level of dignity that the colonists inherently deserved. Even in acknowledging the courtesy to inform others of their actions (i.e., "a decent Respect to the opinions of Mankind requires that they should declare the causes which impel them to the Separation"), they again are appealing to the level of dignity that all humans are due. Further, the level of equality, that is the dignity, to which all mankind is to receive without exception or denial is something the colonists claimed and enumerated specifically as, among other things, "Life, Liberty, and the Pursuit of Happiness." Since these rights are irrevocable, it becomes nothing less than a "Duty, to throw off such government" whenever they are denied to maintain that level of dignity naturally due to all humankind. Without such dignity of rights, humans would even cease to be who they were created to be. Finally, the Declaration ends with confirmation of a trust or "firm Reliance on the Protection of divine Providence" that comes through realization of the dignity that God Himself provides for those within His will.

While the U.S. Constitution is more practically oriented than its philosophical counterpart (the Declaration of Independence), it nonetheless builds off the level of dignity that a nation under God can expect. Namely, that such a nation could expect to function with "Justice," "domestic tranquility," a "defense" from enemies, overall "Welfare" of its citizens, and all the "Blessings of Liberty," as well as to perpetuate these things for "our Posterity."

Conclusion

The United States was founded on the belief that "all Men are created equal" and "endowed by their Creator with certain unalienable rights." By the nature of this equality, all individuals are bound to respect the proper exercise of the rights of others. Such respect prohibits the arbitrary rulership of some over others.

The concept of equality likewise carries another condition, that of respect for individuality. Equality is not identicalness in all matters; in fact, each person possesses an individuality that seeks to be realized. The destiny of each person, when fulfilled or being fulfilled, brings a level of dignity that each is due, by definition of being human. Anything that stands in the way of the exercise of mankind's divine nature arouses natural resistance and constitutes a violation of the principles upon which this nation was founded. In fact, full recognition of equality means to proactively protect the rights of others as a first step in protecting one's own rights.

Accordingly, some basic foundations for educational policy become apparent. Namely, each person's journey toward the dignity of humankind and toward one's own dignity as an individual calls for liberty in educational policy. Without the granting of or the proper use of this liberty, neither equal freedom of conscience nor freedom of belief can be fully or rightfully pursued and all of mankind loses. Furthermore, the deprivation of this liberty automatically, in and of itself, robs each individual of the enjoyment of Creator-given rights. And the equality of each individual and the reciprocal equality toward one another demands that whatever is desired for self must equally be extended to others. This is not at all the orientation of educational policy in the United States.

Educational policy that violates any or all of the above foundations must be eliminated and replaced with one that honors and promotes the equality and dignity of inalienable self-governance. As Mill said, "Mankind are greater gainers by suffering each other to live as seems good to themselves than by compelling each to live as seems good to the rest" (Rapaport, 1978, p. 12). From this perspective, the paradox of civilly depriving liberty via mandated education to supposedly give liberty is a self-contradictory principle and an intolerable presumption. After all, rulers, in their equality with all other citizens, rule over them only by way of citizen-granted conditional authority. Accordingly, autocracy in education must be abolished for the good of each and every citizen and ultimately for the good of the entire country.

References

Abernethy, George L. (1959). *The idea of equality: An anthology.* Richmond, VA: John Knox Press.

Alley, Robert S. (1985). *James Madison on religious liberty.* Buffalo, NY: Prometheus Books.

Bastiat, Frederic (1985/1950). *The law.* (Translated by Dean Russell, Irvington on Hudson, NY: Foundation for Economic Education, Inc.)

Carlyle, Alexander J. (1968). *The Christian church and liberty. New York:* Burt Franklin.

Corwin, Edward (1978). *Liberty against government.* Westport, CT: Greenwood Press.

Dworkin, Ronald (1977). *Taking rights seriously.* Cambridge: Harvard Univ. Press.

Holy Bible. NIV Study Bible (1985). Grand Rapids, MI: Zondervan.

Jefferson, Thomas (1984). *Writings.* New York: Literary Classics of the U.S., Inc.

Lee, Gordon C. (1961). *Crusade against ignorance: Thomas Jefferson on education.* New York: Teachers College Press.

Mace, George (1979). *Locke, Hobbs, and the Federalist Papers.* Carbondale, IL: Southern Illinois University Press.

Macpherson, Crawford B. (Ed.) (1980). *John Locke: Second treatise of government.* Indianapolis: Hackett Publ.

Mill, John S. (1859/1978). *On liberty.* Indianapolis: Hackett Publ. Edited by Elizabeth Rapaport.

Parry, Geraint (1978). *John Locke.* London: George Allen & Unwin.

Pelczynski, Zbigniew & Gray, John (1984). *Conceptions of liberty in political philosophy.* NY: St. Martin's Press.

Peterson, Walfred H. (1978). *Thy liberty in law.* Nashville, TN: Broadman Press.

Rapaport, Elizabeth (Ed.) (1978). John Stuart Mill: *On liberty.* Indianapolis: Hackett Publ.

Redenius, Charles M. (1981). *The American ideal of equality.* Port Washington, NY: Kennikat Press.

Rushdoony, Rousas J. (1978). *The nature of the American system.* Fairfax, VA: Thoburn Press..

Skinner, Burrhus F. (1971). *Beyond freedom and dignity.* New York: Bantam Books.

Sproul, Robert C. (1983). *In search of dignity.* Ventura, CA: Regal Books.

Thielicke, Helmut (1963). *The freedom of the Christian man.* NY: Harper & Row.

Wills, Gary (1978). *Inventing America: Jefferson's Declaration of Independence.* Garden City, NY: Doubleday & Co.

Chapter 2

Freedom Of Conscience And Freedom Of Religion

The natural liberty of men is to be free from any superior power on earth and not to be under the will or legislative authority of man, but to have only the law of nature for his rule. (Macpherson, 1980, p. 17/ von Eckardt, 1959, p. 232)

[T]he operations of the mind as well as the acts of the body, are subject to the coercion of the laws. But our rulers can have authority over such natural rights, only as we have submitted to them. The rights of conscience we never submitted, we could not submit. We are answerable for them to our God. (Lee, 1961, p. 63)

If philosophical ideas ever had practical consequences, the above quotes from John Locke and Thomas Jefferson, respectively, would certainly be a case in point. It was ideas such as these that gave philosophical foundation to the U.S. Declaration of Independence and, in turn, became practically manifest in The Constitution of the

United States.

To be specific, the philosophical ideas typified in the quotes above include the following beliefs: (a) man, by the nature of his being, has certain inherent natural rights and liberties; (b) God-created natural laws supersede laws made by man; (c) the conscience of man, as one of these rights, is answerable only to God and never to human authority; (d) government over self by self takes precedence over government over self by others; and (e) government receives its right to govern from those whom it represents.

Not at all by coincidence, these philosophical ideas are stated (respectively) more formally in the U.S. Declaration of Independence as follows: (a) "They are endowed by their Creator with certain 'unalienable' Rights"; (b) "the laws of nature and of nature's God" entitled the colonists to be independent of the oppressive laws of Great Britain; (c) "We, therefore, the representatives of the United States of America ... appealing to the Supreme Judge of the World for the Rectitude of our Intentions": (d) "that whenever any form of Government becomes destructive of these ends [i.e., 'unalienable' rights]," it is the Right of the People to alter or abolish it"; and (e) Governments are instituted among men, deriving their just powers from the Consent of the Governed." (The reader should note that the word "inalienable" was penned in the U.S. Declaration of Independence as the word "unalienable.")

Human Nature

As basic and foundational as these philosophical ideas and formal statements are, there is a deeper level of ideas that we must acknowledge. In fact, it is because of these deeper realities that the Declaration of Independence was even necessary. These more basic ideas relate to the very central nature of mankind. Specifically, humans are characterized by a dual set of properties that actually stand in contrast to each other. The one property, positive in orientation, is the inherent right to be, to do, and to know those things for which one was created. In essence, mankind has certain natural liberties that enable the process of living out a divinely implanted image. Thomas Aquinas spoke of this image that inclines us to do the will of God as a natural law: "The light of natural reason, whereby we discern what is good and what is evil, which is the function of the natural law, is nothing else than an imprint on us of the divine light (von Eckardt, 1959, p. 24).

The other property, generally negative in orientation, is that, in a state of imperfectness, each person tries to proselytize others to believe and to do what he or she either believes or wants to believe as truth. It is as if the personally interpreted divine image is identically meant for all as interpreted by the few. Such perverted self-interest or self-love, Jefferson says, "is the sole antagonist of virtue, leading us constantly by our propensities to self-gratification in violation of our moral duties to others" (von Eckardt, p. 76). The words of Johann Fichte, an 18th century German philosopher, embody this perverted self-interest: "To compel men to adopt the right form of government, to impose Right on them by force, is not only the right, but the sacred duty of every man who has both the insight and the power to do so" (Roche, 1969, pp. 259, 290).

Nontransferrable Rights

In the context of the U.S. Declaration of Independence, the King of Great Britain, by trying to conform the colonists to the role he had for them, was depriving them of the basic liberties which were sovereignly and nontransferrably the right of each individual. Thus the Declaration bears witness to the conflict that results when attempts to control others, as when perceived by rulers to be their legitimate right, run counter to those rights of personhood retained naturally and inherently by those being governed.

The crucial concern then is that if only certain and not all powers can be given by individuals to any governmental form, who is to ultimately determine what is the right course of action for an individual or collection of individuals? More specific to the educational concerns examined in this book, it is important to ascertain whether inalienable rights are involved regarding the question of who controls or should control education.

Believing that education is ultimately based in the inalienable rights of freedom of conscience and religion, we need to exposit the nature of these freedoms. Accordingly, this chapter develops the following propositions:

1. Each individual is sovereign over his or her own life in relationship to the rights of all humans.
2. There are certain rights naturally and irrevocably guaranteed to mankind among which is freedom of conscience.
3. Because of the debased nature of mankind, some will attempt to reduce the rights of others.
4. A primary role of government is to ensure that the basic rights of each individual are protected and safeguarded.
5. Civil protest is proper and even a duty where a government denies its citizens their basic inalienable rights.
6. The operation of conscience is ultimately based on religious values.
7. The U.S. Declaration of Independence guarantees and, in fact, is even founded on the principle of freedom of religion which includes freedom of conscience.

Before proceeding further, the crucial role of conscience in all these matters must be discussed.

Conscience

The emphasis in this section is on the U.S. Declaration of Independence as the beginning point in understanding the crucial nature of freedom of conscience. In speaking their conviction about the need for independence, the authors of the Declaration ended the document by "appealing to the Supreme Judge of the world for the Rectitude of our Intentions..." In other words, they were acting according to their conscience, and in this compatibility of their action with their conscience, they were asking that ultimate spokesman to their conscience be the judge of their actions. There should be no doubt that they were, first, acting according to their conscience and, second, recognizing the Creator and Supreme Judge of the World as the guiding light to their conscience. But just to be sure these two points are clear, we elaborate on them as follows.

The authors of the Declaration based their actions regarding independence on the prerogative of God's intentions for all peoples, as follows: that all people were created equal and, moreso, that they were created equal by a Creator; that certain rights were endowed to all humans by their Creator; that according to the laws of nature, as implanted by nature's God, all peoples have equal status as nations; and that governmental forms of nations can be replaced or started anew when their duty before their Creator is severely thwarted. In acting according to their conscience as they thought their Creator intended, the authors of the Declaration appealed to Him for the correctness (i.e., Rectitude) of their intentions.

Surely, in basing their actions on this obvious free exercise of conscience, the authors would undoubtedly make provision for the same free exercise to all the people subsumed under this document. To do otherwise would be to violate the concept of equality they themselves held as a self-evident, nondebatable truth.

In the final analysis, the authors of the Declaration were saying to the King of Great Britain and to the "Opinions of Mankind" that they had the right to act according to their consciences in regard to the deprivation of inalienable rights. They then formally published that rationale as a foundation upon which "to institute [a] new Government." Embodied in this rationale of freedom of conscience are certain tenets needful of explanation.

Basic Tenets

First, it is in the basic nature of mankind to live according to one's conscience. As such, conscience serves the triple function of being that place (sometimes referred to as the mind and/or heart) where moral laws are written; where comparisons are made between our moral understandings and our thoughts, actions, etc.; and where the compatibility of our behavior is weighed against what we believe to be right and wrong. And because conscience is personal attribute, each individual person has to decide finally what to accept as truth and non-truth. Each person is thereby created to live according to his or her conscience, even though each may choose otherwise.

Second, in resisting the throne of Great Britain, the authors of the Declaration were further saying that so central is the role of conscience in exercising these inalienable rights that it actually supersedes the role of civil (and even religious) government in terms of self-governance. Governmental laws, after all, are an aggregate of others' thoughts and, by the very nature of equality (as discussed in Chapter 1), cannot override the conscience of any other individual. It is never the role of a person or group of people, and government in particular, to be the governor of another person's conscience—behavior yes, but conscience never.

Even deeper, each person in his or her own conscience is the final determiner of what is truth. Even in the presence of absolute truths, each person still has the final say regarding whether or not to believe such truths; further, each is accountable to his or her conscience *only* for those things believed to be truth. As is evident in everyday life, forcing someone to act contrary to his conscience does not change the conscience but more likely actually strengthens the inner resolve not to change. As Cobb (1968, p. 6) says, "The man convinced against his will is of the same opinion still." Education, discourse, and the like are the more natural and appropriate means for enabling someone to change his or her conscience. Truth, even absolute truth, becomes a guide to conscience only when it is accepted as truth by that individual.

Fourth, the signers of the Declaration in following their own consciences to effect the separation from Great Britain were acknowledging even another basic fact about human nature. Namely, conscience directs the person to some purpose in life. As they wrote, each person has the right to the "Pursuit of Happiness" and "whenever any Form of Government becomes destructive of these Ends ... it is their Right, it is their Duty to throw off such Government...." Obedience to conscience thus becomes translated into a duty to follow a purpose or purposes in life. It is, after all, hardly debatable that mankind has an inward yearning to know what life is all about and how to impact the future.

Last, the authors of the Declaration acknowledged that their behaviors were not ultimately judged by any natural worldly power but instead by the "Supreme Judge of the World," "their Creator," that is, "God." This has to mean that conscience is that place that hears the voice of God (Albornoz, 1967, p. 70) or where the laws of God are imprinted (von Eckardt, 1959, p. 77). Because conscience is the internal residence of God's laws, if we act against these laws, whether correctly or incorrectly received, then we, in effect, have sinned against God, the assumed author of these laws. As Jefferson's opening quote affirms, we answer only to God for our conscience. Interestingly, in keeping with their concepts of liberty and equality, the authors did not ask God to judge the leadership of Great Britain. They asked the God they believed in to judge only themselves. They thus were not setting themselves up to judge the King's conscience since, as we have seen earlier, that was a matter strictly and solely between the King and his God.

By extension, freedom of conscience is founded in a religious orientation. The signers of the Declaration were behaving as they thought God would expect. This is why they based their argument on "The Laws of Nature and of Nature's God" and then appealed to Him for judgment (i.e., "Rectitude") regarding the correctness of their intentions.

A Religious Duty

To behave as God would have them behave means that they were actually performing a religious duty. They, in fact, said that "it is their duty to throw off such Government, and to provide new Guards for their future Security." Freedom of conscience thus means the freedom to act as expected by God. As these colonists themselves dramatically demonstrated, they were engaging in a religious duty by compellingly following their consciences. Parenthetically, it is interesting to note that not one of the many grievances listed against the King related to a purely religious function. The grieved actions, though seemingly secular in nature, were seen by the writers as founded in inalienable rights given by their Creator. Because the independence declared in the document is founded in the Creator-given duty to protect other Creator-given inalienable rights, the U.S. Declaration of Independence can rightfully be called a religiously-derived document. And because the grieved activities were nonetheless "secular," it ultimately means that religious freedom applies to behaviors other than just those externally religious such as church attendance. Following one's conscience in the everyday affairs of life (witness the list of abuses suffered from the King) is just as much and perhaps even more typically a religious duty as the text of the Declaration so eloquently indicates. Twentieth century English journalist G. K. Chesterton said, "America is the only nation in the world that is founded on a creed. That creed is set forth with dogmatic and even theological lucidity in the Declaration of Independence" (Wills, 1978, p. xxi).

Thus the liberty spoken of as an inalienable right must include the freedom to follow one's own conscience and to dutifully act consistent with one's own religious beliefs. Because humans direct and judge their moral behavior, each from his or her own conscience, freedom of conscience is perhaps the most important inalienable right outside of life itself. Any abridgment of this right is worse than even servitude through slavery, which in fact the original draft of the Declaration vehemently protested (cf., Peterson, 1984, pp. 19-20).

As the Declaration itself attests, there was a contest or battle over freedom of conscience. At the very opening of the Declaration, the antagonistic trait inherent within each person to control others was acknowledged. This conflict of man against man is obviously not new nor unique and is perhaps epitomized in the classic clash over the separation of church and state. Basically the church or one's religion is to be the teacher of righteousness and the state the guardian of good social order. As human institutions, they reflect human nature. Accordingly, when reflective of humanity's adverse controlling tendencies, these institutions compete for dominion over mind and behavior as we are about to see.

History of Religious Freedom

With a focus on the foundations of the United States, our study of religious freedom is pertinently confined to the western church. More specifically, we focus on Christendom since it is likely the only religious heritage to have as a major tenet the delineation of the spheres of church and state. The message from Christ that "My kingdom is not of this world" (John 18:36) is a bold historical expression by a religious order regarding the distinction between civil and ecclesiastical authority. Prior to this point in time, the non-Christian religions as well as the Hebrew culture—as predecessor to Christianity—usually had either of the two authorities as the outgrowth of the other. Whereas the Hebrew state got its civil authority from its religion, that is from God, most if not all other civil authorities in one degree or another were themselves the ordainers of appropriate institutions for worship. But with the advent of the Christian church, the lines of authority of church and state were seen as basically separate and delineated in their actions. Important as it is to understand the proscribing of civil and religious authority in terms of their joint relationship, it is even more important to see this conflict in terms of human self-governance.

The words of Christ delineating church and state authority reveal that human institutions were no longer to be the prescribers of what to believe in one's heart and conscience. Since the kingdom of God is primarily over the heart rather than just external behavior, it is "legitimate" to view the heart as the determiner of behavior instead of vice versa. This perspective makes it possible to have integrity or alignment of the heart and behavior of an individual since officially decreed "truths" that run counter to the God-intended directions of the heart and conscience are not the only choice for the individual. With the kingdom of heaven now at hand, an individual can choose to behave consistent with heart and conscience rather than having the external authority decree the "appropriate" behavior to which the heart "must" align itself or be in conflict with (either open or covertly).

European Traditions

This interaction and possible conflict between freedom of conscience (which includes freedom of religion), or in other words, self-rule, and the limited role of church and state is illustrated in a somewhat quick sweep across history. In this historical sweep across Western society we see the human trait that invariably tries to define how others should think and believe.

For approximately 300 years into the era Anno Domino (the year of our Lord), the civil power continued to exercise either passive or aggressive contempt against the Christian church. The effect of this contempt was civil overrule of the rightful moral authority of the church and, therefore, automatically over the freedom of conscience and more specifically freedom of religious worship. In spite of this oppression, the church flourished and, likely by virtue of the numerical magnitude of its followers, was allowed to exist by the state but not as the religion of the state. Freedom of worship actually occurred through the emperors Licinius and Constantine in their Edict of Milan in the year 313 A.D. The edict gave "both to Christians and to all others free power of following whatever religion each man may have preferred" (Cobb, 1968, p. 25). The consequence of this edict in disestablishing paganism and establishing no religion allowed freedom of worship and thus freedom of conscience.

This emancipation of all religions from the state was, however, short-lived. After Constantine's death, his sons, with their decree that heathen temples should be closed, reinstituted religious persecution. This time, however, the persecution was against the "heathen" religions instead of the Christian religions. The decree in effect served to establish Christianity as the religion of the state. Over the next several centuries, the two institutions of church and state existed somewhat separately yet all the while depending on each other for support and alliance against their common enemy—the pagan culture. As the influence of either grew, so grew the other.

The balance was not long to last, however. It went in either one direction or the other depending on the relative strength of respective civil and religious leaders. By the end of the 6th century, the church, led primarily by Gregory the Great, had clearly expanded its authority over the state. By the 9th century, however, the balance shifted back to state control primarily under the civil leadership of Charlemagne. This condition lasted until the rise of Hildebrand as the Pontiff Gregory VII (from 1073 to 1085) who turned the power back to the church. Later, under Pope Innocent III (from 1198 to 1216), kings and emperors were declared to be vassals of the Pope. With the church's authority and motives questioned and with a foretaste of national liberties experienced at the beginning of the Renaissance, the balance of power shifted back again to state control. By the mid to late 1600s, this reversal was so complete that the Pope was considered subject to civil government councils both in terms of authority and matters of doctrine.

The swing back and forth between church and state rule did little to advance the potential of freedom of conscience inherent to their joint existence. The battle for control of authority laterally between church and state likewise was exerted vertically over the people who invariably were the ultimate victims of this authoritarianism. For instance, when the Catholic church was subjected to state control, as under Henry VIII, its followers were persecuted, yet so too were those who did not follow the basic religious teachings espoused by that very church. The Protestant rulers disallowed the authority of Rome yet nonetheless insisted on belief in the faith that Rome stood for as the means to hold together civil rule. In close time proximity, the divisions in Protestantism brought more religious diversity but scant little actual religious choice. This was so because the national ruler, in authority over the church, looked to unity of religious belief to perpetuate the state. Since the existence of more than one religious system in a nation constituted civil impurity in the eyes of the national ruler, it could not be allowed. Therefore, to live under a king was to accept his faith; thus freedom of conscience and religious worship were sacrificed at the altar of battle between civil versus ecclesiastical authority. In the country of England, for instance, it was King Henry VIII, and not the people themselves, who broke from the Roman church, establishing the state institution known as the Church of England.

By the time of the Reformation, the matter was even more complex. Whereas individual freedom of conscience was previously at the mercy of the battle between two lines of authority (civil versus ecclesiastical), it now additionally suffered because of the battle within civil and religious institutions. As noted above, national leaders chose the religious beliefs for their citizens, and religious leaders battled for conformity in the minds of believers, often enlisting the aid of the civilian authorities in the process. Martin Luther, for instance, was reluctant to allow church self-government in Germany and so advocated the exercise of certain civilian powers over it. John Calvin in Switzerland likewise demanded that the civil authorities punish those censured by the church, as did John Knox in Scotland.

While the church professed to believe in the statement that "God alone is the Lord of the conscience," it, at the same time, endorsed powers to the civil realm. The end state of affairs was an institution that spoke the language of religion yet endorsed enforcement by the state, that is, by the sword.

There were dissenters. The Pilgrims and later the Puritans fled such persecution. George Fox led the group known as Quakers in proclaiming liberty of conscience even to the extreme. Also received as extreme but which formed the basis for the eventual separation of church and state in America was the freedom of conscience doctrine proposed by the Anabaptists two hundred and fifty years after Luther. They firmly believed that "The magistrate is not to meddle with religion or matters of conscience, nor compel men to this or that form of religion; because Christ is the King and Lawgiver of the Church and conscience" (Cobb, 1968, p. 64).

However, for the most part, dissension was not for true liberty but only for liberty of the protesting group at the expense of others. We can see the repetition of this biased form of liberty over the approximately 19 centuries since the birth of Christ. Namely, the church, the state, or a vocal minority all insisted on their liberties— and only, or at least, primarily, their liberties.

In fact, the mindset at the founding of the United States reflected the orientation that existed for at least the 19 centuries of humanity just reviewed. Namely, that the controlling authority had the truth and could prescribe this truth for all others. The crucial concern then for any group was how to get and then keep this authority. Thus, while our founding fathers often specifically came to this country to worship God, it was more the case that they came to worship God their own way and to have everyone else do likewise.

Colonial Traditions

As the colonies were founded, three separate orientations surfaced along the lines of authority just discussed—namely among church, state, and individual conscience.

Beginning with the region first settled, Virginia and the Carolinas decreed, by charter and also by colonial legislative action, the Church of England as the state religion. As such, the civil state was the governing body, and the church was its subject. Citizens were to obey the church as a prime indication of their duty as a state citizen. The state decreed its official religion, and the state had the prime responsibility for care of that religion. Freedom of worship was not allowed for any other religious belief. In fact, the Baptist in Virginia probably suffered "the worst and most inexcusable assault on freedom of conscience and worship" (Cobb, 1968, p. 111) that our Colonial history can describe. Cobb notes that official church in Virginia ultimately failed because of its self-promoting efforts at the expense of the citizens of the state.

Most of the New England colonies stand in contrast. While a particular religion (i.e., the Congregational church) was likewise established by state law, it was in conformity with the majority will of the people rather than autocratically by a ruling elite. The orientation, while still a union of church and state, was more of a theocracy for the purpose of bringing God's will on earth. Yet even while we may ascribe a purer religious motive to these New England settlements than to the Virginia region, they were alike in persecuting dissenters. Fearful that "this wilderness might be looked on as a place of liberty, and, therefore, might in time be troubled with erroneous spirits," the magistrate was given certain powers in matters of religion (Cobb, 1968, p. 158) which included punishing, excluding, or banishing from its borders anyone who professed heretical religious beliefs. For example, the preamble to early Massachusetts law read, "although no human power be lord over the conscience, yet because such as bring indamnable heresies ... ought duly to be restrained.." As Cobb (1968, p. 177) writes, the ruling authority demanded for themselves a power of conscience which they denied to all other men.

A third major orientation, prefiguring the ideas resident in the U.S. Declaration of Independence, arose from religious persecution in New England. A fervent advocate of freedom of religious liberty, Roger Williams quickly incurred the displeasure of the

Massachusetts magistrates for his denunciation of any civil involvement in religious matters. He claimed that civil mandates in religion violated the dignity of the conscience and the natural freedom of the mind (Cobb, 1968, p. 183). "The straining of men's consciences by the civil power is so far from making men faithful to God or man, that it is the ready way to render them false to both" (Cobb, 1968, p. 185), said Williams.

Banished from Massachusetts, Williams settled in what was to become the state of Rhode Island, calling his new settlement Providence. He believed that here "the most wise God hath provided and cut out this part of His world for a refuge and receptacle for all kinds of consciences" (Cobb, 1968, p. 425). Whereas the Puritans in Massachusetts objected not to secular control over the church but just secular control for what they deemed to be wrong ends, Williams wanted "liberty for all kinds of consciences" (Cobb, 1968, p. 426) in his principled belief that God alone was the Lord over the conscience. To Williams, this principle of freedom of conscience was essential both to true religion and true humanity.

Williams's argument for the complete uncoupling of church from state control is cited as follows (Cobb, 1968, p. 426):

As it would be confusion for the Church to censor such matters and acts of such persons as belong not to the Church; so it is confusion for the State to punish spiritual offenses for they are not within the sphere of a civil jurisdiction... The civil state and magistrate are merely and essentially civil, and, therefore, cannot reach (without transgressing the bounds of civility) to judge in matters spiritual, which are of another sphere and nature than civility is.

Regarding the tragic consequences of civil intrusion, Williams writes,

Civil and corporate punishments do usually cause men to play the hypocrite and dissemble in their Religion, to turn and return with the tide, as all experience in the nations of the world do testify now. This binding and rebinding of conscience, contrary or without its own persuasion, so weakens and defiles it, that it (as all other faculties) loseth its strength and the very nature of a common honest conscience... This Tenet of the Magistrates keeping the Church from Apostatizing, by practicing civil force upon the consciences of men, is so far from preserving Religion pure, that it is a mighty Bulwark or Barricado to keep out all true Religion. (Cobb, 1968, p. 427)

The section on religion in the Rhode Island charter of 1663 read: "No person within the said colony, at any time hereafter, shall be any wise molested, punished, disqualified, or called in question for any difference of opinion in matters of religion: every person may at all times freely and fully enjoy his own judgement and Conscience in matters of religious concernments" (Cobb, 1968, p. 436). Official representatives of England who visited Rhode Island in 1665 reported that "They allow liberty of conscience to all who live civilly: they admit of all religions" (Cobb, 1968, p. 437).

In this same grouping of colonies that separated religious conscience from state authority, we also must include with Rhode Island the colonies Pennsylvania and Delaware. While not as open in matters of religious conscience as Rhode Island, Pennsylvania nonetheless made no attempt to establish a state church. Similarly, Delaware made no legal provision for managing men's religious opinions nor apparently did its laws ever violate anyone's rights of conscience.

The remaining colonies fit into none of the above three categories in any neat or tidy way since they are all marked by the characteristics of general instability regarding church-state relationships.

By the time of the Revolution, practically all colonies had individually and uniquely lived through such experiences as to make them all generally receptive to freedom from state control of conscience and religious worship. The orientation toward national independence naturally severed those affiliations to a church-state in the old country. Cobb (1968, p. 485), however, claims that the most pervasive mindset against a church-state originated through the preaching of Jonathan Edwards. In his messages on the "divine character of the Church and the absolute necessity for the purity" (p. 487), he elevated thinking about the Church to a position beyond state authority and human contrivances. Up to this point the church was defined—either by the individual or a collection of individuals known politically as the state—according to temporal standards. However, according to Edwards, one was admitted into church membership only by a heart repentant before God, was received only by the grace of God, and was ruled over only by Him. Edwards, through these messages, made it clear that while the conscience of man is to be free from external coercion, it can pursue and discover but not define truth since truth is already established by God. What man can do in the freedom of his conscience is to decide whether or not to accept truth. According to Cobb, these teachings turned the minds of that generation to the disestablishment of the church in America.

Philosophy of Natural Rights

The receptivity for religious disestablishment and freedom of conscience wrought through the pragmatics of colonial life was similarly enhanced by philosophical orientations of the time. We focus in this section on the thinking that guaranteed mankind certain rights, like freedom of conscience, which by nature were undeniably privileged. These rights were, in fact, called natural rights.

The practical philosopher and statesman, Thomas Jefferson, reflected the mindset of his time with the belief that all men were equal in the sense that no one is naturally entitled to any more power or privilege than any other. Since each person is nonetheless unequal in talents, abilities, etc., his rights cannot be based on such inequalities since the logical consequence of doing so is clear discrimination and a denial of the basic humanness of those considered less privileged or talented in one way or another (von Eckardt, 1959, p. 71). Thus all men are considered to have some natural rights that are self-evident and that should not, in fact, be based on apparent inequalities. The sole determining fact for equal natural rights is that all are equal in their status as humans.

The philosophical basis for self-evident natural rights goes back at least to the Greek philosopher Socrates (Carson, 1973, p. 57). The Greeks concluded that governing or at least accounting for the physical reality of change, alteration, and deterioration in life was a metaphysical or spiritual reality of constancy, fixedness, and order, or in other words a fixed natural law governing and explaining an ever-changing reality. The Romans amplified this concept in their belief that the order of law was applicable everywhere even when cultures and circumstances were not the same. More recently, the rationality of the universe as revealed in scientific, political, and artistic thought during the 15th to approximately the 18th centuries served to support what is known as the natural law philosophy.

The natural law philosophy applies equally to the nature of mankind. That is, to know the nature of humanity, as with the nature of all physical phenomenon, means that all accidental or incidental characteristics must be stripped away to reveal only those things that a person or thing shares in common with all others of the same kind. As Cicero would say, "whatever definition we give to man will be applicable to the entire race" (Corwin, 1978, p. 19). To see man in this state of nature or natural self is to thus know the nature of humanity. For instance, humans are naturally considered to be rational creatures since they operate by reason and are unique in this characteristic.

As a system of way of thinking, this natural law philosophy is arrived at by observation and deduction—interestingly, all from humanity's mental and perceptual orientation. In America, the natural law orientation did not derive solely from that methodology. The biblical understanding of the time went beyond this methodology in two ways. One, the natural order of things and the nature of humans in particular was thought to be from God and not exclusively just a "natural" phenomenon. Secondly, the deduced natural characteristics were not an end in themselves but were, in fact, evidences of their prior credibility as first created by the Word of God (Whipple, 1972, p. 29). The methodology of observation and deduction was not then the prime vehicle for original thought but instead was in the instrument for uncovering God's preexisting truths.

The natural rights philosophy was compatible with the prevailing biblical view since numerous Scripture verses attest to the fact that all people are equal before God and all are equally responsible in the exercise of decisions and actions. To be responsible for making correct decisions and actions means that there is a natural, even God-given, right to engage in such behaviors and actions. This is an important point to acknowledge since apparently most of the thinking in the United States at the time of the Revolution was biblically oriented and not exclusively philosophically derived. In fact, according to Cooley (Cobb, 1968, p. 525), it is not possible to label this country unchristian since "In a certain sense and for certain purposes it is true that Christianity is part of the law of the land." More specifically, de Tocqueville, in the 1800s, wrote, "there is no country in the whole world in which the Christian religion retains a greater influence over the souls of men than in America. By regulating domestic life it regulates the state. Religion is the foremost of the institutions of the country. I am certain that the Americans hold religion to be indispensable to the maintenance of republican institutions" (Cobb, 1968, p. 525). Thomas Jefferson also reflected on this matter: "Can the liberties of a nation be sure when we remove their only firm basis, a conviction in the minds of the people, that these liberties are the gift of God? That they are not to be violated but with His wrath? Indeed I tremble for my country, when I reflect that God is just..." (Rushdoony, 1978, p. 6).

This biblical revelatory overlay to the "natural" natural rights philosophy has important ramifications for understanding the events both of that time as well as of our current time. Namely, these natural rights become not so much a license to practice or behave as one individually and egocentrically pleases, but rather these rights are God-given for God-ordained purposes. In other words, to be "endowed by their Creator with certain unalienable rights" means that precisely because God is a completely moral being, the granting of certain rights by Him will axiomatically have moral purposes. As nations and individuals are too often needfully reminded, rights and freedoms imply responsibilities. Specifically, freedom of conscience and of religion have moral purposes— whether or not such purposes are acknowledged.

Interestingly, these historical events and philosophical orientations all seemed to converge at the event of the Revolution in America. The repeated acts of deprivation of rights by the King of England over the colonies were met, after much perseverance (i.e., after "a long Train of Abuses and Usurpations"), with a formal defense of the rights of humans everywhere and of the colonists in particular. These rights included, as discussed earlier, "Life, Liberty, and the Pursuit of Happiness" and "Consent of the

Governed." The ratification by the thirteen colonies attests that these rights were held in agreement by the majority of the population. Bypassing the first as tangential to our interests, we discuss the remaining three rights in reverse order.

Consent of the Governed

Probably the most basic and foundational of all those rights enumerated in the Declaration is that of self-governance. While nowhere is it specifically stated, the right to self-governance or of personal sovereignty is woven throughout the fabric of the Declaration. Recalling our discussion of equality in Chapter 1, each person is created equal as a person and is equally entitled to pursue the calling and to receive the dignity for which he or she is created. It is important to note that the reference point for self-governance is not primarily a country or a nation but rather each individual person. As the Declaration clearly notes, men (e.g., humans), are all created equal as men and not first as nations. And as individual creations of their Creator, each is fully and equally entitled to exercise certain basic rights. It is, however, not just appropriate but in fact lawful and natural (e.g., according to the "Laws of Nature and of Nature's God") for individuals to join collectively into some form of government to ensure these rights. As stated in the Declaration, "That to secure these Rights, Governments are instituted among men, deriving their just powers from the Consent of the Governed." So a major purpose of government is to ensure and thus not take away these rights. That governments are to ensure these rights quite obviously means that some rights, in fact, are not to be turned over to the government.

One of the nontransferable rights relates to freedom of conscience and religion. As already mentioned, government cannot force opinions or conscience. But conversely, government cannot allow for any other institutional deprivation of these rights. Specifically, government must be the guardian against religious oppression while at the same time not prescribing religious orthodoxy. The conscience answers to God and God alone.

Whenever government oversteps its bounds vis a vis its citizens, it no longer operates within its granted (from the citizens themselves) authority. According to the Declaration, whenever government "becomes destructive of these Ends [inalienable rights], it is the Right of the People to alter or to abolish it and to institute new Government ... it is their Right; it is their Duty to throw off such Government, and to provide new Guards for their future Security." The right to "throw off such government" or to engage in civil disobedience is not by any means a right to be taken casually. In fact, as Locke notes, people are basically partial to the status quo and not inclined to rebel against every mismanagement but rather to suffer the wrongs instead (Pelczynski & Gray, 1984, p. 77). But as the Declaration reads, "when a long train of Abuses and Usurpations ... evinces a design to reduce them under absolute Despotism, it is their Right, it is their Duty, to throw off such Government..." It would seem that justification for citizen disobedience must approach the magnitude of large scale despotism over a long duration as agreed upon by a considerable number of the citizens (von Eckardt, 1959, p. 172), or as John Lock says, where "The precedent and consequences seem to threaten all" (Pelczynski & Gray, 1984, p. 77).

It cannot be stressed often enough that the philosophy and the practices of government emanate from inalienable rights of individuals. And these rights of individuals are based on the basic nature of humans. Therefore, since human nature determines the form of government, then government obviously is derived from the people for the people. It cannot be a truth that people exist to serve the state, but in fact the state exists to serve the people.

The two major principles embodied in these statements are that:

1. Each individual is sovereign over self and personally entitled to the exercise of certain basic rights.
2. That government among the people has as one of its primary purposes the securing of these rights for each individual against encroachments by others acting either individually or collectively.

Happiness

According to the Declaration, man has an inalienable right to the "Pursuit of Happiness." This is one of the rights, in fact, that John Hancock and the others were saying that the King was not allowing them. However, activities they were not allowed as specified in their list of grievances do not seem to be immediately pertinent to the emotion of happiness or fun and enjoyment as we are initially prone to think of those terms. They do, however, relate to the notion of happiness-as-fulfillment as we shall soon see.

Even so, it is accurate to say that humans prefer pleasurable activities and avoid those that are unpleasurable. Because of this fact it is easy to see why the company of friends is preferred over the company of enemies, why sweetened medicine sells better than castor oil, and why "doing your own thing" is typically preferred over submission to authority. But these transitory pleasures and states bear little relevance to the basic desires of the colonists as illustrated by their list of grievances in the Declaration of Independence. Obviously something about happiness of deeper import was being addressed in that monumental document.

It seems that a chief goal in life is happiness. According to the Swiss justist and philosopher Emmerich Vattel, "Happiness is the center to which all the duties of man and a people tend: this is the great end of the law of nature. The desire of happiness is the power spring that puts all men in motion..." (von Eckardt, 1959, p. 172). Locke suggests that the pursuit of happiness is man's chief obligation (von Eckardt, 1959, p. 254), English statesman and political writer Henry St. John Bolingbroke says that happiness is the instinctive object of all humans (p. 271), and Jefferson opines that happiness is the maximum human fulfillment (p. 80). Jefferson further notes that it is the pursuit of happiness and not happiness itself that is our right (von Eckardt, 1959, p. 80). That is what the colonists were requesting of the King. But it is erroneous to think that they wanted carte blanche privilege to happiness or that they conceived of happiness as merely an emotionally blissful state.

It is likewise inaccurate to insist that the truism which says that human capabilities automatically make for inalienable rights is the sole reason why they are included in the Declaration (von Eckardt, 1959, pp. 112, 231). The mere ability to do something does not automatically make it a legitimate right as our forefathers so fervently petitioned the King to recognize about his own unlawful behavior.

Moral Basis

What is true is that humans primarily experience happiness as they are compatible with the moral purposes of their lives. As Jefferson says, "Without virtue, happiness cannot be" (von Eckardt, 1959, p. 111). It was accordingly the purpose-subverting nature of the King's restrictions that led the colonists to "throw off such Government ... as to them shall seem most likely to effect their ... Happiness." They were deprived of seeking happiness in the exercise of their God-given, hence morally directed rights.

The happiness they were seeking was not specifically defined, but there can be no doubt that they saw it as being inextricably linked to God-given ends. As Locke has indicated, humans are to pursue temporal and eternal happiness, both of which are related to God's purposes: "Every man has an immortal soul, capable of eternal happiness or misery, whose happiness depending upon his believing and doing these things in this life which are necessary to the obtaining of God's favor, and are prescribed by God to that end" (von Eckardt, 1959, p. 152). Since "... men cannot be forced to be saved whether they will or no ... when all is done, they must be left to their own conscience" (von Eckardt, 1959, p. 153).

The very words of the U.S. Declaration of Independence reveal this God-oriented concept. The Declaration opens with a justification based on God's entitlement to mankind of an equal station among nations with equality of God-given rights, and it ends with an appeal to that "Supreme Judge of the World" to grant their intentions, placing "firm Reliance on the Protection of Divine Providence." Thus, the Declaration itself is a religiously oriented document. It provides the rationale for what was perceived as an actual "Duty" before God and hence places the "Pursuit of Happiness" within God-directed purposes.

Philosophers who were foundational to the thinking evidenced within the Declaration saw virtue and happiness as interdependent, and Jefferson wrote it that way. Bolingbroke said that "human nature is so constituted that morality alone makes happiness possible" (von Eckardt, 1959, p. 271). God, he continued, "has made us happy, and he has put it into our power to make ourselves happier by a due use of our reason, which leads us to the practice of moral virtue..." (p. 275). According to Jean Jacques Burlamaqui, the pursuit of happiness is "of the will which the creator himself has planted in us" (p. 190). William Blackstone, the noted English lawyer of the time, opined that "God so intimately connected, so inseparably interwove, the laws of eternal justice with the happiness of each individual, that the latter cannot be obtained but by observing the former; and if the former be punctually obeyed, it cannot but induce the latter" (p. 176). Locke says that "virtue and public happiness" are joined together (pp. 240 & 254), and in fact, without virtue man "will be happy neither in this, nor the other world" (Axtell, 1968). Jefferson, as the prime author of the Declaration, said, "From the practice of the purest virtue, you may be assured you will derive the most sublime comforts..." (p. 113).

Ultimately, the pursuit of happiness through virtuous or moral behavior addresses freedom of conscience. As noted at the beginning of this chapter, conscience or heart is that place where the laws of God are thought to be written. As actions accord with conscience, the person will have inner peace. Jefferson noted, "our greatest happiness does not depend on the condition of life in which chance has placed us, but is always the result of a good conscience, good health, occupation and freedom in all just pursuits" (von Eckardt, 1959, p. 101).

As the seat of virtue, conscience must necessarily be afforded the liberty of personal determination. Each person must be allowed the equal opportunity to act according to what he or she believes is right and correct before God. Then and only then can a person truly pursue happiness.

This pursuit of happiness is obviously a matter of some individual interpretation. Each person, as a moral creature, is responsible for determining what to believe to be true and for acting accordingly. Further, each person's conscience actually has to guard the integrity of his or her own beliefs from adverse influence. Obviously the conscience references more than just a limited number of moral absolutes; it is also a guide to personal behavior and beliefs. So to carry out one's ongoing role in life and achieve happiness in it, freedom of conscience is necessary.

Government Protections

As the authors wrote in the Declaration, the new government was to provide "Guards for their future security." This certainly had to include the protection of happiness via freedom of conscience. This would include freedom from encroachment by civil authorities like the King of Great Britain as well as by religious authorities. The case against civil intrusion into the pursuit of happiness is clearly documented in the very cause for the Declaration. Regarding religious intrusion, Jefferson said, "The varieties in the structure and action of the human mind ... are the work of our Creator, against which it cannot be a religious duty to erect the standard of uniformity" (von Eckardt, 1959, p. 115). Since conscience is founded on religious beliefs, freedom of religion will contribute to the guaranteed pursuit of happiness.

Equally relevant to government's role in the right to pursue happiness is the protection of all that is individually possessed. For example, government is to be a protector of taxes ensuring that they are utilized consistent with the moral pursuit of happiness. Taxing against one's conscience would certainly be foreign to one's pursuit of happiness. Likewise, to contribute to the pursuit of happiness, government generally should not do for others what they can do for themselves—to do otherwise nullifies the pursuit of happiness derived from living out life's intended role (von Eckardt, 1959, p. 122).

Jefferson sums up the relation between pursuit of happiness and freedom of conscience with the note that God enabled individuals to "promote the happiness of those with whom he has placed us in society, by acting honestly towards all, benevolently to those who fall within our way, respecting sacredly their rights, bodily and mental, and cherishing especially their freedom of conscience, as we value our own" (von Eckardt, 1959, p. 114).

If happiness or the pursuit of it is the goal or fulfillment and thus "the First law of every government" (von Eckardt, 1959, p. 146), then liberty is the means to this end.

<u>Liberty</u>

Abraham Lincoln once said (Hayek, 1960, p. 11), "The world has never had a good definition of the word liberty." Rather than examine all the possible meanings of the word, we restrict our discussion only to its meaning in reference to freedom of religion and freedom of conscience. Basically, we refer to "the possibility of a person acting according to his own decisions and plans, in contrast to the position of one who was irrevocably subject to the will of another..." (Hayek, 1960, p. 12). We assume with this definition that because an individual can shape his or her actions based on his intentions, each individual has an "assured private sphere" (p. 13) into which others cannot intrude. As Frederick Bastiat (1950), French economist, author, and statesman, defines it, liberty is the right to use one's faculties and property to the extent that such liberty does not interfere with the equal liberty of another.

To be even more specific, we can use Pennsylvania founder William Penn's 1670 description of liberty of conscience: "The free and uninterrupted exercise of our consciences, in that way of worship we are most clearly persuaded God requires us to serve him in, without endangering our undoubted birth-right of English freedoms" (Blau, 1950, p. 53).

Liberty of conscience goes beyond liberty of the mind, extending into outward modes of expression. Were this only a right of the mind, it would not even be in need of publication in the U.S. Declaration of Independence as a basic right. After all, the mind is always free. Quoting again from William Penn,

> By Liberty of Conscience, we understand not only a mere Liberty of the Mind, in believing or disbelieving this or that principle or doctrine; but 'the exercise of ourselves in a visible way of worship, upon our believing

it to be indispensably required at our hands, that if we neglect it for fear or favor of any mortal man, we sin and incur divine wrath.' (Blau, 1950, p. 57)

This liberty of conscience and religion to which we refer is not to be conceived of as primarily anti-government as Penn goes on to say:

> Yet we would be so understood to extended and justify the lawfulness of our so meeting to worship God, as not to contrive, or abet any contrivance destructive of the government and laws of the land, tending to matters of an external nature, directly or indirectly, but so far only as it may refer to religious matters, and a life to come, and consequently wholly independent of the secular affairs of this, wherein we are supposed to transgress. (Blau, 1950, p. 57)

To understand the word liberty as spoken of in the Declaration, we look at how Jefferson and his contemporaries used the term, specifically in regard to freedoms of conscience and religion. We start by summarizing our earlier historical account with the proposition that the pure liberty of conscience and religion that is guaranteed as from God and nature is an American production (Cobb, 1968, p. 2). While the idea is not American, the practice of certainly is. For instance, Dutch philosopher Baruch Spinoza (1632-1677) said, "The mind of the individual belongs to himself, not the state" (Cobb, 1968, p. 7).

Discriminatory Liberty

Yet our historical review shows a constant battle over the minds of men that occurred even up to our country's founding. As late as 1687, King James revealed his intent for the colonies: "I hope by a Parliament to obtain a Magna Carta for Liberty of Conscience" (Cobb, 1968, p. 233). Yet, the practical realities of limited freedom spoken to thus far are again revealed in the new charter of Massachusetts as issued by James's brother, King William, in 1691.

It read, "forever hereafter there shall be liberty of conscience allowed, in the worship of God..." But, unfortunately, the quote doesn't stop there. It ends with the liberty-qualifying phrase, "to all Christians (except Papists)" (Cobb, 1968, p. 233).

This discriminatory granting of liberty of conscience occurred, as we have seen, throughout young America. In Virginia, the Baptists were a prime target for the deprivation of freedom of conscience at the hands of the Church of England in Virginia.

The Baptists seemed to light the fire that ultimately led to the declaration of full religious liberty in America. Similarly, the Quakers took exception to laws in New England that extracted taxes to support ministers of the established Congregational church. Isaac Backus, minister and spokesman for the Baptists, believed that God had appointed civil and religious authorities which should not be mixed under the contention that the equal liberty of conscience was a right given by God and that civil representatives were not their representatives in religious affairs. In defending his stand against the paying of these taxes, Backus said, "It is absolutely a point of conscience with me, for I cannot give in the certificates they require without implicitly acknowledging that power to man which I believe belongs to God" (Pole, 1978, p. 75). The occurrence of this type of thinking by the Baptists in Virginia brought them persecution. Grieved over these persecutions, James Madison wrote to a friend saying, "That diabolical, hell-conceived principle of persecution rages among some ... I have squabbled and scolded, abused and ridiculed so long about it, that I am without common patience. So I must beg you to pity me, and pray for liberty of conscience for all" (Cobb, 1968, p. 490; Alley, 1985, p. 48). Similarly, Thomas Jefferson was appalled at the cruelty and absurdity of religious persecution. He firmly believed, from both his intellectual and religious orientations, that people could never be led to the truth by coercion (Pole, 1978, p. 80). As he said later, "Reason and free inquiry are the only effectual agents against error" (Lee, 1961, p. 63); "It is error alone which needs the support of government. Truth can stand by itself" (Lee, 1961, p. 64); and "what has been the effect of coercion? To make one half the world fools, and the other half hypocrites" (Lee, 1961, p. 64).

Against this background of persecution, the 1774 Virginia State convention received citizen petitions for "protection in the full exercise of their modes of worship" and exemption from "payment of all taxes for any Church whatever" (Cobb, 1968, pp. 490-491). In response to these petitions, the 16th section to the Virginia Bill of Rights proposed by Patrick Henry, drafted by George Mason, and modified by James Madison, specifically allowed for full exercise of freedom of conscience in matters of religion. It reads,

> That religion, or the duty which we owe to our Creator, and the manner of discharging it, can be directed only by reason and conviction, not by force or violence; and, therefore, all men are equally entitled to the free exercise of religion, according to the dictates of conscience; and that it is the mutual duty of all to practice Christian forbearance, love, and charity, towards each other. (Alley, 1985, p. 52)

Counterfeit Liberty

So ingrained, however, was the mindset or attitude of religious freedom for the privileged few that the first draft of this 16th article saw religious freedom as something to be merely tolerated. In its original wording, the article included the phrase, "and, therefore, that all men shou'd enjoy the fullest Toleration in the Exercise of Religion..." (Alley, 1985, p. 51). Madison, seeing through this affront to liberty and equality, had the very concept of toleration stricken from the article. While toleration in immediate practice might satisfy, by definition, toleration actually denies the very principle of religious liberty. The word tolerate implies that all are not equal and that for the sake of harmony a certain privileged granting of rights is allowed for those who are different. But more than implying a gift from a superior, it also suggests that the superior has to endure or bear something otherwise not desired.

The best exposing of the attitude behind the use of the word toleration came from Thomas Paine: "Toleration is not the opposite of intolerance, but is the counterfeit of it. Both are despotisms. The one assumes to itself the right of withholding liberty of conscience, the other of granting it" (Cobb, 1968, p. 9).

It is within this historical context that Thomas Jefferson includes the "unalienable Rights of ... Liberty ..." in the U.S. Declaration of Independence. That he was of the same mind as Madison regarding religious freedom can hardly be questioned. He, in fact, called the state of affairs in Virginia an instance of "religious slavery" (Cobb, 1968, p. 493). And it was Madison and Jefferson who successfully stood together against a bill that would allow for taxes to be collected in support of teachers of the Christian religion even though it provided for each taxpayer to indicate the church to whom his amount of the tax should go.

Moral Liberty

Upon defeat of this bill, Jefferson, in 1777, drafted what some call one of the greatest charters of human liberty (Cobb, 1968, p. 491) to specifically "render impossible all future attempts at civil interference with religion." Entitled "An Act Establishing Religious Freedom," and passed in 1785, it includes the following statements in its preamble (Lee, 1961, pp. 66-68):

> that almighty God hath created the mind free, and mani-
> fested his supreme will that free it shall remain by making
> it altogether insusceptible of restraint; that all attempts to
> influence it by temporal punishments, or burthens, or by
> civil incapacitations, tend only to beget habits of hypo-
> crisy and meanness ... that the impious presumption of
> legislators and rulers, civil as well as ecclesiastical, who,
> being themselves but fallible and uninspired men, have
> assumed dominion over the faith of others setting up their
> own opinions and modes of thinking as the only true and
> infallible, and as such endeavoring to improve them on
> others, hath established and maintained false religions ...
> that to compel a man to furnish contributions of money for
> the propagation of opinions which he disbelieves and

abhors, is sinful and tyrannical; that even the forcing him
to support this or that teacher of his own religious persuasion is depriving him of the comfortable liberty ... that the
opinions of men are not the object of civil government,
nor under its jurisdiction.

The act itself includes the following: "all men shall be free to
profess, and by argument to maintain, their opinions in matters of
religion..." Jefferson ends the Act with statements reminiscent of
his wording in the U.S. Declaration of Independence: "that the
rights hereby asserted are of the natural rights of mankind, and that,
if any act shall hereafter be passed to repeal the present or to narrow
its operation, such act will be an infringement of natural right."

Obvious by now, a correct understanding of the word liberty is
that it is not simply a license to do as one pleases. As Governor
Winthrop of Massachusetts said,

> There is a two-fold liberty, natural (I mean as our
> nature is now corrupt) and civil or federal... By this, man,
> as he stands in relation to man simply, hath liberty to do
> what he likes; it is a liberty to evil as well as good... The
> exercise of this liberty makes men grow more evil. This is
> that great enemy of truth and peace, that wild beast, which
> all the ordinances of God are bent against to restrain and
> subdue it. The other kind of liberty I call civil or federal; it
> may also be termed moral... This liberty is the proper end
> and object of authority ... and it is a liberty to that only
> which is good, just, and honest... This liberty is main-
> tained and exercised in a way of subjection to authority; it
> is of the same kind of liberty wherewith Christ hath made
> us free. (de Tocqueville, 1976, pp. 42-43)

Liberty thus means an equal right to be free and to benefit from
the reciprocal respect for autonomy. Liberty equips man to believe
and to act from his conscience. For the particular liberty known as
freedom of religion, it is a freedom to do as that person believes
God would have him or her do. It does not just mean freedom to go

to church, it means much more. It means to be able to do all those things for which the person was individually created by God to do. Hence, it is not simply a freedom from restraint or coercion by others nor to be oblivious to others but is more appropriately a freedom to act consistently with the laws of nature and of nature's God as interpreted by that person. With this liberty, the person is thus entitled to participate in a divinely ordered plan and to achieve temporal and eternal happiness in the process (Pelczynski & Gray, p. 65). As Locke said, "The moral use of liberty involves obligations to God to follow natural law or reason, and a motive to gain eternal happiness" (p. 70).

Conclusion

The crucial relevance of this chapter involves the role of inalienable rights regarding the question as to who should control education. The answer to the matter is found in the structure of the U.S. Declaration of Independence, America's philosophical creed on government and the nature of mankind.

The wording of the Declaration illustrates that the term freedom of conscience invariably means freedom of religious conscience. The injustices that impelled the colonists to separate from Great Britain and that are listed in the Declaration appear on first glance to be "secular" or nonreligious in nature. Yet the deeper truth is that all men are to be free of such injustices precisely because of religious reasons. Namely, they are endowed by a Supreme Creator with certain foundational liberties and rights which supersede the rightful authority of civil leaders and institutions.

In the enjoyment of these rights, mankind has the reciprocal responsibility to use them for their Creator-intended purposes. Conscience is the internal agent of accountability in this regard, and each person answers to God and God alone for his or her conscience. The Declaration's ultimate appeal to religious conscience to justify liberty sets in place the irrevocable precedent for each American citizen to equally appeal to the right of religious conscience in attaining divinely ordained personal liberty. Each matter of conscience is a matter of religious conscience.

Accordingly, education should never violate the conscience. And since conscience is ultimately religious in nature, even in "worldly" matters, education should not be under control of civil authority. In fact, the role of civil authority is that of a guardian of religious freedoms but not a determiner of religious, hence educational, practice and orthodoxy. To promote anything to the contrary would be to reincarnate the tyrannical spirit typified in King George III.

References

Albornoz, Carrillo De A.F. (1967). *Religious liberty.* (J. Drury translator) NY: Sheed & Ward.

Alley, Robert S. (1985). *James Madison on religious liberty.* Buffalo: Prometheus Books.

Axtell, James L. (Ed.) (1968). *Educational writings of John Locke.* Cambridge: Cambridge Univ. Press. Cited in Cremen, L.A. (1970). *American education: The colonial experience.* 1607-1783. NY: Harper & Row, p. 277.

Bastiat, Frederic (1850/1950). *The law.* Irvington-on-Hudson, NY: Foundation for Economic Education.

Blau, Joseph L. (Ed.) (1950). *Cornerstones of religious freedom in America.* Boston: Beacon Press.

Carson, Clarence B. (1973). *The rebirth of liberty.* New Rochelle, NY: Arlington House.

Cobb, Sanford H. (1968). *The rise of religious liberty in America.* New York: Cooper Square Publ. Inc.

Corwin, Edward S. (1978). *Liberty against government.* Westport, CT: Greenwood Press.

de Tocqueville, Alexis (1945/1976). *Democracy in America.* New York: Alfred A. Knopf.

Hayek, Friedrich A. (1960). *The constitution of liberty.* Chicago: The University of Chicago Press.

Lee, Gordon C. (1961). *Crusade against ignorance: Thomas Jefferson education.* NY: Teachers College Press.

Macpherson, Crawford B. (Ed.) (1980). *John Locke: Second treatise of government.* Indianapolis, IN: Hackett Publ.

Pelczynski, Zbigniew & Gray, John (1984). *Conceptions of liberty in political philosophy.* NY: St. Martin's Press.

Peterson, Merrill D. (Ed.) (1984). *Thomas Jefferson, writings.* New York: Library Classics of the United States.

Pole, Jack R. (1978). *The pursuit of equality in American history.* Berkeley: Univ. of Calif. Press.

Roche III, George C. (1969). *Legacy of freedom.* Hillsdale, MI: Hillsdale College Press.

Rushdoony, Rousas J. (1978). *The nature of the American system.*

Fairfax, VA: Thoburn Press (or *This independent republic*).

von Eckardt, Ursula M. (1959). *The pursuit of happiness in the democratic creed*. New York: Frederick A. Praeger.

Whipple, Leon (1972). *Our ancient liberties*. NY: DeCapo Press.

Wills, Garry (1978). *Inventing America: Jefferson's Declaration of Independence*. Garden City, NJ: Doubleday & Co.

Chapter 3

Parents' Rights

... and no father shall either send his own son as a pupil or keep him away from the training school at his own sweet will, but every 'man jack' of them all (as the saying goes) must, so far as possible, be compelled to be educated, inasmuch as they are children of the State, even more than children of their parents (*The Laws,* Book VII, p. 5, from Ulich, 1950, p. 16)

This quote from Plato, the Roman, is to be contrasted with the following quote from Thomas Jefferson:

A question of some doubt might be raised ... as to the rights and duties of society toward its members, infant and adults. Is it a right or a duty in society to take care of their infant members in opposition to the will of the parent? How far does this right and duty extend?—to guard the life of the infant, his property, his instruction, his morals? The Roman father was supreme in all these: we draw a line, but where?—public sentiment does not seem to have traced it precisely. Nor is it necessary in the present case. It is better to tolerate the rare instance of a parent refusing to let his child be educated, than to shock the common feelings and ideas by the forcible asportation and education of the infant against the will of the father. (Padover, 1943, p. 1074)

The intent of this chapter is to examine the rights of parents over their children in specific regard to educational matters. More precisely, the rights of parents in this regard will be contrasted with the rights of the state.

The approach, consistent with that in Chapters 1 and 2, is to reason from ideas contained in the U.S. Declaration of Independence and that were operationalized in the U.S. Constitution. Also consistent with the approach taken in the earlier two chapters, the philosophy of Thomas Jefferson, author of the Declaration, and his contemporaries and mentors are examined to ascertain the full meaning of the words penned in the Declaration.

Our first activity in this chapter is to reveal an underlying orientation of the Declaration that ultimately bears on the question of who has educational authority over children—the parents or the state? Accordingly, we start first by looking at the nature of humans as portrayed in the Declaration.

Nature of Human Authority

The human is considered to be an independent political entity who is self-governing and unbounded by the ultimate rulership of others. As the Declaration indicates, all men are created equal. This does not mean all men in the world together as a single unit since, if true, there would be no other unit left with which to be equal. It means instead that all people are *each* individually equal to each other. Further, in the state of being equal, each person has a number of rights, some of which cannot be given to or taken away by anyone. In fact, at least some of those rights that can be transferred are expressly done so to enable each individual to enjoy the full benefit of those rights that are not transferable. Quoting from the

Declaration, "That to secure these Rights [Life, Liberty and the Pursuit of Happiness], Governments are instituted among Men, deriving their just Powers from the Consent of the Governed..." Governments exist then to enable the basic inalienable rights of each individual person.

The Declaration's claim that each individual (adult) person is entitled to the full and equal benefits of life, liberty, governmental protection and responsibility, and pursuit of happiness is a clear indication that each person is considered to the administrator of one's own self. Each person is considered to be capable of and is expressly protected in the opportunity for maximum self-governance. This maturity ascribed to each individual applies both to managing one's own life and to responsibly ensuring that one's actions do not infringe on the equal rights of others.

It is only because each person is basically a governmental entity that it is possible for certain individual rights to be transferred to civil government. As the Declaration indicates, the civil government derives its "Powers from the Consent of the Governed."

Implicit in the statement that each person is a government unto or a governor over self is the notion that men are considered naturally capable to exercise reasonable self-governance. But it also means that humans are capable of overseeing those rights they have conditionally transferred to a civil authority. So the nature of man as described in the Declaration is someone who has by natural right the property and practice of self-governance, but even more basic, the capability to oversee that which he has created and for which he is responsible.

The nature of man as someone inherently responsible for that which he creates is seen in two ways in the Declaration. First, given that civil government is created by consent of the governed, each person is thus held responsible on an ongoing basis for ensuring that his or her transferred rights are being appropriately exercised. Since our forefathers held the natural prerogative to "alter or abolish" any government "destructive of these Ends" (e.g., Life, Liberty and the Pursuit of Happiness), they obviously viewed each man as responsible to that monitoring activity. Second, in the process of reclaiming a proper government, our forefathers held themselves mutually and unequivocally responsible to the new form of government ("Free and Independent States") that they declared: "And for the support of this Declaration ... we mutually pledge to each other our Lives, our Fortunes, and our sacred Honor." Obviously, this responsibility is not conceived of as existing in isolation but is to be exercised in concert with others suggesting a level of social maturity beyond an individually isolated existence.

Thus, from the Declaration we see that man is envisioned as one endowed with self-governance, particularly in the exercise of certain individually applicable rights, and as one responsible for that which he creates by natural right. Accordingly, the colonists held the King of Great Britain responsible for the welfare of the colonies. As the King was the one who commissioned them, he naturally was the one to be held accountable for them.

Creator-Founded

This reference to the King's responsibility brings us to two important corollaries regarding the nature of man as recognized in the U.S. Declaration of Independence. First, authority, even when rightfully bestowed, can only be legitimately exercised when it is consistent with the inalienable rights of men as given by God. The colonists obviously thought the King was administering otherwise: "The History of the present King of Great Britain is a History of repeated Injuries and Usurpations, all having in direct Object the Establishment of an absolute Tyranny over these States." Accordingly, they set about to reclaim their God-given rights. While it is true that the King was indeed tending to their affairs, it was not in a way consistent with their natural God-given rights. Thus, inalienable rights serve as the value system by which actions of authority are evaluated.

Both the King and the colonists claimed to be operating within their rights, even their God-given rights. Obviously, both parties could not be correct given the level of disunity they were experiencing. The colonists, in raising the evaluation to the level of standards based in God's laws, signal that man can only legitimately exercise his authority when he is consistent with God's standards for that authority. Authority exercised according to other standards makes the perpetrator a tyrant and a candidate for being deposed, but even then legitimately and consistent with God's standards. Thus, the nature of authority invested in man must, according to the principles in the Declaration, be exercised according to the standards implicit to God-given rights else it is not a legitimate or just authority: "Governments are instituted among men deriving their just powers from the consent of the governed..."

<u>Government Accountability</u>

The second corollary interacts in this particular case with the first in that the government is accountable to its constituents and not primarily vice versa. In relation to our discussion on the joint natures of man and government, man is defined as having primary and irrevocable authority and the government as having derived and conditional authority. The colonists demonstrated the primacy of their authority by "repeated Petitions" to the King and further by appealing to their "British Brethren" to exert their authority over the legislature and the King to treat the colonists fairly:" ... we have conjured them by the Ties of our common Kindred to disavow these Usurpations." The British subjects were thus recognized as having authority to hold the King accountable on behalf of fellow subjects living in America.

Even as man is recognized as having authority that flows to civil government and not primarily vice versa, there is a deeper level of authority that is documented in the Declaration that undergirds both these authority structures. The documentation of this undergirding appears in several different ways. First, the Declaration plainly asserts and in fact bases all statements on the authority which comes ultimately from Creator God. It is man's Creator, as the Declaration acknowledges, who fashioned the Laws of Nature (as evidenced in the phrase Nature's God), and it is man's Creator who gives man those inalienable rights which governments are in turn formed to protect.

Supreme Authority

This acknowledgment of God as the source of the authority for the U.S. Declaration of Independence removes the bind implied in statements we have made that man is an independent political entity. While man is, he is not a totally self-sufficient nor a completely independent entity—just more so than the governments he establishes. Without recognition of God as the supreme authority, there really is no way to resolve the dilemma wherein man in governmental authority (e.g., King of Great Britain) has to answer, politically speaking, to man as civilian (e.g., the colonists). The dilemma arises in that both parties to the dispute are men who, while created as equal, are nonetheless intended to function in different roles. Naturally the men on both sides would want their own respective interpretations of authority to prevail. After all, while the King of Great Britain felt he could unilaterally rule over other men, the colonists, at the same time, felt they had a right to be treated differently.

Resolution of the dilemma does not reside in assuming that the majority opinion or the most powerful should prevail. The Declaration gives no hint that either is the key to the correct solution. Instead, the acknowledgment in the Declaration that God is the source of authority places the entire matter in a realm beyond the natural orientations of men. That is, the line of authority is taken out of a foundation in man and is located in God instead, allowing man to operate from higher principles than those he only subjectively and/or experientially derives. Conflicts can then be appealed to God as the one ultimately responsible, just as the colonists did with assurance of resolution: "with a firm Reliance on the Protection of divine Providence."

To summarize, the following can be said about the nature of humans as revealed in the Declaration of Independence. Namely, each person is seen as the basic foundational governing unit over self, possessing certain rights that are absolute and nontransferable. It is from each individual person that certain authority is transferred to give government its limited and revocable authority to be used to protect mankind's God-given rights. Further, nontransferable authority includes the responsibility to care for and oversee, both individually and collectively, that which man creates, whether it be an actual government or a statement of purpose and intent, as revealed in a legal document. Finally, the Creator-endowed absolute rights embodied in man actually comprise an inherent value system by which actions can be evaluated as legitimate or not. This places the exercise of man's authority within some definable and objective value system that ultimately resides outside of self as opposed to being subjectively derived and interpreted. In this sense then, the person is defined as one who is irrevocably authorized by God to exercise the nontransferable rights of Life, Liberty and the Pursuit of Happiness for self with the corollary right to both institute and manage civil government toward that end.

Relation to Education

By extension, because we are concerned about the role of parent and state over the child, we can make certain implications in this regard from the nature of human authority as described above. Namely, since governments are instituted from and answerable to those governed regarding their inalienable rights, the parent, as the instituting authority, and not the state has total educational authority over children. The state can never claim rights to children equal to or greater than that which belongs to the parents any more than the King of Great Britain could override the rights of those over whom he governed.

Parental Authority

A different way to say the same thing comes through recognition that what humans created by natural right is their responsibility. That is, the form of government instituted by man was something that he had the responsibility to oversee to ensure compatibility with the standards of man's inalienable rights. (The inalienable rights of man actually prescribe the operation of government.) Accordingly, as man has the natural right from God to reproduce children in his own nature, then he has the responsibility to

God and not to the state nor to the child to oversee his offspring consistent with the standards of life, liberty and the pursuit of happiness that this child has an inalienable (but qualified as we shall soon see) right to also. The fact that children are a natural fruit of parents and not of the state is evidence enough to ascribe parental and not states' rights over children.

Montgomery (1889/1972, pp. 50-52) summarizes the opinions of a number of writers on this subject: "Every standard writer on the subject of either law or morals proclaims with one voice that *parents* are bound by the natural law to feed, clothe, and *educate* their own children." John Bouvier says: "The principal obligations which parents owe their children are their maintenance, their protection, and their education." Chancellor of the New York Court of Chancery, James Kent, says: "The duties of the parents to their children, as being their natural guardians, consist in maintaining and educating them during their season of infancy and youth." English jurist Sir William Blackstone says,

> The last duty of the parents to their children is that of giving them an education suitable to their station in life; a duty pointed out by reason, and of far the greatest importance of any. For, as Puffendorf [German jurist, historian, and law professor] very well observes, 'it is not easy to imagine or allow that a parent has conferred any considerable benefit upon his child by bringing him into the world if he afterwards entirely neglects his culture and education, and suffers him to grow up like a mere beast, to lead a life useless to others and shameful to himself.'

Dr. Francis Wayland, American Clergyman and educator, in his *Elements of Moral Science*, says, "The duty of parents is generally to educate or to bring up their children in such manner as *they believe* will be most for their future happiness, both temporal and eternal... He [the parent] is bound to inform himself of the peculiar habits and reflect upon the probable future situation of his child, and deliberately to consider *what sort of education* will most conduce to his future happiness and usefulness...

The duties of a parent are established by God, and God requires us not to violate them." According to the laws of nature, says Wayland, "the teacher is only the *agent*; the *parent* is the principal..." Dr. Wayland continues, "that the relaxation of parental authority has always been found one of the surest indications of the decline of social order and the unfailing precursor of public turbulence and anarchy. Now, under the law, as we have already seen, parental authority is not merely *relaxed,* but it is utterly set at defiance."

Not the State

In terms of education specifically, it is the parent and not the state who has authority regarding education of the child. If the parent decides to send his child to other than a state sponsored school, it is not the right of the State to prohibit or penalize this action. Even if the parent decided to keep the school out of school for reasons pertinent to the inalienable rights of the parent and/or the child, the state, as an instrument to enable each person to rightly live by his or her conscience, has no right to compel the parent to do otherwise. Again, in matters regarding inalienable rights, the state serves rather than rules over its citizens. Montgomery (1889/1972, p. 52) asks the summarizing question,

> What, we would ask, does parental authority amount to, in the matter of educating children, when a parent is not recognized as having any '*remedy, as against the teacher,*' for the wrongs he may perpetuate against his child, and when ... the parent is, in the eye of the law, a criminal who ventures to send his own child to a school of his own choice, and at his own expense, without first going with his hat under his arm to a board of petty officials to beg their *permission* so to do?

With this documentation that the Declaration was written from the perspective that government is to serve man and not primarily vice versa, there should be no doubt that parents and not the state were and are to have educational authority over their children. This conclusion is even further substantiated with the orientation in the Declaration that man is responsible for what he creates.

Further understanding on the matter comes through writings of the colonial era. As discussed next, the way the child was typically thought of during colonial times complements the writings contained within the Declaration regarding the nature of man and the role of civil government.

Nature of the Child

The nature of the adult individual with the capacity for mature guardianship of his/her inalienable rights is contrasted with the nature of the child as a person unable to properly steward these inherent rights. Even for the most basic of these rights, that of Life, the very young child, if not provided for, would be unable to properly subsist and would surely die. The role of the parent is just that—to provide for the basics (e.g., by first providing, and then teaching how to provide). In a similar way, the child must be equipped to manage autonomously other inalienable rights including Liberty, the Pursuit of Happiness and, collectively with others, "the Right ... to alter or abolish" any form of government in violation of these rights. This view of leading the child out of natural dependence and into mature self-governance is reflected in the writings of those influential of the Declaration.

Potential for Liberty

In examining the literature, we see two different but not at all contradictory aspects of the nature of the child and thus the reason for educational guidance. First, the child is acknowledged as someone who, while born free and rational, is not yet able to behave according to the standards of freedom and rationality. This is a subtle yet important point that needs clarification. At any point in an infant's life, he is only able to be free and rational consistent with his capabilities at that point, minimal as they may be. Without external guidance and supervision, this freedom would likely lead to the loss of that very freedom if not life itself. Imagine, for instance, a two year old who is totally "free" to do whatever he or she wants. Obviously, this young child would soon be in much trouble. The inescapable conclusion can only be that freedom or liberty cannot mean license to do whatever one pleases. As discussed earlier, liberty and freedom has to be construed to mean the ability to live within constraints appropriate to the nature of humanity as Creator given. The example applies equally to the adult just as to the child, except generally at a more responsible level.

In his *Two Treatises of Government, Part II*, Locke addresses the role of the parent in nurturing these elements in children and the need for freedom to be guided by reason plus an external standard:

> The freedom then of man and the liberty of acting according to his own will, is grounded on his having reason, which is able to instruct him in that law he is to govern himself by, and make him know how far he is left to the freedom of his own will. To turn him loose to an unrestrained liberty, before he has reason to guide him, is not allowing him the privilege of his nature to be free; but to thrust him out amongst brutes, and abandon him to a state as wretched, and as much beneath that of a man, as theirs. This is that which puts the authority into the parents' hands to govern the minority of their children. God hath made it their business to employ this care on their offspring, and hath placed in them suitable inclinations of tenderness and concern to temper this power, to apply it, as his wisdom designed it, to the children's good, as long as they should need to be under it. (cited in Yolton, 1977, p. 234)

It is this way, says Locke, because children are born into the world with, practically speaking, a total lack of knowledge and understanding of the world. In this state, the child is thought of as a blank slate, or tabula rasa, upon which are to be written the ways of the world (see also Garforth, 1964, p. 51). Similarly, English philosopher Thomas Hobbes says that "the Common-peoples minds ... are like clean paper, fit to receive whatsoever by Publique Authority shall be imprinted in them" (Tarcov, 1984, p. 47).

Jefferson likewise believed that each individual needed to exercise his dispositions to become mature in the ways of the world. He believed that next to an honest heart, a well-educated mind was most important: "An honest heart being the first blessing, a knowing head is the second" (Jefferson, 1984, p. 815). Accordingly, Jefferson was fervent in his "crusade against ignorance" (p. 859). As he said, "I think by far the most important bill in our whole code is that for the diffusion of knowledge among the people. No other sure foundation can be devised, for the preservation of freedom and happiness" (Jefferson, 1984, p. 859). Man, according to Jefferson, must have his inner resources and primarily his mind developed to that self-sufficiency from whence comes his freedom (Lee, 1961, p. 19). While we do not seem to have evidence as to Jefferson's view on the nature of the mind at birth, he clearly sees the human mind as "perfectible to a degree" (1984, p. 1064) in its transformation from ignorance to enlightenment:

> There is a certain period of life, say from eight to fifteen or sixteen years of age, when the mind, like the body, is not yet firm enough for laborious and close operations. If applied to such, it falls an early victim to premature exertion; exhibiting indeed at first, in these young and tender subjects the flattering appearance of their being men while they are yet children, but ending in reducing them to be children when they should be men. Yet should this period be suffered to pass in idleness, the mind becomes lethargic and impotent, as would the body it inhabits if unexercised during the same time. (Jefferson, 1984, p. 274)

Memory, he thought, could be developed through language learning "while that and no other faculty is that matured," with mathematics to follow as soon as reason has "acquired a certain degree of strength" (1984, p. 861).

Jefferson sees this development occurring for both the individual and for each generation:

> We should be far, too, from the discouraging persua-
> sion that man is fixed, by the law of his nature, at a given
> point; that his improvement is a chimera, and the hope
> delusive of rendering ourselves wiser, happier or better
> than our forefathers were... Education ... engrafts a new
> man on the native stock, and improves what in his nature
> was vicious and perverse into qualities of virtue and
> social worth. And it cannot be but that each generation
> succeeding to the knowledge acquired by all those who
> preceded it, adding to it their own acquisitions and
> discoveries, and handing the mass down for successive
> and constant accumulation, must advance the knowledge
> and well-being of mankind, not *infinitely*, as some have
> said, but *indefinitely*..." (Padover, 1943, p. 1099)

Jefferson did believe that man was endowed or born not totally blank but with "the general existence of a moral instinct" (1984, p. 1338) or "a sense of right and wrong" (Padover, 1943, p. 1057) and that it was to be brought to fruition through education. As evident in his plan for education, this process should begin formally at the elementary school level (1984, p. 1348) and informally at the hands of the mothers (1984, p. 1411). In summary, Jefferson's views are that "the qualifications for self-government are not innate. They are the result of habit and long training" (Lee, 1961, p. 19).

Prideful Tendency

In contrast to this positive nature of mankind in general and children in particular that calls for the development of knowledge and the enhancement of virtues, there is another side of the human species in need of a different remedy. Specifically, the same general literature of the time also references the fact "that men are by nature willful and proud and filled with desire to master themselves and others" (Tarcov, 1984, p. 89). It is easy to see via the example of the King of Great Britain why the desire to be master over others can be wrong. Regarding the desire to master themselves, Locke says that "men desire specifically that others should not be their masters and if fully realized having their own will in everything, they will not easily be restrained and curbed" (Tarcov, 1984, p. 89). The child, he says, should not be permitted to "have what he cries for, and do what he pleases" (p. 89). Obviously a balance must be struck; otherwise the one who does whatever he pleases is a tyrant while the one who is entirely mastered by others is a slave.

Locke goes on to say that

> He that has not a mastery over his inclinations, he that knows not how to resist the importunity of present pleasure or pain for the sake of what reason tells him is fit to be done, wants the true principle of virtue and industry and is in danger never to be good for anything. This temper, therefore, so contrary to unguided nature, is to be got betimes; and this habit, as the true foundation of future ability and happiness, is to be wrought into the mind as early as may be, even from the first dawnings of any knowledge or apprehension in children... (Garforth, 1964, p. 64)

So for Locke, man as child must learn or be taught so that his mind has "Mastery over itself" (p. 90). Locke is, in the final analysis, addressing the corrupt nature of humanity. All this suggests that there is a need to teach children how to deny those prideful desires that go against what is right.

Locke goes further to say that children love both liberty and dominion. Liberty he says needs to be accommodated, but love of dominion (over others) ought to be repressed. This love of dominion shows up very early in evidence that they "cry, grow peevish, sullen, and out of humour, for nothing but to have their wills" (p. 131). Ultimately, this desire for dominion shows itself in the desire to have others submit to one's own will and even a desire to use property as power over others (p. 132).

Hobbes, while differing with Locke on the details, sees this same prideful need for liberty and dominion over others but also sees power to get objects and security as another nonvirtuous inclination. He speaks to the selfish desire in children that makes them "think that everything ought to be given them which they desire" (Tarcov, 1984, p. 46). And "unless you give children all they ask for, they are peevish and cry, aye, and strike their parents sometimes" (p. 46).

Jefferson says much the same things about this selfish nature of humans when he speaks of self-love. As he says,

> Self-love, therefore, is no part of morality. Indeed it is exactly its counterpart. It is the sole antagonist of virtue, leading us constantly by our propensities to self-gratification in violation of our moral duties to others. Accordingly, it is against this enemy that are erected the batteries of moralists and religionists, as the only obstacle to the practice of morality. Take from man his selfish propensities, and he can have nothing to seduce him from the practice of virtue. Or subdue those propensities by education, instruction, or restraint, and virtue remains without a competitor... When it is wanting, we endeavor to supply the defect by education, by appeals to reason and calculation... (Jefferson, 1984, pp. 1337-1338)

As Jefferson's statement summarizes, the natural good within that needs to be encouraged, and selfishness, its natural antagonist, which is also part of human nature, calls for education, instruction, or restraint. "Education ... controls, by force of habit, any innate obliquities in our moral organization" (Padover, 1943, p. 1099). The message seems very clear—some or various forms of adult guidance are needed, on the one hand, to enhance the positive or virtuous predispositions of mankind, and of children in particular, and, on the other hand, to override the negative, selfish orientations that are a part of us all. Jefferson saw these contrasting natures clearly revealed in public affairs as follows: "In every government on earth is some trace of human weakness, some germ of corruption and degeneracy... Every government degenerates when trusted to the rulers of the people alone. The people themselves therefore are its only safe depositories" (Jefferson, 1984, p. 274). Jefferson continues, "I know of no safe depository of the ultimate power of the society but the people themselves; and if we think them not enlightened enough to exercise their control with a wholesome discretion, the remedy is not to take it from them, but to inform their discretion by education" (Lee, 1961, p. 17).

With the above quote from Jefferson regarding a major purpose of education, we come full circle to the inferred characteristics of humans as revealed in the Declaration. Maturity is characterized as being responsibly self-disciplined; the child is in need of help to reach this type of maturity. Until the child reaches some level of maturity, this help must occur in a form both to build and enhance ways for the child to become competent in the world as well as to enable the child to exert self-discipline over those internal tendencies that operate counter to virtuous behavior.

Paradox of Rights

It is because of this latter point regarding the selfish nature of children (and indeed of all humanity) that educational efforts may even take on a form that may appear to actually violate the child's right to certain basic rights. While in the process of equipping the child to exercise the inalienable rights of life, liberty, and pursuit of happiness, the child's education may take on a form that to the child and to others may even appear to deprive the child of those very same rights. Discipline falls into this paradoxical area.

Locke speaks to this point when he labels the proper balance between freedom and authority in a child's upbringing as the "true secret of education" (Garforth, 1964, p. 11). We must "keep up a child's spirit easy, active and free, and yet at the same time to restrain him from many things he has a mind to..." (Garforth, 1964, p. 60). A great mistake in children's upbringing, he says, is "that the mind has not been made obedient to discipline and pliant to reason when at first it was most tender" (Garforth, 1964, p. 11). Children must, while little, hold their parents in awe and respect, but as they grow older, this awe and obedience gives way to friendship and self-responsibility. We quote extensively here on Locke's view about the selfish nature of the child and the parents' role in educating the child in this regard:

> This much for the settling your authority over your children in general. Fear and awe ought to give you the first power over their minds, and love and friendship in riper years to hold it; for the time must come when they will be past the rod and correction; and then, if the love of you make them not obedient and dutiful, if the love of virtue and reputation keep them not in laudable courses, I ask, what hold will you have upon them to turn them to it? Indeed, fear of having a scanty portion if they displease you may make them slaves to your estate, but they will be nevertheless ill and wicked in private; and that restraint will not last always. Every man must some time or other be trusted to himself and his own conduct; and he that is a good, a virtuous and able man must be made so within. And therefore what he is to receive from education, what is to sway and influence his life must be something put into him betimes, habits woven into the very principles of his nature... (Garforth, 1964, pp. 53-54)

All of this Locke says is necessary because the child really does not have the actual liberty, through self-discipline, to keep from doing what would sometimes amount to nonvirtuous behavior: "Our first actions being guided more by self-love than reason or reflection, 'tis no wonder that in childhood they should be very apt to deviate from the just measures of right and wrong" (Garforth, 1964, p. 14). Thus, relating to the major theme of this manuscript, a child needs to be equipped for liberty to be able to "deny himself his own desires, cross his own inclinations and purely follow what reason directs as best, though the appetite lean the other way" (Garforth, 1964, p. 40). Parenthetically, this self-denial is what Locke calls "the great principle and foundation of all virtue" (Garforth, 1964, p. 40); and the foundation of this virtue, he says, is "a true notion of God, as of the independent Supreme Being, Author and Maker of all things, from whom we receive all our good, who loves us and gives us all things.

And consequent to this, [is] a love and reverence of this Supreme Being" (Garforth, 1964, p. 123).

Jefferson likewise sees the practice of liberty and the development of or education in self-discipline against selfishness integrally related: "The human character ... requires in general constant and immediate control, to prevent its being biased from right by the seduction of self-love" (von Eckardt, 1959, p. 120). That kind of control functions, according to Jefferson, to preserve the equality of all people by preventing the invasion of individual rights of others. This self-discipline is also defined by Jefferson as virtue, and again, like Locke, it is considered to be that which makes liberty and happiness possible.

Beyond the taming of selfishness that both Locke and Jefferson see as necessary for liberty, the development of knowledge and truth is likewise needed to perpetuate liberty. Locke would say that a child is not free until it reaches the age of discretion (Parry, 1978, p. 82). Exactly what point or age that would be is not precisely defined by Locke. He does consistently characterize it though as being able to manage one's own affairs in a rational manner and to understand moral and civil laws (Parry, 1978, p. 82). Jefferson likewise sees a mature person as one who can operate according to rationality and conscience.

To be able to enter into that liberty which is granted by God and protected by civil authority is to be educated for responsible stewardship. Without some level of maturity in this area, humans will not be able to personally rule over selfish desires or to correctly discern right morality.

As seen above, a certain amount of corrective education is needed to enable children to be master over their selfish desires. Because by nature they do not fully welcome submission to authority, the result may actually deprive children, at least temporarily, of what appears to be certain basic rights. Hence we have labeled this section as the paradox of rights—i.e., withholding rights to enable rights.

Beyond the Paradox

Yet the paradox of rights is in reality not a paradox at all according to Locke and others. It is not a paradox for two complementary, in fact, interlocking reasons. First, God has ordained it as a duty for parents to raise their children a certain way, and hence, this duty of parents could not in God's providence contradict the rights of children since they are just as much God's creatures as are the parents. Second, because of the immaturity of children, they do not in actuality (but only potentially) have the same rights to exercise as do their parents via their own maturity. Obviously, more explanation is necessary.

<u>Parental Higher Duty</u>

Regarding the first point, parents have a certain relationship toward children not because the children are theirs, but because they have a God-given duty regarding their children. Children, just as adults, are not the absolute property of anyone but of "one sovereign master, sent into the world by his order, and about his business; they are his property," (Macpherson, 1980, p. 9). But "Children," Locke goes on to say,

> are not born in this full state of equality, though they are born to it. Their parents have a sort of rule and jurisdiction over them ... but it is a temporary one... Parents are 'by the law of nature,' under an obligation to preserve, nourish, and educate their children they had begotten; not as their own workmanship, but the workmanship of their own maker, the Almighty, to whom they were accountable for them. (p. 31-31)

Thus it is, according to Locke, more correct to say that parents have a duty unto God to raise their children as He intends then to say that parents have some type of arbitrary, self-determined rights over children. But most importantly, it is not a responsibility that parents have invented and thus ever have to, but it is instead a God-given and thus inalienable right. Also, it is a right to be exercised on behalf of children, as opposed to over children.

Children's Reciprocal Duty

On the second and interacting point, children, according to Locke, do not have full right to exercise liberty or free will. Liberty and freedom of will come only with reason and a mind matured to guide actions according to the "law of reason" (p. 32). Locke explains, "For God having given man an understanding to direct his actions, has allowed him a freedom of will, and liberty of acting, as properly belonging thereunto, within the bounds of that law he is under" (pp. 32-33). But while "he has not understanding of his own to direct his will, he is not to have any will of his own to follow: he that understands for him, must will for him too; he must prescribe to his will, and regulate his actions; but when he comes to the estate that made his father a freeman, the son is a freeman too" (p. 33). Thus in some sense of the word, children do not have the same rights as adults. Therefore, those educational actions that might by initial appearances violate the rights of adults do not violate children's rights which as yet do not exist. According to Locke, "The power, then, that parents have over their children, arises from that duty which is incumbent on them, to take care of their offspring, during the imperfect state of childhood" (p. 32). The one right that children evidently do have is the right to be parented.

Thus, what may appear as a paradox or conflict of rights between parents and children is not. Parents and children operate from two different "legal" positions: parents carrying out God-given duties to children with children not having parallel rights that can be violated (assuming of course the appropriate actions by the parents) but possessing the right to, in fact, be recipients of these proper parental duties. Children are "not present free: for law, in its true notion is not so much the limitation as the direction of a free and intelligent agent... The end of law is not to abolish or restrain, but to preserve and enlarge freedom: for in all the states of created beings capable of laws, where there is no law there is no freedom" (p. 32).

While no evidence seems to be available regarding Jefferson's views on the interactive rights of parents and children, what has been said so far regarding the philosophy of the time fits nicely with those assumptions inherent to the Declaration as well as his personal views as indicated at the beginning of the chapter.

Standards of Education and Parenting

The Declaration intends for adults to operate from their conscience according to godly convictions. Those responsible for raising and educating children have to prepare them to do likewise. Education should therefore, within the philosophy undergirding the Declaration, develop maturity consistent with these godly standards. This last sentence has to be true as demonstrated through logical if not practical reasoning.

That is, it is a truism to say that the founders of this country separated from Great Britain because they were operating from their consciences according to the way they felt Creator God would have them behave. Similarly, they purposely and expressly indicated that the major purpose of forming the United States of America was to not just permissively allow lawlessness but to positively and dynamically effect the ability of each person to exercise the God-given rights of Life, Liberty and the Pursuit of Happiness—all of which are to be guided by God's "Truths." We have just seen in this chapter how the major thinkers behind the Declaration conceived of the child as coming into the world virtually empty of knowledge and understanding yet with a sinful predisposition. Thus the child needs to be developed in several major ways—first, to be informed of and made competent in the rightful ways of the world and, second, to be placed in control of nonvirtuous tendencies. Bluntly put, without proper education in these two arenas, the child will fail to achieve the self-governing maturity the Declaration assumed. Obviously then the logical conclusion is that the child has to be equipped to be a manager of what the Declaration was written to guarantee. In other words, if the child is to mature into someone who can exercise rights given inalienably by God, which actually translate into duties before God, then the child's education must be founded on such truths.

This "logical" interpretation of the Declaration is as the authors intended. Jefferson, in his First Inaugural Address (March, 1801), recounts that this country's struggle for independence was through "a due sense of our equal right to the use of our own faculties, to the acquisitions of our own industry, to honor and confidence from our fellow-citizens," which resulted from being

> enlightened by a benign religion, professed, indeed, and practiced in various forms, yet all of them inculcating honesty, truth, temperance, gratitude, and the love of man; acknowledging and adoring an overruling Providence, which by all its dispensations proves that it delights in the happiness of man here and his greater happiness here-after—with all these blessings, what more is necessary to make us a happy and a prosperous people? (Jefferson, 1984, p. 494)

As to the source of this benign religion and this overruling Providence, Jefferson indicates that the religion of this country is based on the Bible. Jefferson's letter, in 1787, to his nephew Peter Carr, says, in discussing religion, "You will naturally examine first, the religion of your own country. Read the Bible, then ..." (Padover, 1943, p. 1058).

Jefferson's words in the Declaration—the "laws of nature and of nature's God"—are explained in the writings of John Locke: "The law of nature stands as an eternal rule of all men ... legislators as well as others. The rules that they make for other men's actions must ... be conformable to the law of nature ... i.e., to the will of God" (Macpherson, 1980, p. 71).

The level as well as the type of maturity inherent in the conceptualization of human ability via the U.S. Declaration of Independence and the understood lack thereof in children leads naturally to the conclusion that education of children is not only necessary but must be based on the truths of God. We have touched also on the position that education of children is the specific responsibility of the parent. We now expand this last point to indicate that it is not the role of the state to educate children.

Parental versus Governmental Responsibility

Thomas Jefferson indicated that the role of government as conceived in both the Declaration and Constitution does not include any direct responsibility to educate children. His one-sentence statement in his First Inaugural Address regarding what he calls "the sum of good government" reads, "a wise and frugal Government ... shall restrain men from injuring one another, shall leave them otherwise free to regulate their own pursuits of industry and improvement, and shall not take from the mouth of labor the bread it has earned" (Jefferson, 1984, p. 494). Even as he further elaborates on this sentence in describing "the essential principles of our Government," he at no time addresses educational activities as a granted part of government.

So central, however, was education for guarding "the sacred deposit of the rights and liberties of ... citizens" (Jefferson, 1984, p. 365) that Jefferson did call for a general system of education to be implemented within the State of Virginia (p. 1346) and to be made available to all up through the third grade. He also went so far as to propose at least under certain conditions that students be "educated at the common expense of all" (p. 365) believing that the necessary tax would be only the "thousandth part" of that paid to tyrants who would rise up if the people were to be left ignorant (Malone, 1948, p. 283).

Yet as crucial as education was for Jefferson to the welfare of both the state and the individual, he clearly noted that it could not be made compulsory. His quote opening this chapter declares that education should not occur "against the will of the father" (Padover, 1943, p. 1074). So for Jefferson, the parent rather than the state had educational authority over the child. In fact, Jefferson was not "tenacious of the form" that his idea of education should take (Slossen, 1921, p. 78).

While not attempting to violate parents' rights over children regarding compulsory educational attendance, Jefferson favored mandatory taxation for education. The Virginia Assembly noted of his education bill in 1786 that the taxation requirements that he proposed were beyond the powers of the state (Malone, 1948, p.

283). In fact, it should be noted that in 1781 and again in '82, he wrote that an amendment to the constitution of that state was necessary in order to come to the financial aid of public education (Jefferson, 1984, p. 274). Furthermore, in his role of President of the United States, he likewise indicated that an amendment to the Constitution of the United States would be necessary to enter the field of education (Richardson, Vol. I, 1897, pp. 397-398).

Conclusion

The tenor of the Declaration is that parents, not the civil government, have authority over children's education. Furthermore, by the nature of the standard appealed to in the Declaration, the assumption was that children were expected to be raised to reason from a Creator-granted natural rights framework to maintain consistency with all the rights of mankind as given by God.

If one of the capabilities of natural rights reasoning is to be able to hold government responsible as an agent of the people, government logically cannot be the teacher of these responsibilities. (The servant is not greater than the master.) The principle of vested interest would invariably lead government to self-protection rather than self-abasement and, by extension, the self-promoter rather than the citizen-promoter in the education process. It is unlikely that government would teach its citizens the truths and principles necessary to change or abolish that very government if it ever deprived those same citizens of their inalienable rights. Has there even been a government so humble?

Any government that claims educational sovereignty for itself instead of securing and maintaining it for parents has, in that action alone, violated the inalienable rights of its citizens. Any superseding government sponsorship of education thereafter can only magnify this initial injustice.

References

Garforth, Francis W. (1964). *John Locke: Some thoughts concerning education.* Woodbury, NY: Barron's Educational Series, Inc.

Jefferson, Thomas (1984). *Writings.* NY: Literary classics of the U.S. Inc.

Lee, Gordon C. (1961). *Crusade against ignorance: Thomas Jefferson on education.* New York: Teachers College Press.

Macpherson, Crawford B. (Ed.) (1980). *John Locke: Second treatise of government.* Indianapolis: Hackett Publ.

Malone, Dumas (1948). *Jefferson the Virginian.* Boston: Little, Brown & Co.

Montgomery, Zach. (1889/1972). *The school question.* New York: Arno Press & The New York Times.

Padover, Saul K. (1943). *The complete Jefferson.* Freeport, NY: Books for Libraries Press.

Parry, Geraint (1978). *John Locke.* London: George Allen & Unwin.

Richardson, James D. (1897). *A compilation of messages and papers of the Presidents.* Vol. I. New York: Bureau of National Literature, Inc.

Slossen, Edwin E. (1921). *The American spirit in education.* New Haven: Yale Univ. Press.

Tarcov, Nathan (1984). *Locke's education for liberty.* Chicago: Univ. of Chicago Press.

Ulich, Robert (1950). *History of educational thought.* New York: American Book Co.

von Eckardt, Ursula M. (1959). *The pursuit of happiness in the democratic creed.* NY: Frederick A. Praeger.

Yolton, John W. (1977). *The Locke reader.* Cambridge: Cambridge Univ. Press.

Chapter 4

Religious Foundations

If 'all men are by nature equally free and independent,' all men are to be considered as entering into Society on equal conditions; as relinquishing no more, and therefore retaining no less, one than another, of their natural rights. Above all are they to be considered as retaining an 'equal title to the free exercise of Religion according to the dictates of Conscience.' Whilst we assert for ourselves a freedom to embrace, to profess and to observe the Religion which we believe to be of divine origin, we cannot deny an equal freedom to those whose minds have not yet yielded to the evidence which has convinced us. If this freedom be abused it is an offence against God, not against man: To God, therefore, not man must an account of it be rendered. (Memorial and Remonstrance, James Madison, 1785)

Well aware that the opinions and beliefs of men depend not on their own will, but follow involuntarily the evidence proposed to their minds; that almighty God hath created the mind free; that all attempts to influence

it by temporal punishments or burthens, or by civil incapacitations, tend only to beget habits of hypocrisy and
meanness, and are a departure from the plan of the Holy
author of our religion, who being Lord both of body and
mind, yet chose not to propagate it by coercion on
either, as was in his almighty power to do, but to extend
it by its influence or reason alone. (Bill for Establishing
Religious Freedom, Thomas Jefferson, 1779)

The above two quotes favoring freedom of religion give, for the
most part, the thinking that eventually formed the underpinnings of
the First Amendment to the U.S. Constitution. As we elaborate on
these underpinnings, the foundation is laid for understanding the
First Amendment—a major influence on educational decisions—
with implications for educational policy.

Examination of the content of the two opening quotes from
Madison and Jefferson bring us closer to understanding the true
meaning of the First Amendment.

Paraphrasing from Madison's "Memorial and Remonstrance"
(Alley, 1985, p. 57),

1. Each person is to have the equal right to exercise religious
   conscience.
2. The founding fathers believed that their religion was
   founded in God as their Creator.
3. That man's mind is the locus of his decision-making particularly regarding religious beliefs.
4. Man answers to God and not to other men regarding the use
   of his, and the guarding of others, religious liberty.
5. God is the author of religious freedom, not man.

Paraphrasing from Jefferson's Bill for Establishing Religious
Freedom (Padover, 1943, p. 946),

1. God has created the mind free.
2. True religion is founded in God.
3. Neither can man who does not have the right nor does God

who has the right, coerce anyone to believe in God.
4. Reason alone is the vehicle for believing in God.
5. Influences or pressures designed to force or coerce man into a way of believing about God result in negative reactions or rebellions.

There is an obviously high if not perfect degree of similarity between the two sets of five points. Collapsing across the two lists, two major points appear central toward understanding the meaning of the First Amendment. Basically these two points are, first, that America was founded on biblical principles and, second, that religious liberty means freedom from coercion.

There are two main thrusts of this chapter on the religious foundations of the United States. First, we intend to document the double standard and thus the injustice that results from governmental control of religion. Second, we intend to chart the progression in the U.S. from religious coercion to religious freedom for all faiths. The U.S. Declaration of Independence and the First Amendment to the U.S. Constitution affirm the premise that all people are to be free or uncoerced in their religious beliefs. This premise is based on the complementary facts regarding, first, the nature or principle of religious liberty as a hallmark expression of the Christian religion and, second, the nature of man's conscience as created by Christianity's God. In fact, it will be demonstrated that when that liberty of belief (as embodied for instance in the Christian religion) is not expressly protected, coercion of one form or another is the inevitable outcome. We will eventually draw some parallels regarding the necessity for freedom from coercion in education just as in religion.

Extant guarantees of religious freedom notwithstanding, the First Amendment is an outcome of intense struggle and compromise between conflicting opinions. Already noted in Chapter 2, the early colonies and then states were actually intolerant of any religion not of their own regionally accepted or authorized religion. For instance, in the debate over the U.S. Constitution and its amendments, the New England states wanted to retain a test of religious belief condition to office holding to specifically keep out the "infidels." Likewise the Virginian Patrick Henry was noted as an outstanding spokesman for the sole establishment of the Christian religion in his own state. Given these circumstances we are indeed fortunate that the First Amendment does capture the purest truth of religious liberty rather than promoting self-serving parochial ends.

Religion in Early America

There is ample evidence, both from a collective or governmental and from an individualistic perspective to confirm that this country was founded specifically on a belief in God and according to Christian principles.

Ecclesiastical Vision

Organizationally, the early settlers to this country shared a common vision. For the most part, they were motivated by a sense of divine guidance and divine call on this nation.

> Christopher Columbus, for example, wrote about God in his diary:
> It was the Lord who put into my mind (I could feel his hand upon me) the fact that it would be possible to sail from here to the Indies. All who heard of my project rejected it with laughter, ridiculing me. There is no question that the inspiration was from the Holy Spirit, because He comforted me with rays of marvelous inspiration from the Holy Scriptures...
> ... For the execution of the journey to the Indies, I did not make use of intelligence, mathematics or maps. It is simply the fulfillment of what Isaiah had prophesied...
> No one should fear to undertake any task in the name of our Saviour, if it is just and if the intention is purely for His holy service. (Marshall & Manuel, 1977, p. 17)

Regarding the verses in Isaiah that Columbus references, he believed that God had called him to deliver the light of Christ to undiscovered heathen lands. He likewise cites in his journal Isaiah,

49:;;1,6: "List to me, o coastlands, and harken, you peoples from afar. The Lord called me from the womb, from the body of my mother he named my name... I will give you as a light to the nations, that my salvation may reach to the end of the earth" (Marshall & Manuel, 1977, p. 31). He wrote about the natives he first encountered: "for I knew that they were a people to be delivered and converted to our holy faith rather by love than by force... I believe that they would easily be made Christians for it seemed to me that they had no religion of their own" (Marshall & Manual, 1977, p. 42).

On every island that Columbus encountered, he erected a wooden cross "as a token of Jesus Christ our Lord, and in honor of the Christian faith" (p. 43). When he apparently strayed from this purpose, being caught in the allure of abundant gold, he records the following as part of a voice heard in the midst of a troubled sleep: "O fool and slow to believe and to serve thy God, the God of all... When he saw thee arrive at an age with which He was content, He caused thy name to sound marvelously in the land. The Indies, which are so rich in a part of the world, He gave thee for thine own; thou hast divided them as it pleased thee, and He enabled thee to do this" (Marshall & Manuel, 1977, p. 64).

As if to testify to the reality of God's sovereignty over His purposes, the Jamestown, Virginia settlement of 1607 encountered one frustration after another because of what has been interpreted as a lack of godly submission. While beginning with the covenant that "... from these very shores the Gospel shall go forth to not only this New World but the entire world" (Gyertson, 1979, pp. 8-10), these early settlers very quickly left God out of their activities. According to Marshall and Manuel (1977, p. 105), their efforts were characterized by religious hypocrisy and self-aggrandizement, particularly in light of their charter which read (in part),

> We, greatly commending and graciously accepting of the desires of the furtherance of so noble a work, which may be the providence of almighty God hereafter tend to the glory of His divine majesty, in propagating of Christian religion to such people as yet live in darkness

and miserable ignorance of the true knowledge and worship of God, and may in time bring the infidels and savages living in those parts, to human civility and to a settled and quiet government. (Johnston, 1987, p. 12)

While founded on a similar godly zeal, the story of the Pilgrims is a picture of steady consistency. These Separatists remained in Holland only twelve years after separating from the Church of England. In their dissatisfaction with living conditions in Holland, they sensed that God intended they journey to America on a mission similar to the Israelites' journey out of Babylon and into Jerusalem. Quoting from their leader, John Robinson,

Now as the people of God in old time were called out of Babylon civil, the place of their bodily bondage, and were to come to Jerusalem, and there to build the Lord's temple or tabernacle ... so are the people of God now to go out of Babylon spiritually to Jerusalem ... and to build themselves as lively stones into a spiritual house, or temple, for the Lord to dwell in... (Marshall & Manual, 1977, p. 110)

Intending to land in Virginia and settle under the authority of the Virginia Company, they landed instead at Cape Cod after being blown off course. No longer under the jurisdiction of the Virginia Company because of their location, they, for the first time in the course of recorded history, voluntarily covenanted together between themselves and God to create their own civil government. The resulting Mayflower Compact of 1620 reads in part,

Having undertaken, for the glory of God and advancement of the Christian faith and honor of our King and country, a voyage to plant the first colony in the northern parts of Virginia, do by these presents solemnly and mutually in the presence of God and one another, covenant and combine ourselves together into a civill body politic, for our better ordering and preservation and furtherance of the ends aforesaid... (Commager, 1973, p. 15)

These "ends aforesaid" certainly must have included the goal (originally purposed by the Puritans) that they "maie wynn and incite the Natives of Country, to the Knowledge and Obedience of the onlie true God and Savior of Mankinde, and the Christian fayth" (Perry, 1978, p. 94).

The account of the Puritan migration to America reveals similar Christian-oriented goals. The Puritans, like the Pilgrims, were dissatisfied with the Church of England yet, unlike the Pilgrims, did not wish to separate from the Church. Like the Pilgrims, they saw America as a land where they could practice their religion with freedom of conscience; yet unlike the Pilgrims, they wanted to reform the Church starting at some geographic distance from its control. On departing England, the Reverend Francis Higginson proclaimed, "We do not go to New England as Separatists from the Church of England, though we cannot but separate from the corruptions in it, but we go to practice the positive part of church reformation, and propagate the Gospel in America" (Marshall & Manuel, 1977, p. 155).

Over the period of several generations, the population of the colonies, and especially the northern colonies, expanded consistent with the religious intent of these Pilgrims and Puritans. For instance, as the population increased twenty-fold, from 75,000 in 1660 to nearly 1,600,000 in 1760, the number of churches in eight major denominations multiplied by the same factor over the same general time period (Noll, Hatch, Marsden, Wells, & Woodbridge, 1983, p. 97). Further, it is estimated that during the era of the Great Awakening (1730s and 40s), anywhere from several thousand to a half million people were converted to Christianity (p. 114). In this same general time period, the number of new colleges increased dramatically, whereas prior to 1740, only three colleges existed in colonial America: Harvard, William and Mary, and Yale. The first colleges added after this time included Princeton, Rhode Island College (later to be called Brown University), Queen's College (later to be Rutgers), and Dartmouth. All of these institutions of higher learning claimed a dependence on Christ as the source of wisdom and truth.

Governmental Documents

The First Charter of Virginia, issued in April 1606, said, "for the Furtherance of so noble a Work, which may, by the Providence of God, hereafter tend to the Glory of his divine Majesty, in propagating of Christian Religion to such people, as yet live in Darkness and miserable Ignorance of the true Knowledge and Worship of God..." (Commager, 1973, p. 8)

The Second Charter of Virginia, issued in May 1609, said, "And lastly, because the principal Effect, which we can desire or expect of this action, is the Conversion and Reduction of the People in those Parts unto the true Worship of God and Christian Religion..." (p. 12)

In Virginia, the Christian religion was an integral part of the civil governance structure. Looking past the emotional impact of statements in the Virginia Laws Divine, Moral and Martial (1614), there was an obvious strict keeping of Christian beliefs. For instance, "To speak impiously of the Trinity or one of the Divine Persons, or against the known articles of Christian faith, was punishable with death" (Pfeffer, 1997, p. 8). The Ordinance for Virginia dated 1621 said,

> first and principally in the Advancement of the Honour and Service of God, and the Enlargement of his Kingdom amongst the Heathen People; and next, in erecting of the said Colony in due obedience to his Majesty, and all lawful authority from his Majesty's Directions; and lastly, in maintaining the said Peoples in Justice and Christian Conversation amongst themselves... (Commager, 1973, pp. 13-14)

In 1629, the First Charter of Massachusetts ends with the following words:

"whereby our said People ... may be soe religiously, peaceablie, and civilly governed, as their good Life and orderlie Conversacon, maie wynn and incite the Natives of Country, to the Knowledge and Obedience to the onlie true God and Savior of

Mankinde, and the Christian Fayth..." (Commager, 1973, p. 18). When the Massachusetts Bay Company took its charter to America, its leaders, via The Cambridge Agreement (1629), said, "it is fully and faithfully agreed amongst us, and every of us doth hereby freely and sincerely promise and bind himselfe in the word of a christian and in the presence of God who is the searcher of all hearts..." (Commager, 1973, p. 18). In the Charter of Freedom and Exemptions to Patroons which established the patroon system of land tenure in New Netherland and New York in 1629, specific provision was made for Christian worship: "The Patroons and colonists shall in particular, and in the speediest manner, endeavor to find out ways and means whereby they may support a Minister and School-master, that thus the service of God and zeal for religion may not grow cool and be neglected among them..." (Commager, 1973, p. 20). In 1632 The Charter of Maryland made a similar provision: "and further more the Patronages, and Advowsons of all Churches which (with the increasing Worship and Religion of Christ) within the said Region ... hereafter shall happen to be built, together with License, and Faculty of erecting and founding Churches, Chapels, and Places of Worship..." (Commager, 1973, p. 21)

The first written constitution that created a government in America was the Fundamental Orders of Connecticut, dated 1639. This document begins,

> Forasmuch as it hath pleased the almighty God by the wise disposition of his divyne providence... And well knowing where a people are gathered together the word of God requires that to mayntayne the peace and vision of such a people there should be an orderly and decent Government established according to God ... to mayntayne and presearve the liberty and purity of the gospel of our Lord Jesus which we now profess, as also the disciplyne of the Churches, which according to the truth of the said gospell is now practised amongst us. (Commager, 1973, p. 23)

When the various colonies of the New England area (Massachusetts, new Plymouth, Connecticut, and New Haven) agreed to form a union, they noted in the 1643 articles of the New England Confederation, "whereas we all came into these parts of America with one and the same end and aim, namely, to advance the Kingdom of our Lord Jesus Christ and to enjoy the liberties of the Gospel in purity with peace..." (Commager, 1973, p. 26)

The General Laws and Liberties of the Massachusetts Colony, dated 1646, were similar in rigidity to the early Virginia laws. Acknowledging that "no human power be Lord over the faith and consciences of men," they nonetheless made laws to punish blasphemers of the Christian religion. For instance, "if any Christian ... [deny] the immortality of the soul, or resurrection of the body, or any sin to be repented of in the regenerate, or any evil done by the outward man to be accounted sin, or denying that Christ gave Himself a ransom for our sins, or shall affirm that we are not justified by His death and righteousness..." (Pfeffer, 1977, p. 5). The Rhode Island Charter of 1663 noted the motivations of its settlers to pursue "the holie Christian faith and worshipp" and acknowledged, in its 1663 Charter with the Providence Plantations, the purpose "to preserve them that liberty, in the true Christian faith and worship of God, which they have sought with so much travail..." (Perry, 1978, p. 170).

The law that established the first system of public education in America acknowledged the Christian purpose of doing so. The Massachusetts School of Law of 1647 said, "it being one chiefe project of ye ould deluder, Satan, to keepe men from the knowledge of ye Scriptures..." (Commager, 1973, p. 29)

The several acts uniting church and state equally referenced a Christian rationale. For instance, the Cambridge Platform (1648) gave civil magistrates ecclesiastical authority regarding "open contempt of the word preached, profanation of the Lords day, disturbing the peaceable administration and exercise of the worship and holy things of God..." (Commager, 1973, p. 31). Similarly, the Maryland Toleration Act (1649) gave civil authority to punish those who "shall from henceforth blaspheme God ... or shall deny our Saviour Jesus Christ to bee the sonne of God, or shall deny the holy

Trinity the ffather sonne and holy Ghost, or the Godhead of any of the said Three persons of the Trinity or the Unity of the Godhead..." (Commager, 1973, p. 31)

The colony (i.e., Providence) earliest to claim independence of religion from civil government management is now known as Rhode Island. While contrary to the biblical mindset of most other colonies, this orientation was likewise based in the Christian religion. Their charter of 1663 read, "To encourage the hopeful undertaking of our said loyal and loving subjects, and to secure them in the free exercise and enjoyment of all their civil and religious rights, appertaining to them, as our loving subjects; and to preserve unto them that liberty, in the true Christian faith and worship of God" (Perry, 1978, p. 170).

When Massachusetts declared its independence from England, it declared its patent to be "under God" (Commager, 1973, p. 34) and its industry to prosper "by God's special blessing" (p. 35). William Penn in drafting certain conditions and concessions relevant to the settling of Pennsylvania (1681) acknowledged God's hand in the matter: "That so soon as it pleaseth God that the abovesaid persons arrive there..." (Commager, 1973, p. 35). Later (1701), when the Pennsylvania Charter of Privileges was published, it amplified the previous statement as follows:

BECAUSE no People can be truly happy, though under the greatest Enjoyment of Civil Liberties, if abridged of the Freedom of their Consciences, as to their Religious Profession and Worship: and Almighty God being the only Lord of Conscience, Father of Lights and Spirits; and the Author as well as Object of all divine Knowledge, Faith and Worship, who only doth enlighten the Minds and persuade and convince the Understandings of People, I do hereby grant and declare, That no Person or Persons, inhabiting in this province or Territories, who shall confess and acknowledge *One* almighty God, then Creator, Upholder and Ruler of the World; and profess him are themselves obliged to live quietly under the Civil Government, shall be in any Case molested or prejudiced, in his or their Person or Estate...

AND that all Persons who also profess to believe in *Jesus Christ,* the Savior of the World (notwithstanding their other Persuasions and Practices in Point of Conscience and Religion) to serve this Government in any Capacity... (Commager, 1973, pp. 40-41)

As this country began to assert itself toward that final act of independence from England, the major documents of that cause likewise reflected this Christian orientation. In 1775, the Declaration of the Causes and Necessity of Taking Up Arms, published out of the Continental Congress, references God in several places:

But a reverence for our great Creator ... must convince all those who reflect upon the subject, that government was instituted to promote the welfare of mankind, and ought to be administered for the attainment of that end.

We gratefully acknowledge, as signal instances of the Divine favour towards us, that his Providence would not permit us to be called into this severe controversy, until we were grown up... With hearts fortified with these animating reflections, we most solemnly, before God and the world, declare, that, exerting the utmost energy of those powers, which our beneficent Creator hath graciously bestowed upon us...

With an humble confidence in the mercies of the supreme and impartial Judge and Ruler of the Universe, we most devoutly implore his divine goodness to protect us... (Commager, 1973, pp. 93-95)

Likewise, the instructions from the Town of Malden, Massachusetts, for a Declaration of Independence (May 27, 1776), note, "that the present age would be deficient in their duty to God, their posterity and themselves, if they do not establish an American republic ... for we can never be willingly subject to any other King than he who, being possessed of infinite wisdom, goodness and rectitude, is alone fit to possess unlimited power" (Commager, 1973, pp. 97-98)

The U.S. Declaration of Independence abundantly references religious concepts; namely, "nature's God," endowment of inalienable Rights from the Creator including the right and duty to throw off a despotic government, "the Supreme Judge of the world," and "the Protection of Divine Providence." (Commager, 1973, pp. 100-102)

After the Declaration, still more civil affirmations in God followed. The 1780 Massachusetts Bill of Rights indicated, "It is the right as well as the duty of all men in society, publicly, and at stated seasons, to worship the Supreme Being, the great Creator and Preserver of the universe." (Commager, 1973, p. 107)

Finally, both the Articles of Confederation and the Constitution of the United States close with the phrase "in the year of our Lord..."

<u>Individually</u>

The consistency of governmental pronouncements regarding biblical orientations is fairly well replicated in the personal statements of the early leaders. The focus here is on revealing a biblical mindset such that at least on the surface it would appear to call for a theocratic government; that is, a government specifically fostering a particularly religious and in fact biblical value system.

Starting with George Washington, the Father of our country, he, on numerous occasions, declared his trust in God and Jesus Christ. A contemporary of his said in a biographical sketch that "he was an humble, earnest Christian." (Johnston, 1987, p. 101) From his diary at the age of twenty, Washington's prayer was

> since thou art a God of pure eyes, and wilt be sanctified in all who draw near unto thee, who doest not regard the sacrifice of fools, nor hear sinners who tread in thy courts, pardon, I beseech thee, my sins, remove them from thy presence, as far as the east is from the west, and accept of me for the merits of thy son Jesus Christ ... to the saving of my soul in the day of the Lord Jesus... (Johnston, 1987, p. 104)

When called to an important military position, he wrote to his objecting mother, "The God to whom you commended me, madam, when I set out upon a more perilous errand, defended me from all harm, and I trust he will do so now. Do not you?" (p. 105). When in battle he revealed to his brother John, "by the all-powerful dispensations of Providence, I have been protected beyond all human probability or expectation; for I had four bullets through my coat, and two horses shot under me, yet escaped unhurt..." (p. 105). As commander of the Continental Army, he required of "all officers and soldiers not engaged in actual duty, a punctual attendance on Divine service, to implore the blessing of Heaven..." (p. 112). At Valley Forge he told his men, "To the distinguished character of a Patriot, it should be our highest glory to add the more distinguished character of a Christian" (p. 123). Regarding the final surrender of the British army, Washington wrote, "I take particular pleasure in acknowledging that the interposing Hand of Heaven ... has been most conspicuous and remarkable" (p. 127). As he resigned his Commission he said, "I consider it an indispensable duty to close this last solemn act of my official life by commending the interests of our dearest country to the protection of Almighty God" (p. 131). In his First Inaugural Address, he said, "it would be particularly improper to omit, in this first official act, my fervent supplication to that Almighty Being who rules over the universe ... that His benediction may consecrate to the liberties and happiness of the people." (p. 142)

Other leaders' religious views were similarly reverential.

John Hancock, President of the Continental Congress, described the British troops as "men whom sceptered robbers now employ to frustrate the design of God..." (Johnson, 1987, p. 68). The June 12, 1775, proclamation of the Second Continental Congress signed by John Hancock called for a national "day of public HUMILIATION, FASTING AND PRAYER, that we may ... offer up our joint supplications to the All-wise, Omnipotent and merciful Disposer of all Events..." (p. 75). While governor of Massachusetts, he called for prayer saying, "We think it is incumbent upon this people to humble themselves before God on account of their sins." (p. 77)

John Adams, the man declared to be "the Atlas of American

Independence" (p. 85), spoke for independence saying, "Before God, I believe the hour has come... It is my living sentiment, and by the blessing of God it shall be my dying sentiment, Independence, now, and Independence forever!" (p. 83). When the Declaration of Independence was passed by Congress on July 2, he wrote to his wife that the day "ought to be commemorated as the Day of Deliverance, by solemn acts of devotion to God Almighty." (p. 87)

Jefferson's Bill for Establishing Religious Freedom, authored in 1779 but not passed by the Virginia Assembly until 1786, said, "Almighty God hath created the mind free..." (Padover, 1943, p. 946). As he wrote about religion in the 1780s (Jefferson, 1984, p. 285) regarding the rights of conscience, he said that we "are answerable for them to our God." And in 1802, he said "that religion is a matter which lies solely between man and his God..." (Jefferson, 1984, p. 510). He also believed that man's "social dispositions" (p. 1337) were placed there by God.

The oldest man to sign the Declaration was Benjamin Franklin. It was he who proposed, when the Constitutional Convention was deadlocked, "Sir, we have not hitherto once thought of humbly appealing to the father of lights to illuminate our understanding. In the beginning of the contest with Great Britain, when we were sensible to danger, we had daily prayer in this room for Divine protection... The longer I live, the more convincing proofs I see of this truth—that God govern in the affairs of man" (Johnston, 1987, p. 69). Shortly before his death, he wrote, "You desire to know something of my religion... Here is my creed. I believe in one God, creator of the universe. That He governs it by His providence. That He ought to be worshipped." (Johnston, 1987, pp. 69-70)

Samuel Adams, known as "The Father of the American Revolution," made similar professions of belief. Immediately after the signing of the Declaration of Independence, he said, "We have this day restored the Sovereign, to Whom alone men ought to be obedient. He reigns in heaven and ... from the rising to the setting sun, may his Kingdom come" (Johnston, 1987, p. 86). When confronted with a bribe against his patriotism, he said, "I trust I have long since made my peace with the King of Kings." Earlier he had written that "Just and true liberty, equal impartial liberty, in matters spiritual and temporary, is a thing that all men are clearly entitled to by the external and immutable laws of God and nature, as well as by the law of nations and all well-ground municipal laws, which must have their foundation in the former." (p. 79)

The outspoken patriot Patrick Henry said, "If we wish to be free, we must fight! An appeal to arms and to the God of Hosts is all that is left us! ... There is a just God who presides over the destinies of nations, and who will raise up friends for us. Is life so dear, or peace so sweet, as to be purchased at the price of chains and slavery? Forbid it, Almighty God." (Johnston, 1987, p. 65)

Richard Henry Lee of Virginia spoke against slavery at this same time by saying, "Christianity, by introducing into Europe the truest principles of humanity, universal benevolence, and brotherly love, had happily abolished slavery." (Johnston, 1987, p. 80)

William Prescott, leader of the patriot forces at Bunker Hill, said to them, "Let us all be of one heart, and stand fast in the liberty wherewith Christ has made us free. And may He, of His infinite mercy, grant us deliverance out of all our troubles." (Johnston, 1987, p. 76). Colonel Ethan Allen, when he confronted the British at Fort Ticonderoga, demanded their surrender "In the name of the great Jehovah and the Continental Congress." (Johnston, 1987, p. 78). Thomas Paine, in speaking against the burdens imposed by Great Britain, said, "if being bound in that manner, is not slavery, then there is not such a thing as slavery upon earth. Even the expression is impious, for so unlimited a power can belong only to God..." Paine also said, "I am as confident, as I am that God governs the world, that America will never be happy till she gets clear of foreign dominion." (Johnston, 1987, pp. 87-88)

The one clergyman to sign the Declaration, John Witherspoon, easily represented the ministers of the time in his faith that God was the author of this country's beginnings.

From Religious Coercion to Religious Liberty

Two threatening situations existed in the early stages of this country to work against the religious freedom now embodied in the First Amendment. Even so, the struggles inherent in these situations gave the First Amendment its purest possible meaning. The one struggle, that from without, was dominion by Great Britain; the other, that from within, was religious or denominational intolerance. Externally, freedom from the rulers of Great Britain was achieved through the Revolutionary War and, as discussed in Chapter 2, was established in the U.S. Declaration of Independence. Internally, freedom from the tyranny of fellow Americans, particularly in the area of religion, was achieved in the Bill of Rights to the U.S. Constitution and particularly in the First Amendment of this Bill of Rights.

Before examining these struggles, it is important to emphasize that they emanate fundamentally from two primary issues that in fact have been addressed by every generation of humanity. The first issue is related to the question of whose view of reality and eternity is true, and the second issue is related to the question of who has the legitimate authority to enforce "truth." Various groups, both religious and civil, proclaimed their rightful authority in these two areas.

Religious Intolerance

Practically each Christian denomination or worldly philosophy in colonial America claimed (as it seems they invariably do) to be the prime possessor of truth and almost the same number claimed authority to convince others of that truth. However, those who played a pivotal role in the formation of the First Amendment generally disavowed this latter claim of authority.

By far, the major religious orientation in colonial America was Christianity. In fact, up to the time of the Revolution, at least 75% of the colonists, and even more if we include the related orientation of Calvinism, grew up with the Puritan influence in their homes (Reichley, 1985, p. 53). Puritanism was the creed of the New England Congregational churches, but it also exerted a major influence throughout all the colonies, including the Anglican establishment in the south.

A major characteristic of all those who came to this country for religious freedom was that each group considered its dogma to be the truth. Typically, these groups were also of the persuasion that the best way to maintain their dogma was to enforce it through both civil and religious requirements. Persecution was not wrong under this mentality as long as it was for the "right" cause. It was not uncommon to hear the spokesman of one sect say of another that the only liberty they deserved was the "liberty to keep away from us." (Reichley, 1985, p. 56)

In the New England states, the charitable behavior of the Pilgrims who immigrated to Plymouth from Holland contrasted sharply with their Puritan brethren who settled in other parts of Massachusetts: "However rigid the Plymouth colonists may have been at their first separation from the Church of England, they never discovered that persecuting spirit which we have seen in [other parts of] Massachusetts." (Cobb, 1968, p. 139). The Plymouth colony was "never betrayed into excesses of religious persecution" (p. 139) and never established their religious order through any civil regulations. Those who settled elsewhere around the Bay made a fundamental error in linking church and state and in refusing liberty to any form of worship inconsistent with their interpretation of the Church of England (p. 161). Ministers were given house and provisions "at the publicke expense" (p. 169), and in 1638 a law was enacted such that "all inhabitants are lyable to assessment for Church as for State" (p. 169) and further that civil authorities were to collect these fees even by force if necessary. So intertwined was this church-state relationship that the qualification to vote in civil elections was to be certified by a minister as a member of a Congregational Church "in good and regular standing" (p. 171). Furthermore, in 1641 the civil courts adopted the policy that the civil authority "... hath power and liberty to see the peace, ordinances, and rules of Christ observed in every church..." (p. 174).

The use of civil authority in Massachusetts to bring about the theocratic notion of a pure biblical city led to some of the following violations of civil rights. On numerous occasions, those who spoke against this ecclesiastical authority were fined for their infractions. In 1650, William Pynchow was fined 20 pounds for writing an unauthorized book on atonement (Cobb, 1968, p. 203), and in 1651 Reverend Matthews was fined 10 pounds for preaching in an unauthorized congregation. More drastically, banishment from the settlement resulted for dissension from official doctrine. For instance, both Roger Williams and Anne Hutchinson were forced to leave in the 1630s when they spoke against what they believed to be erroneous biblical teachings. Persecution likewise resulted from minor events such as not having one's child baptized (p. 204) or for celebrating Christmas (p. 209).

Most systematically oppressed were those particular groups declared as blasphemous. Such groups included the Quakers, Catholics, and Baptists. The Roman Catholics were by law forbidden residence, and in 1647 Jesuits were to be put to death if returning to Massachusetts after once being banished (Cobb, 1968, p. 177). Perhaps the Quakers suffered more than any other group. Treated as the "pestilent sect" (p. 221), they were immediately arrested upon their first arrival in Boston. Four Quakers, three men and one woman, were executed in Massachusetts in 1659 when they returned after earlier being banished on threat of execution. While the civil authorities were obviously acting out of a desire for biblical purity, these Quakers felt they were under a "religious restraint" (p. 218) from God to give up their lives to bear witness against these laws. The Baptists were also fined, imprisoned, and sentenced to banishment. Yet after public outcry over the Quaker executions, the injustices began to abate.

Eventually, in 1691, King William issued a new charter of Massachusetts and decreed that "forever hereafter there shall be liberty of conscience allowed, in the worship of God to all Christians (except Papists)" (Cobb, 1968, p. 233). Long beforehand and even a while thereafter, the Puritans thought they but no others were lord over one's own conscience. As the preamble to the 1646 Act of Heresy declared, "although no human power be lord over the conscience, yet because such as bring in damnable heresies ... ought duly to be restrained" (p. 177). They obviously thought they had the final truth and the power to enforce it.

Connecticut, founded in protest against the theocratic nature of Massachusetts, never attempted to make civil and political privileges conditioned to the church, except for the office of governor. While the "Civil authority here established hath power and liberty to see that the peace, ordinances, and rules of Christ be observed in every Church according to His word" (Cobb, 1968, p. 243), this submission of civil government for the benefit and support of the Church was never a cause for injustice. Even while civil governance was to be for the benefit and purity of the Puritan Congregational Church, other dissenting Churches were allowed to exist outside the system. As in Massachusetts, the Quakers were considered undesirable elements not to be entertained by the population, although they were not persecuted as in Massachusetts. Also, while dissenters could worship as they pleased, they still had to pay for the support of the Established Church. Additionally, laws in 1708 provided for the whipping and fining of anyone not a minister for administering the sacraments, yet there is no record of this ever happening. Toleration to Roman Catholics was denied in an act of 1743 to Roman Catholics, and Moravians were forbidden altogether from preaching without permission partially on the grounds that "there were too many Episcopalians in Connecticut already." (p. 278)

The colony of New Haven, before annexed to be a part of Connecticut, was more rigid in enforcement of orthodoxy than Massachusetts. The first duty of their general court was "to provide for the maintenance of the purity of religion, and to suppress the contrary" (Cobb, 1968, p. 283). As in many other colonies, the church was mandatorily supported by all inhabitants and only church members were entitled to vote in civil matters. Examples of the total control exerted by the civil authorities include the rebuking of someone "for building a cellar and selling it without leave" (p. 285) and the banishment of a family for keeping the company of a lewd person who had previously been whipped. Regarding the Quakers, they were allowed briefly in the colony for business only but had to be accompanied by a guard. Refusal of these and related conditions brought upon the Quaker imprisonment, whipping, and hard work. If the Quaker so punished then returned, his hand was to be branded with an "H." On third offense, the other hand was to be branded, and on fourth offense, the tongue bored with a hot iron.

New Hampshire's founders, being some of those banished from Massachusetts, agreed

in the name of Christ and in the sight of God,
combine ourselves together to erect and set up among us

such government as shall be, to our best discerning, agreeable to the will of God ... binding ourselves solemnly by the grace and help of Christ and in His name and fear, to submit ourselves to such godly and Christian laws as are established in the realm of England to our best knowledge ... Cobb (1968, p. 291)

Seeing the injustices of Massachusetts, they did not make civic privileges contingent upon religion and allowed every respectable man to vote. Even so, the church was supported by tithes as assessed and collected through civil magistrates. For the period from 1641 to 1679, New Hampshire was administratively joined to Massachusetts and, through this connection, engaged in the whipping and banishing of three Quaker women. Roman Catholics, as might be expected, were not welcome to the colony. Disregard of church policy was made punishable by law in 1680. For example, in 1681 Robert Briney was sentenced to nine lashes for being absent from church services. When the Reverend Moody disobeyed orders of Governor Cranfield regarding administering the sacrament, he was imprisoned for three months.

New York was founded from motives unlike most other colonies. While the Dutch founders were loyal to the ordinances of the Reformed Church of Holland, the motive for establishment was political colonization rather than for propagating the gospel. Even so, the Articles for Colonization exclusively established the Church of Holland with the clause, "No other Religion shall be publicly admitted in New Netherland except the Reformed..." (Cobb, 1968, p. 304). When those of the Lutheran persuasion petitioned for their own minister in 1653, they were denied by the governor and the council. Then when they held religious services in their homes without a minister, they were imprisoned. Regarding Jews, Governor Stuyvesant refused their residence in the colony, and the Dutch overseeing West India Company forbade them the right to have a synagogue, restricting their worship instead to within their own houses (p. 317). In 1656 when the sheriff of Flusing held Baptist meetings in his own house, he was removed from office and fined on threat of banishment. The Baptist minister was likewise fined and then banished. In 1657, those engaged in Quaker service were thrown in jail. One who escaped was arrested in another town, sentenced to two years hard labor, beaten on several successive days, and strung by his hands with a log tied to his feet (p. 318). Those who refused to side against the Quakers were likewise fined on threat of banishment. When the prominent citizen John Bowne refused to pay a fine for harboring Quakers in his house, he was jailed for several months and then deported to Holland (p. 320).

With the takeover of New Netherland by the English in 1664 (and renamed New York), other forms of persecution followed. Previously allowed establishment by the Dutch, the Presbyterians were now denied their church property by the Episcopalians and repeatedly denied a charter (in 1719, 1766, and 1775). Under English rule, the Dutch church was supposed to enjoy an independent and higher status than that of other non-Anglican congregations. Yet the English governor in 1679 was able to force the Dutch clergy to ordain someone in violation of the Reformed Church ordination policies. Finally, we note that during 1673 and 1674 when the Dutch briefly returned to power, they issued the very ambiguous policy to English settlers according them "Freedom of Conscience as the same is permitted in the Netherlands," but the magistrates had to be those "such only as are of the Reformed Christian Religion, or at least well affected thereto." (Cobb, 1968, p. 324)

Maryland, because of the vicissitudes born of jealous factions, was both, in turn, a colony favorable and then hostile to the Roman Catholics. When first chartered, Maryland was under the authority of Lord Baltimore (Sir George Calvert) and later his son Lord Baltimore II (Cecil Calvert) whose sovereignty was "subject only to one condition, namely; that it should not be such as might prejudice the true Christian Religion or allegiance to the crown" (Cobb, 1968, p. 364). While it seems that the charter of Maryland was intended to secure "liberty of conscience to Roman Catholics," it was equally the case "that the principle of toleration was to be adopted as one of the fundamental institutions of the province" (Cobb, 1968, p. 368). Lord Baltimore, a Catholic himself, was said to be "the first in the history of the Christian world to seek for religious security and peace by the practice of justice and not by the exercise of power" (p. 366). Baltimore prescribed in 1636 that the officers of the colony affirm that,

> I will not, by myself or any, directly or indirectly, trouble, molest, or discountinance any person, professing to believe in Jesus Christ for, or in respect of, religion; but merely as they shall be found faithful and well-deserving; my aim shall be public unity, and if any person or officer shall molest any person, professing to believe in Jesus Christ, on account of his religion, I will protect the person molested and punish the offender. (p. 372)

In Maryland, the Roman Catholics found security, and the "Protestants were sheltered from Protestant intolerance" (p. 373). By 1648, the Protestants so outnumbered the Catholic citizens that Lord Baltimore replaced the Catholic government officials with Protestants. Even so, there was still no toleration for the Unitarian, the Jew, the Infidel, or the Pagan.

Not satisfied with religious liberty, the Maryland Puritans took control of the government in 1652 and in 1654 repealed the toleration act of 1649, replacing it with the declaration that "None who profess the exercise of the Papish Religion, commonly known by the name of the Roman Catholic Religion, can be protected in this Province" (Cobb, 1968, p. 369). Though the overthrow was disallowed by Oliver Cromwell, lord protector of England, the discontent continued. By 1675 the discontent was heartily received in England where Catholics were generally in disfavor. The order from the English ministry to Lord Baltimore the third (Charles Calvert) was that government was to revert entirely to the Protestants. The end result was to disenfranchise the Catholics in the very colony they started.

By 1692, beset with so many charges and countercharges, King William III revoked the charter of Maryland and set up the Church of England as the state-church of Maryland forcing a tax for support of the clergy. In 1704, an act was passed to punish any bishop or priest for practicing under penalty of fine or six months imprisonment. On second offense, the offender was banished to

England. By 1715, the child of a Protestant father and a Roman Catholic mother could be taken from the mother if the father died. After 1716, anyone elected to office had to renounce his Catholic faith, and after 1718, the Romanists were denied the right to vote if they did not abjure their faith.

New Jersey, started under the Dutch Reformed influence but deinstitutionalized by English takeover and influenced by the resident Puritans, required membership in the Congregational Church as a condition both for voting and for office holding. The Puritan influence did not long prevail however against the Quakers in the western part of the state and against the Scottish Presbyterian influence in the eastern part. The Quakers, consistent with their desire for full religious freedom, declared by law in 1681 that "Liberty of conscience in matters of faith and worship shall be granted to all people within this Province, who shall live peaceable and quietly therein, and none of the free people of the Province shall be rendered incapable of office in respect to their faith and worship." (Cobb, 1968, p. 402)

The eastern part of the state limited this liberty only to persons "acknowledging one Almighty and Eternal God, and professing faith in Christ Jesus" (p. 402). In 1702, when the English authority joined both colonies and linked them to New York, liberty of conscience was supposedly allowed for all but the Papists. Yet even then the tone of the English authority was toward the establishment of the Church of England in New Jersey. Such an effort never succeeded however because of the resolute persistence of the Quakers against the attempts at disenfranchisement by the English churchmen.

The colony of Georgia, begun only forty years before the Revolution, obviously has a short history. Its charter of 1732 allowed freedom of worship except for the Catholics: "We do, by these Presents, for Us, our Heirs and Successors grant, establish, and ordain, That forever hereafter there shall be a Liberty of Conscience allowed in the Worship of God to all Persons ... within our said Province, and that all such Persons, except Papists, shall have a free exercise of Religion" (Cobb, 1968, p. 419). However, by 1758, the Church of England was formally established by the colonial legislature. With the onset of the Revolution, establishment of the Church of England was stymied.

In both North and South Carolina, the Church of England was the established religion. Yet, ample liberty was given to those who could not conform to the ceremonies of the Church. In 1665 the charter from King Charles II both established the Church of England and, though giving reasonable liberties to dissenters, allowed the government the privilege of withdrawing these liberties. For a period of approximately fifteen years, the short-lived "Fundamental Constitutions" prohibited voting rights and land ownership to those not professing a belief in God. Further it declared so-called churches that do not believe in God as unlawful meetings, punishable as riots; it also stated that anyone over the age of seventeen who was not a member of some church or profession would not receive the "benefit or protection of the law" (Cobb, 1968, p. 122). By 1704, all members of the legislature were to be members of the Church of England, and public monies were to be used to support ministers and the building of churches. These laws were voided however by the Queen of England in 1706 with such force that later, when the Church of England was reestablished, there was very little infringement on the rights of dissenters. Yet the taxing of the majority to support the religious establishment of the minority continued until shortly after the War for Independence.

Because Pennsylvania and Delaware are so alike and were one colony until 1702, they can be considered together. Founded by the Quaker William Penn, his purpose was to make a "holy experiment" where all people must be able to experience the liberty that the Quakers wanted for themselves. Penn said, "I abhor two principles of religion and pity them that own them; the first is obedience to authority without conviction; and the other is destroying them that differ from me for God's sake" (Cobb, 1968, p. 441). Even so, the laws of 1682 and 1693 prohibited a non-Christian from voting, holding office, and owning property. Unlike many other colonies, the Roman Catholics were not discriminated against, at least for a time. Orders from England dated 1693, 1701, and 1703 making religious oath a requirement, automatically excluded from public office Catholics, Jews, and Unitarians. When William Penn protested these oaths, he was ridiculed as an instrument of the excluded groups and eventually jailed for several months. From this time on until the Revolution, the Quaker ideal of pure religious liberty for Pennsylvania was never realized. Delaware, after its split from Pennsylvania, seems not to have had anywhere near the same amount of religious discrimination.

Without a doubt, the state that most clearly practiced religious liberty was Rhode Island. In fact, religious liberty was the very reason Roger Williams founded Rhode Island after being expelled from Massachusetts in 1636 because of his critical statements regarding the Massachusetts theocracy. Williams felt that civil law had nothing to say about religion other than to guarantee that each person be able to follow his own religious conscience. The charter of 1663 merging Providence and Rhode Island said, "It is much in our hearts to hold forth a lively experiment, that a most flourishing civil State may stand, and best be maintained, with a full liberty of religious concernments" (Cobb, 1968, p. 435). It was said of Rhode Island in 1665 that "They allow liberty of conscience to all who live civilly: they admit of all religions" (p. 437). Two potential exceptions to full liberty occurred when Quakers were to be outlawed because they would not bear arms and when Catholics were to be denied citizenship. Neither deprivations actually occurred however. The charter of Rhode Island passed through the Revolutionary War, remaining for an additional two generations without alteration.

The last colony examined is Virginia. While Rhode Island was the colony with the purest form of religious liberty prior to the American Revolution, Virginia was the colony from which the crucial federal documents on religious freedom were birthed. The birthing process was not easy however. The first Virginia charter dated 1606 stated "that the Word and Science of God be preached, planted, and used ... according to the rites and doctrine of the Church of England" (Cobb, 1968, p. 75). Because of the apparent moral laxity in the young colony, Governor Dale instituted certain laws which provided the following penalties and offenses: "Non-attendance on religious services entailed a penalty, for the first offense, of the stoppage of allowance; for the second, whipping; for the third, the galleys for six months... For Sabbath-breaking the first offense brought the stoppage of allowance; the second, whipping; and the third, death." It was also ruled that every person in the colony was to visit a minister to be examined in the faith and if necessary so instructed. Refusal to do so brought a whipping every day until compliant (p. 78).

When Lord Baltimore visited Virginia in 1628 to wait for his own patent from the King, he was required to take the oath of supremacy of the King of England in religious matters. Unable to do this because of his Catholic beliefs, Lord Baltimore was forced to leave Virginia. By 1642, Catholics were denied the vote, and priests were only allowed to stay in the colony a maximum of five days. Similarly, the Puritans, though once accepted, were treated as rebels and denied admission to the colony when the English Puritans sided with parliament against the King and the Church. About this same time, however, the leaders in the local churches were able to wrest from the governor the power to appoint their ministers themselves.

Quakers were treated much as in other colonies. In 1659 it was ordered that they be arrested and imprisoned until they agreed to leave the colony. If they returned, they were to be treated as common criminals. When the Presbyterians first began preaching in the colony, they were arrested for not being licensed and at times suffered banishment. The Baptists seemed to be the most persecuted of all. Strangely, in Virginia the Baptists were being persecuted at a time when other religious groups were beginning to enjoy some liberties. Besides being beaten and imprisoned, they were tried by law as criminals even as late as 1770.

Even beyond the persecution of these religious groups, Virginia was also guilty of persecution within the established church. This persecution occurred in several different ways. For instance, the clergy were often so licentious and injurious of their congregations' morality that the laws of 1669 and 1705 against immorality and many other acts specifically noted that guilty clergymen were *not* to be exempted from penalties. The legislature, however, often in defense of the established church, magnified the sad conditions by inducing immoral clergy to come to this country. Even at times, because of the legally imposed methods of paying the ministers and the unjust method of establishing monetary values, the clergy would end up bringing suit against their vestries for non-payment of salaries.

Religious Liberty

By the time of the Revolution practically all states were experiencing some kind of religious liberty. In Massachusetts, even one hundred years earlier, all sects were able to worship as they pleased even though the Church establishment of the Puritans remained. By 1780, the Massachusetts legislature required that towns support at their own expense a place for the worship of God. Each taxpayer was able to designate which church would receive his tax share. More rigid however were the laws of Connecticut. While the laws of 1784 granted freedom of religious worship to all Christians, it was not until 1818 that a state constitution for complete religious freedom was attempted. New York, in 1777, asserted that "The free exercise and enjoyment of religious profession and worship, without discrimination or preference, shall forever hereafter be allowed within this State to all mankind" (p. 502). While certain exceptions seemed to discriminate against Catholics and prohibit clergy from holding public office, these restrictions were later abolished. By 1781, New Hampshire adopted a Bill of Rights similar to Massachusetts but even as late as 1784 still had the Church supported by public taxes. By 1775, Maryland extended the right to vote to all within the Christian religion, including the previously excluded Catholics, but still gave civil authority certain taxing powers to support the Christian religion. New Jersey, in its constitution of 1776, decreed freedom of worship yet still made office holding contingent upon test of religious belief. Georgia, in 1777, instituted freedom of conscience but did require that legislators be of the Protestant faith. North Carolina guaranteed freedom of conscience but, along with South Carolina, made office-holding a matter of religious discrimination. Pennsylvania and Delaware stayed relatively similar through the years in allowing religious freedom to those who believed in God or who were Christians, and Delaware additionally tied Christian doctrine to the oath of office.

From its founding onward, Rhode Island maintained full religious freedom. While Virginia declared religious liberty in 1785, events in the time period between 1774 and 1786 intricately relate to the development of the First Amendment to the U.S. Constitution.

Pre-First Amendment Mentality

Early America was characterized by a tension that existed between the vision, on the one hand, to make, force, legislate, cause, or decree that this country be godly and the paradoxical Christian principle, on the other hand, to promote freedom of religious conscience. There were almost as many interpretations of the truth of the Bible as there were Christian denominations. Added to this diversity were the few other groups who had religious beliefs founded on other than the Bible of the Christians. This ambiguity of interpretation, coupled with what seems to be an innate human tendency to declare one's own religious interpretations as more correct than the interpretations of others, resulted in the religious discrimination described in the earlier portions of this chapter. Yet, because each person or sect or denomination thought its interpretation most correct, and because each responded with a type of righteous resistance against being forced into how to believe religiously, a balancing force was naturally energized against whatever opinion or interpretation happened to be in power. Thus from the early beginnings of this country up to and beyond the time of the writing of the Constitution, most states evolved toward more and more religious freedom.

A most perplexing aspect for the early colonists was how to perpetuate the faith thought to be so vital to the success of the nation without constraining the natural liberty of its citizens. To allow freedom of worship and religious expression would seemingly do anything but bring the uniformity of belief desired in this nation and perhaps even necessitated by personal and communal covenants with this nation's God. The events in Virginia around the time of American independence probably best reflect the dynamics of this struggle. As we study these events more closely we can see the tenor of the time particularly regarding the intent and meaning behind the First Amendment to the U.S. Constitution. We will come to see that the affairs of religion and religious conscience are not within the authority of any civil governmental unit. As we have seen so far in this chapter, each colony was progressively moving in this direction. Likewise, the arguments for American independence are based on the same principle. The principle is always the same— each person is his own authority regarding religious conscience; this authority never resides at any higher human level(s).

Rhode Island's Religious Freedom

Rhode Island started and then consistently maintained its stand on full religious liberty. We turn briefly to the ideas of Roger Williams to set the stage for what ultimately happened in the pivotal state of Virginia and also with the U.S. Constitution's First Amendment.

Williams labeled as persecution the molestation of any person "for either professing doctrine, or practising worship merely religious or spirituall ... even if his doctrine or worship is false, or is presumed to be false" (Alley, 1985, p. 126). Persecutions have persisted, he maintains, "despite the fact that Christ has armed his truth with none other than spiritual weapons" (p. 127). He would ask those who persecute supposedly for Christ whether they have "fought against God, that I have not persecuted Jesus in some of them?" (p.127). He claimed that God gave the church what it needed against heresy, but never did He appoint the civil sword for such work. Only when the civil magistrate withdraws from jurisdiction over religion can persecution be avoided. To Williams, any civil control over religion or any official state-church arrangement was patently wrong.

Virginia's Religious Freedom

Unlike Rhode Island, Virginia went through an evolutionary process to gain religious freedom. Three distinct events substantially comprise this evolutionary process. Up to 1774, Virginia operated by the principle that the established Church (of England) set the correct form of worship. Each and every other persuasion had to fight for its own liberties and liberties once won hardly ever transferred to any other groups. Such liberties, where they existed, were more like tolerations than the natural principle of true liberty.

The severe persecution of the Baptists up through 1774, even while the Presbyterians were being granted more and more freedom, because the straw on the proverbial camel's back of religious intolerance. With several Baptist preachers beaten and imprisoned, Madison ran out of patience over these matters, writing to his friend William Bradford,

> I have ... nothing to brag of as to the State and Liberty of my Country... That diabolical Hell conceived principle of persecution rages among some and to their eternal Infamy the Clergy can furnish their quota of Imps for such business. There are ... five or six well-meaning men in close Goal for publishing their religious Sentiments which in the main are very orthodox. I have neither patience to hear talk or think any thing relative to this matter, for I have squabbled and scolded abused and ridiculed so long about it ... that I am without common patience ... pray for the Liberty of Conscience... (Alley, 1985, p. 48)

When the Virginia state convention met in 1776, petitions from all over the state asked for "protection in the full exercise of their modes of worship," release from "payment of all taxes for any Church whatever," disestablishment of the Church of England, and the granting of the "right of private judgment" (p. 491). The Presbytery of Hanover petitioned "that when our blessed Savior declares His kingdom not of this world, He renounces all dependence on state power... We are persuaded that, if mankind were left in quite possession of their inalienable rights and privileges, Christianity, as in the days of the apostles, would continue to prevail and flourish in the greatest purity by its own native excellence and under the all-disposing providence of God" (p. 491).

In response to these petitions, George Mason drafted a Bill of Rights. Its sixteenth section, authored by Patrick Henry, read,

That Religion or the duty that we owe our Creator, and the Manner of discharging it, can be directed only by Reason and Conviction, and not by Force or Violence; and therefore that all Men shou'd enjoy the fullest Toleration in the Exercise of Religion, according to the Dictates of Conscience, unpunished and unrestrained by the Magistrate, unless, under Colour of Religion, any Man disturb the Peace, the Happiness, or Safety of Society, or of Individuals. And that it is the mutual Duty of all, to practice Christian Forbearance, Love and Charity towards Each other. (Alley, 1985, p. 51)

In the spirit that underlies full religious freedom, Madison objected to the clause because it contained the word toleration. He said that the term belongs in a system where liberty of worship is granted or permitted but is not thought of as a right and, therefore, can be rescinded. For that portion of the sentence, Madison substituted the following: "all men are equally entitled to the full and free exercise of religion, according to the dictation of conscience" (Cobb, 1968, p. 492). According to some, "The Amendment by Madison itself forms an era in the history of American liberty. In discarding a term hitherto consecrated in some degree as an symbol of liberty, but intrinsically fallacious, it erected a new and loftier platform for the fabric of religious freedom" (p. 492).

Thomas Paine ably expressed it this way: "Toleration is not the opposite of intolerance, but it is the counterfeit of it. Both are despotisms. The one assumes to itself the right of withholding liberty of conscience, the other of granting it." (Alley, 1985, p. 148)

Thomas Jefferson joined with Madison in affirming the exercise of religion according to the dictates of one's conscience. Writing, in 1782, on the state of religious affairs in Virginia, Jefferson said, "The rights of conscience we never submitted, we could not submit. We are answerable for them to our God." He even labeled the injustices in Virginia as amounting to a state of "religious slavery." Jefferson maintained that submitting our conscience to others and particularly to government is wrong: "It is error alone which needs the support of government. Truth can stand by itself." Attempts to produce uniformity in this area, on grounds that it is a good thing, are wrong. Actually, the effect of religious coercion has been "To make one half the world fools, and the other half hypocrites." (Jefferson, 1984, p. 286)

The second major event toward full religious liberty in Virginia with direct implication for all of America involves two contingently occurring (1784 & 1785) legislative acts. By 1784, the previously official Church of Virginia was financially in trouble because of the loss of assessments through disestablishment in 1779. Its supporters tried to meet the need through incorporation, but this act for "Incorporating the Protestant Episcopal Church" was almost immediately repealed. Even so, there was still strong sentiment for supporting some form of worship. Thus in 1785, Patrick Henry proposed a "Bill for establishing a provision for teachers of the Christian religion." This bill seemed to guarantee religious freedom in that it favored no sects in allowing each individual the choice of which church would receive his tax share. When no church was so designated, the tax went to maintain a local school (p. 67). But it certainly did not contribute to disestablishment since it was for the financial benefit of those of the Christian persuasion only, just as we have already noted regarding the predominant Christian nature of this country. This bill was supported by George Washington, Patrick Henry, Richard Henry Lee, and John Marshall. Principally opposed to it were Madison and Jefferson. Their opposition was based on the notion that total religious freedom included the concept of complete disestablishment. Arguing very strongly against the bill, Madison drafted the now famous document entitled "A Memorial and Remonstrance." In this document, Madison builds off on the Virginia Bill of Rights for his foundational position. Specifically, he declared

> that Religion or the duty which we owe to our Creator and the manner of discharging it, can be directed by reason and conviction, not by force or violence. The Religion then of every man must be left to the conviction and conscience of every man; and it is the right of every man to exercise it as these may dictate. This right is in its

nature an inalienable right. It is inalienable because the opinions of men, depending only on the evidence contemplated by their own minds, cannot follow the dictates of other men: It is inalienable also, because what is here a right towards men, is a duty towards the Creator. It is the duty of every man to render to the Creator such homage and such only as he believes to be acceptable to him ... Before any man can be considered as a member of Civil Society, he must be considered as a subject of the Governour of the Universe... We maintain therefore that in matters of Religion, no mans right is abridged by the institution of Civil Society and that Religion is wholly exempt from its cognizance. (Alley, 1985, p. 56)

Further, Madison writes that all men are to enjoy

equal title to the free exercise of Religion according to the dictates of Conscience. While we assert for ourselves a freedom to embrace, to profess and to observe the Religion which we believe to be of divine origin, we cannot deny an equal freedom to those whose minds have not yet yielded to the evidence which has convinced us. If this freedom be abused, it is an offense against God, not against man: To God, therefore, not to man, must an account of it be rendered. (Alley, 1985, p. 57)

Widespread support of the Memorial and Remonstrance (signed by over 10,000 citizens) resulted in quick legislative abandonment of the bill to provide for teachers of the Christian religion (with approximately 1200 citizens supporting it). Madison, apparently a Christian himself and thus one who would seemingly favor such a bill, as did contemporaries like George Washington, nonetheless remonstrated fervently against it. The several major objections that Madison held included the immediate question regarding how men could judge other men over a body of religious teaching that man did not himself invent. It is a question of "what is orthodoxy, what is heresy" (Alley, 1985, p. 55). The overriding concern for

Madison, however, as his document reveals, is that religion is not at all "within the purview of Civil Authority" (Alley, 1985, p. 54). Whereas those in favor of the bill were operating from the belief that it was a governmental function to provide for religion, Madison felt that religion would survive full well without governmental establishment of religion. In fact, any claim that the bill was necessary for the support of the Christian religion was, Madison said, "a contradiction to the Christian Religion itself, for every page of it disavows a dependence on the powers of this world ... it is a contradiction in terms; for a Religion not invented by human policy, must have pre-existed and been supported, before it was established by human policy" (Alley, 1985, p. 57).

The essence of Madison's argument was that while religion occupied a central role in their lives, it was not the place of government to provide for its existence, its continuation, or its enforcement. The crucial dilemma for the lawmakers of that time was in preserving the country's Christian identity while at the same time respecting the religious freedom of all its inhabitants. The earlier-cited religious section in the Bill of Rights that was proposed by Patrick Henry but modified by James Madison to rid it of "toleration" seems to typify this dilemma. The article, as adopted by the Virginia Convention, embodies the two horns of this dilemma in that it declares that "all men are equally entitled to the free exercise of religion" while at the same time declares that "it is the mutual duty of all to practice Christian forbearances, love, and charity, towards each other" (Alley, 1985, p. 52). Thus men's actions should be evaluated by the standards of Christianity while men, at the same time, should enjoy freedom from religious coercion.

In actuality, the contents of the religious section of the 1776 Bill of Rights are totally consistent with Christian principles. A government that operates according to Christian principles is expected to allow complete religious freedom to all. This is an extremely important point to remember as we come closer (in the next chapter) to considering the meaning of the First Amendment. Specifically, the government was created to run according to Christian principles, which means, among other things, that it can do no less than safeguard religious freedom for all its citizens. While not founded as a theocracy, the United States nonetheless was founded to reflect biblical principles.

With the defeat of the assessment bill via Madison's "Memorial and Remonstrance," the last event toward understanding full freedom of religion was positioned to occur. That last event was passage of the "Declaratory Act," which became entitled "An Act Establishing Religious Freedom." This act was intended to guarantee that in the future no further efforts at civil interference with religion would occur in the state of Virginia. The victory won via Madison's "Memorial and Remonstrance" was to be safeguarded legislatively.

Portions of this act read as follows:

> Whereas Almighty God hath created the mind free; that all attempts to influence it by temporal punishments or burthens, or by civil incapacitations, tend only to beget habits of hypocrisy and meanness, and are a departure from the plan of the Holy author of our religion, who being Lord both of body and mind, yet chose not to propagate it by coercions on either, as was in his Almighty power to do; that the impious presumption of legislators and rulers ... have assumed dominion over the faith of others ... that to compel a man to furnish contributions of money for the propagation of opinions which he disbelieves, is sinful and tyrannical that even the forcing him to support this or that teacher of his own religious persuasion, is depriving him of the comfortable liberty of giving his contributions ... that our civil rights have no dependence on our religious opinions ... but that all men shall be free to profess, and by argument to maintain, their opinion in matters of religion...
>
> ... this assembly ... have no power to restrain the acts of succeeding assemblies ... yet we are free to declare, and do declare, that the rights hereby asserted are of the natural rights of mankind, and that of any act shall be hereafter passed to repeal the present, or to narrow its operation, such act will be an infringement of natural right. (Alley, 1985, pp. 60-61).

Interestingly the proposal to change the first sentence of this Act from "Holy author of our religion" to "Jesus Christ, the holy author of our religion" was rejected. In his autobiography Jefferson, (see Alley, 1985, p. 62) contends the defeat was "meant to comprehend, within the mantle of its protection, the Jew and the Gentile, the Christian and the Mahomaton, the Hindoo, and infidel of every denomination."

The contents of this bill were actually written by Jefferson in 1779. However, it remained in limbo until passage in 1786 when it secured, once and for all, religious liberty in Virginia. Madison, living true to his Christian beliefs, is credited with the success of its passage. On January 22, 1786 he wrote to Jefferson saying, "I flatter myself have in this Country extinguished for ever the ambitious hope of making laws for the human mind ..." (Alley, 1985, p. 62). Writing back to Madison, Jefferson said, "it is honorable for us to have produced the first legislature who has had the courage to declare that the reason of man may be trusted with the formation of his own opinions" (Alley, 1985, p. 69).

Several things are to be emphasized regarding the meaning of both the Religious Assessments proposal and the follow-up "Memorial and Remonstrance." First, for Madison, Jefferson, and the majority of citizens, religious liberty included the freedom not to be forced by civil authority to tithe even to one's own church. Richard Henry Lee, for instance, initially thought it acceptable to word the Virginia Declaration of Rights to compel contributions "for the support of religion in general just as long as there was no forcing modes of faith and form of worship." believing that "the experience of all times shows Religion to be the guardian of morals," there needed to be "a legal obligation to contribute something to its support" since, as he observed, otherwise "avarice is accomplishing the destruction of religion." He held this view of mandatory tax support even while believing "that true freedom embraces the Mahomitan and the Gentoo as well as the Christian religion" (Alley, 1985, p. 65). We see, however, that Madison and Jefferson both believed that forced tax support of churches was wrong, as revealed in "Memorial and Remonstrance" by Madison and the Act for Establishing Religious Freedom by Jefferson.

Conclusion

The various colonies of the United States began predominantly out of a motivation for religious freedom for their Christian founders. John Marshall, Chief Justice of the U.S. Supreme Court, wrote in 1833 that "The American population is entirely Christian, and with us, Christianity and religion are identified" (Alley, 1985, p. 87). The then president of the College of Charleston, Jasper Adams, also wrote, "the people of the United States have retained the Christian religion as the foundation of their civil, legal, and political institutions." Agreeing with these two gentlemen, Justice Joseph Story added, "My own private judgment has long been (and every day's experience more and more confirms me in it) that government can not long exist without an alliance with religion; and that Christianity is indispensable to the true interests and solid foundations of free government." As Judge Cooley said (Cobb, 1968, p. 525), "in a certain sense and for certain purposes it is true that Christianity is part of the law of the land." Frenchman Alexis de Tocqueville also wrote (in 1842), "There is no country in the whole world in which the Christian religion retains a greater influence over the souls of men than in America. By regulating domestic life it regulates the state. Religion is the foremost of the institutions of the country. I am certain that the Americans hold religion to be indispensable to the maintenance of republican institutions" (Cobb, 1968, p. 525). God's name was included in thirty-four state constitutions, and each constitution either invoked the blessings of or expressed gratitude to "almighty God." (Cobb, 1968, p. 518)

As we have seen, religious freedom was not easily obtained. In their religious zeal, the colonists often jealously extended religious freedom only to the denomination in control of civil power. The Quakers and the Baptists seemed most apt to urge religious freedoms for all. Roger Williams, James Madison, and Thomas Jefferson were key leaders in the battle for nondiscriminatory religious liberty.

The problem for the states and their leaders was to maintain and foster the general good of society via religious conformity while gradually coming to the realization that the state has no calling or authority to make men religious. This realization is evidenced through writings like those by Roger Williams to the effect "1. that forced worship stenches in God's nostrils; 2. that it denies Christ Jesus yet to come; 3. that in these flames about religion, there is no other prudent, Christian way of preserving peace in the world but by permission of differing consciences" (Cobb, 1968, p. 427). Also instrumental were the thoughts like those of Madison to the effect that the religion of Jesus Christ can never be "the means of abridging the natural and equal rights of all men, in defiance of his own declaration that his Kingdom was not of this world" (Alley, 1985, p. 90)

Thus as this country entered into the time of its Constitution, it knew full well by the religious persecutions suffered both in England and at home and by the urgings of its leaders, that religion and morality were necessary for its survival, yet they "must be left to the conviction and conscience of everyman" (Alley, 1985, p. 26). And this must be so for every citizen whether "the Jew and the Gentile, the Christian and Mahometan, the Hindu and Infidel of every denomination" (Cobb, 1968, p. 498).

The implications from this chapter for education are foreboding indeed. The early religious history of the United States reveals a tendency or predisposition in humans to impose beliefs of conscience onto others. As we have seen, this tendency to impose is exacerbated by possession of unchecked power even for those who would contend that religious freedom is an inalienable human right of all people. With evidence of this impositional tendency across other matters through the course of human history, it is reasonable to caution that the field of education is not exempt from its grip. After all, education is in the best interests of a society, is vulnerable to government control, and is frequently rooted in matters of conscience. These matters of conscience include issues like defining the good life, purpose of life, moral rights and wrongs, metaphysical truths, proper human interactions, and rights of all created beings.

As we have also seen, a reasonable route to guaranteeing religious freedom is not the removal of government involvement. To the contrary, it is the re-orienting of government power away from imposition, control, and taxation for religion, to instead, protection from that very tendency by governmental entities. Likewise it is reasonable to suggest that the route to educational freedom is not in governmental control but in governmental protection from educational control especially by governmental organisms themselves.

Similarly, full religious freedom holds no place for the perspective that toleration is the highest expression of this freedom. Since the concept of toleration assumes a superior right to grant or withhold freedom, it contradicts the basic inalienable right of freedom of conscience to which each person is entitled. Likewise, the requirement of taxation to support selected beliefs of conscience both betray the attitude of toleration and allow civil government to tax its citizens for religious purposes quite against the nature of true religious freedom. Application of this perspective to education argues against taxation and compulsion over matters of content that are under the purview of freedom of conscience. After all, teachings that address ultimate world view issues like purpose of life are not, as Madison said, "within the purview of civil authority." These matters of conscience cannot, as Jefferson claimed, be submitted to government control— "We are answerable for them to God." To the extent that they have been submitted to governmental jurisdiction is the extent to which citizens have come into educational bondage. In this same line of reasoning, no matter how fervently educational authorities may be convinced of the rightness of their own views, they "cannot deny an equal freedom to those minds that have not yet yielded to the evidence which has convinced them." It is as "sinful and tyrannical" in education as in religion to compel citizens to support opinions they disbelieve *as well as* believe since this constitutes government deprivation of liberty of conscience. As with Madison, we remonstrate against such practices.

Finally, as we also have seen, the battle to extricate religion from government control was initially unpopular even to the extent of being considered unpatriotic and ungodly, costly, and time consuming. To the degree that education is under government control, its liberation will be similarly unpopular. Even so, there is no cost too great for the freedom of conscience that would come through the disestablishment of education.

References

Alley, Robert S. (1985). *James Madison on religious liberty.* Buffalo, NY: Prometheus Books.

Cobb, Sanford H. (1968). *The rise of religious liberty in America.* NY: Cooper Square Publ.

Commager, Henry S. (1973). *Documents of American history Vol. I.* 9th ed. Englewood Cliffs, NJ: Prentice-Hall.

Cord, Robert L. (1982). *Separation of church and state.* New York: Lambeth Press.

Dreisbach, Daniel L. (1987). *Real threat and mere shadow.* Westchester, IL: Crossway Books.

Gyertson, David J. (1979). Historic roots. *Focus 1* (1) Winter, 8-10.

Jefferson, Thomas (1984). *Writings.* NY: Literary Classics of the U.S., Inc.

Johnston, Lucile (1987). *Celebrations of a nation.* Willmar, MN: Biword Publ.

Marshall, Peter & Manuel, David (1977). *The light and the glory.* Old Tappan, NJ: Fleming H. Revell.

Noll, Mark A., Hatch, Nathan O., Marsden, George M., Wells, David F., & Woodbridge, John D. (Eds.) (1983). *Eerdman's handbook to Christianity in America.* Grand Rapids, MI: William B. Eerdmans Publ. Co.

Padover, Saul K. (1943). *The complete Jefferson.* Freeport, NY: Books for Libraries Press.

Perry, Richard L. (Ed.) (1978). *Sources of our liberties.* Chicago, IL: American Bar Foundation.

Pfeffer, Leo (1977). *Religious freedom.* Skokie, IL: National Textbook Co.

Reichley, A. James (1985). *Religion in American public life.* Washington, DC: The Brookings Institute.

Chapter 5

The First Amendment

Congress shall make no law respecting an establishment of religion, or prohibiting the free exercise thereof. (Religion clauses of the First Amendment to the U.S. Constitution—ratified December 15, 1791)

Believing with you that religion is a matter which lies solely between man and his God, that he owes account to none other for his faith or his worship; that the legislative powers of government reach actions only, and not opinions, I contemplate with sovereign reverence that act of the whole American People which declared that their legislature should 'make no law respecting an establishment of religion, or prohibiting the free exercise thereof,' thus building a wall of separation between church and State. (Cord, 1982, p. 115; Jefferson, 1984, p. 510)

Mr. Madison said, he apprehended the meaning of the words [of the First Amendment] to be, that Congress should not establish a religion, and enforce the legal observation of it by law, nor compel men to worship God in any manner contrary to their conscience. The First Amendment, he said, had been required by some of the State Conventions, who seemed to entertain an opinion that under the clause of the Constitution, which gave power to Congress to make all laws necessary and proper to carry into execution the Constitution, and the laws made under it, enabled them to make laws of such a nature as might infringe the rights of conscience, and establish a national religion; to prevent these effects he presumed the amendment was intended... (Cord, 1982, p. 10)

The first quote comes from Thomas Jefferson's 1802 letter to the Danbury Connecticut Baptist Association. From it we have the oft-cited phrase regarding the separation of church and state. The second quote is from official minutes when James Madison, the originator of the First Amendment, explained to the U.S. House of Representatives his understanding of the amended version of his First Amendment proposal.

The seeming contradiction between these quotes from Jefferson (i.e., total separation of church and state) and Madison (i.e., separation limited to prohibiting laws against rights of conscience, and from establishing a national religion) have led to the following more recent contradictions from the U.S. Supreme Court. Speaking for the Court majority in the 1947 *Everson* v. *Board of Education* decision, Justice Black said (Warshaw, 1979, p. 27),

Neither a state nor the Federal Government can set up a church. Neither can pass laws which aid one religion, aid all religions, or prefer one religion over another... Neither a state nor the Federal Government can, openly or secretly, participate in the affairs of any religious organizations or groups and vice versa. In the words of Jefferson, the Clause against establishment of religion by law was intended to erect a 'wall of separation between church and state' (pp. 15, 16). That wall must be kept high and impregnable. (p. 18)

In contradiction, Justice Douglas, also speaking for the Court in the 1952 *Zorach* v. *Clauson* case, said (Warshaw, 1979, p. 33),

> The first Amendment, however, does not say that in every and all respects there shall be a separation of Church and State... Otherwise the state and religion would be aliens to each other—hostile, suspicious, even unfriendly. (p. 312)
>
> When the state encourages religious instruction or cooperates by adjusting the schedule of public events to sectarian needs, it follows the best of our tradition. For it then respects the religious nature of our people and accommodates the public service to their spiritual needs. To hold that it may not would be to find in the Constitution a requirement that the government show a callous indifference to religious groups. That would be preferring those who believe in no religion over those who do believe ... [S]eparation of Church and State [does not] mean that public institutions can make no adjustments of their schedules to accommodate the religious needs of the people. We cannot read into the Bill of Rights such a philosophy of hostility to religion. pp. 313ff)

In *Walz* v. *Tax Commission* (1970), Justice Burger likewise said,

> No perfect or absolute separation is really possible between church and state... The Court has struggled to find a neutral course between the two Religion Clauses, both of which are cast in absolute terms, and either of which, if expanded to a logical extreme, would tend to clash with the other. (Warshaw, p. 55)

If there is to be no cooperation or accommodation between the federal government and religion as some Justices obviously hold, consider the following current day legal practices to the contrary (see Warshaw, 1979, p. 10; Boles, 1965, p. 198).

1. Chaplains are paid to provide services to the armed forces,
2. Clergy perform civilly legal marriages,
3. The birth of Christ is celebrated as a national holiday,
4. The words "under God" are a part of the pledge of allegiance to the flag as of 1954,
5. The phrase "In God We Trust" appears on all currency as of 1955,
6. The phrase "In God We Trust" was adopted in 1955 as our national motto,
7. The National Anthem (adopted in 1931) contains the stanza, "And this be our Motto 'in God is our Trust',"
8. Public funds aid church-controlled hospitals, orphanages, housing for the elderly, and homes for delinquent children,
9. Homes for the elderly have publicly constructed chapels,
10. The U.S. Supreme Court and Congress open their sessions with prayer,
11. Legislation of 1952 calls upon the President to proclaim each year a National Day of Prayer,
12. Public funds provide sectarian schools with lunches, bus transportation, textbooks, and health and diagnostic services,
13. The federal government funds secular programs, new buildings, and equipment at sectarian colleges,
14. GI veterans' education benefits go to public and sectarian colleges,
15. Churches use public school buildings,
16. Individuals are exempted from military service based on their religious beliefs,
17. Most church property and incomes are tax exempt,
18. Churches receive tax-supported police and fire protection services,
19. Contributions to religious institutions are tax deductible.

This chapter examines whether the First Amendment was intended to totally separate church and state as Jefferson is broadly interpreted (though not necessarily accurately), or, more narrowly, to only prohibit the establishment of a national or federal church as

Madison stated. With the resolution of this question, we then discuss subsequent interpretations including those relating to the Fourteenth Amendment to shed light on the current day misunderstanding of both amendments. The chapter concludes with implications for education regarding these two amendments and their misinterpretations.

Historical Setting

By 1787, the year of the U.S. Constitutional convention, the various states were far from being alike regarding religious freedom. Of the original thirteen, only two—Virginia and Rhode Island—allowed full religious freedom. Delaware and Maryland favored the Christian religion in general; New Hampshire, Connecticut, New Jersey, North and South Carolina, and Georgia insisted on Protestantism; Pennsylvania required agreement to the holy inspiration of the Bible; and Massachusetts maintained the specific religious establishment of Congregationalism (Cobb, 1968, p. 507). Practically every state had institutional sponsorship of religion.

Entering the Constitutional Convention of 1787, the various states were wrestling with two orientations internal to their own policies on religion. For one, some were moving away from state mandated religious establishments toward full religious freedom for all. But on the way, six states—Massachusetts, New Hampshire, Connecticut, Maryland, South Carolina, and Georgia—had, at least for a time, multiple establishments. That is, aid was provided to all churches "nonpreferentially" as long as their religions were Christian in nature (Cord, 1982, p. 10). In fact, it actually wasn't until as late as 1790 in South Carolina, 1810 in Maryland, 1818 in Connecticut, 1819 in New Hampshire, and 1833 in Massachusetts that state establishments finally ended (Reichley, 1985, p. 111). Most of the states were wrestling with the long-standing issue regarding the role of individual freedom of conscience and religion as contrasted with the assumed prerogative of each political unit to institutionalize the religion of its citizens.

Second, intermingled with this issue of religious establishments was the issue of state versus national power. Some wanted the federal government via the Constitution to be a powerful institution (i.e., the Federalists), while others were adamant to retain most of the power at the state level (i.e., the anti-Federalists). So the inter-mix of these two issues resulted in some congressmen insisting on freedom of conscience at both the state and national levels; some insisting on protecting freedom of conscience through established state religions; some arguing against either a national religion or the federal power to prohibit even state religions; and some wanting federal support for but not nationalization of any one religion. So in this historical setting, the two issues interacted to ultimately result in the production of sixteen powerful but seemingly ambiguous words of the first part of the First Amendment.

Associate U.S. Supreme Court Justice and Harvard Law School professor Joseph Story summarizes the dilemma regarding these two issues:

> The real object of the First Amendment was not to countenance, much less to advance. Mahometanism, or Judaism, or infidelity, by prostrating Christianity; but to exclude all rivalry among Christian sects, and to prevent any national ecclesiastical establishment which should give to a hierarchy the exclusive patronage of the national government. It thus cut off the means of religious perse-cution ... and of the subversion of the rights of conscience in matters of religion ... (Cord, 1982, p. 13)

Because of these conflicting issues, it is important to note that the First Amendment as finally adopted by the First U.S. Congress was not the sole product of one man's thinking (i.e., James Madison), but was the outcome of some degree of compromise to balance the two conflicting issues of mandated religion and state versus national power.

State versus Federal Powers

When the Constitution was presented to the states for ratifica-tion, it specifically made no mention of religious expectations. The federal government, according to the framers of the Constitution, was not authorized to speak on this matter since it was thought a prerogative of the states. So clear were the framers on this matter that they affirmed their position by prohibiting, in Article VI, a religious test for holding national office. In discussing the matter of religious involvement by the federal government, Madison told the Virginia Convention prior to their ratification of the U.S. Constitution that it had no such power: "There is not a shadow of right in the general [federal] government to intermeddle with religion. Its least interference with it, would be a most flagrant usurpation" (Cord, 1982, p. 8). Later when the matter was discussed in the U.S. House of Representatives in relation to the proposed First Amendment, Roger Sherman of Connecticut stated that there was no need for the amendment at all "inasmuch as Congress had no authority whatever delegated to them by the Constitution to make religious establishments..." (Cord, 1982, p. 9). Madison believed likewise but was convinced by Thomas Jefferson that passage of a Bill of Rights would be enhanced by an amendment on religious freedom.

It is important to recall that the religious safeguards embodied in the First Amendment were called for by various states specifically to insure that the federal government did not violate either the individual rights of its citizens or the established religions of those respective states. For example, the Maryland Ratifying Convention proposed "there be no national religion established by law..." (Cord, 1982, p. 6). When Benjamin Huntington of Connecticut expressed fear that the wording "no religion shall be established by law" (Berns, 1976, p. 4) might be construed to operate against certain state laws requiring religious contributions (which is a component of an establishment of religion), Madison proposed (unsuccessfully) that the word "national" be inserted before the word religion. Yet this was objected to by Elbridge Gerry of Massachusetts since the word national implied the creation of a strong as opposed to a limited national government (Malbin, 1981, p. 10). To guarantee states rights, the House even at one point in the continuing debate adopted a version of the First Amendment that would have prevented national laws from interfering with state laws on religion even when those laws would have established religion at the state level (Berns, 1976, p. 5).

While the above actions were designed to protect state rights, there were also proposals designed to limit state powers in the realm of religion. For instance, Madison's original two amendments that formed the basis for the First Amendment read as follows: "The Civil Rights of none shall be abridged on account of religious belief or worship, nor shall any national religion be established, nor shall the full and equal rights of conscience be in any manner, nor or any pretext infringed" and "No state shall inviolate the equal rights of conscience or the freedom of the press, or the trial by jury in criminal cases" (Dreisbach, 1987, p. 58). The first proposal addressed the desire of the state ratifying conventions to prevent the federal government from using its constitutionally delegated power to interfere with state prerogatives. But wary of the potential within the states to violate freedom of conscience, Madison added the second proposal without any apparent request to do so by the states. He in fact thought this restriction on the states was "the most valuable amendment in the whole list" of nine that he submitted (Berns, 1976, p. 5). Obviously, this second proposal was not uniformly held since it was defeated in the Senate (Berns, 1976, p. 5).

So, regarding the first issue of state versus federal power, attempts were made both to protect the existing state laws by restricting federal power and also to restrict state efforts through federal authority. Obviously by the end of the debate, the amendment was worded to apply to the federal Congress exclusively (i.e., "Congress shall make no law...") without any reference at all to the states. Thomas Jefferson, speaking much later (1808), correctly recognized the nonapplicability of the First Amendment to each of the states:

> I consider the Government of the United States as interdicted by the Constitution from meddling with religious institutions, their doctrines, discipline or exercises. This results not only from the provision that no law shall be made respecting the establishment, or free exercise, of

religion; but from that also which reserves to the States the powers not delegated to the United States. Certainly no power to prescribe any religious exercise, or to assume authority in religious discipline has been delegated to the general government. It must then rest with the State, as far as it can be in any human authority. (Cord, 1982, p. 14)

In his *Commentaries on the Constitution,* Justice Joseph Story (1851) explains, It was under a solemn consciousness of the dangers from ecclesiastical ambition, the bigotry of spiritual pride, and the intolerance of sects, thus exemplified in our domestic and foreign annals, that it deemed advisable to exclude from the national government all power to act upon the subject... It was impossible that there should not arise perpetual strife and perpetual jealousy on the subject of ecclesiastical ascendancy; if the national government were left free to create a religious establishment. The only security was in extirpating the power. But this alone would have been an imperfect security, if it had not been followed up by a declaration of the right of the free exercise of religion, and a prohibition (as we have seen) of all religious tests. Thus the whole power over the subject of religion is left exclusively to the State governments, to be acted upon according to their own sense of justice and the State Constitution... (Cord, 1982, p.15)

Federal Involvement versus Individual Rights

The second major concern surrounding the First Amendment was the extent of involvement, if any, the federal government should have in religious matters. While resolving that the federal government should not be allowed to assume that which the states already had as their prerogative, the legislators were equally concerned regarding what nondiscriminatory and inoffensive role the federal government should have, if any, in fostering religion. We need to reiterate that almost every state had at one time in their history established some form of Christian religion as the "official" state religion. So when the various states called for a Bill of Rights to accompany the Constitution, some of them specifically urged protection of the rights of conscience and religious liberty. For instance, the Maryland Convention proposed "that all persons be equally entitled to protection in their religious liberty." The New York Convention proposed "that the people have an equal, natural and inalienable right freely and peaceably to exercise their religion, according to the dictates of conscience; and that no particular religious sect or society ought to be favored or established by law in preference to others." The Virginia Ratifying Convention proposed that "all men have an equal, natural and unalienable right to the free exercise of religion, according to the dictates of conscience, and that no particular religious sect or society ought to be favored or established, by law, in preference to others." The North Carolina and Rhode Island Conventions proposed amendments similar to that from Virginia (Cord, 1982, pp. 6-7).

These proposals protected the rights of conscience but within the context of already established state religious institutions. After all, these proposals were not couched in multi-religious guarantees but in terms of ensuring that any one particular Christian sect or orientation was not empowered over all others.. According to Justice Story, "The real difficulty lies in ascertaining the limits to which government may rightfully go in fostering and encouraging religion..." (Cord, 1982, p. 13). At the same time that religion was to be protected and even fostered, a delicate balance was maintained to not infringe on the rights of religious conscience. This eventually takes us into the matter of the Free Exercise Clause of the First Amendment which shall be covered later.

The debates in the House and Senate reveal that the framers, at the insistence of the colonists themselves, wanted to protect and foster religion. From the outset of the floor debate in the House about Madison's amendment, the concern was to protect religion. Opening the debate, Peter Sylvester of New York noted his unhappiness with the Committee's version of Madison's amendment, which said that "no religion shall be established by law" (Malbin, 1981, p. 5). Sylvester feared that it "might be thought to have a tendency to abolish religion altogether" (Malbin, 1981, p. 7). When Elbridge Gerry of Massachusetts proposed the substitute wording "no religious doctrine shall be established by law" (Malbin, 1981, p. 7), he apparently was attempting to prohibit an official religion yet leave open nonestablishment forms of religious assistance. Benjamin Huntington of Connecticut expressed the similar concern "that the words might be taken in such latitude as to be extremely hurtful to the cause of religion" and "hoped, therefore, the amendment would be made in such a way as to secure the rights of conscience, and a free exercise of the rights of religion, but not to patronize those who professed no religion at all" (Malbin, 1981, pp. 8-9). As Malbin interprets Huntington, "the amendment should not require the government to be neutral to all differences between religion and irreligion." The prevention of nondiscriminatory assistance to religion was interpreted by the legislators, says Malbin, as "the equivalent of active hostility to religion" (p. 9). In attempting to resolve these objections about the possibility of offending religion, Madison proposed using the term "national" to describe the kind of institutional control that should not be legally permitted. He explained that this change would meet the concerns of the people that any one sect or combination of sects would be able to "establish a religion to which they would compel others to conform" (Malbin, 1981, p. 9). The concern never related to prohibiting religious assistance, only to preventing the establishment of a national religion. This is further confirmed through the rejection of the proposal by Samuel Livermore of New Hampshire prohibiting Congress from making any laws "touching" religion. Use of the word "touching" would seem to prohibit all forms of help to religion which obviously was not the framers' intention.

The final version, which was accepted by the House on September 24th and by the Senate on September 25, 1789, contains one additional clue as to the intent of the framers to prohibit a national religion while allowing nondiscriminatory aid to religion. The framers chose to use the word "an" instead of the word "the" to modify the word "establishment" in the Establishment Clause: "Congress shall make no law respecting an establishment of religion..." Their choice of words also substantiates the position that it was not *the* entire sphere of religion that was to be prohibited thereby placing religion totally off limits or on a par with no religion, but rather what was prohibited was *an* establishment of religion—that is, an exclusive, nationalized sect. Similarly, when Madison defended the need for the amendment against Sherman's charge that an amendment was not needed (on the basis that the Constitution never gave Congress the authority to make religious establishments), he twice noted that Congress should not establish *a* religion. Because of the small but important word "a," this is obviously different than merely saying not to establish religion. Had this little word been in the amendment which originally only said that religion not be established, then Sylvester's underlying concern that religion may be abolished altogether would not even have been an issue.

The other evidence, though meager, in support of allowing federal assistance to religion relates to the Free Exercise Clause. The clause "... or prohibiting the free exercise thereof" seems to mean that Congress can do nothing to inhibit the free exercise of religion including religious establishments. As Malbin (1981) notes, there is little if any historical evidence as to what the phrase means. Consistent with the protection of states' rights, the Free Exercise Clause would most likely mean that Congress could not in any way disestablish or prohibit any religious practice already in existence or even any that may ever come into existence. This clause thus keeps Congress from prohibiting the rightful business of each state, just as the various states had originally desired through their ratifying conventions. As much as Congress may want to disestablish state religions for the full exercise of individual religious freedom, the federal government had no authority in this area.

Post-Amendment Actions

As a check on the veracity of the First Amendment interpretation offered above, we now examine subsequent actions of the federal government for consistency with this interpretation.

We look, for instance, at an action of the House of Representatives on September 25, 1789—only one day after it approved the First Amendment for ratification by the states. On this day, Elias Boudinot of New Jersey, who voted for adoption of the First Amendment, proposed that they ask President Washington for a

Thanksgiving Day Proclamation. The account of his recommendation reads,

> Mr. Boudinot said, he could not think of letting the session pass over without offering an opportunity to all the citizens of the United States of joining, with one voice, in returning to Almighty God their sincere thanks for the many blessings he had poured down upon them. With this view, therefore, he would move the following resolutions:
>
> 'Resolved, that a joint committee of both Houses be directed to wait upon the President of the United States, to request that he could recommend to the people of the United States a day of public thanksgiving and prayer, to be observed by acknowledging, with grateful hearts, the many signal favors of Almighty God, especially by affording them an opportunity peaceably to establish a Constitution of government for their safety and happiness.' (Cord, 1982, pp. 51-52)

It is important to note several things about Boudinot's proposal. First, both Houses of Congress passed the resolution, and President Washington followed through exactly as requested. (The text of his proclamation follows shortly.) Second, there is no record of Mr. Madison objecting to such a proclamation, and in fact Roger Sherman, the one who saw no need for a bill of rights (since government was never granted authority to legislate regarding religion anyway), not only voted for but also spoke in favor of the resolution:

> Mr. Sherman justified the practice of thanksgiving, on any signal event, not only as a laudable one in itself, but as warranted by a number of precedents in holy writ: for instance, the solemn thanksgivings and rejoicings which took place in the time of Solomon, after the building of the temple, was a case in point. This example, he thought, worthy of Christian imitation on the present occasion; and he would agree with the gentleman who moved the resolution. (Cord, 1982, p. 28)

Obviously for Sherman, the resolution could be supported from a religious perspective and yet not violate the First Amendment that had passed in final form just one day earlier. We would be remiss if we attempted to explain the passage of this resolution as a slip of congressional memory, confusion, or reversal of their First Amendment position. Instead, passage of the resolution demonstrates that the unofficial religion of this country was Protestant Christianity, that Congress and the President could foster religion as long as laws to nationalize Christianity were not so made, that this was a federal not a state action, and that the First Amendment was not violated in the process as judged by those who passed the First Amendment affirmatively out of both Houses of Congress.

This proclamation of President Washington, dated October 3, 1789, and entitled "A National Thanksgiving," reads as follows:

> Whereas it is the duty of all nations to acknowledge the providence of Almighty God, to obey His will, to be grateful for His benefits, and humbly to implore His protection and favor; and Whereas both Houses of Congress have, by their joint committee, requested me 'to recommend to the people of the United States a day of public thanksgiving and prayer, to be observed by acknowledging with grateful hearts the many and signal favors of Almighty God especially by affording them an opportunity peaceably to establish a form of government for their safety and happiness.'
>
> Now, therefore, I do recommend and assign Thursday, the 26th day of November next, to be devoted by the people of these States to the service of that great and glorious Being who is the beneficent author of all the good that was, that is, or that will be; that we may then all unite in rendering unto Him our sincere and humble thanks for His kind care and protection of the people of this country previous to their becoming a nation; for the signal and manifold mercies and the favorable interpositions of His providence in the course and conclusion of the late war; for the degree of tranquility, union, and plenty which we

have since enjoyed; for the peaceable and rational manner in which we have been enabled to establish constitutions of government for our safety and happiness, and particularly the national one now lately instituted; for the civil and religious liberty with which we are blessed, and the means we have of acquiring and diffusing useful knowledge; and, in general, for all the great and various favors which He has been pleased to confer upon us.

And also that we may then unite in most humbly offering our prayers and supplications to the great Lord and Ruler of Nations, and beseech Him to pardon our national and other transgressions; to enable us all whether in public or private stations, to perform our several and relative duties properly and punctually; to render our National Government a blessing to all the people by constantly being a Government of wise, just, and constitutional laws, discreetly and faithfully executed and obeyed; to protect and guide all sovereigns and nations (especially such as have shown kindness to us), and to bless them with good governments, peace, and concord; to promote the knowledge and practice of true religion and virtue, and the increase of science among them and us; and, generally, to grant unto all mankind such a degree of temporal prosperity as He alone knows to be best.

Given under my hand, at the city of New York, the 3rd day of October, A.D. 1789. (Cord, p. 251)

The importance of the proclamation has to rank as highly as the very first Thanksgiving itself. In apparently pure conscience, the legislative and executive branches of the U.S. called upon the people of the United States to devote a day to "thanksgiving and prayer" to God just one day after the House and on the very same day that the Senate recommended to the states that they ratify the First Amendment to the Constitution. Further, the colonists never requested the intervention of the judicial branch of the U.S. government to declare unconstitutional continued proclamations of this type after the First Amendment was ratified. But neither could this intervention legitimately occur because, first, Congress never made a law out of the proclamation much less one that forced a religious practice and, second, there was nothing in the proclamation to prevent the free exercise of religion.

The position that religion could be fostered just not nationalized was also supported as follows by the fourth President of the United States, John Quincy Adams. Speaking about the use of federal funds to proselytize American Indians to the Christian faith, his Fourth Annual Message to Congress (1828) included these words: The Indians "were, moreover, considered as savages, whom it was our policy and our duty to use our influence in converting to Christianity and in bringing within the pale of civilization" (see Dreisbach, 1987, p. 129). Statements like those of Sherman and Adams and the actions of all the early presidents give validity to interpretative statements by Justice Story and Judge Thomas Cooley. Justice Joseph Story, a Unitarian, believed that at the time of the writing of the Constitution and the First Amendment,

> the general, if not universal sentiment in America was, that Christianity ought to receive encouragement from the state, so far as it was not incompatible with the private rights of conscience, and the freedom of religious worship. An attempt to level all religions, and to make it a matter of state policy to hold all in utter indifference, would have created universal disapprobation, if not universal indignation. (see Dreisbach, 1987, p. 50)

Cited earlier, the real object of the First Amendment, said Justice Story, was "to exclude all rivalry among Christian sects, and to prevent any national ecclesiastical establishment which should give to a hierarchy the exclusive patronage of the national government" (see Whitehead, 1982, p. 98). Similarly, Judge Cooley wrote (1880),

> It was never intended that by the Constitution the government should be prohibited from recognizing religion, or that religious worship should never be provided for in cases where a proper recognition of Divine

Providence in the working of government might seem to require it, and where it might be done without drawing any invidious distinctions between different religious beliefs, organizations, or sects. The Christian religion was always recognized in the administrations of the common law; and so far that law continues to be the law of the land, the fundamental principles of that religion must continue to be recognized in the same cases and to the same extent as formerly. (see Dreisbach, 1987, p. 51)

Further evidence that Congress held a very constrained meaning of the First Amendment is found in the Northwest Ordinance. Adopted in 1787 by the Continental Congress and then reenacted in 1789 by the First Congress, its purpose was to establish territorial governments under federal authority in the newly acquired western portions of the U.S. Included in its articles was the following: "Religion, morality, and knowledge, being necessary to good government and the happiness of mankind, schools and the means of learning shall be forever encouraged" (Reichley, 1985, p. 112). Obviously, the First Amendment was not intended to prohibit the federal government from encouraging religion and morality since the same Congress that reenacted the Ordinance also authored the First Amendment.

A third example refuting the concept of total separation of church and state is found in the origination of the Congressional Chaplain program. The provision for federally-paid chaplains to the House and Senate was approved by Congress in May of 1789. While the First Amendment did not make its appearance as a Congressional item until later (June 7, 1789), it is important to note that James Madison, the man who felt so fervently over a long period of time (recall that he authored the "Memorial and Remonstrance" for the state of Virginia in 1785) about freedom of religious conscience, was a member of the Congressional Committee that recommended the Chaplain System (Cord, 1982, p. 23). For Madison to propose a chaplain system in one month and in the next month propose the First Amendment suggests that he construed the meaning of the First Amendment narrowly instead of broadly as it generally is today. Similarly, this system of chaplaincy must have been consistent with the religious consciences of the great majority of the legislators. Note that this law of Congress regarding the chaplain system was no more a violation of the First Amendment than the Thanksgiving Day proclamation since neither established a national religion nor interfered with state religions.

More recently, in 1948, one year after the Supreme Court said that "neither a state nor the federal government can set up a church. Neither can pass laws which aid one religion, aid all religions, or prefer one religion over another" (*Everson* v. *Board of Education*, 1947), Congress proposed and President Truman authorized $500,000 to erect a religious chapel at the U.S. Merchant Marine Academy in Kemp Point, New York. Interestingly, this is the same dollar amount that Congress was spending annually by 1896 to support sectarian education by religious organizations to American Indians (see Dreisbach, 1987, p. 129).

Framers' Intentions

Next we turn to certain specific personalities of the time to compare their actions with the purpose of the First Amendment. Two major personalities considered are Thomas Jefferson and James Madison. Prior to that, however, we look briefly at President Washington and several others.

Serving as President when the First Amendment was both proposed and then adopted as part of the Constitution, George Washington issued at least two proclamations for the nation to join in "public Thanksgiving" and prayer. Then the second President of the U.S., John Adams, followed by issuing at least two proclamations himself. These men, who were both close to the debates occasioned by the First Amendment, apparently never expressed that they were in danger of violating the First Amendment or the oath they took to uphold the entire Constitution.

The man closest to the development of the First Amendment and who also had an opportunity to practice it at the highest level was James Madison. We can fairly well understand his personal views on the role of religion in government through his writings on matters in the state of Virginia. Objecting to the bias inherent in the word toleration, Madison reworded Mason's "fullest Toleration in the Exercise of Religion" clause of a state document to read "all men are equally entitled to the free exercise of religion, according to the dictates of conscience, unpunished and unrestrained by the magistrate" (Alley, 1985, p. 52). In his "Memorial and Remonstrance" of 1785, Madison placed civil citizenship second to being considered "as a subject of the Governour of the Universe" (Alley, 1985, p. 56). In fact, this priority of citizenship had legal or direct governmental implications for Madison as we see in two other legislative acts that he presented in the same year (1785). Madison's Bill No. 84 was entitled "A Bill for Punishing Disturbers of Religious Worship and Sabbath Breakers." Accepted by the Virginia Assembly with only the change in wording from "Sunday" to "Sabbath Day," it read in part, "If any person on Sunday shall himself be found laboring at his own or any other trade or calling ... he shall forfeit the sum of ten shillings for every such offense..." (Cord, 1982, p. 217). In this same year Madison also presented but failed to have adopted Bill No. 85 entitled "A Bill for Appointing Days of Public Fasting and Thanksgiving" (Cord, 1982, p. 220). It gave the Virginia General Assembly "the power of appointing days of public fasting and humiliation, or thanksgiving" and directed each "minister of the gospel" to "perform divine service" which would be "suited to the occasion, in his church, on pain of forfeiting fifty pounds for each failure..." (Cord, 1982, p. 220). So even as late as 1785, Madison was obviously not a proponent of total separation of church and state. He envisioned the state working amenably not only for religion but also for church functions (as in Bill No. 85).

When serving in the U.S. House of Representatives, Madison was on the committee (in 1789) that established the Congressional Chaplain System and apparently voiced no objection to the provisions of the Northwest Ordinance for encouraging religion and morality. Likewise, there is no record that he objected to the Congressional recommendation that President Washington declare a national day of fasting and thanksgiving to God. In Madison's initial First Amendment proposal, he wanted the federal government to insure that state governments allowed the free exercise of religious conscience. Obviously Madison thought there was a legitimate interaction between civil and religious institutions.

Madison's actions while President of the U.S. provide an indication of his understanding of the First Amendment which seems at variance with personal views on the matter that he expressed later in life. In 1811, while President, he vetoed both an attempt to incorporate the Episcopal Church in Alexandria, located in Washington, D.C., and an attempt to reserve a parcel of land of the United States for the use of a Baptist Church. His veto message of the first enactment stated, "This particular church, therefore, would so far be a religious establishment by law" (Cord, 1982, p. 33) because the act gave Congress the right to determine church affairs including selection and removal of the pastor. He rejected the second proposal because it "comprises a principle and precedent for the appropriation of funds of the United States for the use and support of religious societies" (Cord, 1982, p. 34). While he saw these bills as making a law in violation of the First Amendment prohibition against making laws "respecting a religious establishment" (Cord, 1982, p. 34), he did sign into effect certain proclamations that were very clearly religious but not legally binding. Specifically, Madison while President issued at least four different "Thanksgiving Day" proclamations (in 1812, 1813, 1814, and 1815) to set aside, for instance, "a day of public humiliation and fasting and prayer to Almighty God" (Cord, 1982, p. 260) "for the devout purposes of rendering the Sovereign of the Universe and the Benefactor of Mankind the public homage due to His holy attributes" (Cord, 1982, p. 257). These proclamations he saw as "recommendatory; or rather mere designation of a day, on which all who thought proper might unite in consecrating it to religious purposes... In this sense, I presume you reserve to the Gov't a right to appoint particular days for religious worship through the State, without any penal sanction enforcing the worship." (Alley, 1985, p. 82)

Since Madison considered these proclamations as "absolutely indiscriminate, and merely recommendatory" (Alley, 1985, p. 82), they were for him within the boundaries of the First Amendment. Madison's actions and verbally stated position is consistent with the framers' intent for the First Amendment as interpreted earlier in this Chapter.

We should note however that in correspondence to Edward Livingston in 1822, Madison also said that "Every new and successful example therefore of a perfect separation between ecclesiastical and civil matters is of importance." Furthermore, he continues, "religion and Gov't will both exist in greater purity, the less they are mixed together" (Alley, 1985, p. 83). Not only that, but Madison's writings in 1819 speak favorably to "the total separation of the Church from the State" (Alley, 1985, p. 81). Finally, writing in the "Detached Memoranda" sometime between 1817 and 1832, he notes how "Strongly guarded as is the separation between Religion and Gov't in the Constitution of the United States" and even suggests that the appointment of Congressional and Military Chaplains and the Executive Religious Proclamations violate both the First Amendment and "the pure principle of religious freedom" (Alley, 1985, p. 91-93).

The views of Madison as presented in the paragraph immediately above stand in direct opposition to his legislative work in the state of Virginia and appear to be at variance with his Presidential proclamations. From even a comparison of his actions in the Virginia Assembly and as a U.S. Representative, it is obvious that his views changed over time. Recall, for instance, his Virginia Bill to punish Sabbath breakers and then his U.S. House of Representatives attempt to stifle similar legislative actions at the state level. Even so, his actions as President seemed to match the founder's intent for the First Amendment even while, at least later in life, his personal philosophy in this regard was more conservative. Recall also that in his initial draft of the First Amendment, he went against (unsuccessfully) the requests of the states by attempting to authorize federal protection of individual rights of conscience from state injustices. This seems to be an extremely important point toward understanding the First Amendment's guarantee of states' rights in religion given contemporary interpretations to the contrary.

In the spirit of this conservatism, our next individual is considered to have reached its zenith. Thomas Jefferson, as most have heard, clearly felt in 1802 as President of the United States that there was, because of the First Amendment, a "wall of separation between church and state" (Jefferson, 1984, p. 510). (See comments later in this chapter on the likely true meaning of this phrase.) However, for Jefferson as with Madison, a clear understanding regarding their interpretation of the First Amendment or their personal philosophy is not accurately gauged by any one set of statements.

Recall Jefferson's actions before he became President. The 1786 Virginia statute (originally penned by Jefferson in 1779) entitled "A Bill for Establishing Religious Freedom," states, after a lengthy philosophical preface,

> that no man shall be compelled to frequent or support any religious worship, place, or ministry whatsoever, nor shall be enforced, restrained, molested, or burthened in his body or goods, nor shall otherwise suffer, on account of his religious opinions or belief; but that all men shall be free to profess, and by argument to maintain, their opinions in matters of religion, and that the same shall in no wise diminish, enlarge, or affect their civil capacities. (Cord, 1982, p. 250)

Yet in the very same year (1785) this bill (with which Jefferson was so personally identified) was being considered for adoption, so too was the Virginia Revisal Bill No. 84. While presented by Madison, it supposedly was authored by Jefferson. Actually Bill No. 84 for punishing Sabbath breakers and Bill No. 85 for appointing public fast and thanksgiving days (both discussed earlier) were reportedly both authored by Jefferson but had to be presented by Madison since Jefferson was out of the country as U.S. Ambassador to France.

Jefferson apparently did not believe in a complete separation between church and state if he had anything to do at all with Bills 84 and 85, contrary to what his Religious Freedom bill implies.

When considering Thomas Jefferson the President of the United States, it is important to recall that he never had any direct role in forming either the Constitution or the First Amendment. He was in France as the United States Ambassador to France during that entire time period. When he became President, Jefferson departed from his predecessors Washington and Adams in not issuing any "Thanksgiving" proclamations since he believed they violated the First Amendment (Cord, 1982, p. 45). While acknowledging that these proclamations were recommendations and not prescriptions, he still believed that they were "a law of conduct for those to whom it is directed" carrying at least "some degree of proscription, perhaps in public opinion" and thus were not within the civil authority as granted by the Constitution (Cord, 1982, p. 40. While the amendment restricted Congress from making certain laws, it did not restrict Presidents from making Proclamations. Further, it would be wrong to read Jefferson's words as a total prohibition of government involvement in religion because in this same letter (to a Presbyterian clergyman in 1808), he acknowledges the right of the states to make such proclamations: "Certainly, no power to prescribe any religious exercise, or to assume authority in religious discipline, has been delegated to the General Government. It must then rest with the States, as far as it can be in any human authority" (Cord, 1982, p. 40). In spite of his professed aversion to making religious recommendations at the federal level, since they were to him violations in the spirit of the First Amendment, he nonetheless signed into law the 1806 act of the 9th Congress that earnestly *recommended* that all officers and soldiers diligently attend divine services (Public Statutes, p. 194). We have already seen that while legislating at the state level he both prohibited state intervention (through the Bill for Religious Freedom) as well as encouraged state intervention in religious matters (through the Sabbath-breaker and public thanksgiving/fast bills).

At the national level, Jefferson did not always maintain consistency against federal involvement. His "wall of separation" letter as typically interpreted is contrasted with his actions of 1803 regarding a treaty with the Kaskaskia Indians and his actions of 1804 regarding the Moravian Brethren in Pennsylvania. Specifically, Jefferson recommended that Congress ratify a treaty with the Kaskaskia Indians who transferred their country to the U.S. in return for the following conditions: "the United States will give annually for seven years one hundred dollars towards the support of a priest of that religion [the Catholic Church]... And the United

States will further give the sum of three hundred dollars to assist the said tribe in the erection of a church" (Cord, 1982, p. 38). Likewise, on three occasions (1802, 1803, 1804) Jefferson extended a 1796 Law, as did Washington and Adams, originally entitled, "An act regulating the grants of land appropriated for Military services, and for the Society of the United Brethren for propagating the Gospel among the Heathen" (Cord, 1982, p. 44). The act included issuing land for the specifically religious activity of spreading Christianity among the Indians. Some (cf. Dreisbach, 1987, p. 287) suggest that appealing to the Indian situation is problematic in that Indian tribes were often given the status of foreign nations and thus not under the same Constitutional provisions as U.S. citizens. However, there is no apparent way to equally excuse, for instance, Jefferson's religion-oriented act of signing into law in 1808 (six years after his wall of separation statement) the appointment of a chaplain, with the rank and privilege of an infantry major, to each military brigade (10th Congress, p. 483).

This evidence regarding Jefferson's 1802, 1803, 1804, 1806, and 1808 favorable actions toward religion seems totally contrary to his 1802 "wall of separation between church and state" phrase. For clarification, we look first to the letter to which he responds with his now often quoted "separation of church and state" phrase.

<u>Letter Sent to President Thomas Jefferson</u>
<u>from Danbury Baptist Association</u>
(Library of Congress Reel #24)

[1801, Oct. 7]

The address of the Danbury Baptist Association, in the State of Connecticut; assembled October 7th, AD, 1801. To *Thomas Jefferson* ESQ. President of the united States of America.

Sir.
Among the many millions in America and Europe who rejoice in your Election to office; we embrace the

first opportunity which we have enjoy,d in our collective capacity, since your Inauguration, to express our great satisfaction, in your appointment to the chief Magistracy in the United States: And though our mode of expression may be less courtly and pompious than what many others dothe their addresses with, we beg you, Sir to believe, that none are more sincere. Our Sentiments are uniformly on the side of Religious Liberty-, That Religion is at all times and places a Matter between God and Individuals-That no man ought to suffer in Name, person or effects on account of his religious Opinions-That the legitimate Power of civil Government extends no further than to punish the man who works ill to his neighbour: But Sir, our constitution of government is not specific. Our ancient charter, together with the Laws made coincident therewith, were adopted as the Basis of our government, At the time of our revolution; and such has been our Laws and usages, and such still are; that Religion is consider,d as the first object of Legislation; & therefore what religious privileges we enjoy (as a minor part of the State): we enjoy as favors granted, and not as inalienable rights: and these favors we receive at the expense of such degrading acknowledgments as are inconsistent with the rights of freemen. It is not to be wondered at therefore; if those, who seek after *power & gain* under the pretance of *government & Religion* should reproach their fellow men-should reproach their chief Magistrate, as an enemy of religion Law & good order because he will not, dares not assume the prerogative of Jehovah and make Laws to govern the Kingdom of Christ.

Sir, we are sensible that the President of the united States, is not the national Legislator, & also sensible that the national government cannot destroy the Laws of each State; but our hopes are strong that the sentiments of our beloved President, which we have had such genial Effect already, like the radiant beams of the Sun, will shine & prevail through all these States and all the world till

Hierarchy and Tyranny be destroyed from the Earth. Sir, when we reflect on your past services, and see a glow of philanthropy and good will shining forth in a course of more than thirty years we have reason to believe that America's God has raised you up to fill the chair of State out of that good will which he bears to the Millions which you preside over. May God strengthen you for the arduous task which providence & the voice of the people have cal,d you to sustain and support you in your Administration against all the predetermined,d opposition of those who wish to rise to wealth & importance on the poverty and subjection of the people—

And may the Lord preserve you safe from every evil and bring you at last to his Heavenly Kingdom through Jesus Christ our Glorious Mediator.

Signed on behalf of the Association.

Neh,h Dodge
Eph,m Robbins   The Committee
Stephen S. Nelson

The Danbury Baptists, writing as a collective group, declare both their harmony with Jefferson and their concern over the matter of "Religious Liberty." In the second paragraph they acknowledge the "reproach" they share with President Jefferson from a common source—namely from those who favor a "Hierarchy" of "government & Religion." The Baptists also note the tyrannical nature of their own state government in that it has a legislative control over religious matters such that the Baptists receive religious "favors" at the expense of being treated degradingly, counter to "the rights of freemen." Similarly, they recognize the reproach "as an enemy of religion, law, and good order" that Jefferson suffers from similar sources who desire "power & gain" because he dares not assume to make laws to govern religious matters.

Interestingly, the Baptists did not write to the President to ask for relief. In fact they acknowledge in their third paragraph that he does not have legitimate authority to "destroy the Laws of each

State." Nevertheless cognizant of the "genial Effect" his sentiments and efforts toward religious liberty have had over a long period of time, they write to affirm his call both from providence and the people to stand against those who wish to bring poverty and subjection on the people, particularly regarding government control of religion, i.e., "Hierarchy," as in their own state.

The crucial point to note about this address of the Baptists to the President is the very direct influence they, as a religious group, intended to have on civil government. Particularly, they were requesting that the President correctly and properly use his rightful authority to have the federal or national government protect the religious rights of all its citizens.

Accordingly, the nature of Jefferson's reply to this address should provide evidence as to whether he believes that religious groups have any right at all to influence civil affairs and whether the federal government should have a role in protecting religious liberty.

We cannot help but note, however, that the Baptists have already revealed the mutuality of their and Jefferson's sentiments regarding religious liberty. In fact, they are very poetic and complimentary as to the favorable effect he has had on the cause of religious liberty over such a long time period, i.e., for more than thirty years.

Now, examine Jefferson's letter of reply, dated January 1, 1802, (Peterson, 1984, p. 510) in which he writes about "the separation between church and state":

> Gentlemen: the affectionate sentiments of esteem and approbation which you are so good as to express towards me, on behalf of the Danbury Baptist Association, give me the highest satisfaction. My duties dictate a faithful and zealous pursuit of the interests of my constituents, and in proportion as they are persuaded of my fidelity to those duties, the discharge of them becomes more and more pleasing.
>
> Believe with you that religion is a matter which lies solely between man and his God, that he owes account to none other for his faith or his worship, that the legislative

powers of government reach actions only, and not opinions, I contemplate with sovereign reverence that act of the whole American people which declared that their legislature should 'make no law respecting an establishment of religion, or prohibiting the free exercise thereof,' thus building a wall of separation between church and State. Adhering to this expression of the supreme will of the nation in behalf of the rights of conscience, I shall see with sincere satisfaction the progress of those sentiments which tend to restore to man all his natural rights, convinced he has no natural right in opposition to his social duties.

I reciprocate your kind prayers for the protection and blessing of the common Father and Creator of man, and tender you for yourselves and your religious association; assurances of my high respect and esteem.

Taken in context, the "wall of separation" phrase takes on an entirely new and different meaning than that which it seems to imply. Specifically note the following.

President Jefferson's response starts with an acknowledgment of the pleasure he has in carrying out those very duties that were of interest to the Baptists. He continues in this spirit of compatibility by affirming their belief that the legislative powers of civil government cannot hold man accountable either for his "faith or his worship." Religion, they both agree, is "between man and his God" and not subject to civil governance. In a logically appropriate expansion of the matter, he references the passage of the First Amendment in which the "whole American people declared that their legislature should make no law..." Jefferson is obviously indicating that *the First Amendment is the will of the American people specifically intended to restrict the federal legislature from interfering with religious freedoms* either by establishing a national church (i.e., an establishment of religion) or prohibiting freedom of religious exercise of state establishments. The specific relevance of his letter to this Baptist group was that, because of the First Amendment, the federal government could not stop the religious injustices they received in Connecticut, no matter how much their natural rights were being violated. That is, beyond the issue of prohibiting a national religion, the federal government was restricted from making laws that would prohibit the free exercise of Connecticut's official religion. Jefferson makes clear his sincere respect for this amendment ("I contemplate with sovereign reverence") suggesting that as much as he would like to help bring religious liberty to the disenfranchised Baptists, no federal law could he promote for this purpose.

The above orientation leads inescapably to the conclusion that Jefferson's "wall of separation between church and state" was to be a *one-way wall, only.* That is, he clearly points to the Amendment's restriction on making man's religious beliefs accountable to the federal legislature. It is in no way, however, a prohibition against supportive federal involvement since the making of laws favorable to religious freedom was not excluded. He even says as much by indicating that the "supreme will of the nation" was in behalf of in guarantee of "the rights of conscience." Thus government, just as the Baptists originally wrote, was to protect citizens' rights (i.e., "The legitimate power of civil Government extends no further than to punish the man who works ill to his neighbor ...").

In the last several lines of the second paragraph, Jefferson indicates his desire for the restoration of all natural rights which are not in opposition to social duties. He thereby affirms the social right of the Baptists to appeal that he work for religious freedom at the federal level (they already acknowledged his powerlessness at the state level). This apparently means he believes that they have a Constitutional right to have their religious views bear on civil government. Jefferson did make reference to this religious group as being part of "my constituents." Thus the "wall" is open to religion influencing government (but closed to government mandating a religion or inhibiting religion at any governmental level). Further, Jefferson's last paragraph, echoing his first, reaffirms his compatibility with the Baptists. Namely, that man's natural rights be restored, which he says includes man's freedom from civil interference in religious matters *and* man's right to have government protect and even be responsive to religious freedom.

The thrust of Jefferson's letter is that the First Amendment has erected a one-way wall whereby federal legislation cannot interfere with anyone's faith or worship but that individuals, even organizations, are free to exert their religiously oriented influences onto the federal government.

Federal Amendment Meaning

From the Congressional debate and concurrent actions, we can deduce what the First Amendment means. To make this deduction, several presuppositions need to be stated.

First, because Madison's intention to extend the federal jurisdiction to protect rights of conscience to the individual states was not allowed, we can say that the First Amendment has federal application only. It addressed only the federal Congress. Federal jurisdiction over state prerogatives was negated by directing the amendment only at Congress and by voiding the amendment Madison proposed for overseeing state actions. Second, the pre- and post-Amendment practices of Congress indicate that it had already been making and then continued to make laws *about* religion. For instance, the Northwest Ordinance of 1787 (two years before the First Amendment was drafted), which was reenacted in 1789 (the year of the First Amendment), and the Congressional Chaplain system of 1789 were both laws about religion. Likewise, the 1796 provision that allowed for "propagating the Gospel among the Heathen" Indians was a law about religion enacted directly in the face of the First Amendment. Thus, it was not the case that Congress could make no laws *about* religion or religious establishments. It was only a specific kind of law that Congress could not make. Third, in that time period, the phrase "establishment of religion" meant the institutionalization or incorporation of an official religion. (O'Neill, 1972, p. 56

Since a nationalized religion did not exist at the time of the First Amendment, the prohibition against Congress meant that they could not make a law to start one. By extension, the Free Exercise Clause is necessary to keep Congress from making any other kind of prohibitory laws—namely, laws that would restrict religious practices. Obviously, if the first Establishment Clause meant that Congress could not make any laws about or pertaining to religion in general, then the Free Exercise Clause would not even be necessary. Since Congress thought the Free Exercise Clause necessary, we have to conclude that the Establishment Clause specifically relates to the prohibition of a federally mandated church or religion. As Justice Pirkham said in the 1899 *Bradfield* v. *Roberts* case, the plaintiff's phrase that "Congress had no power to make a law respecting a religious establishment" is not synonymous with the phrase used in the Constitution which prohibits the passage of a law "respecting an establishment of religion" (O'Neill, 1972, p. 132). In that case, the "religious establishment" referred to and legally affirmed by the Court was a religiously affiliated hospital which obviously is not the same as a nationalized religion (i.e., an "establishment of religion").

For the purpose of interpretation, we analyze each section of this part of the amendment: "Congress shall make no law respecting an establishment of religion or prohibiting the free exercise thereof" (cf. Cox, 2000-2001).

"Congress." Very simply, the First Amendment applies to the legislative branch of the Federal Government. It does not apply to states (applicability to the states was expressly denied) nor does it directly apply to the executive or judicial branch of the federal government. This means that only the law-making branch is being addressed. (Simply put, the executive branch "runs" the government and the judicial interprets for legal correctness.)

"Shall make no law." Laws and ordinances cannot be made on the matter about to be specified.

"Respecting." According to Webster's *1828 Dictionary*, respecting means regarding; having regard to; relating to. In context, it references the entire last part of the phrase, i.e., an establishment of religion.

"An Establishment of Religion." According to the *Morris Dictionary of Word and Phrase Origins* (1971), establishment refers to the state church. Klein's *A Comprehensive Etymological Dictionary* (1971) indicates establishment is a noun derived from establish which means to make firm or stable. The 11th Edition of

The Encyclopedia Britannica (1910) indicates

> ... establishment implies the existence of some definite and distinctive relation between the state and a religious society (or conceivably more than one) other than that which is shared in by other societies of the same general character... It denotes any special connexion with the state, or privileges and responsibilities before the law, possessed by one religious society to the exclusion of others; in a word, establishment is of the nature of a monopoly.

"[O]r prohibit the Free Exercise Thereof." Congress cannot prohibit religious activities of an establishment of religion. The word "thereof" refers to establishments of religion but not the religious conscience of a person. As Jefferson implied, the offended consciences of the Danbury Baptists and the misguided consciences of the oppressive Connecticut government were not relevant to the First Amendment. The word "thereof" refers to the clause "an establishment of religion."

Review

Overall, the amendment keeps Congress from making any laws to establish a national religion and also from restricting the free exercise of establishments of religion. At no time does the amendment prohibit nondiscriminatory aid to religion. Also, federal government actions not classified as laws are likewise not prohibited. While in effect legally nondiscriminatory toward religion, in context the amendment existed at a time when Christianity was the accepted religion of the people. As Justice Story has noted,

> Probably at the time of the adoption of the Constitution, and of the amendment to it now under consideration [First Amendment], the general if not the universal sentiment in America was, that Christianity ought to receive encouragement from the State so far as was not incompatible with the private rights of conscience and the

freedom of religious worship. An attempt to level all religions, and to make it a matter of state policy to hold all in utter indifference, would have created universal disapprobation, if not universal indignation. (Cord, 1982, p. 13)

The evidence overwhelmingly favors a reading of the First Amendment such that religion is to be fostered or encouraged but not established by the legislative arm of the federal government. Furthermore, the federal government cannot interfere with the free exercise of religion at any governmental level.

Obviously, neither the writings of Madison nor Jefferson should be consulted exclusively in interpreting the meaning of the First Amendment. Nonetheless, both men engaged in activities especially while Presidents of the U.S. that violate the notion that they believed in a broad or wide reading of a so-called separation of church and state.

The best interpretation of the amendment would seem to be that Congress was forbidden to make any *laws* that would establish a national religion, or that would infringe on the practices, etc., of establishments of religions that existed then or at any time into the future. Also, we need to note that the First Amendment was written in a cultural context where religion and specifically Christianity was favored over other religions, including no religion, although the amendment is worded to prohibit national religious licensing of any kind. Religious assistance was in fact encouraged in this context.

We end this section with an 1868 quote from Constitutional authority Thomas M. Cooley:

No principle of Constitutional law is violated when thanksgiving or fast days are appointed; when Chaplains are designated for the Army and Navy; and when legislative sessions are opened with prayer or the reading of the Scriptures, or when religious teaching is encouraged by exempting houses of religious worship from the taxation for the support of State government. Undoubtedly, the spirit of the Constitution will require, in all these cases, that care be taken to avoid discrimination in favor of any one denomination or sect. (Cord, 1982, p. 14)

U.S. Supreme Court Confusion

The evidence presented above clearly indicates that the First Amendment is directed at keeping the federal government, i.e., Congress, from making any law that would either establish a religion or restrict practices of establishments of religion. Accordingly, the U.S. Supreme Court can adjudicate only those conflicts on First Amendment grounds that relate to Federal legislative laws—not state laws. When the U.S. Supreme Court applies, as it often has, the First Amendment to state laws, it ultimately has to invent reasons for these intrusions since it has no First Amendment grounds for such applications. In fact, as the circumstances surrounding passage of the First Amendment show, the state governments could do exactly what the First Amendment prohibited the federal government from doing. For the federal government to tell the states otherwise would produce confusion and conflicting results precisely because it has no authority and thus no guidelines for doing so.

In support of the above interpretation, consider the following conflicting set of decisions rendered by the U.S. Supreme Court, all based in some way on the First Amendment. The first example concerns whether or not public funds can be used to meet the transportation needs of children attending private schools. One would wonder at the outset how bus transportation even remotely relates to the establishment of a national religion and, second, how conflicting decisions could come out of the First Amendment on such a simple matter. In *Everson* v. *Board of Education* (1947), public funds could be used for transporting students to and from private (i.e., Catholic) schools in New Jersey. The court reasoned that the students benefited more than the schools and hence the Establishment Clause was not violated. Conversely, in *Wolman* v. *Walter* (1977), the court ruled that bus transportation at public expense for field trips of private schools benefited the schools more than the students, apparently violating the Establishment Clause, and hence was disallowed.

The central issue in these cases of child versus school benefit has become known as the "child-benefit criterion." Yet nowhere does the First Amendment make this a criterion. The test regarding establishment is simple: Is a national religion being established or not? The provision of bus transportation can hardly be called an act of establishing a religion much less indoctrination in a religion or making it a mandatory belief.

The second contradictory set of findings resides in the question of whether public funds can be used to purchase instructional materials in sectarian schools. In *Board of Education* v. *Allen* (1968), the court upheld the constitutionality of a New York statute that required local school boards to lend secular books to nonpublic, even sectarian, schools. The First Amendment was not violated, the court said, since the loan was viewed as an aid to the parents and children rather than to the schools. Conversely, the court ruled as unconstitutional (*Meek* v. *Pittenger*, 1975) a Pennsylvania law that allowed the loan of instructional materials (periodicals, maps, recordings, films) and A-V and laboratory equipment since the loan was to schools of a predominantly religious nature and hence would advance religion. The point to be recalled here is that the First Amendment (beyond being addressed to Congress only) does not prohibit aid to an establishment of religion but only aid so discriminatory that is the likely outcome. It seems illogical to suppose that the loan of materials such as lab equipment, as opposed to the loan of books, can be construed as forced religious indoctrination.

The third contradictory set of findings relates to the use of public funds in sectarian schools to meet state-mandated requirements. The court ruled that it was permissible for Ohio to supply sectarian schools with standardized tests (like achievement tests) and subsidies for diagnostic testing (*Wolman* v. *Walter*, 1977) but that the state could not provide counseling and remedial classes (*Meek* v. *Pittenger*, 1975) as a Pennsylvania allowed. The key point in these two cases relates to the court's belief that the opportunity exists for a religious bias to enter into counseling but not into academic testing of activities. Yet this issue, opportunity for religious influence, is not even addressed by the First Amendment. Discriminatory aid that would establish a national religion as opposed to nondiscriminatory aid is the only relevant establishment issue to these above cases. The court ruled against funding counseling not because the counseling actually established a religion but because it allowed the opportunity to religiously indoctrinate. From this same reasoning then counseling in public schools should equally be disallowed since the opportunity is there also for some form of religious indoctrination to occur.

The fourth set of contradictions relates to the use of public funds for building maintenance and repair in sectarian institutions. In *Hunt* v. *McNair* (1973) the court upheld a South Carolina law that authorized state bond issues to help private colleges build nonreligious facilities yet invalidated a New York law (*Pearl* v. *Nyquist*, 1973) that provided direct grants to nonpublic schools for maintenance and repair of facilities that serve the health, welfare, and safety of the pupils. The effect of allowing the New York law, according to the court, "is to subsidize and advance the religious mission of sectarian schools" (Warshaw, 1979, p. 69). Yet again the First Amendment does not prohibit the advancement of religion. It seems unreasonable to believe that either building program advances religion more than the other (which is not even a First Amendment prohibition), much less establishes a national religion.

The fifth set relates to whether or not public schools could release students for religious instruction. In one ruling, the court said that if the instruction was within the public school, even though voluntary and without conflict with other classes, it was unconstitutional (*McCollum* v. *Board of Education*, 1948). To be constitutional, the religious program actually had to occur off school property (*Zorach* v. *Clauson*, 1952); otherwise it would be "a utilization of the tax-established and tax-supported public school system to aid religious groups to spread their faith" (Warshaw, 1979, p. 29). Yet the First Amendment as we have seen does not at all prohibit aid to religious groups. What consistency is there when the court allows voluntary religious instruction out of school but not in school yet declares as constitutional the public school practice of leasing classrooms in religious school (*Nebraska Board of Education* v. *Harrington School District*, 1972)? It would seem that paying rent to religious schools does more to aid religious groups than does allowing voluntary out-of-school religious instruction.

But again, the practice of advancing religion is not prohibited by the First Amendment.

As the examples above indicate, consistency cannot occur where the reason for judgments is not consistent. In the words of Justice Stevens, "corrosive precedents have left us without firm principles on which to decide these cases" (McCarthy, et al., 1982, p. 197). Further, the Supreme Court has read more into the Amendment than was ever intended. Specifically, aid to religion was not prohibited; rather, Congress was prohibited from making laws that violated the free exercise of an establishment of religion. As each example indicates, application of the Establishment Clause, which was intended only for Congress, onto the states violates and brings confusion to the First Amendment. Further, it is not a First Amendment requirement, in spite of what the court said in *Lemon* v. *Kurtzman* (1971), that a "statute must have a secular legislative purpose; second, its principal or primary effect must be one that neither advances nor inhibits religion; finally, the statute must not foster an excessive entanglement with religion." This three-part cumulative criteria was devised by Chief Justice Burger from decisions reached in the 1963 *Schempp*, the 1968 *Epperson*, and the 1970 *Walz* cases and not at all from the First Amendment words or intended meaning. What states do regarding these three criteria is not even a matter open to evaluation by the U.S. Supreme Court via the First Amendment. What the Supreme Court Justices have in effect done is allow, by building upon each other's opinions, the First Amendment to say what they want it to say. The result, in the words of Justice Powell, is that the First Amendment has become "a blurred, indistinct, and variable barrier" (McCarthy, et al., 1982, p. 108). Historical research says the First Amendment means something quite different than what a significant number of recent Supreme Court Justices say it means.

Fourteenth Amendment Applicability

(No state shall make or enforce any law which shall abridge the privileges or immunities of citizens of the United States; nor shall any state deprive any person of life, liberty, or property, without due process of law; nor deny to any person within its jurisdiction the equal protection of the laws...)

The cases presented earlier show that the U.S. Supreme Court has made innumerable First Amendment decisions regarding the practices of individual states. Since we have already demonstrated that the First Amendment is a directive to the Federal *Congress* only, we ask the logical question: How can the U.S. Supreme Court apply the First Amendment to legal actions that reside in state rather than U.S. federal laws? After all, the U.S. Supreme Court has jurisdiction to hear only those cases that relate to provisions of the U.S. Constitution. Matters not addressed by the U.S. Constitution are, by definition, not within the realm of U.S. Supreme Court authority. The answer to the question is that the Fourteenth Amendment, passed in 1868, is now interpreted by the U.S. Supreme Court to extend the restrictions of the First Amendment unto each individual state.

Recall that the initially proposed version of the First Amendment had two major elements. First, the basic rights of religious belief and conscience were to be protected, and a national church was to be prohibited. Second, and crucial to our present concern, the states were to be accountable to the federal government in this regard. Yet states which first called for a Bill of Rights requested only the first set of provisions. Legislative discussions, as well as the approved version of the actual First Amendment, reveal that the Amendment was to be applicable only to the Legislative branch (i.e., Congress) of the federal government and not at all to the individual states. The specific message to Congress on the matter of religion was that it was, first, not to establish a national church and, second, not to infringe on the free exercise of state establishments of religion. Congress had no jurisdiction over the states regardless of whether they had completely allowed freedom of religion or restricted it through state-sponsored religions.

This exclusive application of the First Amendment to the federal government only and not at all to the state governments occurred through the purposeful omission of Madison's original clause ("No state shall inviolate the equal rights of conscience...") allowing federal oversight of state actions. Exclusive federal applicability of the First Amendment was affirmed by the U.S. Supreme Court forty-two years later. In 1833, the U.S. Supreme Court refused to hear a challenge to a state religious institution (*Barron* v. *Baltimore*) on the ground that, as Chief Justice John Marshall said, the First Amendment applied only to the federal government and not to the state governments (Warshaw, 1979, p. 8). In speaking for the court, Chief Justice Marshall affirmed that the ten amendments in the U.S. Bill of Rights had only federal relevance:

> Had the framers of these amendments intended them to be limitations on the powers of the state governments, they would have imitated the framers of the original constitution, and have expressed that intention. Had Congress engaged in the extraordinary occupation of improving the constitutions of the several states by affording the people additional protection from the exercise of power by their own governments in matters which concerned themselves alone, they would have declared this purpose in plain and intelligible language.
>
> ... In almost every convention by which the Constitution was adopted, amendments to guard against the abuse of power were recommended. These amendments demanded security against the apprehended encroachments of the general government—not against those of the local governments.
>
> ... These amendments contain no expression indicating an intention to apply them to the state governments. This court cannot so apply them. (Epstein & Walker, 1992, p. 16)

Immediately after the Civil War, Congress did however get involved with state government jurisdictions through the Civil Rights Act of 1866. The Act was directed primarily at the southern states in their attempt to continue the substance of slavery. The Act entitled every citizen equal rights under the law and gave Congress enforcement power over the states in this regard. The Fourteenth Amendment (1868) was instituted to at least give constitutional legitimacy to the legally questionable Civil Rights Act. It appears that Congressional members of the 39th Congress, in their adoption of the Fourteenth Amendment, as well as members of the 42nd and 43rd Congresses thought they could set aside unequal state laws and, secondarily, protect citizens in certain constitutional rights when states failed to do so (Harris, 1977). In other words, rights inherent to citizenship could be monitored and even ensured by the federal government when deprived by state governments. But we need to say as before that the First Amendment was an imposition on the federal government alone, not even applicable to state governments, and, as such, never guaranteed legal justice at the state level. Thus the due process rights of the Fourteenth Amendment are literally not a guarantee of individual religious conscience. Likewise, the First Amendment religion clauses amount to a protection for state practices in religion even at the expense of individual religious freedoms. Overall, the First Amendment is a restriction on Congress and not a guarantee of religious liberty, per se.

Most significant, the fact that a Civil Rights Act was considered necessary to intervene into state concerns indicates at the outset that the First Amendment did not apply to the states. Further, when the Fourteenth Amendment was drafted, it was done so because the Civil Rights Act may have been unconstitutional—further evidence that the already existing First Amendment did not relate to the Civil Rights Act. Thirdly, if there were an intention of the framers of the Fourteenth Amendment to specifically transfer the First Amendment to the states, evidence of such an intent should be obvious, which it is not. Certainly, the Supreme Court statement of 1833 that the First Amendment did not apply to the states as well as these other evidences presented above would practically mandate that the Fourteenth Amendment be worked to explicitly overturn these evidences. No such wording was made.

The following table (see O'Neill, 1972, pp. 141-142) shows that the year 1868, the date of the Fourteenth Amendment, is not at all the date or even in the decade whereby states subsequently initiated the separation of religion and public education as would likely be the case if the Fourteenth Amendment applied the First Amendment restrictions to the states.

First state action prohibiting sectarian instruction in public schools in certain states	First state action prohibiting public funds to denominational schools	Last date public money was appropriated to religious schools
Dates	No. of states	No. of states	No. of states

Dates	No. of states	No. of states	No. of states
1790s	-	1	-
1810s	-	2	1
1820s	-	2	-
1830s	2	1	1
1840s	3	3	2
1850s	4	8	1
1860-1868	1	5	-
1868	The Fourteenth Amendment		
1870s	7	10	4
1880s	4	7	-
1890s	5	3	1
1900s	1	2	-
1910s	1	1	-
1920s	1	-	-

Over a large and an approximately equal number of decades both before and after the Fourteenth Amendment, state actions are balanced fairly evenly. Obviously, the Fourteenth Amendment did not automatically incorporate First Amendment provisions.

That the First Amendment was not applicable to the states by way of an open door provided via the Fourteenth Amendment is clearly substantiated in two decades of Congressional actions following ratification of the Fourteenth Amendment. Between the years 1870 and 1888, there were eleven attempts at drafting a Constitutional Amendment to restrict states in aiding religion (O'Neill, 1972, p. 40). That all eleven attempts failed is significant;

the higher significance lies in the fact that after ratification of the Fourteenth Amendment, attempts were made to restrict the states' role in religion via a method different than use of the Fourteenth Amendment. This can only mean that those closest in time to understanding the meaning of the Fourteenth Amendment thought it inapplicable as a means to extend First Amendment provisions to the states. Further confirmation comes in the 1922 *Prudential Insurance Company* v. *Cheeks* Supreme Court case. Speaking for the Court, Justice Pitney said, "neither the Fourteenth Amendment nor any other provision of the Constitution of the United States imposes upon the States any restriction about 'freedom of speech'"—one of the First Amendment provisions (O'Neill, 1972, p. 272).

Just three years after the *Prudential* case and fifty-seven years after the Fourteenth Amendment, the U.S. Supreme Court reversed itself by declaring that the Fourteenth Amendment might be used to restrict state authority over freedoms embodied in the First Amendment. In the 1925 *Gitlow* v. *New York* rendering, the Supreme Court said, "freedom of speech and of the press—which are protected by the First Amendment from abridgement by Congress—are among the fundamental personal rights and 'liberties' protected by the due process clause of the Fourteenth Amendment from impairment by the States" (Warshaw, 1979, p. 8). Then in 1940, the Court stated (*Cantwell* v. *Connecticut*) for the very first time that the religious clauses of the First Amendment applied to the state governments specifically because of the Fourteen Amendment. Justice Roberts, speaking for the court, said (Warshaw, 1979, p. 24),

> The fundamental concept of liberty embodied in that [the Fourteenth] Amendment embraces the liberties guaranteed by the First Amendment. The First Amendment declares that Congress shall make no law respecting the [sic] establishment of religion or prohibiting the full exercise thereof. The Fourteenth Amendment has rendered the legislatures of the states as incompetent as Congress to enact such laws. (p. 303)

But later still in 1947, Justice Reed brings the U.S. Supreme Court back to the original interpretation of the interaction between the First and Fourteenth Amendments. In speaking for the court, Reed said (O'Neill, 1972, p. 304),

> Nothing has been called to our attention that either the framers of the Fourteenth Amendment or the states that adopted intended its due process clause to draw within its scope the earlier amendments to the Constitution. Palko [*Palko* v. *Connecticut*, 1937] held that such provisions of the Bill of Rights as were 'implicit in the concept of ordered liberty', p. 325, became secure from state interference by the clause. But it held nothing more.

In other words the basic liberties guaranteed in the Fourteenth Amendment were those that emanate from the nature of a particular social/governmental philosophy and not specifically from the First Amendment. More specifically, both the Fourteenth and the First Amendments are based in a more fundamental set of principles rather than either amendment in the other. Elaborating through a concurring opinion, Justice Frankfurter said (O'Neill, 1972, p. 305),

> Between the incorporation of the Fourteenth Amendment into the Constitution and the beginning of the present membership of the Court—a period of seventy years—the scope of that Amendment was passed upon by forty-three judges. Of all these judges, only one, who may respectfully be called an eccentric exception, ever indicated the belief that the Fourteenth Amendment was a shorthand summary of the first eight Amendments theretofore limiting only the Federal Government, and that due process incorporated those eight Amendments as restrictions upon the powers of the states ... [these judges] were ... mindful of the relation of our federal system to a progressively democratic society and therefore duly regardful of the scope of authority that was left to the States even after the Civil War. The notion that the

Fourteenth Amendment was a covert way of imposing upon the States all the rules which it seemed important to Eighteenth Century statesmen to write into the Federal Amendments, was rejected by judges who were themselves witnesses of the process by which the Fourteenth Amendment became part of the Constitution.

Finally, we reiterate that the First Amendment is literally a restriction on Congress and not a specific protector of individual religious conscience. Not only is this the verbatim wording; it is also confirmed by the fact that the Free Exercise Clause gave no protection against religious conscience injustices of state religious establishments. Since the First Amendment is not a literal protection of liberty (but a restriction on Congress instead), even if the Fourteenth Amendment did incorporate liberties of the amendments, it could not accordingly incorporate the First.

The actual wording of the Fourteenth Amendment never references any other specific provision of the U.S. Constitution. It is presumptuous to assume that the Fourteenth Amendment provides specific license to do (i.e., literally apply the earlier amendments) what it does not specify. The evidence overwhelmingly supports the position that the Fourteenth Amendment was not designed, and literally does not say, to transfer specifically the First Amendment provisions to the states.

Ramification—Supreme Court Priests

When the First Amendment is transferred unto the states via the Fourteenth Amendment, it causes the Supreme Court to violate states' rights which Congress was specifically excluded by the First Amendment from violating. The intent of the First Amendment was to prevent federal interference in state prerogatives regarding religion by way of a national church or by otherwise imposing federal power in state regulated religious matters. When the Supreme Court sits in judgment of religious practices of a state, the Court violates the entire purpose behind the First Amendment. That is, it passes judgment or exercises an ecclesiastical function over hierarchically lower state religious actions that a national church would have exerted but was specifically prohibited from doing. In that sense, Supreme Court evaluations of religious practices actually make the Supreme Court Justices "High Priests." Furthermore, in the process of prohibiting anything that a state has allowed, the Supreme Court has violated not just the intent of the Establishment Clause, but also the actual wording of the Free Exercise Clause. Restricting any state practice which in the Court's opinion would establish a religion cannot help but prohibit the free exercise of that religion. Thus when operating against religion based upon what the Court thinks is a valid Establishment reason, it invariably violates the Free Exercise provision. Surely the framers did not intend competition between these two clauses.

Conclusion

Use of the Fourteenth Amendment to extend the First Amendment provisions to the states violates both the literal meaning as well as the underlying intent of the First Amendment. The First Amendment is directed only at Congress, so it cannot be transferred to the states or any other unit. The Establishment Clause is a specific restriction on the federal government to prevent it from interfering with either state establishment of religious where they exist or individual religious freedoms where state establishments do not exist. Anything whatever that the states do in the way of religious establishments does not violate the Establishment Clause since it refers only to federally directed religion. Accordingly, litigation against state violations of religious conscience stop at the highest state level—they are not federal matters from a First Amendment perspective.

With its often faulty interpretation of the First Amendment, the U.S. Supreme Court has entered into an arena where it has no jurisdiction or authority. *Every* instance where a state law regarding religion has been adjudicated as either constitutional *or* unconstitutional by the U.S. Supreme Court on the basis of the First Amendment to the U.S. Constitution is impermissible. Whether or not the decisions of the five sets of court cases discussed earlier are agreeable with our individual or collective opinions or consciences, these decisions were made without any legitimate jurisdiction. The Supreme Court was outside its authority in even deciding to take on such cases. Decisions from all such cases are actually constitutionally invalid.

From this perspective, there are several things that can be said about the application of the First Amendment to education. But first, we must admit that on face value, with no mention of education in the Amendment, there would seem to be minimal application to begin with. In fact, the immediate conclusion would be that there are only two concerns in this regard. One would be that Congress, as the lawmaking branch of the federal government, would not somehow mandate a religion or exclusively sponsor religious dogma through its education-oriented activities. To do so would violate the prohibition that the federal government cannot nationalize religion. The other would be that Congress, and in fact, without superseding Constitutional authority elsewhere, the entire federal government would not undo religious exercises that occur in educational settings. To do so would be to read into the First Amendment authority that it does not give.

Beyond this, there are no First Amendment grounds for the federal government to connect in any way with educational matters. State-sponsored religious activities in education are in fact not even relevant to the federal government from a First Amendment perspective. Even where there is injustice against religious conscience in education at the state level (e.g., mandatory prayers), the First Amendment provides no basis by which the federal government can come to the rescue. The interpretation here should not be perceived as an endorsement of injustice. It is instead a statement of fact about the provisions, or lack thereof, of the First Amendment to the U.S. Constitution.

The net results of the Supreme Court's misguided interpretations of the First Amendment is to make it the ruling priesthood over religious functions. As the Court dares to tell state and local educational institutions what can and cannot be done according to the First Amendment, it has extended this priesthood into education. By deciding what is orthodoxy in education, the Court has accomplished what the First Amendment was expressly authored to prevent. Such decisions have ironically given credence to the idea that education is a religiously-oriented activity.

References

Alley, Robert S. (1985). *James Madison on religious liberty.* Buffalo, NY: Prometheus Books.

Berns, Walter (1976). *The First Amendment and the future of American democracy.* New York: Basic Books.

Boles, Donald E. (1965). *The Bible, religion and the public schools.* Ames, IA: Iowa State Univ. Press.

Cobb, Sanford H. (1968). *The rise of religious liberty in America.* New York: Cooper Square Publishing.

Cord, Robert L. (1982). *Separation of church and state.* New York: Lambeth Press.

Cox, William F., Jr. (2000-2001). The original meaning of the Establishment Clause and its application to education. *Regent University Law Review,* 13 (1), 111-143.

Dreisbach, Daniel L. (1987). *Real threat and mere shadow.* Westchester, IL: Crossway Books.

Epstein, Lee & Walker, Thomas G. (1992). *Constitutional law for a changing America: Rights, liberties and justice.* Washington, DC: CQ Press.

Harris, Robert J. (1977). *The quest for equality.* Westport, CT: Greenwood Press Publishers.

Jefferson, Thomas (1984). *Writings.* New York: Literary Classics of the U.S., Inc.

Klein, Ernest (1971). *A comprehensive etymological dictionary of the English language.* New York: Elsevier Scientific Publ. Co.

Malbin, Michael J. (June, 1981). *Religion, liberty, and law in the American founding.* (Reprint #123). Washington, DC: American Enterprise Institute.

McCarthy, Rockne M., Skillen, James W. Harper, William P. (1982). *Disestablishment a second time.* Grand Rapids, MI: Eerdmans.

Morris, William (1971). *Morris dictionary of word and phrase origins.* New York: Harper & Row.

O'Neill, James M. (1972). *Religion and education under the Constitution.* New York: DeCapo Press.

Peterson, Merrill D. (Ed.) (1984). *Thomas Jefferson writings.* New

York: Library Classics of the United States.

Reichley, A. James (1985). *Religion in American public life.* Washington, DC: The Brookings Institute.

The Encyclopaedia Britannica (1910). New York: Encyclopaedia Britannica, Inc.

Warshaw, Thayer S. (1979). *Religion education and the Supreme Court.* Nashville: Abingdon.

Whitehead, John W. (1982). *The second American revolution.* Elgin, IL: David C. Cook Publishers.

Chapter 6

Education <u>Must</u> Be Religious

As the happiness of a people, and the good order and preservation of civil government, essentially depend upon piety, religion, and morality.... Therefore, to promote their happiness, and to secure the good order and preservation of their government, the people of this commonwealth have a right to invest their legislature with the power to authorize and require ... for the institution of the public worship of God, and for the support and maintenance of public Protestant teachers of piety, religion, and morality....

Religion, morality and knowledge being necessary to good government and the happiness of mankind, schools and the means of education shall forever be encouraged.

[Religious instruction is necessary] to ensure greater security in the faith of our fathers, to inculcate into the lives of the rising generation the spiritual values necessary to the well-being of our and future generations.

The first quotation comes from the Constitution of Massachusetts dated October 25, 1780 (Perry, 1978, p. 374), the second from the Northwest Ordinance which the Federal Congress passed in 1787 (Cubberley, 1920, p. 523), and the third from the preamble to the law of Maine dated 1923 (Tyack, James, & Benavot, 1987, p. 165). All speak to the union between religion and education. Representative of a larger body of state and federal documents, these sentiments illustrate the link, which spans several hundred years of United States history, between religion and education.

The main thread of this chapter focuses on both the people's need for religious freedom and the need to educate virtuous citizens to enable good government and societal well-being. The chapter begins by describing how the United States was founded as a Christian nation, documenting the innumerable evidences that indicate education was considered as a religious function.

America's Religious Destiny

Recall that in Chapter 4 a review of selected governmental documents and statements by early settlers revealed that this country was founded to be, as the U.S. Supreme Court concluded in 1892, "a Christian nation" (*Church of the Holy Trinity v. United States*). The court again reaffirmed in 1931 that Americans are "a Christian people" (*United States v. Macintosh*). Likewise in 1952 (*Zorach v. Clauson*) the court stated "We are a religious people whose institutions presuppose a Supreme Being" (Hammond, 1984, p. 223). The establishment of this country as a Christian nation represented the fulfillment of a long process that had direct relevance to education. Namely, a driving force known as the doctrine of natural rights provided a major impetus for leaving the mother country and for making education an early and high priority of the founders. The doctrine of natural rights (see Baldwin, 1981, p. 24) held that it was God's law that men govern themselves. Among other things, it was a duty to resist tyranny (Baldwin, 1981, p. 25). The natural rights ideas seen as early as Plato's *Republic* (approximately 370 BC) but astutely developed in the 18th century by political philosophers Locke, Burlamaqui, and others provided a major rationale for the early settlers to resist the king in their mother country and then again in their new country.

In the early 1600s when the line between religion and government was practically nonexistent, rulers exercised their personal prerogatives under license of "divine right." In effect, the king and his cohorts considered themselves to be in office by divine appointment, hence any treason against the king was equally treason against God.

Yet the counter doctrine, that of natural rights, held that those in government ruled by contract or agreement with the citizenry. The Magna Charta of 1215, for instance, resulted from the protest against the selfish, tyrannical, and arbitrary rule of King John. In return for allegiance of the feudal barons, the Magna Charta required the King to recognize their basic or natural liberties. This document served as a generic model for many early state documents and has been called "the exemplar of the Bill of Rights" (Perry, 1978, p. 9). It established and then helped to perpetuate the rule of law and changed resistance to tyranny from rebelliousness to instead a God-given duty.

Part of the philosophy inherent to natural rights was that governments are established by a social compact between the one governing and those governed. The compact established the role of the government and/or the king as the agent of the people. To prevent men in their natural state, that is without any form of government, from brutalizing one another, government is established to administer order and justice for the citizens in return for their loyalty and cooperation. The assumption operative in this compact is that men are basically rational and equal to one another rather than subordinate and thus requiring domination by a leader. According to John Locke (Good & Teller, 1973, p. 81), rulers should govern by consent of the governed and thus remain rulers only so long as they keep their part of the compact. If either party violates the compact, the matter dissolves back to a state of nature, thus calling for a new or modified compact. This reasoning is obviously present in the U.S. Declaration of Independence (1776) and is foundational to the U.S. Constitution (1787). In fact, so prevalent was this form of reasoning, that when Thomas Jefferson penned the Declaration of Independence, he commented that he was not developing anything new but only declaring what was the general sentiment of the time.

Attendant to the natural rights philosophy were ideas like the equality of all mankind, government created by the people, equal standing before the law, and the duty to change a tyrannical government—all of which are contained in the Declaration of Independence. Such principles were not in fact invented by man but are obvious in nature and are even written on the human heart just as Jefferson wrote— "we hold these truths to be self-evident ... men are ... endowed ... with certain inalienable rights...."

In the final analysis this natural rights philosophy made government servant of the citizens and not vice versa. It specifically acknowledges that man, individually and collectively, has a purpose, goal, or calling that government is specifically established to facilitate. As the Declaration of Independence indicates, life, liberty, and the pursuit of happiness are three God-given ends or goals to which each person is entitled and which government is to facilitate.

Obviously, all the above are relevant to explaining the rationale behind this country becoming independent from Great Britain (see Chapter 11). Using natural rights as our lens, we look in this chapter to the practice of religion as a major motive leading to the settlement of the United States and then later also to the role of education in enhancing man's purpose in governing self. It should come as no surprise that historians (see Beale, 1941) claim that the two main motives for education in colonial America were religion (p. 5) and civil obedience (p. 33). In fact, obedience was a major issue in religiously sponsored education.

The motivating religious duty of the early settlers is captured in the following three quotes. John Adams, writing ten years before the Revolution, said, "I always considered the settlement of America as the opening of a grand scheme and design in Providence for the illumination of the ignorant and the emancipation of the slavish part of mankind all over the earth" (Bellah, 1975, p. 33). More recently (January, 1900) Senator Albert J. Beveridge said, in a speech on the floor of the U.S. Senate,

God has not prepared the English-speaking and Teutonic people for a thousand years for nothing but vain and idle self-contemplation and self-admiration. No. He made us master organizers of the world to establish a system where chaos reigned. He has given us the spirit of progress to overwhelm the forces of reaction throughout the earth. He has made us adept in government that we may administer government among savage and senile people. Were it not for such a force as this the world would relapse into barbarism and night. And of all our race He has marked the American people as His chosen nation to finally lead the redemption of the world (Bellah, 1975, p. 38).

If the above quotes seem self-righteous and/or removed from the real intent of the settlers, consider what the Reverend Samuel Danforth meant in 1670 by his phrase, "errand unto the wilderness." According to Bercovitch (1978, p. 12), it was an errand into Satan's wilderness world for Christ—an errand to fulfill God's grand design for humanity. Danforth's address captured the essence of the founders constant reference and mainstay vision that America was the latter-day land of Canaan. The errand into the wilderness of America was for them no different from the role of Moses or of John the Baptist. New England, and America more generally, was to be a harbinger of the return of Christ and the development of New Israel in America.

This journey of promise was to be the final act in preparing the world for the return of Christ. The founders were to "prepare ye the way of the Lord, make his paths straight" for the new kingdom of the Lord that was about to come. Prior to sailing from England in 1630, John Winthrop, a pious and learned London lawyer, declared to the travelers that God had a great work for them: "We shall be as a city set upon a hill ..." (Baldwin, 1981, p. 42). Winthrop located this venture in the following Biblical scheme: from Mount Ararat and Mount Sinai to the New World city on a hill, on to Mount Zion of the Apocalypse and the promise of the millennium (Bercovitch, 1978, p. 8). John Cotton, on this same voyage, spoke of a new promised land reserved by God for His chosen people to be the site for a new heaven and a new earth. The new church-state in America was to be the proper model of Christianity and the precursor of New Jerusalem.

Others were likewise claiming the settling of America as a mission for "the General Restoration of Mankind from the Curse of the Fall" (Bercovitch, 1978, p. 43). It was the beginnings of the last phase of bringing "a blessing on all the Nations of the Earth." It was a time of prophetic fulfillment—"For the set time to favour Zion is come...The time prefixt by the Prophet Jeremiah" (Bercovitch, 1978, p. 44).

This prophetic call was not just for New England but for America as a whole. The same vision prevailed throughout all the newly discovered land because as historian Perry Miller notes, "No nation of Europe had yet divided the state from the church ... society, economics and the will of God were one and the same, and the ultimate authority in human relations was the ethic of Christendom. All the transactions of this world held their rank in the hierarchical structure, with salvation, to which all other activities ministered, at the apex" (Baldwin, 1981, p. 38).

As Baldwin notes, "Catholic Maryland, utopian Pennsylvania, philanthropic Georgia, and Episcopalian Virginia all were based on some form of a holy errand into the wilderness" (p. 35). For example, the sermon preached to those about to sail for Virginia by William Symonds in 1609 titled "Virginiea Britannia" referenced likeness to the journey of Abraham as directed by God (Baldwin, 1981, p. 36). Then about a century later (1740), Jonathan Edwards reaffirms the vision as follows: "Though there has been a glorious fulfillment of ... prophecies already ... other times are only forerunners and preparatories to this." The Great Migration he claimed was coming to fruition: Christ, he said, will have "the heathen for this inheritance, and the uttermost part of the earth for his possession ... [a] nation shall be born in a day ... the Jews shall be called in." According to Bercovitch's interpretation of Edwards (p. 99), Protestant America will become another, greater Mountain of Holiness, "Beautiful as Tirzah, comely as Jerusalem, and terrible as an Army. with Banners.... Put on thy beautiful garments, O

America, the holy city." Then another century later, the American poet Ralph Waldo Emerson saw America as "a last effort of Divine Providence in behalf of the human race" (Bercovitch, 1978, p. 200). "Let us realize," Emerson said, "that this country, the last found, is the great charity of God to the human race" (Bercovitch, 1978, p. 202). Herman Melville, in his novel *White-Jacket*, symbolically used the same kind of language: "Americans are the peculiar, chosen people—the Israel of our time; we bear the ark of the liberties of the world.... God has predestinated, mankind expects, great things from our race; and great things we feel in our souls.... Long enough have we been skeptics with regard to ourselves, and doubted whether, indeed, the political Messiah had come. But he has come in us." (Bercovitch, 1978, p. 177).

This "errand" to bring God's salvation and redemption into the holy city of America is not just revealed in the words of the ministers and visionaries of the time. America's early governing documents capture this zeal in official terms (Perry, 1978). The First Charter of Virginia (1606) claims as a purpose,

> We, greatly commending, and graciously accepting of, their Desires for the Furtherance of so noble a work, which may, by the Providence of Almighty God, hereafter tend to the Glory of his Divine Majesty, in propagating of Christian Religion to such People, as yet live in Darkness and miserable Ignorance of the true Knowledge and Worship of God, and may in time bring the Infidels and Savages, living in those parts, to human Civility, and to a settled and quiet Government....

The Mayflower Compact (1620) reads, "Having undertaken for the Glory of God, and Advancement of the Christian Faith...." The Charter of Maryland (1632) says, "being animated with a laudable, and pious zeal for extending the Christian Religion...." The Fundamental Orders of Connecticut (1639) reads, "there should be an orderly and decent Government established according to God ... to maintain and pursue the liberty and purity of the gospel of our Lord Jesus which we now profess...." The Charter of

Rhode Island and Providence Plantation (1663) said, "That they, pursuing, with peaceable and loyall minds, their sober, serious and religious intentions, of godly edifying themselves, and one another, in the holy Christian faith and worship as they were persuaded; together with the gaining over and conversion of the poor ignorant Indian natives ... transport themselves out of this kingdom of England into America...." The Declaration of the Cause and Necessity of Taking Up Arms (1775) says, "Our fore-fathers, inhabitants of the island of Great-Britain, left their native land, to seek on these shores a residence for civil and religious freedom." The Constitution of Virginia (1776) says, "it is the mutual duty of all to practice Christian forbearance, love, and charity towards each other." The Constitution of Pennsylvania (1776) indicated that "the great Governor of the Universe (who alone knows to what degree of earthly happiness mankind may attain, by perfecting the arts of government) in permitting the people of this State, by common consent, and without violence, deliberately to form for themselves such just rules as they shall think best, for governing their future society...." The above phrasing is repeated again almost verbatim in the Constitution of Vermont (1777) and the Constitution of Massachusetts (1780).

Reflective of these statements above, no small part of the reasoning that justified America's War of Independence was based on the natural rights, errand-into-the-wilderness logic. For many, America's independence was part of the long process of fulfilling God's plan for this nation as the New World. In fact, various historians have confirmed that the seal of the United States, submitted by Benjamin Franklin and Thomas Jefferson, depicted Moses leading the chosen people out of Egypt (Bercovitch, 1978, p. 124). It was Samuel Adams who spoke so boldly that America's constitution was a pledge from Heaven in fulfillment of the New World prophecies. Timothy Dwight, clergyman and President of Yale University, wrote, "This great continent is soon to be filled with the praise, and piety, of the Millennium...." (Bercovitch, 1978, p. 130). And the second president of the U.S., John Adams, likewise saw the Revolution as the ultimate outcome of the Great Migration to a New Jerusalem.

After the Revolution, Daniel Webster declared (1857) that "The

American Revolution is the wonder and blessing of the world.... The last hopes of mankind ... rest with us" (Bercovitch, 1978, p. 144). Baldwin (1981, p. 9) claims that after the Revolution, the Americans regarded themselves as a "peculiar chosen people—the Israel of our time" (in the words of Melville—see Bellah, 1975, p. 38).

Thus, this country was founded as a Christian nation with a religious purpose. The purpose included evangelizing the Indians, unfolding God's New Jerusalem, and modeling true liberty for all mankind.

Role of Education in Religion

Each of these aspects of America's religious base integrally included education. In fact, it can rightly be said that education was perceived as a religious duty for these early citizens of the United States. That is, education was seen as the method by which the Indians would learn of Christ, the means by which man would fully develop his God-given abilities, and the means by which man would be equipped to relate to God and resist Satan.

One of the major attributes of the Puritan errand was that it was seen as covenant with God. Winthrop and others were quick to explain that God would protect and bless his people as long as they were faithful to His call. Any shortcoming or breaking of the bond on their part would "cause him to withdraw his present help from us. ..." (Bercovitch, 1978, p. 3), just as happened to the Israelites in their disobedience in coming out of Egypt. Most of the prophetic messages on this matter were alike in their Jeremiah-like content: i.e., norms of behavior, consequences for disobedience, and the promise of victory. So similar where they over several generations that historian Perry Miller called these religious/political sermons the American Jeremiad.

The Jeremiad reinforced the belief for the colonists of their duties before God. Education was one such duty. Also, the natural rights philosophy mentioned earlier called for self-governing individuals. To be a party to a "rule by consent" agreement meant that the populous had to be literate and capable of understanding basic rights and when these rights are being deprived. The right of equality before the law, for instance, means that a citizen must be knowledgeable about all the nuances of justice, equality, and rule by law and not by opinion and favoritism. Likewise, proper exercise of the rights of liberty and government by the people required that they become fully cognizant of the fact that true liberty depends on an educated citizenry. As one source puts it, "Liberty begins in the mind" (Good & Teller, 1973, p. 81).

Most importantly, obedience to the Bible was what governed the colonists' educational outlook. The need for people to be competent and godly was revealed early in the Bible. Even before God created man, He announced that man was to be in God's image and was to have dominion over all the lesser creatures and the earth itself (Genesis 1:26 and 28). But even before there is any accounting of man having dominion over the environment there is the account of man's dominion over himself. He was to exercise this dominion by not giving in to the lies of the serpent but by obeying God and not eating from the tree of the knowledge of good and evil. Through godly obedience man would enjoy the help, blessings, and favor of God. But because he disobeyed God, in substituting his own reasoning for God's revelation, and ate from the forbidden tree, man was consigned to a broken relationship with God and therefore to living by the source of understanding he chose for himself—that is, his own intellect.

The Old Testament gives abundant testimony that mankind was and is unable to undo the effects of his disobedience to God. Mankind could neither keep the Ten Commandments to reflect God's moral nature nor effectively rule over the physical world. In fact, throughout this great span of time, God was arranging life's circumstances to educate man to the fact that in every way he tried to rely on his own sufficiency, he would fail.

Where man obeyed God, he was likewise educated to the fact that his faith in God would bring favor, wisdom, and blessings, if not always temporally, certainly eternally. Accordingly, the main and central characteristic of colonial education was to equip students to believe in Jesus, the son of God who saved man from his sinfulness, and to know the wisdom of God. God's commandments and laws were taught to the people. Children were educated by the father and mother, primarily since the father was the person God ultimately held responsible for their education (cf. Ephesians 6:4). The main purpose of formal education was to produce ministers of God for the salvation of present and future generations and for their walk with God. So as the noted educational historian Ellwood Cubberley said, it was the

> Puritans, who settled the New England colonies, and who, more than any others, gave direction to the future development of education in the American states. Very many of these early religious groups came to America in little congregations, bringing their ministers with them. Each set up, in the colony in which it settled, what were virtually little religious republics, that through them they might perpetuate the religious principles for which they had left the land of their birth. From the very beginnings, education of the young for membership in the Church and the perpetuation of a learned ministry for the congregation elicited the serious attention of these pioneer settlers. (Cubberley, 1920, p. 357)

And as Benjamin Rush said in the late 1700s, "the only foundation for a useful education in a republic is to be laid in religion. Without this, there can be no virtue, and without virtue there can be no liberty, and liberty is the object and life of all republican governments" (Rudolph, 1965, p. 10). Thus, as commentators generally agree, religious purpose was the predominant characteristic of all early colonial schooling.

In addition to promoting the discipline necessary for self-government, education was used as a tool in early Virginia by the ministers to reach the Indians. As historian Bernard Bailyn notes (1960, p. 37), some of the first and most carefully planned educational efforts in Virginia, Maryland, and especially Massachusetts were directed at the Indians. The education and Christian conversion of the Indians was, after all, one of the major reasons for the "errand into the wilderness."

This two-pronged orientation (i.e., converting and equipping) of colonial education confirmed education as a religious endeavor.

Most formal instruction in the home country was, either directly or indirectly, under the influence of the various churches. Accordingly, the first schools established in America were also supported by the various religious groups (Nettels, 1981, p. 488). The priority of education in colonial times is revealed in the following quote about North Carolina's educational history: "As soon as a group was settled, preparations were made for religious services, and when the log church was erected, it became also a schoolhouse, a community center, and the foundation of a nation" (see Gobbel, 1938, p. 174). And because education was so centrally linked to religion, the various attitudes toward education reflected the religious thinking of the dominant group or groups in the regions of the New World.

Regional Orientations

In the North where the people adhered to one creed, there was uniformity in educational outlook. The Calvinistic Puritan thinking made a major purpose of the school to teach the children to read the Bible and to participate in family and congregational worship. Everything they did, including education, was done for God (Eavey, 1964, p. 191). Formal education was seen as a means for perpetuating the faith. But instruction first started in the home. Every day the Bible was read and God was worshipped. No child, servant, or apprentice was to be allowed to grow up without a reverence for God and His Word. Children were taught biblical truths early in life. At age three, systematic instruction began. Children were to study and memorize short catechisms but more importantly to put into practice the truths they learned. Cotton Mather admonished parents, masters, ministers, and tutors to equip their children with "early knowledge of the Holy Scriptures, so that they may be wise unto salvation" (Cremin, 1970, p. 290). Children were equally taught obedience to civil laws, not just to be good citizens but because civil society was seen as part of the community of God.

Because of the uniformity of both religious belief and social strata in the northern colonies, the formal schooling that resulted was highly similar in content and was intended for all. However, the educational institutions of the middle colonies was characterized by religious diversity. The diversity was due not to the presence of non-believers but to the presence of different Christian sects or denominations. The German Reformed, Dutch Reformed, Quakers, Anglicans, Presbyterians, Scotch Presbyterians, Baptists, Methodists, German Lutherans, Moravians, Mennonites, and others each believed the Bible, but differently (Beale, 1941, p. 22).

The expected outcome of education was similar among the middle Atlantic colonies and basically similar to that of the northern colonies (Eavey, 1964, p. 198). These colonists believed in the necessity of learning to read the Bible for personal salvation. Schools generally were considered as part of the church organization. Characteristics shared by these schools included praying, prohibiting non-Christian teachers, learning the catechism, and forming Christian character. The main difference of these middle colonies from the New England colonies was that the state was not considered as a servant of the church, so educational problems were handled not by the state but by the sponsoring church or philanthropic organization (Cubberley, 1920, p. 368).

In the south, the parochial form of education of the middle colonies was replaced by a laissez faire form of education. The poor often did not receive good education in the southern states because the quest was often not for religious freedom. Instead, education affiliated with established churches for worldly gain. Most of the southern settlers were adherents to the Anglican church and had emigrated to gain wealth as opposed to the northern neighbors who had come to America, in dissension from the church, primarily to gain freedom of religion. Even so, as Beale (1941, p. 22) notes, the religious basis of education was just as real in the south since the clerics had the responsibility to perpetuate church as well as the crown. The Society for the Propagation of the Gospel in Foreign Parts also fostered the establishment of schools in the south.

Throughout the colonies, whether the north, south, or middle, the people shared the common belief that education was a religious function particularly for self and civil government. As Benjamin Rush said in 1786,

I proceed, in the next place, to inquire, what mode of education we shall adopt so as to secure to the state all the advantages that are to be derived from the proper instruction of growth; and here I beg leave to remark that the only foundation for a useful education in a republic is to be laid in Religion. Without this, there can be no virtue, and without virtue there can be no liberty, and liberty is the object and life of all republican governments.

Such is my veneration for religion that reveals the attributes of the Deity, or a future state or rewards and punishments, that I had rather see the opinions of Confucins or Mohamed included upon our youth, than see them grow up wholly devoid of a system of religious principles. But the religion I mean to recommend in this place is the religion of Jesus Christ. (Smith, 1973, p. 244)

Likewise, the governor of North Carolina, John W. Ellis, said in 1859 (Gobbel, 1938, p. 62), "Christians, in teaching the great truth of practical religion among the people ... is an essential preparation to their expressing properly the function of self government." And in 1860, he said, "the natural friends of education are to be found among those who are engaged in the advancement of religion and morals."

Similarly, the first superintendent of North Carolina common schools and highly respected leader said,

The object of all education, therefore, should not be to learn to dispense with the agency of God, in our affairs, but to lead us more directly to Him.... Education is only a blessing as a means of leading to these results, and the improper prejudice raised against it are due to the fact that promoters of 'vain babblings, and oppositions of science, falsely so called,' have in certain places, confounded the means with the end. (Gobbel, 1938, p. 182)

The early attitude of the mix between education and religion through the first several hundred years of this country is reflected by Abraham Lincoln as late as 1832:

> Upon the subject of education ... I can only say that I view it as the most important subject which we as a people can be engaged in. That every man may receive at least a moderate education, and thereby be enabled to read ... to say nothing of the advantages and satisfactions to be derived from all being able to read the Scriptures and other work, both of a religious and moral nature.... (Reeder, 1958, p. 30)

Benjamin Franklin, on this same matter, quotes Milton: "The End of Learning is to repair the Ruins of our first Parents by regaining to know God aright...." (Tyack, 1967, p. 53).

George Washington said, "Whatever may be conceded to the influence of refined education on the minds of particular structure; reason and experience both forbid us to expect that national morality can prevail in exclusion of religious principle" (Boles, 1965, p. 17).

Those who taught in the school had to be ministers or church members. An edict of 1688 in Virginia, for instance, called all school masters to a meeting to present evidence "that they were upright and sober in their lives, and conformable in their religious opinions to the doctrines of the Church of England" (see Curti, 1978, p. 11). A similar law of 1654 in Massachusetts charged the officers of the town "not to admit or suffer any such to be continued in the office or place of teaching, educating or instructing of youth or children in the college or schools, that have manifested themselves unsound in the faith, or scandalous in their lives, and not giving due satisfaction according to the rules of Christ" (Curti, 1978, p. 11-12). In 1692 and again in 1701-1702, the law in Massachusetts required a ministerial certificate for all grammar school teachers (Beale, 1941, p. 26). During the time the Dutch ruled the middle colony of New Netherlands, every teacher was to be licensed by the civil and ecclesiastical authorities. When New York became a province, the Bishop of London had to approve its teachers (p. 28). New Jersey and Maryland had similar laws; Virginia followed suit but did exempt the Friends and the Presbyterians. Similarly, wherever the Church of England was established in the southern colonies, a license from the Bishop of

London was required of all teachers. Even exceptions arising from teacher shortages still required local clergy approval (Beale, 1941, p. 27). In North Carolina, the first free school of 1766 required that teachers be Anglicans. Colonies like South Carolina, New Jersey, and Virginia (see Knight and Hall, 1951) had similar requirements for teachers to be religiously affiliated.

Curriculum for Religion

Much has also been written by educational historians documenting the biblical foundation of school curriculum materials. The dominance of the religious purpose in all instruction throughout all the colonies, says Cubberley (1920, p. 374), is illustrated in the universally accepted school book, *The New England Primer.* Described as "The Little Bible of New England," its prose, poetry, and pictures all taught salvation and the necessity of obedience to God. Also very popular was Digglesworth's (1662) *The Day of Doom*, which described in lurid detail the terrible torments of hell and the fruitless pleas of sinners.

Reading was learned "chiefly that one might be able to read the Catechism and the Bible, and to know the will of the Heavenly Father.... Religious matter constituted the only reading matter, outside the instruction in Latin in the grammar schools" (Cubberley, 1920, pp. 374-5). Even as late as 1848, Webster's *Elementary Spelling Book*, which sold millions of copies annually and totaled over 20 million new sales between 1782 and 1847 (Smith, 1973, p. 32), was religious through and through. The *Elementary Spelling Book* taught that "God governs the world with infinite wisdom," that He is to be worshipped at the beginning and ending of the day, that the devil is the great enemy of mankind, and that we will all appear before God for judgment (Curti, 1978, p. 17).

Other school books equally made the Bible their content reference point. The Lord's Prayer and the twelve articles of the Christian faith were memorized, principles of religion were catechized, and prayers from the *Book of Common Prayer* were read. In Jonathan Fisher's *The Youth's Primer* (1817), the letter Y is illustrated with the following poem:

Take ye my Yoke
To Jesus spoke
Borne with delight
'Tis easy quite. (Curti, 1978, p. 17)

The *New England Primer* included pictures and verses like the following to teach the alphabet:

A - In *Adam's* Fall
We sinned all.

B - Thy Life to Mind
This *Book* [the Bible] attend.

J - *Job* feels the Rod
Yet blesses God.

P - *Peter* denies
His Lord and cries.
(Pfeffer, 1967, p. 325)

But it was not just the textbooks alone that emphasized biblical morality. One of the first manuals on teacher training, Hall's *Lectures* of 1829, stated that whoever "regards it as a matter of indifference, whether his children can read the sacred Scripture understandingly or not, whether they form their moral taste from the writings of inspired men or heathen philosopher, must be considered as not realizing his own moral accountability" (Curti, 1978, p. 18).

Spokesmen for the profession of education and teacher training openly professed the value of a biblically based education. The Western Institute and College, which had a profound impact on education in the Ohio Valley in the 1830s, vigorously denounced the licentious books of Voltaire, Diderot, and others, maintaining that a nation to remain free must have its people trained in "a sound Christian education." B.P. Aydelott, an early education leader, stated that "the Christianity of the Bible is the salvation of our country." The father of Indiana's school system, Caleb Mills, maintained that the first essential of a sound public school system is that its moral base be the Word of God. The early educational journals such as the *Academician* (1818-1820), the *American Journal of Education* (1826-1830), and the *American Annals of Education and the Institution* (1831-1839) likewise paid respect to the moral and religious elements of education.

A good example of the typical school day is found in Pierre Samuel DuPont de Nemours' book of 1800 entitled *National Education in the United States of America* (1923). This "scheme for national education" (p.v) was requested and then approved by Vice President Thomas Jefferson. The intent of primary schools, DuPont de Nemours claimed, was for moral instruction based in God. In the secondary schools or colleges, he recommended that the day start with a prayer from the head student inspired by the Lord's Prayer, the noon meal begin and end with prayer, and the evening meal also end with prayer. Instruction during the day should develop students' consciences to guide them in their relationship to the Supreme Intelligence. Then at night, time was specifically to be spent to face the Creator. Even for those schools not connected with the state, Dupont de Nemours said that such schools should do nothing to harm morals or inspire atheism:

> But, since a school of atheism would be a school of false reasoning and would weaken one of the foundations of morality, which is the agreement of action with universal reason and with supreme beneficence, I do not think that the government should permit that the doctrine which supposes that there is no Higher or Greater Benefactor should be taught to young people in class.... Their education should no more be trusted to an atheist than to a libertine. (p. 149-150)

Overall, a purpose of school for DuPont de Nemours was for students to "realize the benevolence of the Creator, [and] the necessity of living honestly in the presence and power of the Supreme Intelligence...." (p. 154).

When DuPont de Nemours wrote in 1800, he claimed that

> most young Americans, therefore, can read, write, and cipher. Not more than four in a thousand are unable to write legibly—even neatly; while in Spain, Portugal, Italy, only a sixth of the population can read; in Germany, even in France, not more than a third; in Poland, about two men in a hundred; and in Austria not one in two Hundred.
>
> England, Holland, the Protestant Cantons of Switzerland, more nearly approach the standard of the United States, because it is in those countries the Bible is read; it is considered a duty to read it to children; and in that form of religion the sermons and liturgy in the language of the people tend to increase and formulate ideas of responsibility. (pp. 3-4)

DuPont de Nemours' figures compare favorably with those of Cremin (1970), who asserts that adult male literacy in the United States during the eighteenth century was better than in Ireland but relatively equivalent to that in England. He cites, but with qualification, other figures suggesting the adult male literacy rate in England at this time was only 50-75% but 70-100% in the colonies (p. 546).

As suggested by the DuPont de Nemours account, all levels of schooling had a religious foundation. Early colleges and universities explicitly referenced biblical themes in their purpose statements. The purpose of the first college, Henrico College in Virginia, was "for the education of the children of those barbarian Indians" (Cremin, 1970, p. 12). By 1621 the founders expanded it to include English children for the "grounding of them in the principles of religion, civility of life and humane learning" (Cremin, 1970, p. 13). With Henrico's demise, Harvard, the next college to be founded (1636), was the only existing English-speaking college in America for about sixty years. Its founding is described in *New England's First Fruits* (1643):

> after God had carried us safe to New England, and we

had builded our houses, provided necessaries for our livli-
hood, rear'd convenient places for Gods worship, and
settled the Civil Government; one of the next things we
longed for, and looked after was to advance Learning, and
perpetuate it to Posterity; dreading to leave an illiterate
Ministry to the Churches.... It pleased God to stir up the
heart of one Mr. Harvard to give the one halfe of his
Estate ... toward the erecting of a College...." (French,
1964, pp. 30-31).

Among the expectations for Harvard's students were the following (Knight & Hall, 1951, pp. 60-61):

1. Everyone shall consider the main end of his life and studies,
   to know God and Jesus Christ, which is eternal life; John
   xvii. 3.
2. Seeing the Lord giveth wisdom, every one shall seriously, by
   prayer in secret, seek wisdom of Him; Proverbs ii 2, 3, etc.
3. Everyone shall so exercise himself in readying the Scripture
   twice a day, that they be ready to give an account of their
   proficiency therein, both in theoretical observations of
   language and lyric, and in practical and spiritual truths, as
   their tutor shall require, according to their several abilities
   respectively, seeing the entrance of the word giveth light,
   etc.; Psalm cxix.130.
4. In the public church assembly, they shall carefully shun all
   jestures that show any contempt or neglect of God's ordinances....
5. They shall eschew all profanation of God's holy name,
   attributes, word, ordinances, and times of worship; and
   study, with reverence and love, carefully to retain God and
   his truth in their minds.

Other colleges had similar biblical foundations. For instance,
the announcement of King's College, in 1754, stated that "The
chief theory that is aimed at in this College, is, to teach and engage
the children to know God in Jesus Christ, and to love and serve him

in all Sobriety, Godliness, and Richness of Life, with a perfect Heart and a Willing Mind ..." (Cubberley, 1920, p. 703).

The nine colleges that existed at the end of the colonial period and their religious affiliation are listed below (Reeder, 1958, p. 140):

1636	Harvard College	MA Puritan
1693	William & Mary	VA Anglican
1701	Yale College	CT Congregational
1746	Princeton	NJ Presbyterian
1753-55	Academy and College	PA Non-denominational
1754	King's College (Columbia)	NY Anglican
1764	Brown	RI Baptist
1766	Rutgers	NJ Reformed Dutch
1769	Dartmouth	NH Congregational

Legislation

The interdependence of education and religion is also revealed in some of the governing documents of early America. The Massachusetts Bill of Rights said,

> As the happiness of a people and the good order and preservation of civil government essentially depend upon piety, religion, and morality, and as these cannot be generally diffused through a community but by the institution of the public worship of God and of public instructions, in piety, religion, and morality: Therefore, to promote their happiness, and to serve the good order and preservation of their government, the people of this commonwealth have a right to invest their legislature with power to authorize and require, and the legislature shall, from time to time, authorize and require, the several towns, parishes, precincts, and other bodies politic; or religious societies, to make suitable provision, at their own expense, for the institution of the public worship of God, and for the support and maintenance of public Protestant teachers of piety, religion, and morality, in all cases where such provision shall not be

made voluntarily.

And the people of this commonwealth have also a right to, and do, invest their legislature with authority to enjoin upon all the subjects an attendance upon the instructions they can conscientiously and conveniently attend. (Perry, 1978, p. 374)

The Pennsylvania Constitution of 1776, Section 45, reads, "Laws for the encouragement of virtue, and prevention of vice and immorality, shall be made and constantly kept in force ... and all religious societies or bodies of men heretofore limited or incorporated for the advancement of religion or learning ... shall be encouraged and protected..." (Knight & Hall, 1951, p. 113). The Constitution of Vermont (1777), Section XLI, reads exactly the same. The Constitution of New Hampshire (1784) reads similarly to the early Massachusetts document. Its essence is as follows:

As morality and piety, rightly grounded on evangelical principles, will give the best and greatest security to government ... is most likely to be propagated through a society by the instruction of public worship of the Deity, and of public instruction in morality and religion ... the people of this state have a right to improve ... for the support and maintenance of public protestant teachers of piety, religion and morality.... (Perry, 1978, p. 382)

Probably the most influential statement comes from the 1787 Northwest ordinance as it was amended in 1789 by the First Federal Congress to read: "Religion, morality, and knowledge being necessary to good government and the happiness of mankind, schools, and the means of education shall forever be encouraged" (Sharpes, 1987, p. 16). This ordinance controlled activities in all the land between Pennsylvania and the Mississippi River north of the Ohio River to Canada (now includes Illinois, Indiana, Ohio, Michigan, Wisconsin and part of Minnesota). The same phrasing was repeated again the Ohio Constitution of 1803 (Knight & Hall, 1951, p. 117).

The laws of the various states were even more explicit than the constitutions in linking education and religion. For example, as early as 1647, Massachusetts law required towns of 50 householders or more to provide a school master of education precisely because of a religious purpose—that is, so children could learn how to read the Scriptures and thus keep from being deluded by Satan (Boles, 1965, p. 6). Known as the "Old Deluder Satan Act," it has been called the "mother of all school laws" (Reeder, 1958, p. 12). The 1684 Plymouth Massachusetts law required children and servants "at least to be able duely to read the Scriptures ... and in some competent measure the main Grounds and Principles of Christian Religion, necessary to Salvation" (Beale, 1941, p. 23).

In 1629, the Dutch East India Company wanted the colonists "to find out ways and means whereby they may support a minister and schoolmaster, that thus the service of God and zeal for religion may not grow cool...." Similarly, in the famous remonstrance of 1649 in New York, the colonists asked that "the youth be well taught and brought up, not only reading and writing; but also in the knowledge and fear of the Lord." In 1694, schools in Maryland were expressly established for "instructing our youth in the orthodox religion ... fitting them for the service of the church and state." And in 1661-62, when the General Assembly granted land for a free school, it did so "for the advancement of learning, education of youth, supply of ministry, and promotion of piety" (see Beale, 1941, p. 24).

As recent as the time period between 1913 and 1930, eleven states and the District of Columbia passed laws that required the Bible to be read in public schools (Tyack, James & Benavot, 1987, p. 164). (The Pennsylvania law was declared unconstitutional by the U.S. Supreme Court in the 1963 *Abington v. Schempp* case—see Boles, 1965, p. 49.) Between the 17th and 20th centuries, instances like the South Carolina statute of 1710 abound: "... free school be erected for the instruction of the youth of this province in Grammar, and other arts and sciences and useful learning and also in the principles of the Christian religion." The North Carolina statute of 1766 states that "a proper school of learning [be] established whereby the rising generation may be brought up and instructed in the principles of the Christian religion...." (Boles, 1965, p. 9).

Loss of Biblical Homogeneity

Clearly, the founding of the United States of America was influenced by belief in a divine calling and education was a primary vehicle to equip individuals in this religious quest. Educational materials, teacher qualifications, student requirements, church control, and governing documents and laws across all and not just a few of the colonies (and the states) are consistent in this theme.

Yet this is not the whole picture. Two accompanying phenomena appear approximately 100 years after America's settlement to dilute this biblical homogeneity. The two phenomena were civil takeover of educational authority and the move from a narrow to a broad biblical interpretation in schools.

Early Unifying Forces

For the early settlers, the home was the prime but informal seat of education. Children were raised in large extended families all under one roof and under the headship of the father. The home was much like a complex form of civil government for the child. The child's attitudes, morals, respect for authority, vocational training, and introduction to the social world occurred in kinship groupings of the family. Because of the slow pace and stable nature of life, the community, where neighbors were often relatives, was for many just a larger family that also aided in the educational process.

According to Cremin (1970, p. 480), the family was the "single most fundamental unit" of socialization and cultural transmission in early America. The home was the central place for the child to learn business and work ethic, to be trained for earning a living, to worship, and to learn piety. Overall, the household was the institution for education.

There was, to be sure, an economic payoff for the home in educating the children. Somewhere between age seven and puberty, children were considered fully able, productive members of the family work force. In fact, if the son left home to work elsewhere, he was expected to pay a substitute to labor in his place (Spring, 1986, p. 24).

Still, the primary purpose of education was to raise the child to keep God's commandments. The typical belief was that the child needed to be saved from the effects of the sin nature. Thus parents had the primary task of equipping the child to avoid the entrapments of sin and to be fully self-governed according to God's laws. The following poem of the 1600s by Anne Bradstreet illustrates how the child was viewed in light of Original Sin:

> "Stained by birth from Adam's sinful fact,
> Thence I began to sin as soon as act:
> A perverse will, a lobe of what forbid,
> A serpents sting in pleasing face lay hid."
>
> (see Button & Provenzo, 1983, p. 12)

This practice of raising the child to resist sinful temptations and the idle life certainly did not start in colonial America but was carried over from the old country. For instance, in 1536, Henry VIII charged the clergy to "admonish the fathers and mothers, masters and governors of youth, being under their care, to teach, or cause to be taught, their children and servants, even from their infancy, their Pater Noster, the articles of our Faith, and the Ten Commandments, in their mother tongue...." (see Cremin, 1970, p. 119). Similar directions, all placing the parent as the religious teacher in the family and the clergy as the encourager and overseer, came from Edward VI in 1547 and Elizabeth I in 1559. King Henry's injunction also required the parents to

> bestow their children and servants, even from their childhood, either to learning, or to some other honest exercise, occupation or husbandry ... to provide and foresee that the said youth be in no manner wise kept or brought up in idleness, lest anytime after they be driven ... to fall to begging, stealing, or some other unthriftiness ... they should, being rulers of their own family, have profited, as well themselves as divers other persons, to the great commodity and ornament of the commonwealth. (Cremin, p. 1970, 170)

Thus the expectation was set even before settling in the new land that parents should mold their children to have godly character and to be fruitful citizens of their land. Coupled with this task for the family was the paradoxical development of schools or, better, workhouses, to educate the children of the poor and vagrants through apprenticeship training. These schools actually formed the laborers for many industries and, as a result, prospered through donations from those well-established families likely to benefit from such institutions.

In fact, colonial families stayed "the most important agency of popular education" (Cremin, 1970, p. 135) well beyond the mid 1600s when England turned more and more to formal institutions for education. The dispersed farms of the southern colonies and the strong ideology of the northern colonies contributed to making the family the most significant educational force in colonial America. Another factor contributing to family based education was that skills for the new agricultural and native industries were not to be found in formal institutions but were primarily transmitted by the family unit.

The church was the primary formal means by which children were educated. In addition to being the main guardian of the morals of the community, it also laid the foundation for the system of thought and imagery that undergirded cultural morals. It provided the child with a higher vision and often was the focus and mechanism of social integration.

The formal mechanism of school as we know it today was very limited. Most often formal instruction was geared to equipping for social roles. Very utilitarian in nature, formal education was for public responsibility not for what we know of as professional training.

The state, while interested and even regulatory and supervisory towards education, did not directly finance or support it. Support for public education usually came from private endorsements and philanthropic efforts.

This is how education was in the Old World and was expected to be in the New World. However, because new social and political arrangements were possible in the New World, education became an instrument of deliberate social purpose.

Later Disruptive Forces

Life was different in the new world. Without existing restraints inherent in the old world setting, many changes erupted. But conditions of the new world were also different. Pressure was placed on the family for mere survival. New opportunities broke apart the extended family. The community, now less permanent, provided less in the way of easy transition to adulthood, thereby making the child less externally guided by healthy social forces. Even apprenticeships, because of the greater demand for workers who themselves had greater employment choices, became less discriminating regarding moral education, Christian character development, and literacy building. All these pressures worked against the success of the family as the primary instrument for education and brought more and more state involvement.

At the same time, the increasingly heterogeneous nature of religious beliefs among the different Christian denominations diminished the singleness of religious outlook. Denominationalism led to disagreements that eventuated in all parties suffering a loss of control. Additionally, the diminishing contact with the American Indian left the missionary zeal without purpose. And the greater understanding of religious freedom for all undercut the narrow-minded concept that education was a godly duty as interpreted exclusively by whichever religious persuasion was in power. Survival of denominational allegiance assumed a higher priority than moral and religious preparation.

Reorienting—Role of Religion in Education

State Control

The precedent for state control of education occurred relatively early in colonial America. Actually, the precedent occurred first in the old world. For example, in 1524 Martin Luther persuaded the civil authority to do what he himself saw as a religious activity. Namely, the German rulers were empowered to legally compel citizens to send their children, under compulsory attendance laws, to school to be equipped in the struggle against Satan. Similarly, in 1536 the public schools in Switzerland were created by the General Assembly for the same religious reasons (Blumenfeld, 1985, pp. 10,11). The Swiss schools, mandated by civil authority, later became refined under the religious direction of the noted theologian John Calvin. The Dutch civil authorities, the Scottish Parliament (in 1633 and 1646), and the Scandinavian countries also ordered the establishment of schools, all for religious purposes (Cubberley, 1920, p. 506).

The reason why, in all these instances, civil authorities commanded religious duties was because civil government was conceived as serving the broader purposes of religion and not vice verse. Schools were clearly established to serve religious rather than state purposes.

In the United States, as early as the 1640s, both Virginia and Massachusetts noted displeasure in the way parents were educating their children. According to Eggleston (1961, p. 233), the second and third generations suffered a great loss of literacy as evidenced in letters, wills, and written records. Apparently the requirements of conquering the land made these settlers good frontiersmen but poor spellers and writers (Eggleston, 1933, p. 233). In 1642, Massachusetts passed the first law in America concerning education in condemnation of "the great neglect of many parents and masters in training up their children...." They were reminded of their duty to provide for the "calling and implyment of their children" and to see to their children's "ability to read and understand the principles of religion and the capitall lawes of this country" (see Bailyn, 1960, p. 26). It was this type of legal action in Massachusetts that made it the forerunner of the public education system in the United States (Eggleston, 1933, p. 231). During this time, Virginia passed laws of the same nature and in 1665 so did New York. In these laws, parents could be reprimanded and even fined for non-compliance.

By the late 1640s, Massachusetts and Connecticut passed a succession of laws whereby the Puritans deliberately turned the educational responsibility of the family over to the state. The 1647 "Ye ould deluder, Satan" Law was passed in Massachusetts requiring every town of fifty householders to maintain a teacher of reading and writing and every town of 100 householders to equip students for the University. The 1647 law was designed to teach children how to read the Bible and thus thwart "one chief project of that old deluder Satan, to keep men from the knowledge of the Scriptures...." (Cremin, 1970, p. 181). The money for the teachers was to come from the parents or masters of the children or from the inhabitants in general. By 1648 the first tax on property for the support of local schools was passed in Massachusetts.

Connecticut passed laws in 1650 requiring that children be taught to read English, instructed in the capital laws, catechized weekly, and equipped with a trade profitable to themselves and society. Joining Connecticut was New Haven in 1655, New York in 1655, Plymouth in 1671, and Pennsylvania in 1683. The Pennsylvania law read that the parents and guardians "shall cause such to be instructed in reading and writing, so that they may be able to read the Scriptures and write by the time they attain to twelve years of age; and that then they be taught some useful trade or skill...." (Cremin, 1970, p. 125). Many others states/colonies soon followed with similar ordinances. By 1689, Virginia had six schools, Maryland at least one, New York approximately eleven, and Massachusetts at least 23 (Cremin, 1970, p. 183).

Presumably because the parents were not diligent about their educational responsibilities, the civil authority felt a need to shoulder that burden. The churches, without any real power, could not force any change but had to rely on the legal power of the state to ensure that children were educated. It soon became a matter of survival of the states for the populous to be educated and to be employable. Education allowed the individual to self-govern and to be governed correctly, and employability kept the individual from being a burden and made him an asset to civil government.

Historian of the Massachusetts public school system, George H. Martin, said that the legislation of the 1640s established the following principles upon which all future similar legislative acts were based:

1. The universal education of youth is essential to the well-being of the state.

2. The obligation to furnish them education rests primarily upon the parent.
3. The State has a right to enforce this obligation.
4. The State may fix a standard which shall determine the kind of education, and the minimum amount.
5. Public money, raised by general tax, may be used to provide such education as the State requires.

The tax may be general, though the school attendance is not.

6. Education higher than the rudiments may be supplied by the State. Opportunity must be provided, at public expense, for youths who wish to be fitted for the University. (Cubberley, 1920, p. 366)

The main thrust of this kind of legislation was, according to historian George Martin, "because the State will suffer if he is not educated. The State does not provide schools to relieve the parents, nor because it can educate better than the parents can, but because it can thereby enforce the obligation which it imposes" (Cubberley, 1920, p. 366). The crucial point was not to remove parents or even religion from education but to acquire the means to enforce education to keep the civil structure from failing. In fact, for the settlers, civil prosperity was contingent upon religious training and understanding.

In addition to parental neglect, a number of other factors led to more state and less religious control of education. Some of these factors were the increased demand for practical competence in a rapidly developing nation, the decline of single-minded orthodoxy because of alternate biblical interpretations, and the breaking of the power of church establishments upon separation from the mother country (see Cubberley, 1920, p. 692).

The outcome of the move toward state control of education was that by 1800 half of the sixteen states forming the Union specifically included provisions for education in their constitutions.

The Pennsylvania Constitution in 1776, Section 44, said in part, "A school or schools shall be established in every county by the legislature ... with such salaries to the masters, paid by the public...." Section 45 continued with "... and all religious societies or bodies of men heretofore united or incorporated for the advancement of religion or learning ... shall be encouraged or protected...." The North Carolina Constitution of 1776 duplicates almost exactly Section 44 of the Pennsylvania Constitution. The Georgia Constitution of 1777, Article 54, says, "Schools shall be erected in each county, and supported at the general expense of the state." The Vermont Constitution of 1777, Sections XL and XLI, repeat very closely Sections 44 and 45, respectively, of the Pennsylvania document. The Constitutions of Massachusetts (1780), New Hampshire (1784, 1792), Vermont (1787), Delaware (1792), Georgia (1798), Ohio (1803), and Indiana (1816) all made provision for public schools and sometimes with specific reference to biblical or Godly foundations (Knight & Hall, 1951, pp. 113-119). By 1912, forty-one of the forty-five states admitted to the Union between 1792 and 1912 provided for some aspect of public education in their constitution (Tyack, et al., 1987, p. 46).

But the civil institutionalization of education in no way meant an automatic loss of the religious foundations of education. As presented earlier, the Northwest Ordinance of 1787 specifically joined religion and education. But without exception, the states and not the Federal government were the location of the seat of responsibility for education.

By the middle of the nineteenth century when the institution of public school became the standard, evangelical Protestantism was the dominant force in American life. The Protestant view was that to survive the republic needed a moral citizenry, that morality was based upon religion, and that the Bible was the religion of America. Thus, the argument went, public school instruction must be based on biblical teachings.

This view was so prevalent that it resulted in the courts ruling against what we would now call religious freedom. For example, when a 15-year-old girl was expelled from school in Maine for refusing to read from the King James version of the Bible, the court upheld the school board's decision (*Donahue v. Richards*, 38 Me. 379 [1854] 387). Even though her refusal was on the Catholic belief of her parents that it was sinful to read the Protestant Bible, the court held that it was used to instill the virtues enumerated in the state constitution (Tyack, et al., 1987, p. 163). It should be noted that while the focus of the court decision was on moral character development and not biblical evangelism (a major focus in earlier schooling), it still remains that the civil authorities held the Bible to be foundational to the educational process. In fact, the state was so much in control of education that it could force someone to read the Bible for moral and character development purposes even against that person's religious convictions. Consider the following state-ment from this Court decision: "this tyrannical doctrine of pure democracy, we generally hear only from the lips of demagogues" (Tyack, et al., 1987, p. 163). Similarly, in the 1850s, a Catholic student in Oswego, New York was whipped and expelled from a public school for refusing to read the King James Bible. In this same time period, a teacher in Boston beat an eleven-year-old boy for thirty minutes, again for refusal to read the King James Bible. In both situations legal action against the teachers was unfruitful (Kaestle, 1983, p. 171).

A number of states specifically included provisions in their laws for Bible reading in the classroom. Up until 1826 only Massachusetts had legally mandated reading of the Bible in public school since a law was apparently never needed. In fact, it was esti-mated in the 1880s that somewhere between 80 percent of American schools to 75 percent of the school districts already permitted the practice (Tyack, et al., 1987, p. 164). By 1903, ten states legally prescribed Bible reading (Beale, 1941, p. 210). Between the years 1913 and 1930, eleven states and Washington, DC, passed laws requiring the Bible to be read in public school classrooms. Seven other states passed laws that permitted but did not require Bible reading. In 1903, four-fifths of the state and city schools across the country required daily chapel (Beale, 1941, p. 214). North Dakota required the schools to place the Ten Commandments in a conspicuous place, and Mississippi required every grade level to have a course in morality which had to include the Ten Commandments (Tyack, et al., 1987, pp. 164-5).

The courts also validated both the practice and the requirement of Bible reading in public schools. In 1884, the Iowa Supreme

Court upheld the legality of forbidding the Bible from being excluded from the schools. In 1904, the Kansas Supreme Court, in upholding use of the Bible and the Lord's Prayer in school, declared, "The noblest ideals of moral character are found in the Bible.... To emulate these is the supreme conception of citizenship" (see Beale, 1941, p. 213). In 1905, the Kentucky Supreme Court denied an injunction to remove the Bible and prayers from school activities. In 1908, the Texas Supreme Court ruled that those who object to the use of the Bible in the classroom have no right to deny such a privilege. The Massachusetts Supreme Court ruled that "one of the chief objects of education ... the principles of piety and justice, and sacred regard for truth," were most appropriately instilled by Bible reading and prayer (pp. 213-24).

At the same time that the state constitutions were linking education and religion, laws were requiring Bible reading in school, and the courts were upholding such laws, a series of counterforces were operating in the country. These forces resulted from religious and denominational pluralism and the philosophy of full religious freedom that went beyond the token conciliations granted through religious toleration. While these counterforces fueled the change from church to state control of education, their impact was even more substantive. This impact has already been implied by the mere fact that laws had to be made to permit Bible reading and that courts had to adjudicate between the effect of these laws and opposing actions based on religious conscience.

Bible Nonsectarianism

Along with the switch from parental, and particularly church, to civil control of formal education, there was the reversal from denominational exclusiveness to denominational openness and a relaxation of the strong salvation message toward, instead, civil religion and morality.

The association between civil control and nondenominational or nonsectarian yet biblically oriented instruction is seen in the way Horace Mann conceptualized education. Mann stood at the juncture of two major streams of educational thought in America in the 1800s. The one stream was the Calvinistic belief, which stressed quite dogmatically the necessity of salvation and forgiveness through the cross. It often had a harsh, judgmental nature that conflicted with the flavor of the second stream of educational thinking. The second stream was the liberal European notion that education and enlightenment focus on growth, grace, and the natural potential for man to develop into the likeness of God.

The conflictful mix of these two streams resulted in what some call a philosophy of "common school religion." It was a distancing from sectarianism with a social integration focus. The emphasis was on developing a common set of religious beliefs that would help integrate society and mold moral character. As Samuel Burnside (an ardent Mann supporter) said, "... Our desire is only to train children to the practice of Christian virtues from Christian motives; that is, from reverence of God, an habitual sense of his perfections, his presence, and of personal accountability, and from a love also of country, and the whole human family... This is all I mean by a religious education..." (see Glenn, 1988, p. 153). Thus, for Samuel Burnside, it was proper to write the 1827 statute in Massachusetts that disallowed school committees to purchase books "which are calculated to favour any particular religious sect or tent" (see Glenn, 1988, p. 152). Doctrinal teaching, Burnside said, was to be eliminated in favor of instruction in which "all sects of Christians might walk harmoniously together..." (p. 152)

One of the problems according to Mann was that the various sects were "so rigorously contending against each other" that the school house needed to be a neutral ground. "Against a tendency to these fatal extremes," he said, "the beautiful and sublime truths of ethics and of natural religion have a poising power" (see Glenn, 1988, p. 163). Education was to be a "culture of our moral affections and religious sensibilities, as in the course of nature and providence shall lead to a subjection or conformity of all our appetites, propensities, and sentiments to the will of Heaven" (p. 163).

In recommending that the Bible be read in school without comment, Mann wanted taught "what all its believers hold to be the rule of faith and practice;" he wanted the peculiarities which just one of a few denominations hold to be true to be excluded (Glenn, 1988,

p. 166). This would make the schools "a system which recognizes religious obligations to their fullest extent ... a system which invokes a religious spirit, and can never be fitly administered without such a spirit" (p. 169).

The immediate successor to Mann, Barnas Sears, repeated (1852) the same flow of ideas in favor of natural or common school religion:

> The most perfect development of the mind, no less than the order of the school and the stability of society, demands a religious education. Massachusetts may be regarded as having settled, at least for herself, this great connection of religion with the Public Schools. She holds that religion is the highest and noblest possession of the mind, and is conducive to all the true interests of man and of society, and therefore he cannot do otherwise than seek to place her schools under its beneficent influence... What it needs for its own safety and well-being is the spirit of the Decalogue as expounded by the Great Teacher of mankind, while varying creeds, which are so much in controversy, are not indispensable as a means of public education... In the exclusion of distinctive creeds from the schools, religious persons, of almost every name, are singularly agreed... (p. 173)

Likewise, in 1854, the Massachusetts *Seventeenth Report* on the schools records the following statement by another educator, George Emerson: "moral instruction must be based on the Gospel, on those great principles of Christianity which are common to all Christians, the great principles of the immorality and accountability of man, of the holiness and omnipresence of God, of the authority of the teachings of Christ" (p. 174).

The Outcome

The conflict over whose interpretation of the Bible or exactly what basis of morality would prevail led to many laws against sectarianism. From the time of the middle 1800s, the states pushed for a prohibition on using public funds for sectarian purposes. For instance, the Maclay Bill (1842) in New York forbade payment of public funds to schools that taught or favored any particular religious or sectarian doctrine (Good & Teller, 1973, p. 131). In 1876 the U.S. Congress passed a law (though dubiously valid) requiring all new states coming into the Union to guarantee in their constitution that public school systems be free from sectarian control (Boles, 1965, p. 37).

The word sectarian generally meant in reference to a particular Christian denomination or sect. Thus, to prohibit sectarianism only meant to prohibit the favoring of any one particular Christian denomination. Many states calling for nonsectarianism nonetheless provided for Bible reading in schools. Virginia, for instance, in 1846-47 required that "no book shall be used nor instruction given in the public schools, calculated to favour the doctrinal tenets of any religious sect or denomination" (see Beale, 1941, p. 95). Similarly, in 1848 Wisconsin guaranteed "the right of every man to worship almighty God according to the dictates of his own conscience..." (Boles, 1965, p. 38) and also that "no sectarian instruction shall be allowed" in their public schools. Alabama in 1853 prohibited sectarian religious views in their schools (Beale, 1941, p. 95) but in a 1940 statute mandated that all schools supported by public funds "shall have once every school day reading from the Bible" (Boles, 1965, p. 49). When a protest was registered in Rhode Island in 1838 that Bible reading violated the rights of conscience, the legislature did nothing since it held that the local community could decide that the Bible ought to be read. Yet by 1854, the schools were allowed to excuse those students who objected to reading the Bible.

Michigan, Indiana, Ohio, Kansas, Massachusetts, and Oregon all had constitutional provisions similar to the following, which was passed in Minnesota in 1857: "In no case shall ... any public moneys or property, be appropriated or used for the support of schools wherein the distinctive doctrines, creeds, or tenets of any particular Christian or other religious sect are promolugated or taught" (Beale, 1941, p. 104).

By 1903, thirty-nine states had laws against both sectarianism in public schools and state aid to religious schools. But in balance, ten states had laws by 19903 that prescribed Bible reading in the public classroom. Before the U.S. Supreme Court invalidated such laws in 1963, thirty-seven states either required, permitted, or condoned Bible reading in public schools. In only eleven states, by 1963, was Bible reading thought to be illegal by the courts or by the people responsible for educational policy. But even in these eleven states, no constitutional or statutory provision existed to forbid Bible reading per se (Boles, 1965, p. 53).

Somewhere around the close of the 1800s and the beginning of the 1900s, Bible reading without comment or denominational/sectarian influence was highly desired, if not legally promoted, by the various states. As the 1898 Wisconsin statute read, "To teach the existence of a supreme being of infinite wisdom, power and goodness and that it is the duty of all men to adore, obey and love him is not sectarian because all religious ... sects so believe and teach..." (Beale, 1941, p. 211). In fact, Kentucky went so far in 1893 as to forbid the teaching of infidel doctrines in the schools.

Conclusion

Educational endeavors in the formative stage of the United States emphasized biblical teachings primarily to enable the perceived divine destiny of the country. The methods, purposes, authority, and goals all reflected biblical underpinnings. Initially, education was viewed within the larger context of religion, and not vice versa, for both the good of the individual and society. This "good" purpose, in fact, justified denominational mandates in education.

After several hundred years, a number of factors contributed to a relaxation of denominationalism or sectarianism. These factors included a laxity of parental responsibility, the influx and growth of rival denominations, an acceptance of the natural philosophy of man, and more civil control over educational matters. Interdenominational conflict was a prime reason why civil control became independent from religious affiliation and oversight.

In all that has been reviewed so far, the turn from denominationalism is not to be equated with a turn away from the Bible and
religion in public schools. There was perhaps as much concern to
protect the school children from no religion at all as there was to
protect against sectarianism. Protectiveness notwithstanding,
control by denominations and then independently by civil authority set the precedent for dishonoring school choice and parental
responsibility in education.

This dual protectiveness is best captured in Wisconsin's
Constitution of 1898. Its prohibition against sectarian teachings
referred "exclusively to instruction ... in religious doctrines which
are believed by some religious sects and rejected by others. To
teach the existence of a supreme being of infinite wisdom, power
and goodness and that it is the duty of all men to adore, obey and
love him, is not sectarianism because all religious ... sects so
believe and teach" (Beale, 1941, pp. 210-211).

We close this chapter noting that public education in America
for all practical purposes made or more precisely mandated education as a religious function. As educator D. Bethume Duffield said
in 1856 at the annual conference of the American Association for
the Advancement of Education,

> If the State is injured by the rearing of immoral and
> lawless citizens, she has a right to protect herself against
> the evil; not alone by prison bars and the hangman's cord,
> but by striking at the root of the evil, and adopting preven-
> tive measures. The only effective way to stop the stream of
> pollution is to close and seal up the fountains whence they
> flow. The only way to protect children from barbarism and
> vice is to furnish them the blessing of religious instruction
> and the elements of knowledge. (Glenn, 1988, p. 175)

Even so, the dilemmas that ultimately reside in aspirations of
equality and order of content (i.e., whose biblical interpretation)
and of control (e.g., parents or the state) did not disappear. In fact,
voices of different persuasions on these issues eventually cast
education into an anti-religious mold, as the next two chapters

246

demonstrate. Suffice it to say, issues of equality and order are not necessarily better served by alternate mandates of discrimination.

References

Bailyn, Bernard (1960). *Education and the forming of American society*. Chapel Hill: University of North Carolina Press and New York: W.W. Norton Co.

Baldwin, Leland D. (1981). *The American quest for the city of God*. Macon, GA: Mercer University Press.

Beale, Howard K. (1941). *A history of freedom of teaching in American schools*. New York: Charles Scribners Sons.

Bellah, Robert N. (1975). *The broken covenant*. New York: The Seabury Press.

Bercovitch, Sacvan (1978). *The American jeremiad*. Madison, WI: The University of Wisconsin Press.

Blumenfeld, Samuel L. (1985). *Is public education necessary?* Boise, ID: Paradigm.

Boles, Donald E. (1965). *The Bible, religion and the public schools*. Ames, IA: Iowa State University Press.

Button, H. Warren & Provenzo, Eugene F. (1983). *History of education and culture in America*. Englewood Cliffs, NJ: Prentice-Hall.

Cubberley, Ellwood P. (1920). *The history of education*. New York: Houghton Mifflin.

Curti, Merle (1978). *The social ideas of American educators*. Totowa, NJ: Littlefield, Adams.

Cremin, Lawrence A. (1970). *American education: The colonial experience, 1607-1783*. New York: Harper & Row.

Dupont de Nemours, Pierre Samuel (1923). *National education in the United States of America*. Newark, DE: University of Delaware Press.

Eavey, Charles B. (1964). *History of Christian education*. Chicago: Moody Press.

Eggleston, Edward (1961). *The transit of civilization*. New York: Appleton & Co.

French, William M. (1964). *America's educational tradition*. Lexington, Heath.

Glenn, Charles L. (1988). *The myth of the common school*. Amherst, MA: The University of Massachusetts Press.

Gobbel, Luther L. (1938). *Church-state relationships in education in North Carolina since 1776*. Durham, NC: Duke University Press.

Good, Harry G. & Teller, James D. (1973). *A history of American education* (3rd ed.). New York: Macmillan.

Hammond, Phillip E. (1984). Pluralism and law in the formation of American religion. In Herbert, Jerry S. (Ed.) *America, christian or secular?* Portland, OR: Multnomah Press.

Kaestle, Carl F. (1983). *Pillars of the republic.* New York: Hill and Wang.

Knight, Edgar W. & Hall, Clifton L. (1951). *Readings in American educational history.* New York: Greenwood Press.

Nettles, Curtis P. (1981). *The roots of American civilization.* (2nd ed.) New York: Irvington Publishers, Inc.

Perry, Richard L. (Ed.) (1978). *Sources of our liberties.* Chicago: American Bar Foundation.

Pfeffer, Leo (1967). *Church, state and freedom.* Boston: Beacon Press.

Reeder, Ward G. (1958). *A first course in education* (4th ed.). New York: Macmillan.

Rudolph, Frederick (Ed.) (1965). *Essays on education in the early republic.* Cambridge, MA: Harvard University Press.

Sharpes, Donald K. (1987). *Education and the U.S. government.* New York: St. Martin's Press.

Smith, Wilson (1973). *Theories of education in early America: 1966-1819.* New York: Bobbs-Merrill.

Spring, Joel (1986). *The American school—1642-1985.* New York: Longman.

Thayer, Vivian T. (1947). *Religion in public education.* Westport, CT: Greenwood Press.

Tyack, David, James, T. & Benavot, A. (1987). *Law and the shaping of public education 1785-1954.* Madison: University of Wisconsin Press.

Tyack, David B. (Ed.) (1967). *Turning points in American educational history.* Waltham, MA: Blaisdell Publ. Co.

Chapter 7

Education <u>Must</u> Be Religiously American

The liberty to worship God according to the dictates of conscience, conceded to our citizens by the Constitution, cannot, by any principle of legitimate interpretation, be construed into a right to embarrass the municipal authorities of this Christian and Protestant nation in the ordering of their district schools (see Beale, 1941, p. 101).

The greater the proportion of our youth who fail to attend our public schools and who receive their education elsewhere, the greater the threat to our democratic unity. To use taxpayers' money to assist private schools is to suggest that American society use its own hands to destroy itself. (cited in Herberg, 1958, p. 127)

[I]t is the duty of a nation to superintend and even coerce the education of children and ... dictate the establishment of a system which shall place under a control,

independent of and superior to parental authority, the
education of the children (Glenn, 1988, p. 91).

The first quote is part of a resolution proposed by Presbyterians
and Congregationalists at their Cleveland, Ohio convention in 1844.
It represents their reaction to the perceived threat or embarrassment
to national interests in education by those whose consciences were
grounded in other than orthodox or "authorized" Christianity. The
second quote comes from the book *Education and Liberty* (1965). It
pinpoints the supposed lack of national unity that arises from any
departure from the singular establishment of public education. The
third quote comes from an award-winning 1795 essay on education.
At a time in this country when educational policy was often
discussed in such position papers, Samuel Harrison Smith captured
a prevailing sentiment that the children belong to the state and
should be trained to serve the state.

All three quotes represent a favored perspective that education
must serve the national interests of the United States. This perspective included the prerogative to deprive citizens of their rights of
religious conscience regarding content of instruction and to
promote this content at taxpayer expense. While James Madison's
Memorial and Remonstrance successfully defeated such practices
in the 18th century, the victory was obviously not long-lasting.

In many ways, the history of education in the United States
reveals two categories of control (Skillen, 1987). Primacy of
parental influence lasted until approximately the mid-1800s.
Governmental priority has prevailed since then. In this regard,
Herberg (1958, p. 119) claims that public education in the United
States grew out of the principle of subsidiarity. That is, when the
independent sponsoring agencies (e.g., parents, charities, religions)
were declared as unable to meet certain educational expectations,
the government unilaterally claimed justification for intervention to
meet those expectations. Even in the early period of parental
primacy, government often reserved for itself the self-proclaimed
privilege of superseding parental prerogatives.

While this battle over control is invariably a major determining
issue in educational policy, the issue that typically and deceptively

occupies center stage of the public's attention is that of secular versus religious content. When continually cast in light of First Amendment and other considerations, the secular (usually associated with governmental primacy) versus sectarian/religious (usually associated with family or denomination primacy) content issue keeps the more crucial matter of parental versus government control subtly disguised. Continued focus on the issue of religious versus secular content of instruction as primary results in treating the hidden assumption of the rightfulness of government control as if it were a foregone conclusion or not at issue at all (cf. Lewis, 1947). The following comments by a State Superintendent of Public Instruction (1992) illustrates this perspective. When informed that only a minority of the citizens in his state would take advantage of school choice he said, "Why thrust this particular reform [school choice] across the state when the vast majority ... have no interest?" (Editorial—*Virginian Pilot Ledger Star*, 12/2/92). The Superintendent's comment betrays the assumption that government has the final say over all children particularly as the majority are allowed to speak for the minority. We need to be reminded of James Madison's observation that the Bill of Rights protects "against the majority in favor of the minority" (Gales, 1834, p. 454.

The key point of this chapter is that those who worked to liberate education from denominational and hierarchical control nonetheless fostered a different and self-promoting system of control but similar dogmatic perspective. After having fought the War of Independence to achieve freedom from centralized authority, the colonists sought a new kind of unity. But the goal of unity soon turned protectively to that of uniformity wherein leaders like Thomas Jefferson, Benjamin Rush, and Noah Webster defined "the free American [as] the uniform American" (Tyack, 1967, p. 84). Thus, the control of belief changed but the authoritarian structure for instilling beliefs did not. In the words of U.S. Supreme Court Justice Robert H. Jackson (*West Virginia State Board of Education* v. *Barnette*, 1943, 319 US 624), "Probably no deeper division of our people could proceed from any provocation than from finding it necessary to choose what doctrine and whose program public education officials shall compel youth to unit in embracing... Compulsory unification of opinion achieves only the unanimity of the graveyard."

As a case in point, Thomas Jefferson, "chief prophet of public education" (Malone, 1948, p. 280), is thought to have absorbed a particular pattern of thought about education from his Scottish professor William Small. Just as Scotsman John Knox promoted a national school system to produce "conforming Christians," Jefferson promoted state schools to produce "conforming republicans" (Conant, 1963, p. 40). Knox's plan has been classified as a scheme "to perpetuate a spiritual tyranny" (Conant, 1963, p. 19); Jefferson's might be classified as a national tyranny.

This chapter examines the history of public education to understand how education transitioned from being founded in biblical religion to civil religion instead. The former, as discussed in Chapter 6, was relatively coincident with state or regional establishments of religion (cf. Garrison, 1948, p. 16). The latter is coincident with governmental disestablishment of religion as reflected in the U.S. Constitution and the Bill of Rights. The prime characteristic to be discussed is that, by governmental mandate, education must not be sectarian but must be religious and primarily for the good of the nation.

Religious But Not Sectarian

Toward the end of the 17th century, educational policy mirrored the general religious trends in each state. For instance, where a single establishment of religion existed, public funds for education (following the pattern set in Massachusetts) went exclusively to schools of that sect. Connecticut followed Massachusetts' policy in 1650, then New Haven in 1655, Plymouth in 1677, and New Hampshire in 1680 (Butts, 1950, p. 114). Schools of any other sectarian orientation were either not permitted or were entirely dependent upon private funding.

Whenever multiple establishments existed, either as the initial orientation of a colony or because of increased religious pluralism, public and private schools both received public support. In fact, it is difficult to make any clear distinction between these two kinds of schools because these labels as currently used do not fit the conditions of colonial times. For instance, both public and private schools purposely taught from a religious perspective and both received public funds. The fact that private schools were run by other than the civil government (the main reason for being labeled as private) did not hinder their eligibility for public funding. They were, after all, seen as public in the sense that they were performing the same public function as the mainline public schools. Interestingly, Massachusetts, the state forerunner of a singular establishment of religion included in its Constitution (the last of the original colonies to adopt a constitution) of 1780 that "private societies and public institutions" were both to be encouraged in recognition of this very fact (McCarthy, Oppewal, Peterson, & Spykman, 1981, p. 80). After experiencing the terrible religious persecutions of the old country, it was, with hindsight, inevitable that the favored citizens of single establishment states would begin to respect the religious liberty rights for believers of other persuasions. The massive immigration of different believers from Europe and the resettlement of the existing populous were the main catalysts for religious pluralism. Existing establishments were disestablished or prevented from even occurring (cf. Butts, 1950, p. 23). Whether disestablishment occurred easily or forcefully, it was ultimately driven by the majority desire for equal religious liberty.

It should not go unnoticed that schooling and educational policies of this time (17th and 18th centuries) treated education as inextricably tied to religion. Rhetoric continually linked good government and national prosperity with morality, and morality with religion and education. Massachusetts, with the earliest official public educational policy, declared in its mandatory schooling law of 1648, "Forasmuch as the good education is of singular behoof and benefit to any Commonwealth ... to read the english tongue, and knowledge of the Capital laws ... that all masters doe once a week (at the least) catechize their children and servants in the grounds and principles of Religion..." As late as 1787, federal government policy for the newly acquired territories of the Ohio Valley by virtue of the Northwest Ordinance read, "Religion, morality, and knowledge being necessary to good government and the happiness of mankind, schools and the means of education shall forever be encouraged."

As the country grew, so did the diversity of schooling. At the beginning of the 19th century, no state had a statewide system of free schools. Yet by the end of this same century, almost all states had a system of free public education from elementary school up to and sometimes including college (Karier, 1986, p. 43). At the beginning of the 19th century, the southern states maintained the English tradition of private education with the state assuming responsibility only for pauper schools. Massachusetts, as the leader in New England (and then the entire country), started with sectarian schools but eventually opened to public support of Latin grammar schools, private academies, and colleges. While the middle states varied, they too supported private schools with public funds.

From Sectarian to Common Schools

How the various states and the nation as a whole moved from private sectarian schools to the common school movement of public nonsectarian schools is a complex issue. Various authors emphasize multiple dynamics as the answer. We will review several of these proposed dynamics for a general level of understanding. In spite of the diversity of dynamics, a common thread runs through them all.

Some of the factors that led to the common school system include the difficulty of funding all the diverse sectarian institutions of learning; the brute force of religious and cultural pluralism; Enlightenment ideas that emphasize rational, scientific inquiry preeminent over religious revelation and deductive (only) inquiry; the liberating spirit of freedom of religion and disestablishmentism; the perceived threat of ignorant immigrants; the nationalistic desire to build a better republic; and the reconstructionist agenda of social and individual perfectibility. To the individual who feared the effect of universal suffrage on the stability of the new republic, the common school was the saving educational instrument; to the property owner, it was a protective insurance policy against social violence; to the entrepreneur, it was a means for enhancing worker skills as well as consumer awareness; to the laborer, it was a means of social mobility; to the social reformer, it was the great equalizer; to the nativist, it was the Americanizer of many diverse groups. (Karier, 1986, p. 45)

In the final analysis, the rapid growth of common schools in the early 1800s can be attributed to the influence of three major ideas endemic to the American scene. First there was the longstanding belief of an organic, integral connection between religion and politics. John Adams said it well in 1790: "The constitution was made for a moral and religion people. It is wholly inadequate to the government of any other" (Federer, 1996, pp. 10-11). Second, the ideal of exclusive freedom of religion was tempered by the clash of each group's desire to live according to its own religion. Third, the early citizens and particularly their leaders had a vested interest in ensuring that this noble experiment in republican governance succeed.

The interaction of these forces resulted in a uniform system of education of a distinctly Protestant nature. Through this solution, early America's mainstream religious teachings would be fostered in an educational environment designed to produce an intelligent electorate and leaders. While some (cf. Smith, 1967, p. 679) attribute this common school solution to a conscious effort to amalgamate these forces into a consensually approved solution, it was more the result of a give-and-take battle. In fact, it was often not so much even a product of compromise by involved parties so much as it was the imposition of power that effected this outcome.

Leading into this conflictual time period, the majority of Americans entrusted their children to the state for their education. Since the Protestant ethic of the schools naturally appealed to the religious beliefs of the vast majority, the state was considered an honorable servant to the parents for educating their children.

Early Spokesmen

An early though not initially successful spokesman for this amalgamated policy was Thomas Jefferson. He is important because he is the historically recognized spokesman for not just one but for two major streams of thought in this second historical phase.

Jefferson, for one, was a leading spokesman for the right of full religious freedom from establishment practices of religious or governmental groups. He cogently captured this American sentiment regarding freedom from governmental control in the Declaration of Independence and in several collaborative works with Madison to guarantee religious freedom. He was adamantly opposed to religious mandates on the people by governmental enforcements.

Second, Jefferson was an early and chief proponent of public schooling. In 1779, just a few days after being elected as governor of Virginia, Jefferson submitted his "Bill for the More General Diffusion of Knowledge" to the Virginia legislature (Honeywell, 1931, p. 10). In his bill were four main objectives: free elementary schools for all; free advanced education for selected poor boys, publicly paid university education for a few bright students, and the establishment of a public state university (Conant, 1963, p. 3). In support of his bill, he said, "If the condition of man is to be progressively ameliorated, as we fondly hope and believe, education is to be the chief instrument in effecting it" (Honeywell, 1931, pp. 13, 148). Additionally, Jefferson proposed that provisions for a public school be provided in the development of Virginia's Constitution, and then while president of the United States, he proposed that the national constitution be amended to aid public education (Henderson, 1970, p. 351). This latter type of aid was considered outside the authority of the national government by most statesmen of that time, hence the need for a constitutional amendment.

The exact date for the beginning of this phase is difficult to know as it is for any emerging trend. The year 1789 is a good estimate since the writing of the First Amendment symbolically if not officially marks the break of civil government from religious hierarchy. This event also officially signals a change in the major purpose of education. Up to that time it could reasonably be said that religion was a prime force even when the health and success of the "commonwealth" was the prime object. The civil state was after all either an instrument of religion or a partner in pietistic living. But after being shed of religious control, civil government was free to exist independently and in fact to perpetuate itself just as the religions had tried to do earlier via educational efforts. "[W]hen disestablishment and separation secularized the New England township, it was inevitable that the same forces should operate to secularize the township schools. This was the pattern that American education has adopted" (Pfeffer, 1967, p. 324).

The spirit of this phase is probably best captured in the words of Benjamin Rush in 1786. For this signer of The Declaration of Independence and for many early statesmen, the War of Independence was only "the first act of a great drama. We have changed our forms of government, but it remains yet to effect a revolution in our principles, opinions, and manners so as to accommodate them to the forms of government we have adopted. This is the most difficult part of the business of the patriots and legislators of our country" (Tyack, 1967, p. 83).

That business referred to by Rush was focused primarily through a uniform system of education. In 1786, Rush proposed an educational plan for Pennsylvania similar to Jefferson's of 1779 calling for free schools in every town, four colleges throughout the state, and a state-supported university in Philadelphia (Kaestle, 1983, p. 9). Rush said, "Our Schools of learning, by producing one general, and uniform system of education, will render the mass of the people more homogeneous and thereby fit them more easily for uniform and peaceable government" (Tyack, 1967, p. 103). Elaborating at another time he said, "I consider it as possible to convert men into republican machines. This must be done if we expect them to perform their parts properly in the great machine of the government of the state ... the wills of the people ... must be fitted to each other by means of education before they can be made to produce regularity and unison in government" (Glenn, 1987, pp. 30-31). According to Tyack (1967, p. 83), many Americans of this time period purposefully sought via education to develop the "artifact of American nationality."

Herein lies the great dilemma for the leaders of the time. That dilemma was to produce people to function like parts of a machine while at the same time preserving the personal liberties that they fought for so sacrificially. The unfolding of this dilemma bought conformity at the price of liberty and particularly educational liberty.

Consider Rush's statement: "... the only foundation for a useful education in a republic is to be laid in Religion. Without this there can be no virtue, and without virtue there can be no liberty, and liberty is the object and life of all republican governments" (Tyack, 1967, p. 103).

Rush was very specific about the religion of his choice: "... the religion I mean to recommend in this place, is the religion of Jesus Christ ... all its doctrines and precepts are calculated to promote the happiness of society, and the safety and well being of civil government" (Tyack, 1967, p. 103). Herein we can see a major focus of this phase of history—namely, that promotion of the national good was the highest order. This orientation in fact supplants the earlier orientation that the highest good was promotion of the Christian way. For these promoters of republicanism and particularly for those like Rush of a biblical orientation, education became their Tower of Babel. That is, education was revered as the way to be readied for service to the government.

A second major stream is also revealed in Rush's presentation: "I am aware that I dissent from one of those paradoxical opinions with which modern times [1786] abound; that it is improper to fill the minds of youth with religious prejudices of any kind, that they should be left to choose their own principles, after they have arrived at an age in which they are capable of judging for themselves" (Tyack, 1967, p. 103). It would seem that for many, freedom from denominational control was not motivated so much by preference for a different denominational choice but instead for no denominational inculcation at all. Rush's identifications of both this apparently widely held "prejudice" against religious inculcation and the preoccupation with preserving the republic account in large degree for the acceptance of nonsectarian public or common schools. The biblically consistent Protestant ethic of how to live the "good citizen" life without denominational indoctrination could be taught with approval of most if not all Protestant sects.

Initial Forms of Education

For educational vanguard Massachusetts, initial forms of

education had a religious purpose. The civil sphere was used as an instrument of religious policy to enforce certain educational expectations even if that meant that parental authority would be violated. Movement toward pluralism in Massachusetts made its education policies similar to those of many other early colonies. In this emerging phase of educational purpose, civic and religious interests did an about-face from the earlier phase. Now national welfare was the purpose and religion and morality were the method for this purpose. Again, parental authority over children was conditioned within the context of preserving civil government. It did not seem to matter that the Creator-given inalienable right of parenting would, on occasion, be violated by governmental self-perpetuation even when the violation of similar inalienable rights was the Declaration's stated reason for separating from Great Britain.

The Declaration of Independence and its relatives, the Constitution and the Bill of Rights, generally reflected the prevailing spirit of the times. The mutually oppositional forces of disestablishment of religion throughout the colonies versus state sovereignty over establishments eventually freed religion from national control via the First Amendment. This spirit of disestablishment also made government support and financing of sectarian schools highly problematic. Common public schools therefore became the method of schooling as sectarian schools began to lose favor and financial support. With subsidiarity thinking rationalizing educational policies, it was a logical eventuality that governments support public schools and public schools only.

Religion in schools became nonsectarian, that is, nondenominational, with an emphasis on devotional and other exercises nonoffensive to most Protestant groups. It was not that schools actively promoted these activities so much as it was likely to have been the duty of operating "in loco parentis" where devotions were the standard in most Protestant families (Beale, 1941, p. 54).

The public schools around the start of the 19th century assumed they had the right to teach biblical morality, and families expected this to happen. By this time the majority of Protestants held the same beliefs and purposes for their families that the nation held for itself. This same overlap of outlook also existed between the

Protestant church and the nation. While sectarianism had been disestablished, the national disposition was as existed in early Massachusetts (though different in content). That is, families, church, and the nation were again all aligned in common purpose. Patriotism, capitalism, and republicanism as collective goals, and morality and personal enlightenment as individual goals were all rooted in the Protestant ethic. The public school became the chief instrument to effect these common purposes of a more social than ecclesiastical nature. In this regard, educational historian Glenn (1987, p. 47) claims the common school "became the cornerstone of a policy of forced assimilation."

Not all groups were voluntarily part of this common purpose however. Women, blacks, American Indians, Hispanic Americans, the laboring class, Baptists, Catholics, Episcopalians, Lutherans, and Presbyterians all experienced out-group status and reform by imposition at one time or another (cf. Kaestle, 1983, chpt. 7; Rice, 1978, p. 852). While the focus in this chapter is primarily on religion, the authoritarian methodology of the common school movement regarding the working class is briefly summarized here to illustrate its broad, indiscriminate sweep across other groups.

In a Beverly, Massachusetts town meeting in March 1860, the vote was 2-to-1 for abolishing the town's two-year-old high school. According to Katz (1968), the school was imposed on the working class by reformers who wanted "a parental state to sponsor education that would help build modern industrial cities permeated by the values and features of an idealized rural life ... educational change, however, was not a gentle process: educational promoters, convinced of the value of their wares, harangued and badgered the mass of reluctant citizens; the style of reform was imposition" (pp. 49-50). Furthermore, the economic conditions were such that the working class became less and less able to benefit from the very institution that was supposed to help them. As Katz summarizes, "the communal leaders were not answering the demands of a clamorous working class: they were imposing the demands; they were telling the majority, your children shall be educated, and as we see fit" (p. 47).

Dissidents in this Protestant nationalism who went unheeded just as occurred in early Massachusetts. Whereas the unheeded in Massachusetts was anyone outside of Congregationalism, in this later time period it was anyone outside of mainstream Protestantism, and primarily the Catholics. But the matter is now all the more serious since the prevailing intention of the First Amendment was that such religious discrimination should disappear.

Religious Discrimination

The account of religious discrimination in education against the American Catholics in the 1800s is a classic example of how the same prejudicial dynamic as in Puritan Massachusetts continued to operate in spite of the spirit and the guarantees of federal and state constitutions. Except now the shoe was on the other foot, so to speak, because while the Catholics, just like the Puritans, wanted religious purity in education, discrimination worked in the opposite direction. In the case with the Catholics, it was discrimination against this desire for religious purity instead of discrimination to deprive others of the purity favored by the Puritans.

One of the reasons the Catholics were shunned was because the Irish Catholics were seen as illiterate and without any hope of being truly civilized. Some public school textbooks even taught that Irish immigration would make the United States the "common sewer of Ireland" (Kaestle, 1983, p. 163). But the larger factor was that Catholics did not assimilate well into American culture because of their allegiance to a head not of the American civil establishment. Their sovereign, the pope, in fact, gave them their political views and orientations, and their sovereign was not always seen by Protestants as being totally moral. They owed their allegiance to a foreign leader, and they stayed aloof and apart from the Protestant dilemmas; in fact, they even used a different Bible than the Protestants. Many Protestants were suspicious that the Catholics would try to take control of this country and transform it into a "catholic country" such that, from a historical perspective, civil and religious liberties would again be lost (Garrison, 1948, p. 22).

This Protestant hostility to Catholics was not a new phenomenon. American nationalism was closely linked to Protestantism and against Catholicism just as occurred in England prior to the American settlement (Morgan, 1972, p. 7). In England, the 1559 Acts of Supremacy and Uniformity were aimed at excluding Catholics from social and political power. One of the reasons Catholics were not trusted was because of the perceived intolerance of the Catholics toward the Protestants. At any rate, the reciprocal intolerance of the English toward the Catholics was carried to America where it flourished. The situation is summed up well in the words of a leading liberal Protestant of the times: "Manifestly there is an irreconcilable difference between papal principles and the fundamental principles of our free institutions" (see Morgan, 1972, p. 52).

Early in their migration to this country, the Roman Catholics established schools of their own just as did many other groups. By the early 1830s the massive immigration of Irish Catholics into New York City resulted in a significant ethnic community. With the desire for democratic participation on the increase and with their numbers growing, Irish Catholics also desired more direct citizenship participation and particularly educational privileges. But while their tax dollars were used to support the Protestant public schools, they were either purposely excluded from teaching since their particular dogma was shunned in schools, or they chose not to teach because their conscience could not abide with the Protestant content. As a result they naturally expected a share of school funds to operate their own schools, as was the practice with other denominations. But as Beale (1941, p. 99) indicates, Protestants objected to their monies going to the potentially subversive papists, and the country was adamant against supporting schools controlled by a so-called foreign and perhaps even subversive sovereign.

One resolution to this problem was the practice of supporting religious schools with public monies. In 1830, the town of Lowell, Massachusetts granted money to Catholic schools and several years later included two such schools in their school system. Pennsylvania had laws allowing for financial support to parochial schools as did New Jersey (Beale, 1941, p. 99). But overall, the country generally excluded Jews, infidels, pagans, atheists, and Catholics from leadership and recognition in the public school system. The state of Maine even denied Catholic objections to use of the Protestant Bible in mandatory school readings (*Donahoe* v. *Richards*, 1854). In 1858 a Catholic child was beaten for refusing to read the Protestant Bible in a Boston public school (Beale, 1941, p. 102).

At the root of the problem was the contradiction of two different and often opposing doctrines (i.e., Protestantism and Catholicism) competing for public tax support of their respective educational institutions. The Catholics obviously objected to Protestant favoritism, and the Protestants objected to Catholic demands.

In the early 1800s, the few Catholic schools operating in New York City received a portion of the state school subsidy to that city. This was also true for the schools of the Public School Society, the Manumission Society, the Orphan Asylum Society, and several other denominational societies. However, in 1825, the city council restricted the school funds to nondenominational schools only. The Catholics objected with the counter charge that the eligible schools of the Public School Society were not nondenominational as claimed but of a Protestant perspective and thus offensive to the Catholics. Their petitions continued to fail even when Governor Seward supported them with an appeal to the legislature to allow "the children of foreigners" to have schools with teachers of their own language and faith for "qualifying their children for the high responsibilities of citizenship" (Cremin, 1980, p. 167). Not only was the proposal rejected by the legislature, but in 1842 the legislature enacted into law the provision to subsume the schools of the Public School Society into the state school system and forbade the distribution of public funds to any school "in which any religious sectarian doctrine or tenet shall be taught, inculcated, or practised" (Cremin, 1980, p. 168). Similar actions occurred in other states about the same time. For instance, when the Bishop of Philadelphia protested against the Catholic children being required to read the Protestant King James Bible, preferring the Douay Bible instead, the community perceived this to be a "papist attack" on the Bible. This only fueled the ongoing dispute between Protestant Americanism and Catholicism, causing riots in the city and several Catholic schools to be burned (Beale, 1941, p. 101).

The contradiction that comes out of all of this is in the hypocrisy of the Protestants. The Public School Society's teaching manual (McCarthy, Skillen & Harper, 1982, p. 65) reveals that at least some of the instructional content was biblically based. As in most of the nation at this point, most Protestants were willing to trust the state for educating their children because the Protestant religion was a natural characteristic of the culture and the schools alike. Yet the Catholic schools in New York were denied public funds because they failed to pass a secular test that the Public School Society somehow managed to pass (cf. McCarthy, Skillen, & Harper, 1982, p. 65) in spite of their Bible-based instruction.

This national atmosphere of hostility against Catholics soured them against accepting the public school system and encouraged them, instead, to develop their own parochial school system. Highly critical of the decisions in New York, Bishop Hughes urged Catholics to assume responsibility for educating their own children. He charged that the public school system in New York City was not even "suited to a *Christian* land, whether Catholic or Protestant, however admirably it might be adapted to the social condition of an enlightened paganism" (Cremin, 1980, p. 169). The First Plenary Council (1852) of the Catholic church advised parents to "Listen not to those who would persuade you that religion can be separated from secular instruction" (Kaestle, 1983, p. 169). Then in 1884 the Third Plenary Council of the Catholics established their policy that a parochial school be erected near each Catholic church and that parents send their children to these Catholic schools unless excused at the diocese level.

The fate of the Catholics stands as a woeful paradox of the common school movement. With the common schools moving to nondenominational Protestantism, they were actually abandoning the strong biblical foundations upon which the early schools were founded. In this sense, the Catholics were more the perpetuators of the Puritan idea of a strong religious basis for education than were the Protestant inheritors of the Puritan-inspired system. Another ironical aspect of this situation is that in the century after the passage of the First Amendment, Bishop Hughes contended legitimately that mandatory attendance in the public schools was a violation of the religious conscience of Catholic families. With the First Amendment making the spirit of religious freedom such a promoted human right in the nation, it would not be expected that civil authority would have the temerity to position common schools against this right.

Yet not only did the Catholics have to repeatedly petition for the right of religious conscience, they eventually had to withdraw to start their own system just as the colonists did in reaction to King George III's violations of their basic rights. The founding colonists' major appeal of "no taxation without representation" is mirrored all too accurately in Bishop Hughes' request to the New York City Council that they not "take from Catholics their portion of the fund by taxation and hand it over to those who do not give them an equivalent in return ... do not tie them [the Catholics] to a system ... from which they can receive no benefit" (McCarthy, 1987, p. 63).

How such a blatant violation, with civil government endorsement, of this basic right could exist seems at least partially understood through the words of Horace Bushnell. He wrote, in 1853, that "the common school is, in fact, an integral part of the social order... An application against common schools is so far an application for the dismemberment and reorganization of the civil order of the state... Common schools are nurseries thus of a free republic, private schools of factions..." (Glenn, 1987, p. 45). Anyone then, including the Catholics, who could not support the public school system at that time was considered un-American.

To understand the mentality that justified depriving a group of their religious freedom for the cause of expected civil order and national well-being, we look deeper into two interacting phenomena in the early history of the country. One has already been cued through Benjamin Rush's statement regarding the reluctance to foster religious beliefs onto others. This orientation spawns a movement away from doctrinal purity toward civic morality of the majority opinion as typified in Horace Mann's efforts in education. Naturally filling the void was the almost religiously sacred hope—the second phenomenon—that some held out for the role of the new republic. This religion of republicanism was rooted in Enlightenment rationalism "and was articulated in terms of the destiny of America, under God, to be fulfilled by perfecting the democratic way of life for the example and betterment of all mankind" (Mead, 1976, p. 135). The movement was typified by leaders like Benjamin Rush and Thomas Jefferson. Yet because each of these two orientations so intricately involve the other, they are almost impossible to separate. For discussion purposes we will nonetheless try to explain these two forces separately. Since Jefferson's influence precedes Mann's in chronological sequence, Jefferson's ideas will be discussed first.

Civil Religion

By and large Jefferson's ideas reflect those of Enlightenment thinking. The Age of Enlightenment (the 18th century) describes the character of thought that human reason would enable mankind to discover natural laws of human existence by which a glorious if not a utopian society could be achieved. The country of France was a major site for the nurturance of Enlightenment thought. So influential was France's Enlightenment contribution to the world that Thomas Jefferson said every man (including himself) had two homelands, his own and France (Brinton, et al., 1967, p. 46). Proponents of Enlightenment thought were highly critical of religious control of education and religiously motivated practices as in the heavy emphasis on ancient languages and theology. The influential Enlightenment educator and Frenchman Jean Jacques Rousseau (1712-178) rebelled, as did many others, against Calvinist dogma calling instead for toleration and elevation of experiential judgments and practical experience over the decrees of religious authorities.

In a more general way, the notion of Enlightenment philosophers was that reason should replace religious doctrine because, among other reasons, God (if He even existed at all) had abandoned the world to be run by the exalted reason of mankind. Enlightenment driven tolerance and trust in natural law destroyed the dictum of the divine right of King's, elevated the right of individuals, and led to the belief that governments were to operate according to the will of the people. Rousseau's influential work, *The Social Contract*, made the general will of all the people the rule of government. In his conception, the state would receive the allegiance of its citizens that heretofore went to the church. Thus traditional religion would be replaced by civil religion. The general will of the citizens now formulated moral and political standards for the good of the whole community.

Part of the Enlightenment thinking and particularly of the French Revolution (last decade of the 1700s) was that education would be a prime vehicle for setting the people free. The hope of a national school system would enable remaking of the people. Mandatory attendance in these schools by all children would free the children from old aristocratic ideas, even those of their parents (Glenn, 1987, pp. 29-31).

Influential Leaders

The outlook of many influential leaders in the U.S. at that time reflected similar ideas. These leaders included Benjamin Rush, Robert Coram, James Sullivan, Noah Webster, Pierre Samuel DuPont de Nemours, Samuel Knox, and Samuel Harrison Smith (Good & Teller, 1973, p. 77). Two who were highly influenced in this regard were Thomas Jefferson and Benjamin Franklin, both of whom were ambassadors to France toward the end of the 18th century. For Jefferson and others, the new U.S. republic must be perpetuated not by an "artificial aristocracy" as in past times but by a natural one. This "natural aristocracy" would result from the sound preparation of gifted and able leaders as well as the development of a knowledgeable electorate—both through educational efforts. Benjamin Rush believed that education could help "promote the duration of replication forms of government far beyond the terms limited for them by history, or the common opinion of mankind" (see Tyack, 1967, p. 84). The "Bill for the More General Diffusion of Knowledge" that Jefferson submitted to the Virginia legislature in 1779, stated that while "certain forms of government are better calculated than others to protect individuals in the free exercise of their natural rights, and at the same time themselves better guarded against degeneracy, yet experience hath shewn that even under the best forms those entrusted with power have, in time and by slow operations, perverted it into tyranny..." From this backdrop, Jefferson believed that the most effectual means of preventing this would be to illuminate, as far as practicable, the minds of the people at large, and more especially to give them knowledge of those facts which history exhibiteth, that, possessed thereby of the experience of other ages and countries, they may be enabled to know ambition under all its shapes and prompt to exert their natural powers to defeat its purpose.

Laws were expected to be administered wisely and honestly since the leaders would, by Jefferson's educational plan, be made wise and honest: "Those persons whom nature has endowed with genius and virtue should be rendered by liberal education worthy to receive and able to guard the sacred deposit of the rights and liberties of their fellow-citizens" and that these "should be sought for and educated at the common expence of all..." (Knight & Hall, 1951, p. 300). This plan, which did not get accepted until 1870 (Kaestle, 1983, p. 9), was the first attempt to institutionalize a state-wide public school system in the United States. In it, Jefferson proposed that all "free" children "shall be taught, reading, writing, and common arithmetick" as well as be "acquainted with Graecian, Roman, English, and American history" for three years tuition-free and then longer if financed by their parents. Obviously Jefferson's plan was very progressive if not prophetic.

Other leaders and spokesmen of the time were equally concerned about ensuring the longevity of the republic. George Washington favored, as did all of the first six presidents, a federal university so students would not contract the "principles unfavorable to republican government" if they were to study abroad. "The more homogeneous our citizens can be made in their particulars," he said, "the greater will be our prospect of permanent union." Proposed apparently for the first time by Benjamin Rush in 1787, a federal university was specifically omitted from the powers of Congress consistent with Madison's negative motion at the Constitutional Convention (Good & Teller, 1973, p. 89).

The views of Benjamin Franklin coincide closely with those of Thomas Jefferson regarding perpetuation of the republican government through educational efforts. He said in 1749,

The good Education of Youth has been esteemed ... as the surest Foundation of the Happiness both of private Families and Commonwealths. Almost all Governments have therefore made it a principal object of their attention, to establish and endow with proper Revenues such Seminaries of Learning, as might supply the succeeding age with Men qualified to serve the Publick with Honor to themselves, and to their country (Knight & Hall, 1951, p. 75).

Noah Webster similarly wrote (in 1788) that since Americans now had "an empire to raise" and "a national character to establish," they must do it through "a broad system of education" (Knight & Hall, 1951, p. 96). He said, "systems of education should be adopted and ... may implement in the minds of American youth ... just and liberal ideas of government and with an inviolable attachment to their own country... The only practical method to reform mankind is to begin with the children... Education should be the first care of a legislature..." (Glenn, 1988, pp. 76-77). He intended to educate the poorer classes of citizens to be "useful members of society" (p. 77). To protect the purity of this American idealism, Georgia had a law that disbarred its residents from civic office for the number of years spent in study abroad.

Noah Webster's desire "to see America assume a national character" was a prime reason for his writing of textbooks that promoted uniformity, particularly in principles of the written and spoken word. Additionally, students must be taught, according to Webster, "that there can be no desirable liberty but in a republic, and that government, like all other sciences, is of a progressive nature" (Tyack, 1967, p. 87). Obviously, Webster's theory calls for a homogenizing educational system. In his 1798 edition of the *American Spelling Book*, Webster added the "Federal Catechism," which extolled the advantages of republicanism against other major forms of government. According to educational historian David Tyack (1967, p. 88), this instruction in the principles of government was essentially indoctrination.

As mentioned earlier, republic conformity prevailed in its paradoxical relationship with individual liberty—both of which were unique to the American way. In fact, Jefferson envisioned that the University of Virginia would be a "seminary" to keep alive the "vestal flame" of republicanism and to graduate "disciples" to carry its "doctrine" to the various states where they "will have leavened thus the whole mass" (Tyack, 1967, p. 91). It has been suggested that Jefferson was so anxious for the success of the great American experiment in liberty and self-government that any attack on him was interpreted as a threat to this new government (Tyack, 1967, p. 90).

While Benjamin Rush has to be counted in the company of Jefferson and others regarding education of the republic national character in each child, he nonetheless correctly identified the method of intolerance ironically shared with other belief systems in this country's young history: "We only change the names of our vices and follies in different periods of time. Religious bigotry has yielded to political intolerance. The man who used to hate his neighbor for being a Churchman of a Quaker now hates him with equal cordiality for" a different reason (Tyack, 1967, p. 91).

But sad as it is, this intolerance in the cause of national conformity is only part of the picture. The other part is implied in Rush's statement above. That is, political intolerance was in effect religious intolerance. In other words, this zeal for republican conformity of character served a religious purpose for its adherents and even for its opponents as well. One example of this political and religious intolerance is seen in the futile attempts of the Catholics and Bishop Hughes to have the religious liberty to educate their children.

Few, we dare to say, would take exception to Jefferson's statement that any tax which would be collected to pay for a free public school system "is not more than the thousandth part of what will be paid to kings, priests and nobles who will rise up among us if we leave the people in ignorance." It was in this spirit that Jefferson wrote in 1786 to his friend George Wythe to "Preach, my dear sir, a crusade against ignorance; establish & improve the law for educating the common people" (Tyack, 1967, p. 117). While too much can be made of word meanings, Jefferson's use of words like "preach" and "crusade" symbolize, if they don't realistically actualize, his valuation of education as Messianic.

Clues to Jefferson's religious characterization of education are not in just his favorable metaphors from biblical statements. From this evidence of his familiarity with the Bible, it seems unusual that Jefferson would counter his biblical metaphors by proclaiming "that the people alone can protect us against these evils [of despotic rulers]" (Tyack, 1967, p. 117). This statement of the ultimate control of a destiny by the people themselves, while counter to biblical pronouncements that God is in charge of all events, is entirely consistent with Enlightenment thinking. As mentioned earlier, Jefferson's ideas drew heavily from the French Enlightenment philosophy. So not only did education become, for Jefferson and others, the means for guaranteeing republic conformity, it also became the purveyor of a morality and value system that, while Protestant in its roots, was civil in its locus of hope. As Little explains, "the religion of Jefferson should properly be called a 'civil religion'" (1974, p. 194). While this dimension of national character building was noble and desirable, the zeal by which it was proposed and its replacement of bedrock religious teachings was not so noble or desirable to those of conventional religious persuasions.

In addition, the hope that public education was to be the new machinery to effect a successful republic was not universally shared. As a whole, the country was skeptical both of greater control of education by central government and new levels of taxation. The logic of liberty deprivation to protect liberty did not make sense. Many were not at all convinced, in fact, that the already existing educational arrangements were faulty and that the republic would fail unless educational change occurred (Kaestle, 1983, p. 9).

Still, a number of national leaders of the 18th century, when speaking on education, transferred it from a religious to a civil matter. Some, like Benjamin Rush who professed to have the whole counsel of the Bible ("the religion I mean to recommend ... is the religion of Jesus Christ"), nonetheless seemed to make civil government the purpose for religion:

> My only business is to declare, that all its [the Christian revelation] doctrines and precepts are calculated

273

to promote the happiness of society, and the safety and well-being of civil government. A Christian cannot fail of being a republican ... a Christian cannot fail of being wholly inoffensive, for his religion teacheth him, in all things to do to others what he would wish, in like circumstances, they should do to him (Tyack, 1967, p. 103).

Students of the Bible would claim that the preeminence of Rush's civil purpose for religion is directly counter to biblically-inspired priorities. Instead, the preeminence of biblical over civil purpose is evidenced by Christ's disciples disobeying (Acts 4:19-20 and 5:29) civil authority in preference to God's commands as well as to Jesus' own statement that He did not come to bring peace but a sword (Matthew 10:34,35).

The purpose of these character examinations is to suggest how education perspectives of that time incorporated viewpoints only superficially compatible with earlier orientations. Thomas Jefferson's and Horace Mann's views on education help us make this point clearer. In fact, it is widely believed "that the elimination of sectarianism from the American public schools resulted chiefly if indeed not exclusively from the efforts of Horace Mann in Massachusetts" (Pfeffer, 1967, p. 329).

Jefferson's Religion in Education

Jefferson, too, seemed to be oblivious to the contradictions in his position. It was Jefferson who said, "I have sworn upon the altar of God eternal hostility against every form of tyranny over the mind of man" (Koch & Peden, 1972, p. 557). And it was Jefferson who said,

Almighty God hath created the mind free ... that all attempts to influence it by temporal punishments, or burthens, or by civil incapacitations, tend only to beget habits of hypocrisy and meanness, and are a departure from the plan of the holy author of our religion, who ... chose not to propagate it by coercions ... that the impious presumption of legislators and rules, civil as well as ecclesiastical ... have assumed dominion over the faith of others... (Lee, 1961, pp. 66,67)

For all these protestations, Jefferson in his own way did just what he protested—he imposed his religious beliefs on others, as we shall see. Jefferson outwardly projected in many ways a hands-off approach about promoting his religious beliefs. He boasted never using his office or position to openly endorse his particular religious views onto others. For instance, in declining to approve a national day of prayer as a recommendation to the nation's citizens, he conservatively reasoned that such a proclamation, while not law, would have the force of law and thus possibly be injurious to another's religious conscience. He similarly said, "while I claim a right to believe in one God, I yield as freely to others that of believing in three. Both religions, I find, make honest men, and that is the only point society has any right to look to" (Sanford, 1984, p. 90).

Yet, in other ways Jefferson was not so much the neutral leader that he prided himself to be. His phrase "preach a crusade against ignorance, establish and improve the law for educating the common people" (Koch & Peden, 1972, p. 395) reveals the religious qualities that he ascribed to education. Because he saw mankind as capable of solving its own problems, education, for Jefferson, was the way of salvation. As he said in a letter to DuPont de Nemours in 1816, "Enlighten the people generally and tyranny and oppressions of body and mind will vanish like evil spirits at the dawn of day" (Lee, 1961, forward). Similarly, in 1820 he wrote to William Jarvis, "I know no safe depository of the ultimate powers of the society but the people themselves; and if we think them not enlightened enough to exercise their control with a wholesome discretion, the remedy is not to take it from them, but to inform their discretion by education" (Lee, 1961, p. 17).

But the paradox or even contradiction is that Jefferson's activities in education eventually led to taking control from the people. Not only did schooling become mandatory and at public expense, but the Bible began to be forsaken as a source of wisdom and truth.

For Jefferson, reason not revelation was the final determiner of truth. He wrote to Peter Carr from Paris in 1787 (Lee, 1961, p.

148) that "Your own reason is the only oracle given you by heaven, and you are answerable not for the rightness but uprightness of the decision." This Jefferson said to Carr in the context of deciding whether there is even a God and whether Jesus was also a god. This reason, he said, was to be used to decide whether the supernatural facts recorded in the Bible (e.g., virgin birth of Jesus) were true or not. Also, the phrase that we are "answerable not for the rightness" of such decisions reveals that conformity to absolute standards was less important than the proper use of reason (i.e., "uprightness of the decision") to arrive at a conclusion.

In specific reference to education, Jefferson thought that the combined actions (in which he had a direct authorship) of providing religious freedom and of providing public education to all would ensure an orderly government. In other words, as he explained in his 1813 letter to John Adams (Lee, 1961, p. 165), religious freedom would "put down the aristocracy of the clergy" and restore "to the citizen the freedom of the mind..." By default, so to speak, he went on to claim that his educational plan "would have raised the people to the high ground of moral respectability necessary to their own safety, and to orderly government..." Obviously, according to Jefferson, education was to do for the people what the "aristocracy of the clergy" was to be prevented from doing. As it happened, Jefferson's natural religion did become the public philosophy of the new nation (McCarthy, Skillen, & Harper, 1982, p. 28) as it filled the void left by the disestablished denominations.

This attitude of substituting education and the development of reason for religious instruction showed itself in two streams of thought for Jefferson. First and most frequently quoted is his prohibition of a sectarian or denominational professorship at his University of Virginia supposedly but questionably in keeping with "the constitutional reasons against a public establishment of any religious instruction..." (Lee, 1961, p. 79). As a substitute, however, he proposed that a professor of ethics carry the responsibility of

> the proofs of the being of a God, the creator, preserver, and supreme ruler of the universe, the author of all the relations of morality, and of the laws and obligations they infer

... to which adding the developments of the moral obligations of those in which all sects agree, with a knowledge of the languages, Hebrew, Greek, and Latin a basis will be formed common to all sects. (Lee, 1961, p. 126)

Religious instruction was to occur, after all, apparently without doctrinal reference to the Bible and certainly without influence of any particular sectarian spokesman. Denominations were encouraged to establish their own institutions and professorships nearby, with access to but independent of the university. The goal was "by bringing the sects together, and mixing them with the mass of other students, we shall soften their appetites, liberalize and neutralize their prejudices, and make the general religion a religion of peace, reason, and morality" (Lee, 1961, p. 79). As Little has concluded, this "religion of Jefferson should properly be called a 'civil religion'" (Little, 1974, p. 194) because civil order and affirmation of God both arise out of man's nature rather than from an external and divine source.

The preeminence of reason over biblical teaching for Jefferson is impactfully revealed in his bill to provide education for all children in the state of Virginia. Explaining his position in "Notes on the state of Virginia, Query XIV," Jefferson looked to his bill to diffuse knowledge.

wherein the great mass of the people will receive their instruction, the principal foundations of future order will be laid here. Instead, therefore, of putting the Bible and Testament into the hands of the children at an age when their *judgments* [emphasis added] are not sufficiently matured for religious inquiries, their memories may here be stored with the most useful facts from Grecian, Roman, European, and American history. The first elements of morality too may be instilled into their minds such as, when further developed as their judgments advance in strength, may teach them how to work out their own greatest happiness, by showing them that it does not depend on the condition of life in which chance has placed them, but is always the result of good conscience, good health, occupation and freedom in all just pursuits... (Lee, 1961, p. 95)

Obviously Jefferson did have his own view of the way to develop religion and morality and actively promoted this onto others in a somewhat innocuous and seemingly well-intentioned way. As is obvious from the citations above, Jefferson promoted religious teachings he favored but was adamantly opposed to sectarian teaching. Yet his religious beliefs were founded, in short, on the supremacy of reason over revelation. Certainly Jefferson was entitled to whatever religious opinion he had since, just as he taught, man does not answer to other men for his religious beliefs. Yet inconsistent with what he wrote, his liberal/civil/Unitarian religious leanings were promoted onto others by way of "civil incapacitations" for the children in the publicly-supported schools of the state of Virginia and the students at the publicly-supported institution of higher learning—the University of Virginia.

Mann's Religion in Education

The tenor of much of what is said about early proponents, like Jefferson, Franklin, and Mann, of a national public education system is that they were zealous for ensuring the success of the new republic as a guardian of freedom and liberty. The general impression regarding these spokesmen is that they were not antireligious but in fact believed that education could not be separated from religious or moral precepts. Mann said in his Tenth Annual Report (1846) to the Massachusetts school board, "Religion and knowledge—two attributes of the same glorious and eternal truth, and that truth the only one on which immortal or mortal happiness can be securely founded..." (Knight & Hall, 1951, p. 165). It was, in fact, Mann's religious views, just as with Jefferson, that formed his educational views. For instance, he argues for education on theological grounds:

I believe in the existence of a great, immortal, immutable principle of natural law, or natural ethics,-a principle antecedent to all human institutions, and incapable of being abrogated by any ordinance of man,-a principle of divine origin, clearly legible in the ways of Providence as those ways are manifest in the order of nature and in the history of the race, which proves the *absolute right* to an education of every human being that comes into the world, and which, of course, proves the correlative duty of every government to see that the means of that education are provided for all... (Knight & Hall, 1951, p. 165)

Mann similarly argued for the content of education on theological or religious grounds: "Are they so educated that when they grow up, they will make better philanthropists and Christian, or only grander savages?-for, however loftily the intellect of man may have been gifted, however skillfully it may have been trained, if it be not guided by a sense of justice, a love of mankind and a devotion to duty, its possessor is only a more splendid, as he is a more dangerous barbarian" (Cremin, 1980, p. 141).

Mann also argued the purpose of education from a theological basis. Mankind, he believed, was capable of being improved, and education would accelerate that improvement (Blumenfeld, 1985, p. 188). Mann maintained that responsible citizenship and leadership in this free Republican society would be the vehicle for guarding the liberty of all.

Speaking on the topic of government in 1842, he said, "It is the heresy and the blasphemy of believing and avowing, that the infinitely good and all-wise Author of the universe persists in creating and sustaining a race of beings, who, by a law of their nature, are forever doomed to suffer all the atrocities and agonies of misgovernment, either from the hands of others, or from their own." Referring to the new nation of the U.S., he said, "The great experiment of Republicanism,-of the capacity of man for self government,-is to be tried anew... Two dangers then, equally fatal, impend over us.-The danger of ignorance ... and the danger of vice" (Tyack, 1967, p. 132). To correct these two problems, Mann looked to the common schools: "Never will wisdom preside in the halls of legislation and its profound utterances be recorded on the pages of the statute book, until common schools ... create a more far-seeing intelligence and a purer morality than has ever yet existed among communities of men" (Cremin, 1980, p. 137). He continued, "As the child is father to the man, so may the training of the schoolroom expand into the institutions and fortunes of the state" (Cremin, 1980, p. 139). Mann truly believed that

> the common school is the greatest discovery every made by man... Let the common school be expanded to its capabilities, let it be worked with the efficiency of which it is susceptible, and nine-tenths of the crimes in the penal code would become obsolete: the long catalogue of human ills would be abridged; men would walk more safely by day; every pillow would be more inviolable by night; property, life, and character held by a stronger tenure; all rational hopes respecting the future brightened. (Blumenfeld, 1985, p. 211)

Mann obviously followed in the Enlightenment tradition of envisioning mankind as capable of solving all the problems of humanity. This Enlightenment humanism was professed very clearly by Mann in 1837:

> ...but, for myself, natural religion stands as pre-eminent over revealed religion as the deepest experience over the lightest hearsay. The power of natural religion is scarcely begun to be understood or appreciated ... and however much the lights of revealed religion may have guided the generations of men amid this darkness of mortality, yet I believe that the time is come when the light of natural religion will be to that of revealed as the rising sun to the day-star that preceded it. (Blumenfeld, 1985, pp. 199-200)

It would appear that education became, if not God, then at least the divine voice in Mann's continued construction of moral truth. In his First Annual Report (1837) to the Massachusetts Board of Education, he wrote,

> that hereditary opinions on religious subjects are not always coincident with truth ... each sect according to its own creed, maintain separate schools ... where the gospel, instead of being a temple of peace, is converted into an armory of deadly weapons for social, interminable warfare. Of such disastrous consequences, there is but one remedy and one preventive. It is the elevation of the common school. (Cremin, 1957, p. 33)

In his Tenth Annual Report (1846) he declared that "the establishment of Free schools was the boldest every promulgated, since the commencement of the Christian era" (p. 59). Continuing, he said that "any community, whether natural or state, that ventures to organize a government, or to administer a government already organized, without making provision for the free education of all its children, dares the certain vengeance of Heaven..." (p. 76). He declared that the Commonwealth of Massachusetts was duty bound to pledge its property "for the education of all its youth, up to such a point as will save them from poverty and vice, and prepare them for the adequate performance of their social and civil duties" (p. 77).

In his Twelfth and final Annual Report (1848), Mann made common schools the answer to all of mankind's moral problems, saying that "moral education is a primal necessity of social existence" (p. 98). Mann bemoaned the "moral condition of all Christendom ... to say nothing of heathen nations ... that in all the ages of the world the admonitions of good man have been directed ... against these social vices ... they still continue to exist..." He asked, "Now, how best shall this deluge be repelled? What mighty power or combination of powers can prevent its inrushing, or narrow the sweep of its ravages?" Answering his own question, he said,

> The race has existed long enough to try many experiments for the solution of this great problem... Mankind have tried despotisms, monarchies, and republican forms

of government... They have established theological standards, claiming for them the sanction of Divine authority... These and other great system of measures have been adopted as barriers against error and guilt ... and yet the great ocean of vice and crime overlaps every embankment, pours down upon our heads, saps the foundations under our feet, and sweeps away the securities of social order, of property, liberty, and life.

But to all doubters, disbelievers, or dispairers, in human progress, it may still be said, there is one experiment which has never been tried... Education has never yet been brought to bear with one hundredth part of its potential force, upon the nature of children... Here then, is a new agency, whose powers are but just beginning to be understood ... we do know that far beyond any other earthly instrumentality, it is comprehensive and decisive... (Cremin, 1957, p. 101)

On first glance, it could be argued that Mann was not against but actually promoted biblical teachings. Proponents can actually quote Mann to support this viewpoint. In his Eleventh Report (1848), he denied excluding the Bible from classroom instruction: "It is not known that there is, or ever has been, a member of the Board of Education who would not be disposed to recommend the daily reading of the Bible, devotional exercises, and the constant inculcation of the precepts of Christian morality in all The Public schools... I suppose there is not, at the present time, a single town in the Commonwealth in whose schools it is not read..." (Glenn, 1988, p. 166).

In his Eighth Report (1844) he wrote, "... it is the duty of parents and of religious teachers, to cooperate with the common school teachers in their religious instructions, yet it is only in the Common School that thousands of the children in our Commonwealth can be thus instructed" (Glenn, 1988, p. 82). Even earlier, in 1840, Mann exhorted the common school teachers "to train them [the students] up to the hope of God ... to make the perfect example of Jesus Christ lovely in their eyes..." (Glenn, 1988, p. 104).

But a more complete coverage of Mann's position indicates the Bible was to be selectively used. Only portions of the Bible agreeable to all could be used, but then they could only be read and not taught: "By introducing the Bible, they introduce what all its believers hold to be the rule of faith and practice and although by excluding theological systems of human origin, they may exclude a peculiarity which one denomination believes to be true, they do but exclude what other denominations hold to be erroneous" (Glenn, 1988, p. 166).

Consistent with his personal position of not believing portions of the Bible that spoke of hell, the need for repentance and salvation, and anything other than the joys of heaven and the loving benevolence of God, Mann endorsed only those Bible teachings in the common school that offended no one, including the liberal Unitarians. In supporting the exclusion of teaching about sin and salvation in the common schools, Mann write in his diary, "Pure religion and undefiled is to visit the fatherless and widows in the affliction, etc., and that other definition, 'Do justice, love mercy, and walk humbly with thy God,'—The Orthodox have quite outgrown these obsolete notions, and have got a religion which can at once gratify their self-esteem and destructiveness" (Glenn, 1988, p. 161). In his Twelfth report (1848) he wrote, "I believe that sectarian books and sectarian instruction, if their encroachments were not resisted, would prove the overthrow of the school" (Glenn, 1988, p. 168). But Board member Edward Newton said, "The idea of a religion to be *permitted* to be taught in the schools, in which all are at present agreed, is a mockery. There is really no such thing unless it be what is called natural religion" (Glenn, 1988, p. 141).

It is apparent that Mann, as well as Jefferson and others, allowed their own particular views of religion to influence their educational policies. This phenomenon was not new in the U.S., but its application was. That is, in early Massachusetts, education had to be consistent with the Calvinist perspective. Those of other persuasions who paid taxes to the system had no real say in the matter. Clear and simple, it constituted a religious establishment.

Yet in Mann's time, the shift away from Calvinist orientations in education swung to the opposite extreme of forbidding an exclusive sectarian influence in favor of content unanimity. It was still a religious establishment except that the brand of establishment changed.

Camouflaged Neutrality

There are two troublesome aspects of this shift in exclusivism. First, majority rule in the content of education, particularly in the arena of morals and values, deprives the minority, whether of 49% or 1%, of their inalienable right to freedom of religious conscience. The common school plan proposed by Mann and others made it possible "for 51 percent of voting adults (if not a small dictatorial educational elite) to determine the religious, moral, and political ideas taught to everyone in the entire state, not just a local community" (McCarthy, Skillen & Harper, 1982, p. 55). It is the dictating of one group to another group in matters that Jefferson interestingly said were between God and man only. Such an attitude essentially places those in charge of educational content in the same relative position of indifference and arrogance that King George held toward the colonists.

Secondly, and equally dangerous, the disregard by leaders like Mann and Jefferson to individual religious persuasions as they surface in education seemed to be rooted in their personal rejection of that same religion.

We have already documented how both Mann and Jefferson, as leading spokesmen and trendsetters in education, share idiosyncratic views of religion. They both interpreted the Bible from a highly personal viewpoint. This in itself probably does not distinguish them from most others. But additionally they both apparently actively rejected the prevailing orthodoxy of the day. But, this too presents no need of concern since this has been occurring since time immemorial.

What is a cause for great concern in this matter, however, is the two-fold ramification of their personal religious positions. First, both actually seemed to be blind to the hypocrisy of their own positions, and, second, they both used the good will of their offices to manipulate the freedom of others in the very crucial intersection of religion and education.

On this first point Mann, as we have already seen, placed natural religion above revealed religion. He said in his Twelfth Report, "Our own government is almost a solitary example among the nations of the earth, where freedom of opinion and the inviolability of conscience, have been even theoretically recognized by the law..." Yet he nonetheless decreed that "sectarian books and sectarian instruction if their encroachments were not resisted, would prove the overthrow of the schools." Clearly, these two positions are contradictory. Respecting freedom of religious conscience does not at all equate to prohibiting sectarian instruction. Also, in his Twelfth Report, Mann claimed that citizens were not taxed to support educational institutions "as religious institution ... [but] as a preventive means against dishonesty, against fraud, and against violence..." (Cremin, 1957, p. 103). Yet, in this same report he defends using the Bible in schools by rhetorically asking, "If the Bible makes known those truths, which, according to the faith of Christians, are able to make men wise unto salvation, and if this Bible is in the schools, how can it be said that Christianity is excluded from the schools; or how can it be said that the school system which adopts and uses the Bible is an anti-Christian or an un-Christian system? (p. 106)

Most troublesome is the structural similarity of the behavior of those like Mann and Jefferson to the behavior of those they abhorred. That is, Mann and Jefferson both rejected what they perceived as harshness and conformity imposed by the Calvinists. Yet in the final analysis, Jefferson, and most certainly Mann, began to similarly impose conformity on others by way of their educational plans. Whether it was by the Calvinists or others, aspirations for educational control invariably involve controlling others for some personally decreed expectations.

Jefferson and Mann's perspectives as representative of many other spokesmen of the time are seen as "camouflaged neutrality" toward religious instruction in public schools. Religious for them meant what they wanted it to mean (i.e., civic morality) just as with those of earlier generations of whom they were so critical. Freedom of choice or of representation in education was operative for the majority of citizens as the Protestant ethic, and national survival became relatively synonomous in the immigrant-fed explosive growth of this embryonic nation. Yet certain groups (e.g., Catholics), similarly as pure in religious foundations of education as the founding Pilgrims, suffered the same negative discrimination that the Pilgrims eventually and wisely ceased to levy against others of different religious persuasions.

In 1795, the American Philosophical Society of Philadelphia (of which Jefferson was president from 1797 to 1815) sponsored a contest for the best essay on a national system of education. The prize was awarded jointly to two different authors in the year that Thomas Jefferson and Benjamin Rush were the two chief officers (1797). Samuel Harrison Smith based his essay on the proposition that "children belong to the state and that in their education they [the parents] ought to conform to the rules which it prescribes." He said that "it is the duty of a nation to superintend and even coerce the education of children and ... high consideration of expediency not only justify but dictate the establishment of a system which shall place under a control, independent of and superior to parental authority, the education of children" (Glenn, 1988, p. 91). This civil usurpation of parental authority in education was a fairly widespread orientation. For instance, Ohio school commissioner, Hiram Barney, wrote in 1854 that "the state may with propriety be regarded as one great School District, and the population as constituting but one family, charged with the parental duty of educating its youth." Similarly, the Wisconsin Teachers Association held, in 1865, that "children are the property of the state" (Kaestle, 1983, p. 158).

The co-recipient of the award, Samuel Knox, echoed in his essay what Smith had to say regarding a mandatory system of national education. Knox was also of the same mind as Smith in proposing that the human mind be emancipated "from the tyranny of church authority and church establishments ... theology, so far as the study of it is connected with particular forms of faith, ought to be excluded from a liberal system of national instruction..." Knox proposed, similar to the positions of Jefferson and Mann, "to make use of a well-digested, concise moral catechism" (Glenn, 1988, p. 95). In other words, as Glenn (1987) has so aptly concluded, the state claimed the right to do exactly what it was prohibiting religions from doing with state monies—that is, molding the religious values and morals of the students.

The tragic irony of the matter at this point is not just in the hypocrisy of those like Jefferson and Mann not being able to see that they were headed in the direction of violating individual and particularly parental rights to supposedly save the country. As patriotic as their motives may have been in substituting religion in education for a form of civil or nationalized religion, they were apparently blind to the similarity of their positions with King George III.

No one would contest that part of King George III's motive for his dictatorial stance toward the colonies was to enhance the fortunes and stability of the mother country. Protesting taxation without representation and deprivation of other inalienable rights, according to the colonists, had to assume a higher priority than securing the government. In fact, the colonists initially had no desire to separate from Great Britain but instead to be treated as free citizens of Great Britain just as the Magna Carta and other similar acts guaranteed.

Jefferson and Mann (as our representative examples) were acting similar to King George III. For the good of the country and particularly the success of the first ever republic, they were just as guilty as the King of injustices against the inalienable rights of citizens, including taxation without representation. Specifically their view of the role of religion in education excluded the right of tax-paying parents to have their children raised according to their religious consciences.

Parents did object, but as history shows, they lost the battle. It was reported in Ohio in 1854, for instance, that people opposed the school law "because they think its principles subversive of their constitutional and parental rights." A Massachusetts school committee of 1851 indicated that "Most of the difficulties that occur in school may be traced to one single source and that is the undue interference of parents with government" (Kaestle, 1983, p. 159). One of the acknowledged developments in education during this time period was the strenuous exertion of the state over the authority of the parents (Kaestle, 1983, p. 67).

Resistance to public education started right at the beginning. When Jefferson's plan was first introduced in 1779, he claimed it failed because of economic anxieties and scarce resources. After its third defeat in 1817, he blamed "ignorance, malice, egoism, fanaticism, religious, political, and local perversities." Rush's school plan for Pennsylvania was equally resisted in the 1830s (Kaestle, 1983, p. 9).

Make no mistake about it, however, this trend did not start with Jefferson and Mann. Recall that in the early Massachusetts colony, taxes supported Calvinistic schools in spite of the objections of its non-Calvinistic citizens. Also, recall that later the Catholics were similarly discriminated against by Protestant majorities for the very same reason—the supposed good of the Protestant nation.

From these selected instances, it would seem that religious motivations play a more pervasive role in human affairs than most like to admit or acknowledge. It would be incomplete to say that the views and injustices cited are located solely in national prosperity orientations. Beyond that, it would seem that mankind suffers from the character propensity to make others similar to one's own image particularly regarding the great issues that are ultimately religious in nature. As Katz (1968, p. 215) so succinctly put it, "one gets the impression that .... most people concerned with schools are as sure they see moral truth as were Horace Mann..." It was Mann who said "If we would have improved men, we must have improved means of educating children ... of all the means in our possession, the common school has precedence..." (cf. Glenn, 1988, p. 80).

Read (1964) is more blunt in his description of this phenomena. Without the quality of humility—"The sense of freeing oneself from be-like-meness"—man tends to behave as a demigod. A demigod, according to Read, believes the world would be better off if everyone were a reflection of the demigod himself:

> Each of these millions would have us live in the kind of housing he has in mind, work the hours he prescribes, receive the wages he thinks appropriate, exchange with whom he decrees and on terms he proposes, but, more particularly, he wants us to be educated as he thinks proper! Bear in mind, however, that not a single one of these millions is a demigod in the judgment of any other person than himself. Perhaps he may never think of

himself in such egotistical terms; he merely performs as if he were a demigod: *He would mold us in his own image*!

For Read, the educational system of the U.S. originated from this type of demagoguery:

History reveals the original 'reasoning' to have been somewhat as follows: America is to be a haven for free men. To accomplish this, we must have a people's, not a tyrant's government. However, such a democratic plan will never work unless the people are educated. But free citizens, left to their own resources, will not accomplish their intellectual upbringing. Therefore, 'we' must education 'them': compulsory attendance in school, government dictated curricula, forcible collection to defray the costs. In short, *education for the sake of others*. Of course, the early proponents of government education never put the case in these concise terms. Had they done so, they would have been discovered, at the outset, how illogical they were. Imagine: *We will insure freedom to 'the people' by denying freedom to them in education, for if their education is entrusted to freedom they will remain uneducated and, thus, will not be able to enjoy the blessings of freedom!* (p. 206)

Conclusion

We conclude with the following observations. Several factors, such as the massive immigration of many without the rock-solid biblical faith of the founding generation and the injustices of rigidly interpreted sectarianism, fostered an overall decline in the role of faith in daily life. With this orientation, the cultural atmosphere was ripe for a more direct trust in man's efforts to control his own destiny. The substance of this redirected faith was easily found in the appealing lure of the Enlightenment philosophy as espoused by Jefferson, Mann, and others. Commingled with this was the ascendancy of a trust in economic well-being and the national republican experiment over a trust in God's provision for the nation. Protestant solidarity over suspected Catholic insurgency is one outgrowth of such dynamics. The outcome of all of this for education was a turning from a belief in and a funding of biblically-centered education in favor of non-denominational education based on civil morality.

In essence, two significant positions were stabilized in education by the early to mid-1800s: "the foundations were laid for effective state control, and the historic role of schools in transmitting religious traditions was attenuated into perfunctory observances and moralizing" (Glenn, 1987, p. 28).

An inescapable truth about education is that it is not merely the teaching of truth as much as it is the teaching of truth as someone else defines it. This means that someone or some group ultimately declares what is proper and improper to learn. Given the nature of humanity such that those in authority will perpetuate what they believe and discount what they do not believe, education ultimately amounts to the conforming of one group to what another group expects. The dilemma of this reality is in determining who perpetuates what!

In the early colonies, the church was the corporate representative of the entire community, particularly in the north. The citizens (i.e., believers) promoted the church and chose its leaders to whom they willingly submitted. Thus the directives from the church to the parents regarding children's education was, in the homogeneous culture, largely welcomed and faithfully received.

With religious disestablishment, the civil government was relatively unencumbered in its ability to enforce a religion for national well-being unto citizens and particularly via education. It was not uncommon for those in civil authority to vehemently petition against religious influences in education yet to impose their own "religious" views in education in a structurally parallel way. The disestablishment of religion in education in effect amounted to the establishment of a different religion in education. Freed from religious establishments, religious conscience now fell hostage to the educational establishment.

References

Beale, Howard K. (1941). *A history of freedom of teaching in American schools*. New York: Charles Scribner's Sons.

Blumenfeld, Samuel L. (1985). *Is public education necessary?* Boise, ID: Paradigm.

Brinton, Crane, Christopher, J. B. and Wolff, R. L. (1967). *A history of civilization*. Englewood Cliffs, NJ: Prentice-Hall.

Brownson, Henry F. (1966). *The works of Orestes A. Brownson, Vol. XIX*. New York: AMS Press Inc.

Butts, R. Freeman (1950/1974). *The American tradition in religion and education*. Westport, CT: Greenwood Press Publ.

Conant, James B. (1963). *Thomas Jefferson and the development of American public education*. Berkeley: Univ. of CA Press.

Conant, James B. (1965). *Education and liberty*. Cambridge, MA: Harvard University Press.

Cremin, Lawrence A. (1980). *American education: the national experience, 1783-1876*. New York: Harper & Row.

Federer, William J. (1996). *America's God and country: Encyclopedia of quotations*. Coppell, TX: FAME Publishing Co.

Gales, Joseph (Ed.). (1834). *The debates and proceedings in the Congress of the United States*. Washington, DC: Gales and Seaton.

Garrison, Winfred E. (1948). Characteristics of American organized religion. *Annals of the American Academy of Political & Social Science*. CCLVI, March, 14-24.

Glenn, Jr., Charles L. (1987). "Molding" citizens. In Neuhaus, Richard J. (Ed.) *Democracy and the renewal of public education*: Grand Rapids, MI: Wm. B. Eerdmans Co.

Glenn, Jr., Charles L. (1988). *The myth of the common school*. Amherst, MA: The Univ. of Mass. Press..

Good, Harry G. & Teller, James D. (1973). *A history of American education* (3rd Ed.). New York: Macmillan Publ. Co.

Henderson, John C. (1970). *Thomas Jefferson's views on public education*. New York: AMS Press.

Herberg, Will (1958). Religion, democracy and public education. In Cogley, John (Ed.) *Religion in America*. New York: World Publ. Co.

Honeywell, Roy J. (1931). *The educational work of Thomas Jefferson*. Cambridge, MA: Harvard University Press.

Kaestle, Carl F. (1983). *Pillars of the republic*. New York: Hill & Wang.

Karier, Clarence J. (1986). *The individual society, and education* (2nd Ed.). Chicago: Univ. of Illinois Press.

Katz, Michael B. (1968). *The irony of early school reform*. Cambridge, MA: Harvard Univ. Press.

Knight, Edgar W. & Hall, Clifton L. (1951). *Readings in American educational history*. New York: Greenwood Press.

Koch, Adrienne & Peden, William (1972). *The life and selected writings of Thomas Jefferson*. New York: The Modern Library.

Lee, Gordon C. (1961). *Crusade against ignorance: Thomas Jefferson on education*. New York: Teachers College Press.

Lewis, Clive S. (1947). *The abolition of man*. New York: Macmillan.

Little, David (1974). The origins of perplexity: Civil religion and moral belief in the thought of Thomas Jefferson. In Richey, R. E. & Jones, D. G. (Eds.). *American civil religion*. New York: Harper & Row.

Malone, Dumas (1948). *Jefferson the Virginian*. Boston: Little, Brown & Co.

McCarthy, Rockne, Oppewal, Donald, Peterson, Walfred & Spykman, Gordon (1981). *Society, state & schools*. Grand Rapids, MI: William B. Eerdmans Publ. Co.

McCarthy, Rockne M. (1987). Public schools and public justice. In Neuhaus, Richard J. (Ed.). *Democracy and the renewal of public education*. Grand Rapids, MI: William B. Eerdmans Publ. Co.

McCarthy, Rockne M., Skillen, James W., & Harper, Wm. A. (1982). *Disestablishment a second time*. Grand Rapids, MI: Wm. Eerdmans Publ. Co.

Mead, Sidney E. (1963/1976). *The lively experiment*. New York: Harper & Row.

Montgomery, Zach. (1889/1972). *Poison drops in the Federal Senate: The school question*. New York: Arno Press & The New York Times.

Morgan, Richard E. (1972). *The supreme court and religion*. New

York: The Free Press.

Pfeffer, Leo (1967). *Church, state and freedom* (Rev. Ed.). Boston, MA: Beacon Press.

Read, Leonard E. (1964). *Anything that's peaceful.* Irvington-on-Hudson, NY: The Foundation for Economic Education, Inc.

Rice, Charles E. (1978). Conscientious objection to public education: the grievance and the remedies. *Brigham Young University Law Review,* 847-888.

Sanford, Charles B. (1984). *The religious life of Thomas Jefferson.* Charlottesville: University of Virginia Press.

Skillen, James W. (1987). Changing assumptions in the public governance of education. In Neuhaus, Richard J. (Ed.) *Democracy and the renewal of public education.* Grand Rapids, MI: Wm. B. Eerdmans Co.

Smith, Timothy L. (1967). Protestant schooling and American nationality. *The Journal of American History, 53,* 679-695.

Tyack, David B. (1967) (Ed.). *Turning points in American educational history.* Waltham, MA: Blaisdell Publ. Co.

Chapter 8

Education <u>Must</u> Not Be Religious

Instead of consolidating the education interest of the Commonwealth in one grand central head, and that head be government, let us rather hold on to the good old principles of our ancestors, and diffuse and scatter this interest far and wide, divided and subdivided not only into towns and districts but even into families and individuals. The moment this interest is surrendered to the government, and all responsibility is thrown upon civil power, farewell to the usefulness of common schools, the just pride, honor, and ornament of New England; farewell to religious liberty, for there would be but one church; farewell to political freedom, for nothing but the name of a republic would survive such a catastrophe. (cited in Glenn, 1987, p. 36)

But were an approved system of national education to be established, all these imperfections of its present state would, in a great measure, be remedied and at the same time accompanied with many peculiar advantages hitherto unexperienced in the instruction and improvement of the human mind... It is a happy circumstance peculiarly favorable to a uniform plan of public education that this country both excluded ecclesiastical from civil policy and emancipated the human mind from the tyranny of church authority and church establishments. (cited in Glenn, 1987, p. 34)

The great object was to get rid of Christianity... The plan was to ... establish a system of state—we said *national*—schools, from which all religion was to be excluded, ... and to which all parents were to be compelled by law to send their children (Brownson, 1966, pp. 442-443).

The first quote comes from an 1840 report of the special legislative committee in Massachusetts in their recommendation to abolish the state board of education and Horace Mann's position as its secretary. It not only calls for freedom from government control in education, it likewise notes that without this freedom the education establishment will be the nation's church. Accordingly, in this chapter we will see the reality of government unilaterally deciding what religious content is and is not permitted in education. The second quote is from the award-winning 1797 essay by Samuel Knox as sponsored by the American Philosophical Society of Philadelphia. In taking an opposite perspective, it lauds the benefit of freedom from ecclesiastical control in education while arguing in the larger context for a nationalized, i.e., government controlled system of education. But as we will see in this chapter, our nationalized system provides its own system of control in matters ecclesiastical. The third quote, that from Orestes Brownson, explains the objective of a secret society of Owenites and certain Unitarians operative in New York City in the early to middle 1800s. It represents an extreme perspective regarding the degree to which certain groups disfavored the influence of religion in education. While Brownson departed from membership in the group in 1830, he noted that "the plan has been successfully pursued, the views we put forth have gained great popularity, and the whole action of the country on the subject has taken the direction we sought to give it..." (Brownson, 1966, pp. 442-443).

It would be pure speculation to suggest that the "secret infidel society" which Brownson described has given direct impulse to whatever religiously "neutral" education may currently exist in the public area. However, this we do know. The U.S. Supreme Court has banned the posting of the Ten Commandments in school since they will "induce the school children to read, meditate upon, perhaps to venerate and obey, the Commandments" (*Stone* v. *Graham*, 1980). Similarly, lower courts have declared it is unconstitutional, for instance, for a child to say lunch prayers aloud (*Reed* v. *VanHoven*, 1965). With evidence of decisions like these it is not so speculative to suggest that the spirit of that secret infidel society lives on. As we examine the status of religion in education in these contemporary times, we do so from the perspective of what is Constitutionally authorized as opposed to personal preferences and/or what we would like the Constitution to say.

Hostility to Religion in Education

Education in colonial America, and in New England in particular, served family supported and endorsed religious purposes. Local civil government served to enforce such purposes. Religious purity was maintained via homogeneous religious settlements or by making the will of the minority subservient to the majority or ruling class. While seemingly prohibited by the Bill of Rights, this establishment of religion was surreptitiously repeated through American history via the establishment of education. The prejudicial application of legal force for and against beliefs has regularly prevailed in education.

The first form of religious establishment in education (reviewed in Chapter 6) was Christian denominationalism. With the immigration of peoples not nearly as homogenous or as ardent in their faith, denominationalism gave way to American Protestantism (reviewed in Chapter 7). The civil arm of enforcement was used against those outside the general mainstream of Protestant Christianity. With the decline of doctrinal orthodoxy came the increased reliance on nationalism. All of this together constituted what is often known as civil religion.

In each era, people outside the protected religious orientations were the object of discrimination and deprivation. In this sense, the picture of tyranny was and is no different than the conditions of religious persecution under King George III from which the colonists escaped to find religious freedom. The irony of continued persecution is made worse by the use of the First Amendment to deprive citizens of the very religious freedoms it was designed to protect.

The U.S. Supreme Court, as highest interpreter of federal law, has, starting in the latter half of the 20th century, so reconstructed the First Amendment that traditional religion in general and Christian doctrine more specifically, is now largely removed from education. In effect, a different religion is protected (i.e., secularism) and Christianity, as with formal religion in general, is outlawed.

First Amendment Interpretations

Prior to discussing hostility to religion in education, it is helpful to review the meaning of the First Amendment. It is the First Amendment and particularly the Establishment Clause of that amendment that is so often cited in the court cases germane to religious issues in education. Thomas Jefferson's words of 1823 instruct us in how to interpret the First Amendment: "On every question of construction, carry ourselves back to the time when the Constitution was adopted, recollect the spirit manifested in the debates, and instead of trying what meaning may be squeezed out of the text, or invent against it, conform to the probable one in which it was passed" (Rice, 1978, p. 40 citing Ford, *The Writings of Thomas Jefferson, X*, p. 231 (1899)).

The spirit behind the construction of the First Amendment is found in the promise Madison made to Virginians in his bid for a seat in the First Congress. Namely, he promised to amend the Constitution to protect their rights. The constitutional amendments known as the Bill of Rights basically represented concerns of the various states as expressed in their respective ratification conventions. One such concern was that the federal government might supersede states' rights in religion by mandating a national religion. Madison said in the debate over the initial wording of the Amendment,

> He believed that the people feared one sect might obtain a pre-eminence, or two combine together, and establish a religion to which they would compel others to conform. He thought that if the word 'national' was introduced, it would point the amendment directly to the object it was intended to prevent" (Rice, 1978, p. 42, citing *Annals of Congress I*, 731). The adjective national was attached to the word religion to clarify the meaning of the amendment but then later omitted in the rephrasing process to satisfy the diverse interests not the least of which was the fear, on the part of the anti-federalists, of an overly strong national government. Thus, the most probable intent of the First Amendment is captured in the words of Madison and fellow Congressman Benjamin Huntington: "Mr. Madison said, he apprehended the meaning of the words to be, that Congress should not establish a religion, and enforce the legal observation of it by law, nor compel men to worship God in any manner contrary to their conscience" (Rice, 1978, p. 42, citing *Annals of Congress I*, 730). Contemporary Constitutional historian James O'Neill summarizes the early debate: "The phraseology finally adopted after long discussion accomplished the exact purpose of preventing a national church from taking the place of the dying state churches, and at the same time made possible the support of the Bill of Rights by those who still believed in *state*-established churches" (1972, p. 10).

Mr. Huntington (of Connecticut), expressing fears regarding future interpretations of the original wording, said,

> he feared ... that the words might be taken in such latitude as to be extremely hurtful to the cause of religion. He

understood the amendment to mean what had been expressed by the gentleman from Virginia [Madison]; but others might find it convenient to put another construction upon it... He hoped, therefore, the amendment would be made in such a way as to secure the rights of conscience, and a free exercise of religion, but not to patronize those who professed no religion at all. (Rice, 1978, p. 43 citing *Annals of Congress, I*, pp. 730-731)

Ironically, Madison put, in Huntington's words, a construction on the meaning of the First Amendment that was not intended by the various states. While generally reflecting concerns of the various states, Madison did, however, add his own independently authored phrase that would have equally restricted each state from violating "the equal rights of conscience" (Morgan, 1972, p. 21). Yet symbolic of the very purpose of the amendment in keeping the federal government entirely out of the state's religious orientations (some states had establishments of religions; others did not), Madison's restriction on the states was quickly omitted from and never reintroduced again into the amendment. Concluding his review on this matter, Katz said, "It seems undeniable that the First Amendment operated, and was intended to operate [only] to protect from congressional interference the varying state policies of church establishment" (Morgan, 1972, p. 30). In fact, the U.S. Supreme Court itself ruled in 1845 that "the constitution makes no provision for protecting the citizens of the respective states in their religious liberties; this is left to the state constitution and laws; nor is there any inhibition imposed by the Constitution of the United States in this respect on the states" (*Permoli* v. *First Municipality of New Orleans*—McCarthy, 1983, p. 10).

Parenthetically, with this evidence that the First Amendment does not fully reflect Madison's views on the topic, subsequent commentary by Madison on interpretations and practices relevant to the First (as finally approved) need to be received with caution. Equally to be viewed with caution are those who more recently say that the Fourteenth Amendment makes the First binding on individual states. Since Madison's attempt to do this was specifically voided, this transfer hypothesis would have validity through evidence that framers of the Fourteenth wanted it to override the initial exclusion of the First unto the states. However, "Nothing has been called to our attention that either the framers of the Fourteenth Amendment or the states that adopted intended its due process clause to draw within its scope the earlier amendments to the Constitution," says Justice Reed in the 1947 *Adamson* v. *California* case (O'Neill, 1972, p. 304).

We shall soon see that in spite of the efforts of the legislators of 1789 to have the words of the First Amendment protected from becoming "hurtful to the cause of religion," the prophetic fears of Huntington have become a reality in our time. Specifically, the highest body of federal government decision making—the U.S. Supreme Court—now uses several self-constructed and invalid litmus test standards to decide whether educational/religious practices are in violation of the First Amendment (cf. Cox, 2000-2001).

The first test came in 1930 when the U.S. Supreme Court, in *Cochran* v. *Board of Education*, through Justice Charles Evans Hughes made "child benefit" the primary focus of First Amendment education-related decisions. The child-benefit theory serves to allow apparent sectarian support where it can be arguably demonstrated that the child rather than the sectarian school is the prime beneficiary as when textbooks are furnished for the children's use. This child-benefit criterion for evaluating for potential violations of the First Amendment certainly never had its precedent in First Amendment thinking or in the debates, yet it figures even larger in the 1947 *Everson* busing case and others after that.

The second test comes out of *Everson* v. *Board of Education* (1947). Speaking for the court, Justice Hugo Black set the benchmark meaning of the First Amendment Establishment Clause: "Neither a state nor the Federal Government can set up a church. Neither can pass laws which aid one religion, aid all religions, or prefer one religion over another."

From the just prior discussions and the extended discussion of Chapter 5, the only valid meaning in Black's 1947 dictum is the portion that prohibits the Federal Government from setting up a church and possibly though not necessarily the preferring of one religion over another. Black's restriction on the states is not a part of the First Amendment, even allowing for the Fourteenth Amendment, nor are his restrictions on aiding religions individually or collectively.

A third major litmus test comes out of *Lemon* v. *Kurtzman* (1971). Combining findings from three earlier cases (*Epperson* v. *Arkansas*, 1968; *Abington* v. *Schempp*, 1965; and *Walz* v. *Tax Commission*, 1970), the court ruled that for any statute to be valid it must "first, have a secular legislative purpose; second, its principal or primary effect must be one that neither advances nor inhibits religion; finally, the statute must not foster an excessive entanglement with religion." Again, as discussed earlier, the First Amendment, contrary to the Lemon wording, was specifically designed to have a religious purpose and was intended to advance the free exercise of religion. Obviously, part one and two of the Lemon test are erroneous constructions (just as Congressman Huntington feared would happen), and part three is so fraught with subjective ambiguity it is practically useless as a meaningful standard. As Justice Harvey Blackmun concluded in *Roemer* v. *Maryland* (1976), "There is no exact science in gauging the entanglement of church and state."

Another spurious test is revealed in cases involving post-secondary educational institutions when they are compared to primary or secondary educational institutions. That is, practices decreed as violations of the First Amendment in primary or secondary educational settings are ruled as valid by the Supreme Court in post-secondary settings. For instance, whereas federal grants for the construction of buildings at church-related colleges were allowed (*Tilton* v. *Richardson*, 1971), grants for maintenance and repair of facilities serving the health, welfare and safety of pupils in nonpublic grade schools was disallowed (*PEARL* v. *Nyquist*, 1973). Part of the reasoning, according to Justice Warren Burger's statement for the Court in the *Tilton* case, was that in comparison to pre-college students, "college students are less impressionable and less susceptible to religious indoctrination" and apparently, by extension, support to colleges (versus primary and secondary schools) is less likely to establish a religion.

The test is spurious because it was not the differential suscepti-bilities of the citizens that the First Amendment promoters were concerned about, but only enactments by the federal government that would establish a mandatory religion. In fact, whether all the citizens of that time either totally rejected or accepted the teachings of a single religion, the First Amendment would still be violated if that religion was made mandatory by the federal government.

The existence of these add-ons, or better, the invalidity of such constructions, was spoken to back in the early 1800s by then Chief Justice of the U.S. Supreme Court, John Marshall. Writing in *Osborn* v. *The Bank*, he said, "Courts are mere instruments of the law and can will nothing... Judicial power is never exercised for the purpose of giving effect to the will of the judge; always for the purpose of giving effect ... to the will of the law" (see Whitehead, 1982, p. 54).

There is also the balancing test to evaluate free exercise versus governmental "rights." Explained in *Wisconsin* v. *Yoder* (1972), this test invokes three questions: first, whether the individual acted out of a legitimate and sincerely held religious belief; second, whether such actions are impaired by governmental actions; and third, whether compelling governmental interests justify the burden imposed on the individual's free exercise of religion (see McCarthy, 1983, p. 13). These tests, the court says, are necessary because while the freedom to believe is "absolute," "conduct remains subject to regulation for the protection of society" (*Cantwell* v. *Connecticut*—1940).

Of all the subsequent constructions that have been placed on the original meaning of the First Amendment, perhaps the most insidious is the doctrine of parens patriae. This Old English entitlement that allows civil authorities to protect children against various forms of parental abuse often enjoys a higher priority in the court's eyes than free exercise claims. The Court's position in this regard is voiced in *Prince* v. *Massachusetts* of 1944: "acting to guard the general interest in youth's well-being, the state as *parens patriae* may restrict the parents' control by requiring school attendance... Its authority is not nullified merely because the parent grounds his claim to control the child's course of conduct on religion or conscience" (McCarthy, 1983, p. 142). Not at all a part of the First Amendment intent and a danger to parental authority in education, the parens patriae doctrine allows for civil encroachment on religious schools in direct contradiction to the guarantees of the First Amendment. More specifically, "if the state must satisfy its interest in secular education through the instrument of private schools, it has a proper interest in the manner in which those schools perform their *secular* [emphasis added] educational function" said Justice Byron R. White for the Court in *Board of Education* v. *Allen* (1968), (Alley, 1988, p. 75). Conversely, at other times the Court has denied aid to private schools primarily on the grounds that they were not secular but sectarian in nature. Obviously, with multiple constructions come contradictory results.

Prior to discussing various court decisions in more detail, it is instructive to suggest what reasonably should be permissible regarding the interaction of religion and education. In the spirit of freedom of religious conscience, religion and education can be interrelated in public schools just as long as individuals (i.e, students) are not deprived of their natural right to learn consistent with their (and their parents') religious beliefs. One way this deprivation could occur would be when certain religious practices in school settings directly inhibit the religious practices of some other persuasion. This abridgement of religious liberty is most likely to result from either the overlap of multiple religious orientations or the exclusionary promotion of one religious perspective in the same educational setting. A second area of potential trouble for religious freedom would result from the attempt to eliminate all religions from schools, thereby essentially depriving all pupils (and parents), not just some as above, of their natural right to practice their religion.

Regarding the Establishment Clause of the First Amendment, violations in education are most apt to result whereby legally-oriented mandates from the federal government prefer one religion over the other to the degree that the preferred religion carries with it the exclusivistic force of law as against other religions. The same applies at the state level even where state law allows such governmental force.

Parenthetically, the failed attempt via the 1876 Blaine Amendment to the First Amendment to prohibit the use of public funds of any kind to support any school "under the control of any religious or anti-religious sect, organization, or denomination" (Butts, 1974, p. 143) or where the creeds of such are taught, gives support to the belief that this was not the original intent of the First Amendment as Justice Black and other contend. The Republican platform of this same year (as President Grant considered a third term) equally acknowledged that a constitutional amendment was needed to prohibit public aid to church schools: "The public school system of the several states is a bulwark of the American republic; and, with a view to its security and permanence, we recommend an amendment to the Constitution of the United States, forbidding the application of any public funds or property for the benefit of any school or institution under sectarian control" (cited in Moynihan, 1978, p. 33). Again, this platform recommendation would be unnecessary if the First Amendment already accomplished this purpose as is typically thought nowadays.

Legal Establishment

The Establishment Clause is actually subsidiary to the Free Exercise Clause of the First Amendment, yet it has been scrutinized and accessed the most when education has been the context. It is subsidiary because it was by way of establishing a national religion that the colonists thought that the federal government (i.e., Congress) could, by law, deprive them of their more inclusive right of free exercise of religion. As Jefferson, Madison, and others, while president, have demonstrated, religions and their practices could be funded and promoted without violation of the Amendment. And as Constitutional scholar James O'Neill (1972, p. 10) concludes, "the First Amendment had nothing whatever to do with any theory of public financing or the propriety or impropriety of using public funds for any purpose whatever." The Congressional and military chaplain authorizations are examples in the affirmative as is the construction and maintenance of chapels at our major military educational institutions (e.g., U.S. Naval Academy, West Point, U.S. Air Force Academy).

Facilities and Salaries

The record of the U.S. Supreme Court decisions in this regard is incompatible with the intent of the First Amendment. While the Amendment does allow assistance, just not exclusive endorsement, to matters religious in education, the Supreme Court has generally decreed otherwise. Starting on a positive note, the Court has upheld construction grants to church-related colleges (*Tilton* v. *Richardson*, 1971), the issuing of revenue bonds to aid a church-related college to borrow money (*Hunt* v. *McNair,* 1973), and "noncategorical" institutional grants to church-affiliated colleges (*Roemer* v. *Maryland Board of Public Works*, 1976).

Similarly, at the pre-college level, the U.S. Supreme Court allowed the purchase of books with tax dollars for use in sectarian schools (*Cochran* v. *Board of Education*, 1930); the use of public funds for bus transportation to private school (*Everson* v. *Board of Education*, 1947); the lending of secular public school textbooks to children in sectarian schools (*Board of Education* v. *Allen*, 1968); the loan of textbooks, financing of state-mandated testing, subsidies for diagnostic testing by public officials, and remedial off-site counseling, all for non-public schools (*Wolman* v. *Walter*, 1977); and tuition tax deductions and other expenses by the parent for the child's education in parochial schools (*Mueller* v. *Allen*, 1983).

Most if not all the above decisions are deceptively positive regarding provisions of the First Amendment. They are positive in that they are consistent with the intent of the Amendment to not establish an exclusive national or regional religion. They are deceptive, however, in that almost invariably they are based on reasoning foreign to the intent of the First Amendment. Reasons given in these cases include the following: the service or the product goes primarily to the child and not the institution; the child is the prime beneficiary—not the institution; the purpose is secular—not sectarian; the probability of transmitting religious ideology is low; and the government maintains neutrality toward religion. Each of these expressed reasons go beyond the intent of the First Amendment. Actually, the only major issue that needs to be addressed regarding the Establishment Clause is whether the purpose or effect is to establish a civilly-sanctioned religious hierarchy.

Because the above decisions are based on both error and irrelevant tests of validity, confusion among decisions inevitably results. In our continuing review of Establishment Clause decisions, this conflict of results is apparent.

In spite of the above affirming decisions, the court held, to the contrary, the following similar and even almost identical activities in violation of the First Amendment. Ruled unconstitutional were reimbursements to non-public schools for salaries, textbooks, and instructional materials used to achieve purely secular educational objectives (*Lemon* v. *Kurtzman*, 1971); payments to parents to help offset educational expenses of non-public school pupils (*Essex* v. *Wolman*, 1972); direct grants to non-public sectarian schools for the maintenance and repair of facilities serving the health, welfare, and safety of the pupils (*PEARL* v. *Nyquist*, 1973); direct reimbursements to non-public schools for state-mandated testing, recordkeeping, and recording (*Levitt* v. *PEARL*, 1973); state aid to non-public schools in the form of instructional materials (e.g., maps, films), audiovisual, and laboratory equipment, and for auxiliary services (e.g., counseling (*Meek* v. *Pittenger*, 1975); grants for pupil field trips and instructional materials loaned to parents and pupils in non-public schools (*Wolman* v. *Walter*, 1977); and use of public teachers and other professionals to provide remedial instruction and guidance services to religious schools (*Aguilar* v. *Felton*, 1985). In large part, these findings of unconstitutionality were based on the perception that organized religion would be the substantial beneficiary, thereby wrongly promoting religion, and/or that approval would require too much governmental policing (i.e., "excessive entanglement") of institutional practices. But again, it must be noted that the First Amendment does not prohibit promotion of religion, only the exclusive promotion of religion which apparently was never a reality in these cases. Also, it must be noted that the First Amendment does not make the extensiveness nor expense of monitoring for possible violations a factor at all in determining whether an exclusive religion is being established. In fact, the implication that sectarian schools but not public schools needs policing regarding the expenditure of public funds is a likely betrayal of the court's overall attitude toward those religious by declaration. It would not be unreasonable to conclude that Supreme Court decisions in this regard are tailored after personal preferences about what the First Amendment should say and mean rather than what it actually says and means. Fears that religion may be promoted are exactly opposite of the intent of the framers and thus are constitutionally unfounded.

At the state and district level, similar invalidations have occurred. The rental of classroom space from a parochial school, because of inadequate public school space, was held by a Kentucky federal district court to be against the Establishment Clause because it was only the parochial school students who attended such instruction (*Citizens to Advance Public Education* v. *Porter*, 1976). A New Hampshire federal district court similar invalidated, on the basis of excessive governmental entanglement (*Americans United for the Separation of Church* and *State* v. *Paine*, 1973), the leasing of rooms in parochial schools by public schools for the purpose of instruction in secular subjects (McCarthy, 1983, p. 105). Besides constituting wrong interpretations of the Establishment Clause, the deeper injustice is that of even applying the First Amendment to state practices—the First applies *only* to Congress.

Time and Content

Whereas most of the cases presented above regarding facilities, salaries, and the like are related to sectarian schools, most decisions regarding permissible content and use of time are related to public schools. The focus in both categories, however, remains on the Establishment Clause of the First Amendment.

The court has ruled that it is permissible for public schools to give dismissed time during school hours to attend religious education programs at religious centers (*Zorach* v. *Clauseon*, 1952). However, if the location of the religious education program is within the public school setting, students cannot be released, said the court in *McCollum* v. *Board of Education* (1948). The approval given for off-site but not on-site public school religious instruction was due mainly to the belief by the court that no aid at all was to be given to religions to spread their faith. On-site instruction was thought by the court to provide pupils for religious classes even if they were not mandatory. But the court failed to grasp the intent of the First Amendment, which was to promote and safeguard religion, not to be oblivious toward it. Helping religion even on the so-called neutral ground of public school premises is not to be confused with establishing by law a religion.

From the perspective of maintaining a hands-off policy of neutrality toward religion, the court has elevated the Establishment Clause far above the Free Exercise Clause. The seemingly paranoiac aversion to aiding religion in any way at all has resulted in decisions that deprive citizens of their inalienable right to freely exercise their religious beliefs. For instance, even when objecting school children are excused, reciting a pre-composed prayer in public school is ruled as violating the Establishment Clause and thus cannot be permitted (*Engel* v. *Vitale*, 1962). The court reasoned in this case that the "wall of separation had been breached."

The same type of reasoning has also resulted in the following decisions:

1. Devotional Bible readings and school sponsored prayers are unconstitutional. Speaking for the Court, Justice Tom Clark founded the decision on the belief that the Establishment Clause prohibits placing the official support of the state or federal government behind the tenets of one or of all orthodoxies (*School District of Abington Township* v. *Schempp*, 1963). A similar decision was rendered in *Murray* v. *Curlet* (1963). Even having students arrive at school early to voluntarily read the "remarks" of the chaplain from the *Congressional Record* was judged as violating the First Amendment (*State Board of Education* v. *Board of Education of Netcong*, 1970) (Barton, 1989, p. 156).

2. Forbidding the teaching of evolution is unconstitutional because it, by some strange logic of the court, establishes Christian orthodoxy (*Epperson* v. *Arkansas*, 1968).

3. The mere posting of the Ten Commandments in

public school is unconstitutional because it establishes a religion (*Stone* v. *Graham,* 1980).

4. The teaching of remedial and enrichment classes to nonpublic school students in nonpublic school facilities at public expense is unconstitutional because "the symbolic union of government and religion in one [so-called] sectarian enterprise is an impermissible effect under the Establishment Clause" (*Grand Rapids School District* v. *Ball,* 1985).

5. The requirement that whenever evolution is taught in school, Creation Science must also be taught was ruled unconstitutional "... because the primary purpose of the Creationism Act is to endorse a particular religious doctrine, the act furthers religion in violation of the Establishment Clause" (*Edwards* v. *Aguillard,* 1987).

6. The following verse:

We thank you for the flowers so sweet;
We thank you for the food we eat;
We thank you for the birds that sing;
We thank you for everything.

when said in the morning before snack-time in an Illinois school district was declared unconstitutional (*DeSpain* v. *DeKalb County Community School District,* 1967). The Seventh Court of Appeals claimed it constituted a prayer and thus violated the First Amendment (McCarthy, 1983, p. 22). Regarding the plaintiff's complaint, a dissenting Justice noted that while the word "God" was not in the prayer, it was in the minds of the children. They were thus being asked to rule on "what the plaintiff thinks the children are thinking" (Barton, 1989, p. 160).

7. Ruled unconstitutional was a student prayer said in voluntarily attended student council assemblies. A federal district court of appeals declared (*Collins* v. *Chandler Unified School District,* 1979) that it violated

the First Amendment because it did not have a secular purpose, served to advance religion, and was excessive entanglement because of teacher involvement (McCarthy, 1983, p. 24). The court even permanently prohibited future authorizations by the school for the saying of public prayers by students at school assemblies. This is in spite of the Constitutional provision that the judicial branch can only interpret laws regarding "cases" and "controversies" (Article III, Section 2) not that it can prescribe or proscribe future actions.

Similar invalidations of school prayer have occurred in the Louisiana based *Karen B.* v. *Treen* case of 1982, the Texas based *Lubbock Civil Liberties Union* v. *Lubbock Independent School District* case of 1983, and the *Brandon* v. *Board of Education of Guilderland Central School District* case of 1980. However, in *Widmar* v. *Vincent* (1981, the U.S. Supreme Court said the very same kind of activities (prayer in voluntary student religious meetings) are permissible at the college level. Yet, the Alabama voluntary school prayer law of 1982 was invalidated by the U.S. Supreme Court in 1983 (*Jaffree* v. *Wallace*).

8. A school district's elective course in Bible literature was declared in 1981 as violating the Establishment Clause by the Fifth Circuit Court of Appeals (*Hall* v. *Board of School Commissioners*). The court went so far as to prohibit use of a particular Bible-based text in any future courses. Similarly, a biology text written from a creation-science orientation was prohibited from use in a 1978 Indiana case (*Hendren* v. *Campbell*) (McCarthy, 1983, p. 83).

9. The right to forbid public school teachers from wearing religious clothing was upheld in several cases in the states of Pennsylvania (*Commonwealth* v. *Herr*, 1910), New York (*O'Connor* v. *Hendrick*, 1906), and New Mexico (*Zellers* v. *Huff*, 1951). The reasoning by the court was that religious garb worn by teachers would

insure students' respect if not sympathy for the respective denomination and thus promote religion even if doctrine was never taught (McCarthy, 1983, p. 38).

10. Distribution of religious literature in schools has been declared unconstitutional in a number of cases. The New Jersey Supreme Court disallowed children to receive Gideon Bibles even with parental permission (*Tudor* v. *Board of Education*, 1953) as also did an Arkansas federal district court (*Goodwin* v. *Cross County School District*, 1973). Even the mere availability (not distribution) of Presbyterian religious pamphlets was declared unconstitutional by New Mexico's Supreme Court as unconstitutionally advancing religion (*Miller* v. *Cooper*, 1952).

11. The teaching of content that parents believed to be counter to their own religious beliefs has been upheld in a number of instances, e.g., *Cornwell* v. *State Board of Education* (Maryland, 1969) and *Smith* v. *Ricci* (New Jersey, 1982). This has included the continued use of curriculum materials (*Williams* v. *Board of Education of County of Kanawha,* West Virginia, 1975), literature (*Rosenberg* v. *Board of Education of City of New York*, 1949), novels (*Todd* v. *Rochester Community Schools*, Michigan, 1972), and films (*Pratt* v. *Independent School District,* Minnesota, 1982).

12. Even prayers constructed to be scrupulously neutral have been declared unconstitutional at public school graduations (*Lee* v. *Weisman*, 1992) (Wagner, 1993).

As is obvious from all the above cases, the U.S. Supreme Court and lower courts have, counter to the intended meaning, interpreted the Establishment Clause to mean at least that "Neither a state nor the Federal Government ... can pass laws which aid one religion, aid all religions, or prefer one religion over another." Stated initially by Justice Black in 1947 (*Everson* v. *Board of Education*), this reading has served as a false beacon to literally shipwreck many cases since that time. Prior to a more detailed discussion of this clause, we will look at cases that appealed to the Free Exercise clause.

Free Exercise

In the area of schooling, the number of U.S. Supreme Court cases that appeal to the Free Exercise Clause are substantially less than those that appeal to the Establishment Clause.

In 1940, the U.S. Supreme Court ruled (*Minersville* v. *Gobitis*) that the public school compulsory flag salute law was constitutional because it was secular, applicable to everyone, and necessary for national unity and security. This ruling stood in spite of the complaint by Jehovah's Witnesses that flag salute violated their religious conscience. Just three years later, however (*West Virginia State Board of Education* v. *Barnette*, 1943), the court ruled that it was unconstitutional to force public school students to salute the flag if it violated their religious beliefs (Jehovah's Witnesses again). Siding for religious cause again, the court in 1972 (*Wisconsin* v. *Yoder*) exempted children of Amish and Amish Mennonite sects from the 16-year-old minimum age requirement in education. The minimum age limit at least at the secondary level was held to seriously violate the religious values of these sects thus making it unconstitutional.

As favorable to religion as the Yoder decision appears, it, as with certain other cases reviewed earlier, emanates from a faulty interpretation of the First Amendment as seen through a related case. In *Donner* v. *New York* (1951), the U.S. Supreme Court upheld the compulsory elementary education attendance requirement even if it violated religious beliefs. The basic reason why the secondary education requirement was invalidated (in *Yoder*) while the primary school requirement was not is related to the priority of national over religious interests even when applying the irrelevant-to-nationalism First Amendment. That is, since the Amish had produced responsible self-supporting citizens to that point, their argument was granted as valid. In other words, the First Amendment religious right of free exercise was qualified within the overriding concern of producing responsible citizens even though such qualification has never been a part of the First Amendment.

At the state and district level, a Maryland appeals court, in 1982, ruled that students who attend parochial schools do not have an automatic right of participation in public school programs (*Thomas* v. *Allegany County Board of Education*). Using the irrelevant-to-the-First reason of potential administrative disruptions, the Court effectively penalized the students of their tax-paying right of public school involvement because they exercised their free-exercise right of religion to attend parochial school (McCarthy, 1983, p. 107). Similarly, when denied access to interscholastic athletics because of the failure to seek state accreditation, a Christian academy was disallowed from claiming exemption by virtue of the religious doctrine that forbids serving two masters—e.g., God and the state. The Eighth Circuit Court of Appeals (*Windsor Park Baptist Church* v. *Arkansas Activities Assoc.*, 1981) said the accreditation did not pose any undue burden in the free exercise of religion in spite of their religious position to the contrary (McCarthy, 1983, p. 147).

Similar religious based objections by home schoolers have been disallowed by the courts. Failure to seek approval (*Commonwealth* v. *Renfrew*, 1955) by Buddhist parents in Massachusetts and noncompliance with state procedures by religiously motivated home schoolers in Washington (*Shoreline School District* v. *Superior Court for King County*, 1960), Virginia (*Rice* v. *Commonwealth*, 1948), and West Virginia (*State* v. *Riddle*, 1981) have all been disallowed by the courts. This is particularly troublesome in light of the original mode of schooling (i.e., home and church) in this country.

Other decisions at the lower levels have allowed freedom of speech even when blasphemous. The courts have refused to remove books from curriculum even with their message declaring "Jesus Christ to be a 'poor white trash God' or 'a long-legged white son-of-bitch" (Barton, 1989, p. 180) (*Grove* v. *Mead School District*, 1985). Yet the State of Ohio (*State of Ohio* v. *Whisner*, 1976) will not let the State Board of Education include reference to God in its statement of minimum standards (Barton, 1989, p. 191). Further, a Christmas play where kindergarten children ask questions about the meaning of Christmas was declared (*Florey* v. *Sioux Falls School District*, 1979) in violation of the First Amendment (Barton, 1989, p. 190). Even the prayers offered outloud by a student over his own lunch was declared unconstitutional in *Reed* v. *VanHoven*, 1965 (Barton, 1989, p. 11).

Again, not only has the religion clause of the First Amendment been wrongly interpreted by the Court, but the mere application of this federal amendment to state matters is also in violation of its purpose.

End Result

Taking the Establishment Clause and Free Exercise Clause decisions as a whole, several conclusions are warranted. First, the Establishment Clause has been interpreted so broadly by the Court as to practically exclude any aid to religion whatsoever. Second, the Establishment Clause has been so favored by the Supreme Court that the free exercise right of nonbelievers has priority over the free exercise right of believers. Third, in addition to the above misinterpretations of the literal wording and intent of the First Amendment, the Court has added criteria that were never mentioned by the First's framers and thus has added meaning that was never intended.

The outcome of these misinterpretations and added constructions (Huntington must literally be spinning in his grave by now!) is severely felt in education. Confusion and ambiguity run amuck with constructions such as child benefit, differential effects on ages, and so on. For instance, using public funds to bus students to sectarian schools is permitted, but using public funds to bus sectarian students to museums is prohibited. Similarly, the use of public funds to purchase secular textbooks for use in sectarian institutions is permitted, but the use of public funds for wall maps and charts in sectarian institutions is unconstitutional. Consider the dissenting words of Justice William Rehnquist in the 1985 *Wallace* v. *Jaffree* decision:

These difficulties arise because the Lemon test has no

more grounding in the history of the First Amendment than does the wall theory upon which it rests. The three-part test represents a determined effort to craft a workable rule from a historically faulty doctrine; but the rule can only be as sound as the doctrine it attempts to service. The three-part test has simply not provided adequate standards for deciding Establishment Clause cases, as this Court has slowly come to realize. Even worse, the Lemon test has caused this Court to fracture into unworkable plurality opinions, depending upon how each of the three factors applies to a certain state action. The results from our school services cases show the difficulty we have encountered in making the Lemon test yield principled results.

For example, a State may lend to parochial school children geography textbooks that contains maps of the United States, but the State may not lend maps of the United States for use in geography class. A State may lend textbooks on American colonial history, but it may not lend a film on George Washington, or a film projector to show in history class. A State may lend classroom workbooks, but may not lend workbooks in which the parochial school children write, thus rendering them nonreusable. A State may pay for bus transportation to religious schools but may not pay for bus transportation from the parochial school to the public zoo or natural history museum for a field trip. A State may pay for diagnostic services conducted in the parochial school but therapeutic services must be given in a different building; speech and hearing 'services' conducted by the State inside the sectarian school are forbidden, but the State may conduct speech and hearing diagnostic testing inside the sectarian school. Exceptional parochial school students may receive counseling, but it must take place outside the parochial school such as in a trailer parked down the street. A State may give cash to a parochial school to pay for the administration of state-written tests and state-ordered reporting services, but it may not provide funds for teacher-prepared tests on secular subjects. Religious instruction may not be given in public school, but the public school may release students during the day for religion classes elsewhere, and may enforce attendance at those classes with its truancy laws. These results violate the historically sound principle 'that the Establishment Clause does not forbid governments ... to [provide] general welfare under which benefits are distributed to private individuals, even though many of those individuals may elect to use those benefits in ways that "aid" religious instruction or worship.

The logic of such contradictions is beyond common understanding and certainly not compatible with the First Amendment.

With the overextended broad interpretation of the Establishment Clause (not to mention its total inapplicability to the states), schools are severely restricted in religious-related activities. Even when, for instance, a sectarian school is abiding by state-mandated requirements of recordkeeping, public funds are prohibited for carrying out such requirements. Similarly, public schools are prohibited from providing time and space for voluntary prayer. The essence of the entire matter is telegraphed clearly in statements that speak about "Establishment Clause prohibitions." As originally written and approved, the prohibition that the First Amendment exacted was only on the Congress of the United States. Now because of wrong interpretations about the meaning of the First and Fourteenth Amendments, prohibitions have been placed largely on religions while their protections, as originally intended, have been undone.

Furthermore, when religious practices, even if voluntary, are proclaimed to be offensive to someone excused from the practice, the practice is typically declared in violation of the Establishment Clause and thus disallowed. Yet the issue of offensiveness to any involved parties is not within the jurisdictional purview of the Establishment Clause.

It would seem that anything religious that could occur in school is prohibited, and very little pertaining to sectarian schools is fundable with public monies. But not only is the First Amendment interpreted in a highly restrictive way, it is also interpreted within the constraint of national well-being. That is, in spite of the absence of any such intent by the framers, religion-in-education issues of the First Amendment are made secondary to perceived issues of national citizenship. Justice Robert H. Jackson said it this way in his 1948 *McCollum* v. *Board of Education* concurring opinion:

> Authorities list 256 separate and substantial religious bodies to exist in the continental United States. Each of them ... has as good a right as this plaintiff to demand that the courts compel the schools to sift out of their teaching everything inconsistent with its doctrines. If we are to eliminate everything that is objectionable to any of these warring sects or inconsistent with any of their doctrines, we will leave public education in shreds. Nothing but educational confusion and a discrediting of the public school system can result... (cf. McCarthy, 1983, pp. 76-77)

Thus, matters like religiously motivated exceptions from schooling are cast within the so-called right of the government (not even a part of the Bill of Rights) to insure a productive citizenry.

Conclusion

We have seen in the last several chapters a complete turnabout regarding the role of religion in education. In simple terms the early mandate that education must be biblical and denominational has been reversed in current times such that education must not be biblical or denominational (see accompanying chart entitled Turning Points in American Education). We have likewise seen a turnabout in the degree of sensitivity toward parental prerogatives in education. Initially parents were often the major decision-makers regarding the education of their children. In contemporary times, decisions are typically made at governmental levels far removed from parental oversight, much less control.

In these reversals, several issues arise as highly significant. One, control of education is a constant in the sense that decisions must be made and enforced. This is not a bad thing; this is the way the world operates. With the writing of the Declaration of Independence, the proviso in effect since that time has been that government control is for the protection of citizens' inalienable rights. The religion clauses of the First Amendment enforced that proviso by prohibiting the federal government from interfering with the inalienable right of freedom of religion. In literally denying that which was never authorized in the U.S. Constitution, the federal government was prohibited from installing, in specific terms, a national religion or from interfering more generally with government established religions at non-federal levels. It was a no-control policy on Congress for the good of the religious interests of the citizens.

With the First Amendment now reinterpreted (along with the Fourteenth), the federal government claims the right to decree what religious matters can and cannot be present in education. This of course means that the greater right of free exercise of religion in education is reduced to that which is allowed by the federal government.

The wisdom embodied in the Constitution and the First Amendment was that the federal government would never be in a position to declare and enforce orthodoxy in religion. All religious interests would thus be relatively equivalent in terms of citizen selection and support. The gross abuse of control over religion in Europe prior to America's settlement and subsequently in colonial America was a prime impetus for the religion guarantees embodied in the First Amendment. With its passage, the citizens would be guaranteed that the federal government could not return to an earlier state of religious control and persecution. This was indeed wise—it worked for the good of religion, the nation,citizens, and parents.

The prevailing upside down interpretation of the First Amendment religion clauses has authorized its use to do exactly what it was expressly forbidden. As we have seen in this chapter, the federal government has decreed what religious matters shall be practiced and taught in education. And because the federal government has exercised this power to control it has discriminated— control invariably discriminates. That is why government was not supposed to have this power to begin with.

In its misinterpretation of the constitutional ban against government control of religion, the federal government has in effect exercised control such that education must not be religious. Here we have a contradiction perhaps even greater than the reversed meaning of the First Amendment. The fact that matters of educational relevance are decided via religion statutes makes education a religious activity even when it is declared not to be so. More will be said on this in later chapters.

Finally, as discussed in Chapter 7, as important and pronounced as educational content is, the greater issue is that of control. Content would be far less incendiary if it were not the subject of control factions and mandates. But with control taken from parents regarding the education of their children, and with decrees regarding which religious perspectives are and are not appropriate in education, our government of the people, by the people, and for the people has tyrannized their First Amendment religious protections.

References

Alley, Robert S. (1988). *The supreme court on church and state.* New York: Oxford Univ. Press.

Barton, David (1989). *The myth of separation.* Aledo, TX: Wallbuilder Press.

Brownson, Henry F. (1966). *The works of Orestes A. Brownson, Vol. XIX.* New York: AMS Press Inc.

Butts, R. Freeman (1950/1974). *The American tradition in religion and education.* Westport, CT: Greenwood Press Publ.

Cox, Wm. F. (2000-2001). The original meaning of the Establishment Clause and its application to education. *Regent University Law Review, 13* (1), 111-143.

Glenn, Charles L., Jr. (1987). "Molding" citizens. In Neuhaus, Richard J. (Ed.) *Democracy and the renewal of public education.* Grand Rapids, MI: Wm. B. Eerdmans Co.

McCarthy, Martha M. (1983). *A delicate balance: Church, state, and the schools.* Bloomington, IN: Phi Delta Kappan Educational Foundation.

Morgan, Richard E. (1972). *The supreme court and religion.* New York: The Free Press.

Moynihan, Daniel Patrick (April 1978). *Government and the ruin of private education.* Harper's, 28-38.

O'Neill, James Milton (1972). *Religion and education under the Constitution.* New York: DaCapo Press.

Rice, Charles E. (1978). Conscientious objection to public education: the grievance and the remedies. *Brigham Young University Law Review*, 847-888.

Wagner, David M. (1993). Religious intolerance. *Family Policy.* Washington, DC: Family Research Council.

Whitehead, John W. (1982). *The second American revolution.* Westchester, IL: Crossway Books.

Turning Points in American Education

Control	Major Events	Content/Philosophy
Church/Parents	Founding	Must be Biblical & Denominational
State as institution of church	1640's – Massachusetts laws	Biblical & Denominational
Church & State separate	Declaration of Independence & U.S. Constitution	Moving toward Biblical but Nondenominational
State as institution of national interests	1850 Public school era begins	Civic morality
State as protector from religion	1940 – *Cantwell v. Ct.* (First Amendment "applies" to the States)	Must not be Christian

Chapter 9

Nature of Religion

While we assert for ourselves a freedom to embrace, to profess and to observe the Religion which we believe to be of divine origin, we cannot deny an equal freedom to those whose minds have not yet yielded to the evidence which has convinced us. (James Madison, "A Memorial and Remonstrance," 1785)

[The] Act for Establishing Religious Freedom meant to comprehend, within the mantle of its protection, the Jew and the Gentile, the Christian and Mahomatan, the Hindu, and infidel of every denomination. (Thomas Jefferson's interpretation of his 1786 legislative Act—Alley, 1985, p. 62)

The two quotes above affirm that religious freedom was to be extended to all faiths, even to the infidel, that is, to the one whose religious beliefs would not even fit into the structure characteristic of religions. By definition, infidel means, in its broadest sense, one who acknowledges no religious belief. This definition also incorporates Madison's view that those who have not come to believe in the majority religion (i.e., Christianity) are entitled nonetheless to free-doms equal to those specifically provided for Christian believers.

A major concern in this chapter is to specify what constitutes a religion or religious belief. Our study of freedom of religion and its interplay with education needs this kind of definitional clarity. The first step is to review definitions and characteristics of reli-gion. The chapter concludes with a working understanding of how to characterize religion and how this characterization affects our treatment of education.

Philosophical Definition

Mankind has never been without some form of religion (Hume, 1959, p. 3), and currently every human community has religion or a religion (Smith, 1978, p. 18). Religion is likely one of the major characteristics of man; it serves as one of the most powerful forces or needs in his life. For individuals and societies alike, religion provides a confidence in the outcome of life's struggles through a relationship to a superhuman power or powers. The world religion (Hopfe, 1987, p. 2) actually comes from the Latin *religio* which refers to the awe or fear felt in the presence of a spirit or a god. But religion also describes moral systems that do not reference the supernatural. The term religion originally meant some "band or scruple" uniting those of similar belief (*The Encyclopedia of Religion*, 1987, p. 283).

For all its universality, religion has never acquired a universally accepted definition. Consider the following sample of definitions (Hutchison & Martin, 1953, p. 4): "Religion is the recognition of all duties as divine commands," it is "what the individual does with his solitariness," it is "that we are conscious of ourselves as abso-lutely dependent," it is "a concern about experiences which are regarded as of supreme value..." and it is a "serious and social atti-tude, in individuals and groups, towards the power or powers which they hold to be in ultimate control of their interests and fates" (Ringgren & Strom, 1967, p. xvii).

The above sampling indicates the extreme diversity of definitions on the matter. One book devotes seventy-one pages to definitions of only samples of religions and James Leuba, a psychologist of religion, has identified at least forty-eight different definitions of religion. Philosopher Alfred North Whitehead (1960) sums up the matter this way: "There is no agreement as to the definition of religion in its most general sense, including true and false religion; nor is there any agreement as to the valid religious beliefs, nor even as to what we mean by the truth of religion" (p. 14). Religious writer Wilfred Smith (1978) even suggests that since it has not had a sustained definition, the term should be dropped.

All definitions do however seem to share the common thread that "religion is intimate and ultimate concern—convictions and activities dealing with the ultimate meaning of existence" (Hutchison & Martin, 1953, p. 9). However, all definitions do not fit the traditional western view regarding belief in a Supreme Being as ultimate. In fact, definitions may refer to one Supreme Being, numerous beings, or man himself. For clarification, sample definitions in these various categories are presented below under the two major headings, theistic and atheistic religions.

Theistic Religions

Theistic religions all have their focus on a divine being or beings. Those that focus on a single deity as creator, sustainer, perhaps judge and redeemer of the world yet as not identical with the world are monotheistic. Those that focus on many gods as responsible for nature and society are labeled polytheistic. Those that believe in the divine character of all of reality as constituting God are called pantheistic.

Example religions of a monotheistic nature include Judaism, Christianity, and Islam (Hume, 1959, p. 271). Example religions of a polytheistic nature include Shinto, Hinduism, and the various religious beliefs of the native American Indians. Examples of a pantheistic nature include the Shia Muslims, Hinduism (again) (Hutchison & Martin, 1953, p. 113), and the Sikh religion (Hume, 1959).

Sample definitions from notable philosophers and theologians (Leube, 1912) incorporating the range of theistic beliefs include the following. According to J. A. Comenius, "By religion we understand that inner veneration by which the mind of man attaches and binds itself to the supreme Godhead" (p. 351). For James Martineau, religion is "the belief in an ever living God, that is, in a Divine Mind and Will ruling the Universe and holding moral relations with mankind" (p. 343). For F.D.E. Schleiermacher, Protestant clergyman and theologian, "the essence of religion consists in the feeling of an absolute dependence ... upon the Universe ... or upon God" (p. 348). For Max Muller, religion "is a faculty or disposition, which independent of, nay in spite of, sense and reason, enables man to apprehend the Infinite under different names and under different disguises" (p. 25). For American philosopher Josiah Royce, "Religion is the consciousness of our practical relation to an invisible, spiritual order" (p. 357). For philosopher Emmanuel Kant, "Religion is the recognition of all our duties as divine command" (p. 358). For Siebeck, religion is the "understanding and the practical realization of the existence of God and of the transcendental world, and, in connection with this, of the possibility of salvation" (p. 40). For G.W.F. Hegel, religion places man in relation to God (p. 344).

Atheistic Religions

Not all religions have as their focus an infinite God or even multiple gods. For these, says Euchen, "whether God exists or not, focus on infinite God or even multiple gods is not important to the nature of religion" (Van Til, 1978, p. 78). Such religions are often classified as atheistic. They go under names such as existentialism, materialism, Taoism, Humanism, Ethical Culture, American Naturalism, and Unitarianism (Hutchison & Martin, 1953, p. 455). Sample definitions of such religions include the following. L. A. Feuerbach, a left wing materialist, says "that religion is an illusion, a dream of the human mind. God is no more than the attributes man finds in himself and hence the proper worship of man is man" (*New Catholic Encyclopedia*, 1967, p. 255). For Edward von Hartmann, "religion constitutes the whole of the philosophy of the masses... In fine, religion comprises all the idealism of the masses..." (Leuba, 1912, p. 343). For George Santayana, "God is only a symbol for human ideals" (*New Catholic Encyclopedia,* 1967, p. 256). Theologian George T. Ladd says that religion is "an attempt to explain human experience by relating it to invisible existences that belong, nonetheless, to the real world" (Leuba, 1912). For John Dewey, "the function of religious faith is that of unifying men in the pursuit of the highest ideals" (*New Catholic Encyclopedia,* 1967, p. 256). For Prince Kropotkin, religion is "a passionate desire for working out a new, better form of society" (Leuba, 1912, p. 358). For Herbert Spencer, every form of religion contains "an hypothesis which is supposed to render the Universe comprehensible. Nay, even that which is commonly regarded as the negation of all Religion-even positive Atheism-comes within the definition" (Leuba, 1912, p. 26).

Characteristics of Religion

Just as there is no single definition of religion, there is also no single set of characteristics that is essential to or that defines religion. Depending on the culture and perhaps also the state of social, economic, psychological, emotional, and spiritual development, cultures differ in those characteristics that help to define religion. In fact, *The Encyclopedia of Religion,* volume 12 (1987, p. 282), suggests that the very attempt to define religion is basically the result of the Western world's "speculative, intellectualistic, and scientific disposition." Basically the religion experience is religious for the central reason that it occurs in a context defined by those experiencing it as religious. The *Encyclopedia* notes that similar experiences can also occur outside of religion such as through natural events, psychosomatic events, and drug usage.

Without claiming exclusivity of characteristics of religion versus non-religion, there seem to be elements that all religions commonly share. The common features of religions of the underdeveloped areas of the world include animism, magic, divination, taboo, totems, sacrifice, rites of passage, and ancestor veneration (Hopfe, 1987). Dimensions that seem to characterize religions of current cultures include ritual, mythology, doctrine, ethics, social, and experiential (Smart, 1976). Ringgren and Strom (1967, p. xvii

& viii) suggest there are four essential elements of religion: intellectual, emotional, behavioral, and social. Yet Ringgren and Strom also mention other essential characteristics of religion that include belief in God, institutions, worship, ministry, and concern about last things. *The Encyclopedia of Religion*, volume 12 (1987) describes the following elements as characteristics of religions: traditionalism, myth and symbol, salvation, sacred places and objects, rituals, sacred writings, community, and experience.

Obviously, in the various listings above, none are exactly duplicative of any other. Each expert's opinion varies at least somewhat from each of the others. Furthermore, it seems that these identified characteristics can and do vary by the differences in cultures. For instance, those religions of primitive or underdeveloped countries have different characteristic features than do religions of the more literate or advanced cultures.

Another difficulty in isolating what constitutes or defines a religion is the degree of self-determination of the religion and/or culture. In Western cultures the assumptions of theism have "forced" a dichotomous view of religion. That is, a distinction is made between a transcendent duty and everything else, or between God and His creation, or between the Creator and man (*The Encyclopedia of Religion*, 1987, p. 282). This is not so in other societies where religion is such an integral part of life that it is indistinguishable as something separate or different.

Practical Definitions

Such difficulties of definition and classification have led some to speak about religion in more wholistic, less formal terms. For instance, Fredrich Schluermacher influentially expressed religion as a "feeling of absolute dependence" (*The Encyclopedia of Religion*, 1987, p. 283). William James called it "the enthusiastic temper of espousal." Morris Jastrow (1981) very simply claims that "religion may be defined as the natural belief in a Power or Powers beyond our control, and upon whom we feel dependent." Further, this feeling of dependence prompts us to organization, to specific acts, and to the regulation of conduct. Jastrow apparently comes to this very uncomplicated definition of religion through his review of multifarious ways to classifying religion. Every effort of classification reviewed by Jastrow seemed to be accompanied by an exception or exceptions to whatever scheme was proposed.

Perhaps because of this impossibility to find a scheme of common features among all religions, elementary definitions prevail. In fact, one of the most favored and relatively uncomplicated definitions is proposed by theologian Paul Tillich:

> is the state of being grasped by an ultimate concern, a concern which qualifies all other concerns as preliminary and which itself contains the answer to the question of the meaning of our life. Therefore, the concern is unconditionally serious and shows a willingness to sacrifice any finite concern which is in conflict with it. The predominant religious name for the content of such concern is God—a god or gods. In nontheistic religions divine qualities are ascribed to a sacred object or an all-pervading power or a highest principle such as the Brahma or the One. In secular quasi-religions the ultimate concern is directed towards objects like nation, science, a particular form or stage of society, or a highest ideal of humanity, which are then considered divine. (Tillich, 1964, pp. 4-5)

A property of this ultimate concern is its ability to displace other concerns. It is the point from which other concerns are evaluated: "Practically speaking, religious values are those values for which men are willing to die. Any such values take on religious significance" (Hutchison & Martin, 1953, p. 11).

This ultimate concern is more a quality than a being. In fact, the state of "being grasped by an ultimate concern" is also Tillich's definition of faith (Brown, 1965, p. 4). Since religions are not just theistic, the object of this ultimate concern does not have to be a person. As such, it represents a value that displaces all others.

Universality

Because of this quality of ultimate concern, it is ultimately impossible to *not* possess some sort of religion. All men possess some system of values from which they operate. Similarly, one can deny or critique a religion only from the standpoint of another religion or value system. Since the groundwork from which any criticism emanates must come from an alternative value system, it ultimately constitutes another religion (Hutchison & Martin, 1953, p. 12).

Where theistic religions are addressed, ultimate concern can refer to an absolute dependence on a divine being. For instance, absolute dependence is communicated in the phrase "the fear of the Lord." Because of the ultimateness of this concern, there is an absolute quality of allegiance attached to the object or value cherished: "It seems that men will worship something, and if they can find nothing worthy in traditional religious institutions they will turn to political or other secular concerns in search of an idea to which they can give themselves unreservedly" (Hutchison & Martin, 1953, p. 15).

Because of the universal need of mankind to have a religion, this need is often expressed through avenues that are not typically seen as religious. For instance, the Canaanites of Old Testament time worshipped a sky god (Baal) and earth goddess (Anath). Hick (1982) lists Marxism and Maoism, and Smith (1978) includes Freudianism in their respective listings of the religions of the world. Obviously, the object of worship or allegiance can be theistic God but it can equally be a manmade belief system like, for instance, Communism.

Non-Traditional Religions

Communism

"Communism is a Western religion in the sense that its final goal is a morally perfect society achieved by scientific, economic, and political theory and action ... the heart of its religious character lies in the absolute quality of allegiance which it elicits from its adherents..." (Hutchison & Martin, 1953, p. 15). Elaborating on the question of whether communism is a religion, Bernett gives this classic response:

> If religion is defined as man's relationship to whatever he regards as ultimate or to whatever he trusts most for deliverance from the evils and hazards of life, then communism is undoubtedly religious... It is certainly true to say that communism occupies the place in the life for the convinced communist that religion occupies in the lives of their adherents. Communism offers a goal for life. It offers a faith in redemption from all recognized evils. It offers an interpretation of life's meaning which may be short-sighted and one-sighted but which at least does provide the kind of guidance that the religious believer secures from doctrine. It even offers the kind of authority that the more authoritarian churches provide for their members. Many other features of religion, such as sacred scriptures and saints, have their analogies in communism. The communist, like the Christian ... is a man of faith. He is committed to a cause, and he has ultimate confidence that the highest powers, the existence of which he will admit, are on the side of that cause (Vos, 1959, pp. 323, 324).

Here in the explanation of communism, we see many of the characteristics mentioned earlier. That is, it has a sense of the ultimate as with the more typical religions, it provides for deliverance from evil, it contains doctrine and statements of ethics, it has a social or institutional aspect, and it has an authority structure that functions in a ministry or priestly fashion. Also present is a faith in the potency of the belief system and an interpretative structure to make sense of life.

All of these characteristics obviously make Communism a religion for those who truly believe in it. In fact, there are many belief systems that can qualify as religions.

Democracy

Just as communism has religious characteristics and its religious zealots, so too does a contemporary alternative—democracy. Religious adherents of democracy make claims as to its ability to resolve matters of ultimate concern. They believe it can bring mankind to a world of peace and happiness where there is freedom and no fear (see Williams, 1969, p. 481).

Ultimate concerns addressed by the practice of democracy include issues such as right of rule by the people; liberty for all regardless of race, creed, religion, or class; individual freedoms and purpose; the right to the fruit of one's labors; the surpassing worth of each individual; the superiority of the method of peace versus that of war; possession of the earth by all mankind; and the brotherhood of all men (see Counts, 1941).

Believers in the social salvific promise of democracy propose that it might be taught in schools and by governmental agencies (Williams, 1945, p. 488) as a matter of "ultimate faith" (p. 161). Harold Rugg has concurred that to even make democracy work "we must make a religion out of it" (1941, p. 277). The fact that Democracy does not seem to fit the mold of traditional religions does not deter such proponents from their faith in it. Religion, they claim, can be of at least three types—private, denominational, and societal. While religion has typically been thought of as denominational, the others are equally valid as expressions of religion. Since "democracy is a way of life, the truest vision of social ethics which mankind has dreamed" (Williams, 1969, p. 485), it is a societal form of religion. Americans are urged to devote themselves to democratic ideals just as do the ardent believers of the more traditional religions. Accordingly, the key element as to whether democracy will work or not will be the citizens' faith in it (Dewey, 1939, p. 126).

Nationalism

Hayes (1926) claims that a sure indicator that nationalism is a religion is found in the fact that millions have been ready and willing to die for their nation. For instance, World War I apparently contributed to the death of more men that did the medieval Christian Crusades.

For this magnitude of sacrifice, something beyond a philosophy, a doctrine, or a political process seems to be operating. Nationalism apparently arouses a type of commitment and faith that is, in essence, religious. This has occurred in the past with the deification of the Roman emperor and more recently during the French Revolution where the state had supremacy in everything. Only those clergy who swore allegiance to the Civil Constitution were allowed to perform Christian services. Catholics were persecuted during this time partially because they "had committed the greatest infamy of all—they had defied the national state" (p. 102). France's Declaration of the Rights of Man and of the Citizen was considered to be their national catechism. The Book of the Constitution was considered the Blessed Sacrament of the French. Such governing documents were considered the symbols of their faith; there were also civic baptisms, civic marriages, and civic funerals. Hayes cites a speech made in the 1793 national convention of France where la Patrie—the national state—was to be the common religion, law makers the preachers, and magistrates the pontiffs.

Nationalism can equally share commonalties with other religions. The fatherland becomes one's god, and the mission of the state can be the focus of one's faith. Devotion of its adherents is expected, and symbols such as flags take on holy significance as citizens bow before them. School systems often take on a religious teaching role for the nation in that children are taught to revere the nation, its leaders, and to not blaspheme its policies.

Nationalism during the early 1920s took on religious tones not only in the United States but in many other parts of the world, also. According to Hayes, nationalism during this time period was "the latest and nearest approach to a world-religion" (p. 117). Hayes boldly suggests that American nationalism represented a reaction against historic Christianity—that it served the function of the universal mission of Christ. This substitution of one belief system for another qualifies the latter to be of the same category as the former, i.e., a religion.

Science

According to its proponents, science can be considered as a religion. When the Royal Society of London was confirmed by the Crown in 1623, the pursuit of natural science was considered as a religious duty to the Creator. The Society's charter ruled that scientific studies "are to be applied to further promoting by the authority of experiments the sciences of natural things and of useful arts, so the Glory of the Creator..." (Torrance, 1981, p. 41). Later in 1831, the Royal Society admitted that "true religion and true science ever lead to the same great end, manifesting and exalting the glory and goodness of the great object of our common worship" (Coulson, 1968, p. 61).

More recently, von Weizsacker (1964) maintains that "faith in science plays the role of the dominating religion of our time" (p. 12). He builds his case by relating science to what he calls the three "indispensable elements" of a religion—a common faith, an organized church, and a code of behavior. As we have seen, these are common elements of religion.

Regarding faith, von Weizsacker (1964) says we face science just as a believer does his religion. The atom, for instance, is just another invisible world, and the mathematical formula is the sacred text. According to Jaki (1974, p. 356), the man of science, just like his counterpart in religion, lives ultimately by faith. Eiseley (1961, p. 62) makes the case more directly in noting that it was the faith of the Christian belief that literally gave birth to the experimental method of science. To quote Whitehead, it was "the sheer act of faith that the universe possessed order and could be interpreted by rational minds." For Whitehead, "science is an enterprise in which reason is based on a faith" (Schilling, 1962, p. 25). Einstein similarly held that the fundamental, apriori beliefs of science are intuitive and religious in character. Of these beliefs he said, "To the sphere of religion belongs the faith that the regulations valid for the world of existence are rational, that is comprehensible to reason. I cannot conceive of a genuine scientist without that profound faith" (Torrance, 1981, p. 59). Such faith was so genuinely metaphysical for Einstein that he did not hesitate from describing it as a religious belief. For German physicist Max Planck, "Science demands also the believing spirit. Anybody who has been seriously engaged in scientific work of any kind realizes that over the entrance to the gates of the temple of science are written the words: *Ye must have faith*. It is a quality which the scientist cannot dispense with" (Jaki, 1966, p. 346). German mathematician Hermann Weyl claims that "science would perish without a supporting transcendental faith in truth and reality" (Jaki, 1966, p. 346). Lorsdale, a leading scientist, said, "The scientist, as well as the man of religion lives by faith and not by certainty" (Jaki, 1966, p. 347). Or as Justice Jackson said in *U.S.* v. *Ballard* (1944), "Belief in what one may demonstrate to the senses is not faith."

Regarding the second characteristic, that of an organized church, von Weizsacker says that the church of scientism (i.e., faith in science) has a priesthood—namely, the scientists themselves. While there may not be a formal church, there nonetheless is a common bond (recall one of the early original meanings, i.e., "bond" or "scruple") uniting those who believe in the common truths of science. As scientist W. Weaver said, "There is a special, small priesthood of scientific practitioners; they know the secrets and hold the power" (Jaki, 1966, p. 523).

Third, regarding the last element, a code of behavior, von Weizsacker (1964) claims that there are rituals or sets of right behaviors toward so-called superhuman powers of science. While there may be a void of technical ethics, he does admit to the existence of technological rituals.

In a similar way, Coulson (1968, p. 61) says "that what we conventionally call science and what we conventionally call religion have so much in common that we need fear no dichotomy of experience..." Both science and religion, he says, share three main characteristics. The first is that neither is just a collection of facts but a higher set of statements about what the facts mean. As Schilling (1962, p. 98) says, there are "no bare facts in science." Second, both are full of presupposition, unproven assumptions, or faith statements. Third, the personal elements of humility, devotion, and interpretation are also present in each.

Bower (1944) suggests that science may carry more religious

force than the more traditional religious orientations: "Perhaps it is not going beyond the evidence to suggest that science so conceived is more effective in the evocation of religious attitudes and religious commitment to the realities of life than are the traditional theological formulations..." (p. 63). This science "so conceived" is what Haskell labels unified science; that is, a science that incorporates the interrelatedness of physical, chemical, biological, psychological, or social phenomena. For Haskell, this unified science is a religion: "Unified science is, like all religions, inescapably and directly connected with values, ethics and morals... In short, unified science gives the power of knowledge, of faith, and of efficient action to the individual and to the society. This power is the religious force of unified science" (see Bower, 1944, p. 63).

There are other belief systems that also qualify as religions even though on the surface they are not initially seen as such.

Humanism

There are those views or definitions of religion that make man, rather than things or gods, the center of religious thought. For instance, American psychologist Hugo Munsterberg says that "religion creates God" (Leuba, 1912, p. 345). And for Auguste Comte, the highest stage of religious truth is the worship of humanity. The "religion of humanity is conceived as replacing the worship of God..." (*New Catholic Encyclopedia*, 1967, p. 255). This belief in man and the ultimate righteousness of man is not new. Belief in humanism can be traced back to Democritus and Lucretius, through Spinoza and Hume, and to modern day thinkers like Julian Huxley who explicitly labeled Humanism as a religion (Hutchison & Martin, 1953, p. 446). For Hugo Munsterberg, God is that which is constructed by man's mind (Leuba, 1912, p. 345), making man the highest point of life and the creator of even God. As Comte said, "It is only through the worship of Humanity that we can feel the inward reality and inexpressible sweetness..." (Konvitz, 1968, p. 30).

Claire Chambers (see the Freedom Council, 1984, p. 5) says that "Humanism is not new. It is, in fact, man's second oldest faith. Its promise was whispered in the first days of Creation under the

Tree of the Knowledge of Good and Evil, 'Ye shall be as gods.'"
Julian Huxley, a major spokesman for the Humanist movement,
said, "I use the word 'Humanist' to mean someone who believes
that man is just as much a natural phenomenon as an animal or
plant; that his body, mind and soul were not supernaturally created
but are products of evolution, and that he is not under the control or
guidance of any supernatural being or beings, but has to rely on
himself and his own powers" (Chambers, 1977, p. 53). In an analysis of the words secular humanism, Whitehead and Conlan (1978,
p. 29) indicate,

> The word 'secular' by definition refers to 'the tempo-
> ral rather than spiritual.' 'Secularism' is a doctrinal belief
> that morality is based solely in regard to the temporal
> well-being of mankind to the exclusion of all belief in
> God, a supreme being, or a future eternity. 'Humanism' is
> a philosophy or attitude that is concerned with human
> being human, rather than with the abstract beings and
> problems of theology. 'Secularism' is nontheistic and
> 'humanism' is secular because it excludes the tenets of
> theism. Therefore, secular humanism is nontheistic.
> However, while secular humanism is nontheistic, it is reli-
> gious because it directs itself toward religious beliefs and
> practices that in active opposition to traditional theism.
> Humanism is a doctrine centered solely on human inter-
> ests and values. Therefore, humanism deifies man collec-
> tively and individually, whereas theism worships God.

Past president of the American Humanist Association John
Dewey said in his book, *A Common Faith*, "Here we have all the
elements for a religious faith that shall not be confined to sect, class,
or race. Such a faith has always been implicitly the common faith of
mankind. It remains to make it explicit and militant" (1934, p. 87).
Pfeffer says, "it is not Protestantism, Catholicism, or Judaism which
will emerge the victor, but secular humanism, a cultural force which
in many respects is stronger in the United States than any of the
major religious groups or any alliance among them" (see McCarthy,

Oppewal, Peterson & Spykman, 1981, p. 116).

Humanism is recognized by the U.S. Supreme Court (*Torcaso* v. *Watkins*, 1961) as a religion. Hutchison & Martin (1953, p. 446) suggest that after Judaism, Roman Catholicism, and Protestantism, humanism is perhaps the fourth main religious option in the Western world. The so-called father of humanism, Protagoras, says that "Man is the measure of all things, of things that are that they are, and of things that are not that they are not" (The Freedom Council Foundation, no date, p. 37).

> More specifically, the *Humanist Manifesto* (1933) was written "In order that religious humanism may be better understood..." (Kurtz, 1973, p. 7). The authors of the *Manifesto* said that
>
> Today man's larger understanding of the universe, his scientific achievements and his deeper appreciation of brotherhood, have created a situation which requires a new statement of the means and purposes of religion... While this age does owe a vast debt to the traditional religions, it is nonetheless obvious that any religion that can hope to be a synthesizing and dynamic force for today must be shaped for the needs of this age. To establish such a religion is a major necessity of the present. (Kurtz, 1973, p. 8)

Thus, the major purpose of the *Manifesto* is to articulate the tenets of its religious creed. Finally, the document ends with a clear statement about man's total self-sufficiency: "Though we consider the religious forms and ideas of our fathers no longer adequate, the quest for the good life is still the central task for mankind. Man is at last becoming aware that he alone is responsible for the realization of the world of his dreams, that he has within himself the power for its achievement" (Kurtz, 1973, p. 10).

Humanist Manifesto II (1973) reaffirmed that humanism is a religion and man is to be the object of worship: "We believe, however, that traditional dogmatic or authoritarian religions that place revelation, God, ritual, or creed above human needs and experience do a disservice to the human species... As non-theists, we begin with humans not God, nature not deity... No deity can save us; we must save ourselves" (Kurtz, 1973, pp. 15-16).

Religious Freedom Considerations

Definitions of religion for the founders always started with God as the reference point. Even when religious liberty was initially tolerated for those who did not hold Christian beliefs, the term toleration always referenced Christianity as the standard, thus implying that alternate beliefs were patronized deviations. Just as the term toleration was abandoned in favor of full and equal liberty, the understanding of religion moved along a parallel course from being content to functionally defined.

Content

A sampling of colonial-era definitions of religion follow. George Mason defined religion in a proposal to the Virginia Revolutionary Convention of 1776 as "the Duty which we owe to our divine and omnipotent Creator..." (Alley, 1985, p. 51). Similarly, James Madison defined it in this same meeting and again in the 1785 document, "Memorial and Remonstrance," as "the duty which we owe to our Creator and the manner of discharging it..." (Alley, 1985, p. 56). Thomas Jefferson, in his 1802 letter to the Danbury Baptist Association, said that "religion is a matter which lies solely between man and his God" (Alley, 1988, p. 286) and in his 1822 statement regarding Freedom of Religion at the University of Virginia, that religion concerned "the relations which exist between man and his Maker, and the duties resulting from those relations" (Alley, 1988, p. 284).

With these as only a representative sample of the colonial definitions of religion, it is uniformly obvious that religion denoted a biblical, theocentric orientation. As Jefferson said (1779/1786), God is "the Holy author of our religion" (Alley, 1985, p. 60).. Or as Ezra Stiles wrote in 1761, "in this land of liberty,—the SCRIPTURES are professedly our only RULE..." (Bridenbaugh, 1962, p. 3).

This content-oriented focus on religion also prevailed in the judiciary. In the 1878 *U.S.* v. *Reynolds* decision, Chief Justice Waite, speaking for the Court, summarized the situation at that point in time by appealing to the meaning intended at the time of the writing of the Constitution. Without defining the word religion, the Court reached its conclusion regarding jurisdictional authority between religion and government by using content-based statements of Madison and Jefferson (Konvitz, 1968, p. 32). But shortly after, in 1890, the Court did, through Justice Field in *Davis* v. *Beason*, directly state that religion "has reference to one's views of his relations to his Creator, and to the obligations they impose of reverence for his being and character, and of obedience to his will. It is often confused with the cultus or form of worship of a particular sect, but is distinguished from the latter" (McMillan, 1984, p. 59). While not specific, this definition seems to maintain the traditional Christian theistic orientation.

More recently, Justice Hughes characterized religion in *United States* v. *Macintosh* (1931) as a "belief in a relation to God involving duties superior to those arising from any human relation... One cannot speak of religious liberty, without proper appreciation of its essential and historic significance, without assuming the existence of a belief in supreme allegiance to the will of God" (McMillan, 1984, p. 60). This definition reflects the primary religious belief in this country for at least two hundred years prior, even while it specifically extended religious liberty and freedom of conscience to all inhabitants.

Even more recently, in his dissent from the 1943 *West Virginia* v. *Barnett* decision, Justice Frankfurter characterized religion more loosely but still with reference to content. He referenced the following from lower court Judge Augustus N. Hand (*U.S.* v. *Kauten*— 1943): "Religious belief arises from a sense of the inadequacy of reason as a means of relating the individual to his fellow-men and to his universe...[It] may justly be regarded as a response of the individual to an inward mentor, call it conscience of God" (McMillan, 1984, p. 63). Two cases in 1961 close out this review. First the *McGowan* v. *Maryland* decision spoke of religion as "an aspect of human thought and action which profoundly relates the life of man to the world in which he lives" (McMillan, 1984, p. 64). But very specifically in *Torcaso* v. *Watkins*, Justice Black in a footnote to the court decision labeled as religious those beliefs "which do not teach what would generally be considered a belief in the existence of God are Buddhism, Taoism, Ethical Culture, Secular Humanism and others" (McMillan, 1984, p. 65).

With a certain amount of ambiguity regarding precision of definition, confusion would likely result when attempting to decide which belief systems qualify for religious freedom. Fortunately, the matter is not all that confusing. While it is true that at the outset various colonies/states excluded various religions, religious freedom to all persuasions was ultimately granted within and across all states. This proper outcome is the natural consequence of switching from a content to a functional understanding of religion.

Transition

In the era of the Declaration of Independence and the Constitution/Bill of Rights, these and other similar governing documents were designed to protect all and not just Christian or biblical religious beliefs. These documents codified the cause of religious freedom for all beliefs in a country that was nonetheless of one predominant religious persuasion (i.e., Christian). These documents made concrete and legal the religious freedom principles proclaimed by leaders like Roger Williams, Thomas Jefferson, and James Madison.

Williams declares that

> all civil states with their offers of justice, in their respective constitutions and administrations, are ... essentially civil, and therefore not judges, governors, or defenders of the Spiritual, or Christian, State and worship... It is the will and command of God that, since the coming of His Son, the Lord Jesus, a permission of the most Paganish, Jewish, Turkish, or anti-Christian consciences and worship be granted to all men, in all nations and countries... God requireth not an uniformity of religion to be enacted and

enforced in any civil state; which enforced uniformity, sooner or later, is the greatest occasion of civil water, ravishing consciences... An enforced uniformity of religion throughout a nation or civil states confounds the civil and religion... (Cobb, 1968, pp. 12-13)

In 1779, Thomas Jefferson introduced into the Virginia Assembly the Act for Establishing Religious Freedom in which all religious beliefs were declared free from civil control. The main thrust of this Act reads as follows:

That no man shall be compelled to frequent or support any religious worship, place, or ministry whatsoever, nor shall be enforced restrained, molested, or burthened in his body or goods, nor shall otherwise suffer on account of his religious opinions or belief; but that all men shall be free to profess, and by argument to maintain, their opinion in matters of religion, and that the same shall in no wise diminish, enlarge, or affect their civil capacities. (Alley, 1985, p. 61)

Jefferson's Act extended religious liberty to *all* people against compulsion toward *any* religious belief.

Even further, the religious liberty guaranteed in this Act did not originate in the mind of Thomas Jefferson. In his Act are the words, "all attempts to influence it [the mind] by temporal punishments or burthens, or by civil incapacitations ... are a departure from the plan of the Holy author of our religion..." When the legislators were readying the Act for passage, an amendment was proposed to insert the words "Jesus Christ," so that the above phrase would read instead, "the plan of Jesus Christ, the Holy author." However, consistent with the desire to extend this religious freedom to all, the amendment was defeated. As Jefferson noted in his autobiography, the defeat of the amendment occurred because the legislators "meant to comprehend, within the mangle of its protection, the Jew and the Gentile, the Christian and Mohammedan, the Hindoo, and infidel of every denomination" (Alley, 1985, p. 62).

Another great framer, James Madison, also fought hard for similar nondiscriminatory religious freedom. Consider the events that resulted in his authoring the profound "Memorial and Remonstrance." The essence of this document is contained in the following two phrases: "The Religion then of every man must be left to the conviction and conscience of every man; and it is the right of every man to exercise it as these may dictate"; and "Whilst we assert for ourselves a freedom to embrace, to profess, and to observe the Religion which we believe to be of divine origin, we cannot deny an equal freedom to those whose minds have not yet yielded to the evidence which has convinced us" (Alley, 1985, pp. 56, 57).

These ideas of religious freedom by Madison and Jefferson also appeared in their more extensively felt documents, the Declaration of Independence and the U.S. Constitution. Recall again that the Declaration called for the granting of inalienable rights, including life, liberty, and the pursuit of happiness, to all people. Further, it specified that the role of government was to make these rights possible, and when such government interfered with these rights, the government was at the mercy of the people and not vice versa.

Similarly, the U.S. Constitution was written void of favoritism toward any particular religion and in fact prohibited the making of any particular religious belief a qualification for federal or state public office (Article VI). Supreme Court Justice Joseph Story said of this prohibition on a religious test for public office, "The Catholic and the Protestant, the Calvinist and the Armenian [sic], the infidel and the Jew, may sit down to the Communion-table of the National council, without any inquisition into their faith or mode of worship" (Stokes & Pfeffer, 1964, p. 91). Then, as discussed earlier in Chapter 5, the First Amendment specifically guaranteed freedom of religious worship from federal government interference. As Supreme Court Justice Black recently (1962) indicated in *Engel* v. *Vitale*, religion is far too holy and personal to come under the control of a civil magistrate (McMillan, 1984, p. 58).

So complete was the concept of religious freedom for all peoples that the seemingly synonymous word, toleration, was actually abhorred by our founding fathers. Our country had by the mid-1700s reached the third phase of Lord Stanhope's quote: "The time was when toleration was craved by dissenters as a boon; it is now demanded as a right; but the time will come when it will be spurned as an insult" (Cobb, 1968, p. 8). Locke's intent regarding toleration was in fact one of the few ideas of his that did not become part of our heritage. It was Locke's belief that those who held *opinions* contrary to the moral laws of a society (e.g., denying the existence of a god) were to be denied toleration. Yet Jefferson said in response, "where he stopped short we may go on" (Brauer, Mead & Bellah, 1976, p. 48). It was because of this abhorrence to the concept of toleration that Madison felt the need to revise George Mason's 1776 declaration of rights for Virginia. Mason's proposal read, "all Men shou'd enjoy the fullest toleration in the Exercise of Religion, according to the Dictates of Conscience..." (Alley, 1985, p. 51). As innocent and positive as this phrase seems, the following quote by Thomas Paine reveals the full measure of bias and delusion in Mason's phrase: "Toleration is not the opposite of intolerance, but is the counterfeit of it... The one assumes to itself the right of withholding liberty of conscience, the other of granting it" (Cobb, 1968, p. 9). In this spirit, Madison revised Mason's declaration to read, "all men are equally entitled to the free exercise of religion, according to the dictates of conscience..." (Alley, 1985, p. 52).

George Washington communicated this positive difference between liberty and toleration in his 1790 address to Jewish Americans. To this group, who was outside the mainstream of America's religious orientation and thus a potential target for religious discrimination, he said,

> all possess alike liberty of conscience and immunities of citizenship. It is now no more that toleration is spoken of, as if it were by the indulgence of one class of people, that another enjoyed the exercise of their inherent natural rights. For happily the Government of the United States, which gives to bigotry no sanction, to persecution no assistance, requires only that they who live under its protection should demean themselves as citizens, in giving it on all occasions their effectual support... (Brauer, et al.,

1976, p. 59)

The U.S. Supreme Court decision that reveals this transition to the plurality of religious belief occurs in *Minersville School District* v. *Gobitis* (1940). Justice Frankfurter said, "Government may not interfere with organized or individual expressions of belief or disbelief. Propagation of belief—or even of disbelief in the supernatural—is protected, whether in church or chapel, mosque or synagogue, tabernacle or meeting house" (McMillan, 1984, p. 61).

As Justice Roberts said of the Constitution in the 1940 *Cantwell* case, "the tenets of one man may seem the rankest error to his neighbor. [The Constitution] safeguards the free exercise of the chosen form of religion. Thus the [First] Amendment embraces two concepts—freedom to believe and freedom to act. The first is absolute..." (Blanshard, 1960, p. 63).

By 1944, in *United States* v. *Ballard,* both the official court and the dissenting opinions were confirming of this expansive thinking about religion. For the majority, Justice Douglas noted that freedom of religion "embraces the right to maintain theories of life and death and of the hereafter which are rank heresy to followers of the orthodox faiths. Heresy trials are foreign to our Constitution." He likewise noted that

> Man's relation to his God was made no concern of the state. He was granted the right to worship as he pleased and to answer to no man for the verity of his religious views. The religious views exposed by respondents might seem incredible, if not preposterous, to most people. But if those doctrines are subject to trial before a jury charged with finding their truth or falsity, then the same can be done with the religious beliefs of any sect. (Kovitz, 1968, p. 39)

Dissenting in this case, Justice Jackson nonetheless guaranteed to the individual the same religious rights. In support of these rights, Jackson quotes psychologist William James' explanation of religious experiences:

If religious liberty includes, as it must, the right to communicate such experiences to others, it seems to me an impossible task for juries to separate fancied ones from real ones, dreams from happenings, and hallucination from true clairvoyance. Such experiences, like some tunes and colors, have existence for one, but none at all for another. They cannot be verified to the minds of those whose field of consciousness does not include religious insight. (McMillan, 1984, p. 63)

By this time, the Supreme Court has expanded explanations of religion in ways that totally honor or respect each individual's freedom of conscience and belief. No one can officially or legally pass judgment on another's religion, no matter how unorthodox and personal it may be.

In this same attitude, Justice Frankfurter in the 1952 *Burstyn* v. *Wilson* decision labeled blasphemy as "the chameleon phrase which meant the criticism of whatever the ruling authority of the moment established as orthodox religious doctrine" (Blanshard, 1960, p. 63). In the 1961 *Torcaso* v. *Watkins* case, Justice Black, speaking for the court, put belief and disbelief on equal footing:

We repeat and again reaffirm that neither a State nor a Federal Government can constitutionally force a person 'to profess a belief or disbelief in any religion.' Neither can constitutionally pass laws or impose requirements which aid all religions as against non-believers, and neither can aid those religions based on a belief in the existence of God as against those religions founded on different beliefs. (McMillan, 1984, p. 65)

More recently, Supreme Court Justice Goldberg wrote in the 1963 *Abington* v. *Schempp* decision that "The basic purpose of the religion clause of the First Amendment is to promote and assure the fullest possible scope of religious liberty and tolerance for all and to nurture the conditions which secure the best hope of attainment of that end" (McMillan, 1984, p. 43)

Religion is now firmly established by the U.S. Supreme Court in 1970 (*Welsh* v. *U.S.*) as a matter of "duty of conscience." Speaking for the Court, Justice Black said,

> If an individual deeply and sincerely holds beliefs that are purely ethical or moral in source and content but that nevertheless impose upon him a duty of conscience to refrain from participation in any war at any time, those beliefs certainly occupy in the life of that individual 'a place parallel to that filled by ... God' in traditional religious persons. Because his beliefs function as a religion in his life, such an individual is as much entitled to a 'religious' conscientious objector exemption ... as is someone who derives his conscientious opposition to war from traditional religious convictions. (McMillan, 1984, p. 68)

From this selection of statements, it is readily obvious that religious liberty was not intended just for those of the foundational faith of this country. All religious beliefs are equally protected by our governing documents. This is so, said the framers, precisely because the Christian religion demands it, so to speak. Justice Brewer, in the U.S. Supreme Court decision of the 1892 *Holy Trinity Church* v. *United States* case, said it most eloquently: "The free, equal, and undisturbed enjoyment of religious opinion, whatever it may be, and free and decent discussions on any religious subject, is granted and secured ... and for this plain reason, that the case assumes that we are a Christian people, and the morality of the country is deeply ingrafted upon Christianity..."

Thus we can conclude with confidence that all religious persuasions are guaranteed full religious freedom in the United States. This policy was relatively straightforward and unambiguous for its authors and immediate interpreters primarily because religious denominations were rather easy to identify. That is, the content of the religious belief systems of the day fit rather well into the characteristics of what would be called traditional religions.

While apparently seldom if ever confronted in colonial times, the interesting question of contemporary times is what beliefs of the religious-freedom-guaranteed "infidel" (to use Jefferson's term) would actually be respected with religious freedom. Such a question reopens the door to ascertaining the proper definition of religion. The question is particularly relevant in current times because of the many who do faithfully hope and believe in such other systems of personally meaningful beliefs such as communism, democracy, nationalism, science, or humanism. The answer of highest internal consistency comes with seeing religion from a functional rather than static phenomenon.

Similarly, Smith (1978) makes a distinction between thinking about religion as a system of intellectual constructs and abstractions of objects and ideas as opposed to a personal, inner, and dynamic phenomenon. According to Wilfred Smith, the concept of religion as something impersonal, abstract, and outside the person become standard from about the mid-seventeenth century. Seen in this way, religion abstracts, objectifies, and depersonalizes in the eyes of the observer what actually is experienced by participants of a faith. Commentators are critical about religion being defined in this way. Smith charges that such a notion of religion can easily become the enemy of the faith and the pietistic personal aspect of religion. He suggests that the rise in conceiving of religion as a quantifiable concept may even be correlated with a decline in the very practice of religion. In favor of dropping the concept of religion as a noun and using it instead as an adjectival quality of living faith, he cites numerous authors of the same orientation. For instance, Karl Barth calls religion (as an abstract, outside, and often worshipped thing) unbelief and thus a sin. Emil Brunner says the Christian revelation ought not be called religion, Paul Tillich has apologized for using the term, C. S. Lewis labels it an odious term, and Dietrich Bonhoffer looked forward to a religionless Christianity. In other traditions, a modern Jewish thinker would claim that attempts to reduce Judaism to a religion is to betray its true nature. Muslims would say that Islam is not a religion as the term is understood in the West.

For Smith and others, everything that has ever happened in the religious life of mankind can be explained by the use of two concepts. These concepts can be "used equally by skeptic or believer, by Muslim or Buddhist, Episcopalian or Quaker, Freudian or Marxist or Sufi" (1978, p. 157). The two concepts, cumulative tradition and faith, are used to refer respectively to the observables and to the interaction of the individual with the traditions. The dynamic side of this pair, faith, is what comes from inside the individual. It is the person's relationship to the transcendent; it is what meaning the person derives from his faith journey.

This focus on dropping the term religion in favor of understanding its operation in each individual leads us to conceptualizing religion by its function rather than by its abstract characteristics. When packaged and systematized, religions eventually become nonliving abstractions to be compared and ranked and, as Paul Knitter (1985) humorously but accurately notes, with mine on top of yours. As such, the term then prostitutes the very quality it was intended to convey.

It is for these reasons that we prefer to think of religion in terms of the function it serves for the individual. Following Smith's lead, to participate in a religious movement is to be involved in something that points beyond self. For Arnold Toynbee (see Knitter, 1985, p. 39), the way to be in harmony with the truth of the universe is to give up self-centeredness. Obviously, these self-sacrificing orientations point us to process or function as the hallmark of the religious experience.

Function

In a sense, we have come full circle. Madison's, Jefferson's, and other's ultimate sense of the matter was that one's religious belief was a matter of personal conscience not to be constrained by other individuals or civil institutions. So pure was their conviction in this matter that they would not settle for mere toleration of those beliefs that were different from the one which was the cohesive and driving force of this nation. As a result of living within the early predominant cultural belief system, religion was typically defined from the biblical orientation only—"the duty we owe our Creator." With the onset of more and more religious diversity in this country, society, and the Supreme Court in particular, has now defined religion both from a human experience perspective and from an orientation that all beliefs (and non-beliefs) are on an equal basis. The summary definition abstracted from our sequence of Supreme Court cases is "Religion = Traditional Religion + Its Competitor Ideologies" (The Freedom Council Foundation, no date, p. 25). Religion has its basis for the individual in one's own conscience and thus is perceived as a duty to be obeyed.

It is obvious though that the U.S. Supreme Court is not alone in this expanded view of religion. As support for its decision in *United States* v. *Seeger* (1965), the Court approvingly cited theologian Paul Tillich's definition of God: "Translate it and speak of the depths of your life, the source of your being, of your ultimate concern, of what you take seriously without any reservation" (Warshaw, 1979, p. 44). As Tillich himself elaborates (1964, pp. 4-5),

> Religion is the state of being grasped by an ultimate concern, a concern which qualifies all other concerns as preliminary and which itself contains the answer to the question of the meaning of our life. Therefore, this concern is unconditionally serious and shows a willingness to sacrifice any finite concern which is in conflict with it. The predominate religious name for the content of such concern is God—a god or gods. In nontheistic religions divine qualities are ascribed to a sacred object or an all-pervading power or a highest principle such as the Brahma or the One. In secular quasi-religions the ultimate concern is directed towards objects like nation, science, a particular form or stage of society, or a highest ideal of humanity, which are then considered divine.

Bower (1944) cautions against ignoring the functional aspects of religion through an exclusive focus only on content or structure (pp. 47, 51). Two relatively recent U.S. Supreme Court cases highlight these dangers very cogently. Both cases were concerned with appeals for conscientious objector (CO) religious exemptions from military service. The first case, *U.S.* v. *Seeger* (1965) tested the legitimacy of religious exemptions for three men who professed to not believe in a Supreme Being. Yet the Universal

Military Training and Service Act of 1948 (operative at the time of the appeal) specifically restricted CO exemptions to "an individual's belief in a relation to a Supreme Being..." Objector Seeger claimed his religious disbelief in war was based on a purely ethical creed, "without a belief in God except in the remotest sense." Objector Jakobson claimed religious exemption on the basis of meditation and thought while believing in being related to "Godness" through the world and mankind. The third objector, Peter, based his request on the supreme expression of human nature. A Supreme Being or God for him was "man thinking his highest, feeling his deepest and being his best." Deciding unanimously in favor of the three objectors, the court through Justice Clark stated that "The test of belief in a 'relation to a Supreme Being' is whether a given belief that is sincere and meaningful occupies a place in the life of its possessor parallel to that filled by the orthodox belief in God of one who clearly qualifies for the exemption..." While none of the litigants claimed to be atheists, neither did they claim to be monotheistic as the 1948 act seems to require.

In the 1970 *Welsh* v. *U.S.* decision (again regarding religiously based conscientious objector exemptions), the updated Military Act of 1967 deleted reference to a Supreme Being in favor of deeply and sincerely held beliefs that are purely ethical or moral in both source and content. Claiming that his anti-war beliefs came from readings in history and sociology, not from religious training and belief, the objector was nonetheless granted the exemption by a 5-3 Court. Speaking for the Court, Justice Hugo Black also appealed to the functional definition of religion by noting that Welsh was granted the exemption in that he held his beliefs "with the strength of more traditional religious convictions."

In the final analysis, functional rather than content definitions seem to best convey the intention behind the notion of freedom of religious conscience. First, the static, structural, or more institutionalized definitions of religion always seem to exclude some view that its proponents claim has a religious nature. To remedy this, the characteristics and definition of religion would either have to be so minimal, to ensure including all beliefs, that little substance would remain, or the characterization, while reasonable to most, would in some way offend or exclude a group of believers somewhere, sometime.

As Pratt summarizes after reviewing many definitions by very knowledgeable individuals,

> But the striking thing about these definitions is that, persuasive as many of them are, each learned doctor seems quite unpersuaded by any but his own. And when the doctors disagree what are the rest of us going to do...
>
> The truth is, I suppose, that 'religion' is one of those general and popular terms which have been used for centuries to cover so vague and indefinite a collection of phenomena that no definition can be formed, which will include all its uses and coincide with everyone's meaning of it. Hence, all definitions of religion are more or less arbitrary and should be taken as postulates rather than as axioms. (see Van Til, 1978, p. 129)

Second, and most importantly, use of the functional definition keeps the focus of the definition within the individual conscience of each behavior. That is, each person is entitled to decide what constitutes a religion for him or herself. If religion is, as Thomas Jefferson said, a matter "solely between man and his God," then no other person can even say who or what God is. Even when George Mason and James Madison defined religion as the "duty we owe God," they placed this obligation within the context of each individual's conscience or opinion and not instead as decreed by any other individual. Madison says it so nicely in his "Memorial and Remonstrance":

> While we assert for ourselves a freedom to embrace, to profess and to observe the Religion which we believe to be of divine origin, we cannot deny an equal freedom to those whose minds have not yet yielded to the evidence which has convinced us.

Accordingly, the Bill of Rights guarantee of religious freedom (via the First Amendment) does not even suppose to define religion just as the Constitution purposefully prohibits a test of religion for office-holding (Article VI).

Religion Individualized

To mandatorially define or prescribe religion for another is to violate that person's religious conscience. Each person has that inalienable right to decide on matters that are in the arena of religious truth. Each has a right to believe according to that inward guide known as conscience. As has been said, "A man convinced against his will, is of the same opinion still" (Cobb, 1968, p. 6). As far as religious liberty is concerned, "neither the truth or falsity of religious beliefs, nor the good or bad faith with which they are held or taught can become legal issues..." (Konvitz, 1968, p. 43). According to Justice Douglas (*U.S. v. Ballard*, 1944), "Man's relation to God was made no concern of the state. He was granted the right to worship as he pleased and to answer to no man for the verity of his religious views." Otherwise,

> those who embraced one religious faith rather than another would be subject to penalties: and that kind of discrimination, as we held in *Sherbert* v. *Verner*, would violate the Free Exercise Clause of the First Amendment. It would also result in denial of equal protection by preferring some religions over others—an invidious discrimination that would run afoul of the Due Process Clause of the Fifth Amendment. (*U.S. v. Seeger*, 1965—Justice Douglas)

As Justice Jackson claimed in *West Virginia Board of Education* v. *Barnett* (1943),

> If there is any fixed star in our constitutional constellation, it is that no official, high or petty, can prescribe what shall be orthodox in politics, nationalism, religion, or other matters of opinion or force citizens to confess by word or

act their faith therein. To allow expression of religious views by some and deny the same privilege to others merely because they or their views are unpopular, even deeply so, is a denial of equal protection of the law forbidden by the Fourteenth Amendment. (*Niemotko* v. *Maryland*, 1951)

The psychologist William James is quoted by Justice Jackson (*United States* v. *Ballard*, 1944) on this topic:

If religious liberty includes, as it must, the right to communicate such experiences to others, it seems to me an impossible task for juries to separate fancied ones from real ones, dreams from happenings, and hallucinations from true clairvoyance. Such experiences, like some tunes and colors, have existence for one, but none at all for another. They cannot be verified to the minds of those whose field of consciousness does not include religious insight.

Whenever we define religion for someone else, we deny that person the freedom and integrity of his faith. Defining from the outside is not at all synonymous with living the faith from the inside. In fact, one of the distinguishing features of a religious tradition is that it enables those within it to see things differently from those who are outside of it.

Conclusion

To define religion by way of content of belief is to limit religious freedom. The absolute freedom of religion, according to Justice Douglas (*U.S.* v. *Ballard*, 1944), "embraces the right to maintain theories of life and of death and of the hereafter which are rank heresy to followers of the orthodox faiths. Heresy trials are foreign to our Constitution." This is so even if a religion constitutes a church of only one: "The determination of what is a 'religious' belief or practice ... is not to turn upon a judicial perception of the particular belief or practice in question" (*Thomas* v. *Review Board*, 1981).

Functional definitions of religion, as opposed to content or structural views, protect each individual's freedom of religious conscience from servitude to another's religious conscience. A starting point for conceptualizing religion in this way is to ask whether any belief occupies the same place in the life of the individual as an orthodox belief holds in the life of one typically considered as religious. If the answer to such a question is yes, and if the substance of that faith deals with matters of ultimate concern, of what is the vital and supreme reality in the universe, then such a belief serves a religious purpose for the individual possessor of that belief. To say otherwise would be to deny religious freedom and to set oneself up as the authority over another's conscience. Jefferson's words ring true: "religion is a matter which lies solely between man and God, that he owes account to none other for his faith or his worship" (Peterson, 1984, p. 510).

In full support of the conceptualization of religion as concerned with matters of ultimacy, Phenix (1959) provides six indicators to help decide what is and isn't of an ultimate nature. For him, ultimacy is concerned with importance, value, depth, totality, origin, destiny, and relationship. In each of the six dimensions, the individual makes judgments of a personal nature. They address for instance that which, respectively, is ultimately important, has high personal value, has profound depth and meaning, is related to the totality of existence, explains the origins of life and the individual personality, addresses the consummation of all things, and determines whether individual entities fit into some unified scheme. While too much reliance on analysis from these dimensions would likely move in the direction of a content focus, these dimensions at least provide a way to understand ultimacy. They provide a depth of understanding beyond the ungrounded relativeness of equating what is religious in one person's life to the fervency of belief in another's life.

Because there is conscientiously no other way to define what is a religion for a person other than to ascertain whether it serves a religious purpose, full religious liberties and protections must be accorded all such qualifying beliefs. This is at least partially what

Justice Black was referring to in *Everson* v. *Board of Education* (1947) when he said that the "[First] Amendment requires the state to be neutral in its relations with groups of religious believers and non-believers..." This is also what Black seemed to be addressing when he discussed the theory of evolution from the perspective of those who see it as an "anti-religious" doctrine in *Epperson* v. *Arkansas* (1968). That is, because the theory of evolution substitutes for the Bible's Genesis account, it must therefore be equally as religious as the creation perspective. If evolution contradicts some people's religious convictions, it is not at all a neutral concept. By extension, whatever legal qualifications apply (as in the *Epperson* case) to the teaching of evolution must equally apply to the teaching of creationism and vice versa. If either is excluded, so must the other; if either is permitted, so must the other; and if either is conditioned, so must the other. Removing one, for instance, and not the other does not leave the state in a legally neutral position toward these two religiously functioning beliefs. As Justice Harlan concurringly reported in *Walz* v. *Tax Commission* (1970), whatever tax exemption was extended to groups that were "antitheological, atheistic, or agnostic" should be extended to organized religious groups for neutrality to prevail. Similarly, in *Torcaso* v. *Watkins* (1961), Justice Black claimed it was unconstitutional to "impose requirements that aid all religions as against nonbelievers, and neither can it aid those religions based on a belief in the existence of God as against those religions founded on different beliefs." Also as Justice Brewer said in the decision of *The Holy Trinity* v. *United States* in 1892,

> The free, equal and undisturbed enjoyment of religious opinion, whatever it may be, and free and decent discussions of any religious subject is granted and secured; but to revile with malicious and blasphemous contempt, that religion professed by almost the whole community is an abuse of that right [of religious freedom]. Nor are we bound by any expressions in the constitution, as some have strangely supposed, either not to punish at all, or to punish indiscriminately the like attacks upon the religion of *Mahomet* or of the Grand *Lama*.

Just as the Fourteen Amendment has been used to turn the religious freedom component of the First Amendment on its head, the narrow exclusivist definitions of religion have turned the entire concept of government neutrality to religion on its head. When the Supreme Court ruled, for instance, in 1963 (*Abington* v. *Schempp*) to exclude Bible reading in public schools, since it was at odds with the requirement "that the Government maintain strict neutrality," the decision in effect discriminated in favor all substitute activities of the same general purpose. Justice Stewart called it correctly in dissenting with particular insight into the perversion of neutrality: "... a refusal to permit religious exercises thus is seen, not as the realization of state neutrality, but rather as the establishment of a religion of secularism..." He rightly argues instead that for schools to be truly neutral in the matter of religion, then permission of all religious activities is necessary. Ultimately, for neutrality to be operative, either all religiously functioning practices must be allowed or none allowed—no middle ground is reasonable. And this neutrality to all must include those traditional types of religions as well as any and all beliefs that are functionally matters of ultimacy for such believers.

The obvious conclusion is that there is no such thing as religious neutrality in education. Regardless of whether or not the Christian or any other religion or denominational orthodoxy is taught, ultimate concerns (i.e., religious issues) *are* being addressed and taught in schools everywhere. That is, education is directly involved in transmitting dimensions of religion like, for instance, value, origin, destiny, totality, depth, and relationship (Phenix, 1959).

References

Adams, Charles (Ed.) (1865). *The works of John Adams,* vol. 9.. Little Brown & Co.

Alley, Robert S. (1985). *James Madison on religious liberty.* Buffalo, NY: Prometheus Books.

Alley, Robert S. (Ed.) (1988). *The supreme court on church and state.* New York: Oxford University Press.

Blanshard, Paul (1960). *God and man in Washington.* Boston: Beacon Press.

Bower, William C. (1944). *Church and state in education.* Chicago, IL: University of Chicago Press.

Brauer, Jerald C., Mead, Sidney E. & Bellah, Robert N. (1976). *Religion and the American revolution.*

Bridenbaugh, Charles H. (1962). *Mitre and sceptre.* New York: Oxford University Press.

Brown, D. Mackenzie (1965). *Ultimate concern: Tillich in dialogue.* New York: Columbia University Press.

Chambers, Claire (1977). *The Siecus circle.* Belmont, MA: Western Islands.

Cobb, Sanford H. (1968). *The rise of religious liberty in America.* New York: Cooper Square Publ.

Coulson, Charles A. (1968). The similarity of science and religion. In Barbour, Ian G. *Science and religion.* London: SCM Press Ltd.

Counts, George S. (1941). *The education of free men in American democracy.* Washington, DC: Educational Policies Commission.

Dewey, John (1934). *A common faith.* New Haven: Yale University Press.

Dewey, John (1939). *Freedom and culture.* New York: Paragon Books.

Eidsmoe, John (1987). *Christianity and the constitution.* Grand Rapids, MI: Baker Book House.

Eiseley, Loren (1961). *Darwin's century.* Garden City, NY:: Anchor Books.

The Encyclopedia of Religion, Vol. 12 (1987). New York: Macmillan.

The Freedom Council (1984). *War on religious freedom.* Virginia Beach, VA.

Hayes, Carlton J.H. (1926). *Essays on nationalism.* New York: Macmillan.

Hick, John (1982). *God has many names.* Philadelphia: Westminster Press.

Hopfe, Lewis M. (1987). *Religions of the world* (4th ed.). New York: Macmillan Publ. Co.

Hume, Robert E. (1959). *The worlds living religions.* New York: Charles Scribner's Sons.

Hutchison, John A. & Martin, J., James A. (1953). *Ways of faith.* New York: The Ronald Press Co.

Jaki, Stanley (1966). *The relevance of physics.* Chicago: The University of Chicago Press.

Jaki, Stanley (1974). *Science and creation.* Edinburgh: Scottish Academic Press.

Jastrow, Morris (1981). *The study of religion.* Ann Arbor, MI: Scholars Press.

Knitter, Paul F. (1985). *No other name?* Maryknoll, NY: Orbis Books.

Konvitz, Milton R. (1968). *Religious liberty and conscience.* New York: Viking Press.

Kurtz, Paul (Ed.) (1973). *Humanist Manifestos I and II.* New York: Prometheus Books.

Leuba, James H. (1912). *A psychological study of religion.* New York: AMS Press.

McCarthy, Rockne, Oppewal, Donald, Peterson, Walfred, & Spykman, Gordon (1981). *Society, state & schools.* Grand Rapids, MI: William B. Eerdmans Publ.

McMillan, Richard C. (1984). *Religion in the public schools.* Mercer University Press.

Moehlman, Conrad H. (1944). *School & church: The American way.* New York: Harper & Brothers.

New Catholic Encyclopedia Vol. 12 (1967). New York: McGraw-Hill.

Peterson, Merrill D. (Ed.) (1984). *Thomas Jefferson Writings.* New York: Library Classics of the United States.

Phenix, Philip H. (1959). *Religious concerns in contemporary education.* New York: Teachers College, Columbia University

Bureau of Publications.

Reichley, A. James (1985). *Religion in American public life.* Washington, DC: The Brookings Institute.

Ringgren, Helmer & Strom, Ake V. (1967). *Religions of mankind.* Philadelphia: Fortress Press.

Rugg, Harold (1941). *That men may understand.* New York: Doubleday, Doran & Co.

Rushdoony, Rousas J. (1978). *The nature of the American system.* Fairfax, VA: Thoburn Press.

Schilling, Harold K. (1962). *Science and religion.* New York: Charles Scribner's Sons.

Smart, Ninian (1976). *The religious experience of mankind.* (2nd ed.) New York: Charles Scribner's Sons.

Smith, Wilfred Cantioell (1978). *The meaning and end of religion.* New York: Harper & Row.

Stokes, Anson P. & Pfeffer, Leo (1964). *Church and state in the U.S.* Westport, CT: Greenwood Press.

The Freedom Council Foundation (no date). Memorandum of law of Plaintiff Smith. U.S. District Court, Southern District of Alabama, Southern Division. Civil Action No. 82-0792-H.

Tillich, Paul (1964). *Christianity and the encounter of the world religions.* New York: Columbia University Press.

Torrance, Thomas F. (1981). *Christian theology and scientific culture.* New York: Oxford University Press.

Van Til, Cornelius (1978). *In defense of the faith.* Vol VI. Phillipsbury, NJ: Presbyterian & Reformed Publ. Co.

von Weizsacker, Carl F. (1964). *The relevance of science.* New York: Harper & Row.

Vos, Howard F. (Ed.) (1959). *Religions in a changing world.* Chicago: Moody Press.

Warshaw, Thayer S. (1979). *Religion, education & the Supreme Court.* Nashville: Abingdon.

Webster, Noah (1928/1967). *American dictionary of the English language.* San Francisco, CA: Foundation for American Christian Education.

Whitehead, Alfred North (1960). *Religion in the making.* New York: Meridian.

Whitehead, John W. & Conlan, John (1978). The establishment of the religion of secular humanism and its First Amendment implications. *Texas Tech Law Review*, X(*1*), 1-66.

Williams, J. Paul (1945). *The new education and religion*. New York: Association Press.

Williams, J. Paul (1969). *What Americans believe and how they worship* (3rd ed.). New York: Harper & Row.

Chapter 10

Education Is A
Religious Activity

That religion, or the duty which we owe to our Creator. (Bill of Rights, Section 16, Constitution of Virginia, June 12, 1776)

Religion that God our Father accepts as pure and faultless is this: to look after orphans and widows in their distress and to keep oneself from being polluted by the world. (*Holy Bible*, James 1:27—NIV)

While we assert for ourselves a freedom to embrace, to profess and to observe the Religion which we believe to be of divine origin, we cannot deny an equal freedom to those whose minds have not yet yielded to the evidence which has convinced us. (James Madison's "Memorial and Remonstrance," 20 June 1785)

[The assumption] that the Civil Magistrate is a competent Judge of Religious Truth ... is an arrogant pretension falsified by the contradictory opinion of Rulers in all ages... ("Memorial and Remonstrance," June 20, 1785)

As is the custom in this book, this chapter opens with several quotations to set the stage for what follows. In this group of four quotations, the tone of the chapter is set by way of a contradiction. The contradiction inherent in these quotes is the multiple and even opposing viewpoints regarding the nature of religion.

On first glance, the first (Perry, 1978, p. 312) and second quotes are in agreement that religion is defined in regard to a duty before God the Creator. In fact, both of these quotes put the emphasis on religion as a duty-bound activity unto God rather than as primarily the codification of a set of beliefs. It seems unreasonable, however, to expect that duties are only arbitrarily derived and that they do not emanate from some underlying set of beliefs (cf., I Timothy 5:4). From this it follows that religion cannot be defined merely by way of proper behaviors or duties; it has to have an underlying propositional nature also.

The matter is made even more contradictory by the remaining two quotes. Namely, James Madison, in his "Memorial and Remonstrance" (Dreisbach, 1987, pp. 173-177), expands the definition of religion beyond his own belief in Christianity to include all parallel beliefs that people hold to be true. Madison says this even while affirming in the same document his own support of the duty-to-God definition in the first quote above.

The contradiction attains its highest level in our fourth introductory quote, again from Madison's "Memorial and Remonstrance." Here the hard truth of the matter is revealed in the statement to the effect that no one, and especially civil rulers, can be the determiner of what constitutes a religious truth for anyone else. Justice Jackson said the same thing in the 1943 *Board of Education* v. *Barnette* case: "If there is any fixed star in our constitutional constellation, it is that no official, high or petty, can prescribe what shall be orthodox in ... religion..." (Neuhaus, 1974). As stated by Justice Douglas in *United States* v. *Ballard* (1944),

> The First Amendment ... knows no heresy... It embraces the right to maintain theories of life and of death and of the hereafter which are rank heresy to followers of the orthodox faiths. Heresy trials are foreign to our Constitution. Men may believe what they cannot prove. They may not be put to the proof of their religious doctrines or beliefs. Religious experiences which are as real as life to some may be incomprehensible to others. (Pfeffer, 1967, p. 692)

No matter how much one person's perception and reason may dictate that the object of someone else's belief is untrue or is an illusion, for the one who believes, it is supremely real and unchallengeably true. For this believer, the antagonists may instead be the illusionists. Justice Black wrote of religion (*Engle* v. *Vitale*, 1962) as a sacred, holy, and personal experience, far too holy and personal to come under the control of a civil magistrate (McMillan, 1984). A perfect example of the difficulty inherent in defining what is religious for others comes by way of conflicting statements of the U.S. Supreme Court. In 1838, the Court declared that the First Amendment did not cover atheists (*Commonwealth* v. *Abner Kneeland*) since they "do not believe in God or religion." Yet in 1977 (*Malnak* v. *Yogi*) it declared, "Atheism may be a religion under the establishment clause" (Barton, 1989, p. 182).

Putting the four introductory quotes together, the derived conclusion is that religion is whatever serves as sacred or divine for each person (cf., James, 1982, p. 31). As Madison indicates in the fourth introductory quote, whatever beliefs others may have that parallel his belief in the Christian religion serve as a religion for its adherents. No one has the right, he would say, to determine what is religious for another. Our review in the just prior chapter reached the same conclusion. Further, whereas most definitions of religion in colonial America referenced classic characteristics, the tenor in contemporary America is to acknowledge the religious functions of a diversity of beliefs. For instance, religion scholar Martin Marty notes the wide acceptance of Clifford Geertz's 1968 definition of religion: "A system of symbols that act to establish powerful, pervasive, and long-lasting moods and motivations by men, by formulation conceptions of a general order of existence, and clothing these conceptions with such an aura of factuality, that the moods and motivations seem uniquely realistic" (Marty, 1987, p. 21). Similarly, as Justice Brennan noted in 1963 (*Abington* v. *Schempp*), "Today the Nation is far more heterogeneous religiously, including as it does substantial minorities not only of Catholics and Jews but as well of those who worship according to no version of the Bible and those who worship no God at all." (Rice, 1978, p. 856). Feuerbach wrote (cf., Vitz, 1977, p. 68) that "the historical progress of religion consists in this: that which during an earlier stage of religion was regarded as something objective is now recognized as something subjective, so that which was formerly viewed and worshipped as God is now recognized as something human." In actuality, religion "is to be understood better by observing its function than by analyzing any of its particular doctrines, and that it is to be judged by the way it works rather than to be tested by logical cannons as an intellectual system" (Pratt, 1926, p. 6). According to Kallen (1951), it is the *way* we select and adore things and not *what* we select and adore that makes something religious to us.

Madison's "Memorial and Remonstrance" indicates that even in colonial times, religions were not just conceived of in a strict, biblically orthodox sense. Competing belief systems were even acknowledged back then as being religious in nature. For instance, in 1786 Jefferson remarked that his Act for Establishing *Religious* [emphasis added] Freedom was intended "to comprehend within the mantle of its protection, the Jew, the Gentile, the Christian and Mahometan, the Hindoo, and Infidel of every denomination" (Jefferson, 1984). Similarly in the 1800s, Supreme Court Justice Story, in writing about the First Amendment, clusters Christianity, Mahometanism, Judaism, and *infidelity* [emphasis added] together as religions (Pfeffer, 1967, p. 159). The difference between then and now is not so much some new liberalized view of the definition; rather, it is the availability of pluralistic writings now versus the enforced predominance of singularly Christian writings of colonial times. The evidence of that time suggests the singularity of definition was due to exactly what Madison was opposing—the defining by only one group of what was and was not properly a religion for others.

Given the premise that religion is whatever serves as sacred for each individual person, the logical outcome is that there are many things in life that suddenly acquire religious identity. For instance, whatever is thought to be a duty to a supreme being must be considered a religious activity for that person, regardless of how others may judge it. For some, this may incorporate all of life including education (cf., Spilka, Hood, and Gorsuch, 1985, p. 29).

Working from the above orientation about the nature of religion, the message of this chapter is that education is a religious activity. This will be demonstrated through several different approaches. First, we will see that experts directly claim that education is a religious function. Second, for many, education provides answers to what are considered to be primarily religious questions. Third, even where educational content makes no contact with what are perceived as typical religious pronouncements, its substitutionary function makes it a religion for its adherents. We will call this the doctrine of non-neutrality. Fourth, since the content of educational teachings ultimately rests on faith statements, education serves as a religion from this perspective also.

Historical Introduction

In the beginning, so to speak, the earliest cultures were not compartmentalized as religion plus law, plus science, plus education, and so on. There was no differentiation of one from another; all were intricately linked together in the common desire to live the "indissoluble life" (Coe, 1916, p. 109), the whole of which is best called religious in nature. Augustine's law of concentration that every person is serving gods in his life echoes this notion that life as a whole is religious (McCarthy, Oppewal, Peterson, & Spykman, 1981, p. 9): "Religion deals with 'the meaning of the whole' so that attempting to find meaning to life in anything less than the divine amounts to the idolatry of promoting a partial interest or perspective as ultimate ... making even democracy the center of education [is] idolatrous, because if democracy were an end in itself, that would amount to a political religion" (Marsden, 1994, p. 397). As theologian Niebuhr said, "The religious problem is the ultimate issue in education."

In its contribution to this religious whole, education was an extended initiation ceremony into society. As Jellema (1951) has noted, "education is always education by some kingdom and for citizenship in some kingdom" (p. 112). It is never neutral but always reflects some civitas or kingdom purpose and thus has to both have and promote the value system of that kingdom. Justice Douglas captures this concept in *Lemon* v. *Kurtzman* (1971) with the recognition that the public school cannot be divided into dichotomous categories of secular and religious: "the school is an organism living on one budget. What the taxpayers give for salaries of those who teach only the humanities or science without any trace of proselytizing enables the school to use all of its own funds for religious training."

While on the surface education may not appear to be religiously oriented, it is ultimately governed by a set of convictions religious in nature. The questions of origin and destiny, aims and purposes, what is and is not important or valued, and proper human relationships all address matters of ultimacy. It is these statements of values from which educational objectives are written, according to noted educator Ralph Tyler (1949, p. 34). And, as we have seen in earlier chapters, matters of ultimate concerns are what constitute religious orientations.

But not only does religion provide the basic framework within which education occurs, education, in turn, is the primary field for implementing religious orientations in very practical ways (cf., Phoenix, 1959, p. 19). Education is a primary vehicle of religious inculcation.

Except for very recently, it was an indisputable given that education served a religious function. The colonists transplanted to this country the belief of the Greeks, Romans, and Europeans that public education was to be denominationally controlled (Beard & Beard, 1927). As stated in Justice Frankfurter's concurring opinion in *McCollum* v. *Board of Education* (1948), "organized education in the Western World was Church education ... to the extent that the

State intervened, it used its authority to further the aims of the Church" (Pfeffer, 1967, p. 321). There is perhaps no more obvious evidence of this religious base for education than in the 1647 "Ye Olde Deluder Satan Law" of Massachusetts. The preamble to this law that gave legal force to public schools read, "It being one chief project of that old Deluder, Satan, to keep men from the knowledge of the Scriptures ... that learning may not be buried in the graves of our fathers in the church and commonwealth, the Lord assisting our endeavors... It is therefore ordered ... to teach all children..." (Pfeffer, 1967, p. 323).

Education by and large was considered a religious function throughout early America until the church and state separation of the mid to late 1700s secularized the state and, by extension, the schools.

Even so, the general perception of the teacher's transcendent role was portrayed in the *Massachusetts Teacher* magazine of 1857: "Magnify your office teacher! Higher than the kings of earth;—Are you not the prophet, preacher, to the future giving birth?" (Katz, 1968, p. 157). As late as 1861, statements like the following from the *Wisconsin Journal of Education* were still commonplace: "O, Teacher, reflect!, pause, ere you go further ... have you considered that you are preparing souls for eternal happiness or everlasting misery?" (Jorgenson, 1987, p. 59). Further, Katz (1968) notes that educators of the 1800s saw themselves devoted to an ideology that was crucial for the salvation of mankind (p. 115). But eventually schools, while serving primarily religious and even denominational purposes, went the way of secularization along with the state because they were perceived as properly being under civil jurisdiction. But as we shall see, the secularization of public schools made them no less religious institutions. The truthfulness of this paradoxical concept is seen in various ways including the opinions of those recognized as educational and/or religious experts.

Education Is Religious, Say Experts

No matter that disestablishment occurred—the "public-education system is and always has been teaching religion," says church historian Sidney Mead (1963, p. 68). Since "religion in its most nascent form is seldom ever recognized as religion at all" (Potter, 1930, p. 127), it is often overlooked as such. In fact, with disestablishment, the public schools took over what was earlier the basic responsibility of the established church. For example, Jefferson's faith in a moral system of public education substitutes the dogma of natural religion for the traditional religious ideology that was being squeezed out of public education: "The public school system in America becomes, in the Jeffersonian framework, the established church of the republic" (McCarthy, Skillen & Harper, 1982, p. 41). As a case in point, when this rationally-grounded natural religion took hold, Catholics switched from complaining about offensive Protestantism in public schools (Woltersstorff, 1992) to, in more current times, complaining about its substitute—secularism. But whatever the specific content, it ultimately is still religious in nature. As Baer notes, "It is impossible for schools to be completely or even substantially neutral towards religion" (Baer, undated, p. 5). It is sheer mythology to think otherwise, he says (1983). The "untutored devotion to the concept of neutrality" led Justice Goldberg to say in the *Abington School District* v. *Schempp* case (1963) that the Constitution "prohibited ... a brooding and pervasive devotion to the secular." As New York Secretary of State John C. Spencer said in 1841, "No books can be found, no reading lessons can be selected which do not contain more or less of some principles of religious faith, either directly avowed, or indirectly assumed" (McCarthy, et al., 1981, p. 91). In fact, the removal of religious instruction from public education would, according to education reformer D. Bethune Duffield, create "just what the constitution forbids; viz. a sectarian establishment consisting of schools, in which the tenets and dogma of sect are taught; for Infidels and Deists are as much a *sect* as Presbyterians, Catholics, or Quakers" (1857, p. 97).

This idea is captured in Mead's (1963) thesis that "the public school system of the United States *is* its established church" and the religion is the "democratic faith" (p. 68). He cites from Williams' *What Americans Believe And How They Worship* (1952) to say that a culture is a faith, a set of shared convictions. It is a spiritual entity.

Education is concerned with the sacred and is to "facilitate the quest for what is holy" (Purpel, 1989, p. 78). And because the maintenance of this faith calls for systematic and universal indoctrination, the government must teach it as an object of religious dedication.

This view that democracy is the faith or religion of American education is not primarily the "sour grapes" complaints of religious zealots. It was, in fact, the official view espoused by President Truman's 1946 Commission on Education. The Commission maintained that "It is imperative that American education develop a 'democratic dynamic' that will inspire faith in the democratic way of life." As the report read, "what America needs, what the world needs is a moral, intellectual, and spiritual revolution. Higher education fails unless it does what it can to initiate and carry through this revolution" (Kennedy, 1952, p. 89). In line with this mission, critics were not off the mark in claiming that the "underlying philosophy was that youth should be trained for the democratic state" (cited in Marsden, 1994, p. 393) "and that the democratic state is a sort of religion, with public education as its church." From all appearances, the intended educational goal of having democracy become America's religion has succeeded. According to Herberg (1974),

> [W]e have ... religion and national life so completely identified that it is impossible to distinguish the one from the other. I want to make it clear that when I designate the American Way of Life as America's civil religion, I am not thinking of it as a so-called common-denominator religion; it is not a synthetic system composed of beliefs to be found in all or in a group of religions. It is an organic structure of ideas, values, and beliefs that constitutes a faith common to Americans as Americans, and is genuinely operative in their lives; a faith that markedly influences, and is influenced by, the professed religion of Americans. Sociologically, anthropologically, it is *the* American religion, under-girding American national life and overarching American society, despite all indubitable differences in ethnicity, religion, section, culture, and class. And it is a civil religion in the strictest sense of the

term, for, in it, national life is apotheosized, national values are religionized, national heroes are divinized, national history is experienced as a *Heilsgeschichte*, as a redemptive history. (pp. 77-78)

The education heavy-weight and popular American philosopher John Dewey endorsed the notion that education is a religion: "I see no ground for criticizing those who regard education religiously." He in effect agreed that we do "make a religion out of education." In his article, "Education as a Religion" (1922), he called the education community to task, not because of some wrongful religious worship of education, but because it was promoting the salvivic qualities of education prior to actually being in possession of commensurate methods. True education does lead the student to a "genuine religious conversion" say Adams & Stein (1989, p. 64). Consistent with the language of religion, Dewey proposed that educational representatives allow the conviction of sin to lead them all to *repentance* (truly a religious concept) and to turn to the science of human behavior to keep education from becoming nothing more than "a mass of dogmas ... and ... ritualistic exercises" as one would expect in a religion that lacked vitality.

Educational philosopher Alfred North Whitehead similarly saw that education was essentially religious in nature. Similar to Dewey's ideas, education is religious for Whitehead because it inculcates both duty (in the potential of humanity to control the course of events) and reverence (in the idea that all eternity is held within the present) (Whitehead, 1957, p. 14) for our self-determination.

Others hold to essentially the same viewpoint. Ivan Illich has described the church of North America to be education (Neuhaus, 1974, p. 78). Henry Steele Commanger calls education the American religion (Adams, 1991, p. 9). John Dunphy (1983, p. 26) writes that public school teachers are "the proselytizers of a new faith; a religion of humanity," i.e., secular humanism. These teachers "will be ministers of another sort utilizing a classroom instead of a pulpit to convey humanistic values in whatever subject they teach, regardless of the educational level—preschool day care or large state universities." Philosopher/psychologist W. R. Coulson says this promotion of humanism in the schools amounts to "Unitarianism in the classroom" (Profile, 1990, p. 10). With the prohibition in schools of the Christian perspective, Justice Stewart (*Abington* v. *Schempp*, 1963) says it has led not to true neutrality but the possible "establishment of a religion of secularism" in education (McMillan, 1984, p. 176). Former Harvard president Nathan M. Pusey claims that this secularism has "become a faith" by which man can "solve all the remaining problems which stand between him and a secular paradise on earth" (Blum, 1987, p. 23). Similarly, the banning of teaching religion on public school property by the 1948 *McCollum* v. *Board of Education* Supreme Court decision is really only, according to Neuhaus (1974, p. 74), the teaching of "religion under another name." Finally, testifying in the federal district court case (*Smith* v. *Board of Education*, 1986) sociologist David Hunter stated that the humanism present in public school textbooks is also functionally incorporated into a wide range of religious institutions and that it "is certainly no less religious than transcendental meditation or ESP" (*Educational Week*, 1986, p. 1).

Beyond these statements by lone individuals, education is also declared to be a religious activity by groups of individuals. Those of various religious persuasions and the holy books of these societies equally declare education to be of a religious nature and even a religious mandate. As a case in point, consider the Christian religion.

It has been noted that education is a creation concept. Christian theologians suggest that Adam and Eve, even in their pre-fallen condition, would progressively take on more of the characteristics of God as they continued to live in obedience to Him (cf., Robertson, 1984, p. 55). After the fall, education for obedience was no less a significant factor. The early books of the Old Testament depict education as divinely commanded. In the book of Deuteronomy, Chapters 4 through 6, after God gave His commandments and statutes for all of life, He commanded His people to teach them to their children. Interestingly, this educational process was not restricted to some formal educational setting but was to occur continually— "when you sit in your house, when you walk by the way, when you lie down, and when you rise up" (6:7). In the New Testament, the command for parents to educate their children continues. All that children learn must be interpreted through the Word of God (cf., Ephesians 6:4; Romans 12:2). Educators of the Christian faith write extensively on this topic to parents and teachers alike with admonishments and prescriptions for insuring that all their efforts are consistent with God's Word (cf., Fugate, 1980; Rushdoony, 1981; Stormer, 1984). All hold to the persuasion of "education as religious activity" as sincerely as they hold to any other central concepts of their faith (cf., Titus, 1982).

This matter of education constituting a religious activity does not end with its confirmation by educators, historians, theologians, and Supreme Court Justices. In fact, education is a religious activity not primarily because experts say so but because of its very nature. The next section documents the fact that by its nature education cannot help but address religious world view questions.

Education Answers Religious Questions

At first glance most people would say that matters of education and of religion are different entities. The proposition that education is a religious activity has no intuitive appeal to many people. In fact, the statement typically arouses reactions of disbelief if not suspicion that some radical and unnatural agenda is being promoted. As we shall see in this section, education does provide answers to world view questions that are religious in nature. This perspective is not as far-fetched as it may sound if we remember that education had its origin as part of a religious whole and only became differentiated yet no less religious as the discipline became more self-conscious and self-serving.

The bottom line of the entire matter is that education is a religious activity because it properly and unabashedly makes statements about the sacred and thus about how we ought to live all of life. The fulfillment of this sacred trust is by way of a world view—the confession of that which unifies all of life and thought in a personally meaningful way (Holmes, 1983, p. 34). "... religion cannot be considered simply 'private.' It is an aspect of human thought and action," wrote Justice Frankfurter, "which profoundly relates the life of man to the world in which he lives—all of it, politics, economics, and social reform" (Smith, 1972, p. 320). It is important to note that the absence of belief in a deity does not disqualify world views from being religious. The key element is in the ultimacy of such beliefs (Hand, 1987, p. 45).

Basically, a person's world view does answer questions of ultimate concerns (e.g., the purpose and nature of the universe, the nature of mankind, the reason for man's existence) (cf., Hand, 1987, p. 45) as well as what is wrong with the world and how to fix it (cf., Walsh & Middleton, 184, p. 35). Wherever a world view or "belief system deals with fundamental questions of the nature of reality and man's relationship to reality, it deals with essentially religious questions" (Hand, 1987, p. 45). James in his classic book on religious experience (1982, p. 35) said answers to these questions "belong to the general sphere of religious life, and so should generically be classed as religious." Further, world views perform a religious function in the way they give even the mundane routines in life a meaningful relationship to the divine (Luckmann, 1967, p. 56).

Additionally, while discussed in more detail later, it is important now to see that the answers to these questions are largely based on assumptions rooted in faith more so than on reason and empirical evidence. This is so because in matters metaphysical we cannot ultimately prove what is right and wrong or true and false, but we do act on assumptions about these matters. Human action is even impossible without making these kinds of assumptions (Creel, 1977, p. 39). Reason and evidence relate primarily to the finite, but the meaning of life comes only by relating the finite to the infinite—our finiteness literally forces this on us. Outward behaviors make explicit our implicitly held beliefs and assumptions. In this sense, we are all people of faith.

World views actually determine interpretations more so than do mere facts. Theologian Paul Tillich suggests (1951, p. 34) that even those in his profession do not generally develop their philosophical systems from facts so much as their basic world view perspectives determine their interpretations of these facts. After all, people generally see the same data but interpret it differently—for instance, from the same observed phenomenon, one person will believe in God and another will not. Consider also the work of

Derek Freeman (1983) that refuted the findings of Margaret Mead in her landmark book, *Coming of age in Somoa* (1961). According to Freeman's research, Mead apparently did not see the evidence that was readily available to her because her world view orientations would not let her. Kuhn (1970), whose work on the effect of paradigms is often cited, likewise notes that paradigms, as with world views, functions to determine how we perceive or do not perceive what we see.

But faith and learning are not opposites according to Phenix (1966, p. 14). They are, in fact, "necessarily inclusive of one another." Every program of instruction has some faith basis about what is ultimately true and important. Similarly, every religious orientation, whatever it may be, requires some knowledge learned about the world we live in and people we live with. In this sense there cannot be the possibility of having no religion; people differ in this regard only in the content of their beliefs.

This notion of a world view as a universally applicable scheme unifies religion and education. The root word for religion is the Latin *ligare* which means "to bind together" (Adams & Stein, 1989, p. 59). The actual word "religion" is a transliteration of the Latin word "religio" which again means "to bind together" (Oates, 1973, p. 21). Religion ties everything together, serves as a guide for thought, and provides a unifying perspective on life. This conceptual scheme is called a world view (Holmes, 1983, p. 33): "Religion is an interpretive scheme which provides man with a map that enables him to chart his course in the areas of bafflement he encounters in the course of his life" (Greeley, 1985, p. 84). Midgley claims that systems like Marxism, evolutionism, art, and science serve as religions, as opposed to something like devotion to golf, because by their very nature they are dominant creeds and explicit faiths "by which people live and to which they try to convert others. They tend to alter the world" (1985, p. 16).

Education likewise addresses the same concerns as do religions: "All education pursued with concern for ultimate meaning is religious education, and all teaching and learning dedicated to the highest excellence and the deepest truth are in a fundamental sense acts of worship" (Phenix, 1966, p. 26). And all education practically does concern itself with ultimate meanings and with developing a world view. As our world view determines our values, education has a major role in both developing and establishing these values. Aristotle captures the notion well in his statement "that the aim of education is to make the pupil like and dislike what he ought" (Lewis, 1947, p. 26). From a different professional perspective but with equal cogency, George Washington noted in his Farewell Address, "And let us with caution indulge the supposition that morality can be maintained without religion. Whatever may be conceded to the influence of refined education on minds of peculiar structure, reason and experience both forbid us to expect that national morality can prevail in exclusion of religious principle" (Johnston, 1987, p. 147). The point is that education inculcates a world view value system that is inherently religious in nature. For instance, education is held responsible by society at large for providing a vision of the good, true, and beautiful life and for equipping children for getting there. Interestingly, Creel (1977, p. 38) defines religion in precisely the same terms: "life lived in wholehearted pursuit of the true and the good, and in disciplined commitment to the fruits of that commitment."

While Dewey, Jefferson, and others may have differing perspectives on that issue, all are addressing the same fundamental issues about the good life. To illustrate, Jefferson envisioned education as *the* vehicle for setting people free: "If the condition of man is to be progressively ameliorated, as we fondly hope and believe, education is to be the chief instrument in effecting it" (Pfeffer, 1967, p. 327). It all starts with a will-to-live, says Albert Schweitzer, which becomes reflected in what he calls one's theology (cf., Oates, 1973, p. 48). Similarly, Gordon Allport says religion is "the right of each individual to work out his own philosophy of life, to find his personal niche in creation as best he can" (Abraham, 1982, p. 225). But just a religion starts with this valuing life as life, so too is this a characterization of education as Jefferson has demonstrated. Rushdoony (1963, p. 315) says it this way:

> If education is in any sense a preparation for life, then
> its concern is religious. If education is at all concerned

with truth, it is again religious. If education is vocational, then it deals with calling, a basically religious concept. It would be absurd to reduce preparation for life, truth and calling to an exclusively religious meaning in any parochial sense, but it is obvious that these and other aspects of education are inescapably religious.

Since education is about the business of teaching morality and since "morality is not separable from religion" (Jellema, 1951, p. 121) then we see again that education has to be considered as a religious endeavor. The National Education Association claims without reservation that education is concerned with imparting moral and spiritual values (Pfeffer, 1967, p. 361). The concern over ultimacy is just as relevant for education (cf., Baer, undated) as for religion (Greeley, 1985, p. 64). From Aristotle forward, educators agree that education is concerned with "the transmission and nurturing of truths by which a community would live" (Neuhaus, 1987, p. vi). This means that teachers invariably work at the metaethical level (Baer, undated, p. 15). The weighty responsibility of it all typically astonishes student teachers even while remaining a challenge for veteran teachers. Teachers cannot help but be moral figures in the lives of their students. Regularly, teachers are called upon to answer students' questions such as "What am I supposed to do in life" and "Why they were fated to live where and as they did...?" (Coles, 1994, p. A 64).

A vast amount of evidence regarding the fact that education addresses world view issues is contained in the record of U.S. Department of Education hearings (1984) in the form of violations of the Pupil Rights Amendment (Schlafly, 1984). Only a few of those testimonies are included here. In Bellevue, Washington, thirteen-year-olds were asked at what age is it okay to engage in acts such as (list only sampled here) French kissing, masturbation, having intercourse, having a variety of sexual partners, etc. After answering the questions, the children were then supposed to physically move to the "yes before 14" or "yes after 14" section of the room in answer to each question. Apparently yes before or after age fourteen were the only two answers allowed (p. 39). In a Portland,

Oregon school, students aged fourteen and up were taught in a prob-lem-solving workshop by Oregon Department of Education employ-ees that "There are no objective standards of morality, and that truth is relative and can mean anything they want it to mean" (p. 50). The program, TA for Teens, as taught in North Clackamas, Oregon, promotes autonomy of children from any and all authority. Ways to develop this attitude include teaching the teens to destroy things of value, flashing the middle finger in the air, and spilling things over and over again (p. 60). In a fifth grade Health class in Lincoln City, Oregon, sexual activity among the fifth graders was *not* at all discouraged, and intercourse was described, abstinence was not mentioned, and boys were told to handle a plastic model of female genitalia with a tampon inserted. In Ohio, students were told by their teacher, "If your parents told you there was a God and He made this world, they are lying to you" (p. 126). The Health class curriculum used in East Detroit, Michigan includes a "do it yourself" manual with instructions on foreplay, erections, positions for intercourse, etc. In a writing workshop for grades three through six in Mexico, Missouri, students practice yoga exercises, write their own horo-scopes, role-play book characters such as a warlock, a spiritess, an exorcist, and a poltergeist as well as use powers of concentration to try to move a metal object (p. 204). In the Shawnee Mission public schools, students are taught how to assume various bodily positions for meditation and to vocally recite unknown words and language. Parents of children in this program saw it as a form of occult practice and not just meditation. In Denver, Colorado the test used in certain classes was "so dirty that I cannot repeat it out loud" (p. 258). In a story that seventh graders in one school had to read, an economically poor mother was cast in a positive light for drowning her three chil-dren ("They floated for a while and finally disappeared.") so they could be much happier in heaven: "She smiled for the first time in many months, satisfied that she had fulfilled her maternal duty" (p. 272). In Montgomery County, Maryland, a drama group, trained with federal funds, performed a sociodrama for grades two through six. In one skit, the announcement was made by one actor that God was dead, followed by all the actors using obscene gestures, doing obscene things, and saying obscene words. It was reported that

"When the play was over the students went to recess and mimicked the actor's actions and words" (p. 430). Apparently with the notion that God was dead, it was then considered acceptable to behave any way one wanted.

While many more accounts could be taken from the 440 pages of edited excerpts of the official proceedings, the point hopefully has been made. Namely, that education does directly provide answers to world view issues of an ultimately religious nature even against the objections of parents and even in violation of various federal, state, and local statutes. Now if this is not convincing enough, selections from another investigation (Gabler, Gabler, & Hefley, 1985) into classroom and curriculum teachings should convince the reader that education does address religious matters. Selections from their review follow. An introductory text to the behavioral sciences states, "For a very few, religion can still provide a special sense of embracing belonging and selfhood; but for most, religion is but a Sunday meeting house and nursery school, and a recreation center, which cannot adequately define the entire person" (p. 36). From evidence of many current day polls, this is not even the way most people think about religion!

But, as the reviewers found, texts do more than misrepresent facts; they actively promote various religious perspectives. A high school sociology text says this about Christianity: "[it] didn't help the blacks gain dignity and equality in America, for Christian love was the white's love of themselves and of their own race" (p. 103). Some public school textbooks even rewrite the Bible. Consider this textbook version of Exodus 14:21-22: "Moses may have led them across some shallow swamps and into the Sinai (sigh-nigh) desert. The Hebrews called these swamps the "Sea of Reeds" because of the tall grass that grew in them. It may be that the Sea of Reeds was later called the Red Sea by mistake" (p. 38). Some texts go so far as to classify various holy book accounts as myths: "[M]yths may give a picture of the world as having fallen from a perfect state. The evil of the world, according to these traditions, resulted from man's failure to obey the will of God, and it is only by following the will of God that the world can be restored to its proper state. This is essentially the mythological standpoint of Christianity, Judaism,

Islam, and many other religions" (p. 38). Finally, students in creativity training were asked to question biblical teachings: "... we should teach children to question the Ten Commandments ... monogamy, and the laws against incest" (p. 36).

The curriculum "Children of the Rainbow" has generated lots of controversy in the way it has redefined correct answers to religiously oriented themes. This curriculum takes a very positive stand toward homosexuality (clearly a religious issue for many people) by featuring reading such as "Heather Has Two Mommies" and "Daddy's [male] Roommate" (*Newsweek*, 1992).

This teaching of children to be free from so-called religious superstitions and prejudices with the intent of supposedly making them rational, objective human beings is obvious in the above examples. Daniel Webster is on record as being opposed to a very similar effort attempted at Girard College in Pennsylvania in 1844:

> It has been said ... that there was no teaching *against* religion or Christianity in the system. I deny it ... the children are ... to learn to be suspicious of Christianity and religion: to keep clear of it. They are to be told and taught that religion is not a matter of the heart or conscience, but for the decision of cool judgment of mature years; that at a period when the whole Christian world deems it most desirable to instill the chastening influences of Christianity into the tender and comparatively pure mind and heart of the child. (Glenn, 1988, p. 192)

Ultimately the entire matter of individual existence, while often encountered in an educational setting, is a religious issue, say sociologists like Durkheim and Weber (cf., Luckman, 1967, p. 12). The social interaction process leads to the two complementary aspects of the individuation of consciousness and the giving of moral meaning to life (Luckman, 1967, p. 48). In this sense, the cultural system becomes the means by which life is interpreted—the means by which people are elevated from mere biological existence. In fact, any kind of radical separation from the social world results in the loss of moral bearings and psychological well-being to such an extent that the individual may choose death instead (Berger, 1967, p. 22). The teacher's role in developing the social aspect of humanity was so important for Dewey that he said in his pedagogic creed, "... in this way the teacher always is the prophet of the true God and the usherer in of the true kingdom of God." Here again, this is most appropriately a religious function (cf., Greeley, 1985, p. 53). Yet it is, in final analysis, within the educational setting where this activity is most purposely conducted for a vast majority of students. After all, religion is man's attempt to bring human significance to the entire universe (Berger, 1967, p. 28).

Summarizing this section, the interpretative scheme that guides one through the bafflement of life is called a world view. World views answer religious questions. In this sense all people have a religious orientation; there is no neutral zone. Even for those radical contemporary theologians who say that the Christian religion does not have to presuppose either the existence or non-existence of God nor include any religious beliefs at all, it is still a gospel for them. It is exclusively a secular gospel, a good news world view about "how man should live and think and act and feel and see things..." (Wolterstorff, 1967, p. 13). Convictions over what is good, what is true, what is the ultimate meaning of life, and so on are not simply inborn; instead, they come through experience and more precisely through directed experiences. In a word, they come in no accidental way through education. Since education is the systematic attempt to provide students with answers and orientations to life, it cannot help but be religious in nature.

Yet, critics of this perspective protest saying that there is a distinction to be made between the sacred and the secular. The argument is that orientations to life that are outside of the sacred realm are not generally considered to be religious. They are seen as either secular or as neutral in content—not religious.

Myth of Neutrality

The very fact that education addresses world view questions of a religious nature means that there cannot be religious neutrality in education. This is especially evident in the effect of court decisions that deny religious practices in the school (i.e., teaching of creationism, posting of the Ten Commandments). When such decisions are made, it is not the case that the issue or question addressed by such prohibited practices is also prohibited, nor that students and teachers no longer think about such things, nor that the questions become irrelevant. No, the matter becomes addressed by some alternative answer. For instance, the question of how the human race came into being is not summarily voided with the court rulings that creation science cannot be taught. Instead, some other explanation such as evolution is taught as the answer to the still-relevant question. Such court decisions only deal with answers to questions; they do not and cannot prohibit the question from being asked. The history of mankind, and particularly during times of religious persecution, shows that officially sanctioned answers and/or the restrictions on question-asking do not keep people from seeking personally satisfying answers anyway. Even an imposed silence on a matter ultimately communicates that the matter is of a trivial nature which thus is an answer to the initiating question. In the final analysis, attempts to avoid sectarianism or religious instruction by abolishing it altogether "would be in itself sectarian; because it would be consonant to the views of a particular class, and opposed to the opinions of other classes" (McCarthy, et al., 1981, p. 91). That is why this section appropriately makes synonymous the phrases "non-neutrality" and "the substitutionary function of educational content."

The impossibility for education to be neutral in matters of religion is seen in the education related decisions of the U.S. Supreme Court even while it claims to be "firmly committed to a position of neutrality ... in the relationship between man and religion" (Justice Clark in *Abington School District* v. *Schemmp*, 1963). The totally arbitrary decisions the court has made in this regard are illustrated in *Wolman* v. *Walter* (1977) as summarized in Justice Blackman's main opinion: "In summary, we hold constitutional those portions of the Ohio statute authorizing the state to provide nonpublic school pupils with books, standardized testing and scoring, diagnostic services, and therapeutic and remedial services. We hold unconstitutional those portions relating to instructional materials and equipment and field trip services." Who can say where the logic is! Moynihan's (1978, p.

383

36) tongue-in-cheek observation cannot be improved upon: "Backward reels the mind. Books are constitutional. Maps are unconstitutional. Atlases, which are books of maps, are unconstitutional. Or are they? We must await the next case." He continues, "In this regard, Justice Rehnquist took the court to task for its neutrality inconsistencies. The Court apparently believes that the Establishment Clause of the First Amendment not only mandates religious neutrality on the part of government but also require that this court go further and throw its weight on the side of those who believe that our society as a whole should be a purely secular one" (quoted in McCarthy, et al., 1982, p. 88). This according to Justice Stewart amounts to "the establishment of a religion of secularism" (*Abington School District* v. *Schempp*, 1963). The Chief Justice also chastises his own court in *Meek* v. *Pittinger* (1975):

> The failure of the majority to justify the differing approaches to textbooks and instructional materials and equipment in the above respect is symptomatic of its failure even to attempt to distinguish the Pennsylvania textbook loan program, which it upholds, from the Pennsylvania instructional materials and equipment loan program, which it finds unconstitutional.

At a deeper level, McCarthy, et al. (1982, p. 80) note that the court's attention has been on laws that assume the present political-educational structure of public and private schools. They have not yet questioned the legitimacy of that structure itself. If it turns out, however, that the very existence of the present system of public education alongside independently financed private schools is religiously discriminatory both by inhibiting free exercise and by sustaining an illegitimate establishment, then all of the efforts to find subtle ways to remain 'neutral' within the present system are in vain.

Arons (1976, p. 78) claims that "the notion of value-neutral education implicit in the legal distinction between religious and secular education is untenable" because values inculcation cannot be eliminated from schooling. Justice Stewart noted in *Schempp* that "a compulsory state educational system so structures a child's life that if religious exercises are held to be impermissible activity in schools, religion is placed at an artificial and state-created disadvantage." Similarly, Justice Burger, in *Lemon* v. *Kurtzmann* (1971) revealed his non-neutral world view that governmental concerns are of greater priority than religious concerns:

> To have states or communities divided on the issues presented by state aid to parochial schools would tend to confuse and obscure other issues of great urgency. We have an expanding array of vexing issues, local and national, domestic and international, to debate and devise on. It conflicts with our whole history and traditions to permit questions of the Religious Clauses to assume such importance in our legislatures and in our elections that they could deviate our attention from the myriad issues and problems that confront every level of government.

Obviously as noted elsewhere in this chapter, democracy allows religion to find its place just as long as it doesn't overstep the bounds as determined by democracy. This is hardly non-neutrality! The result of court decisions, according to Justice Stevens, that have tried to comply with the impossible task of maintaining religious non-neutrality in the public schools "has been, as Clarence Darrow predicted, harm to 'both the public and the religion that [this aid] would pretend to serve" (*Wolman* v. *Walter*, 1977).

There is no neutrality regarding the religious content of curriculum and instruction. Education always comes from one religious perspective or another. Lawrence Kohlberg, author of texts, curriculum, and test instruments on morality, says, "My first reaction to the notion that moral education and religious education are identical in their implications for civil liberties was, like that of most lay people, one of incredulity and shock ... [however,] Once the school becomes engaged in teaching a particular moral doctrine belonging to a particular group of citizens organized as a religious, political, or ideological body, it may well be accused of establishing religion" (1981, pp. 294-95).

It is important to see that in claiming "that schools cannot be 'value-neutral' but must be engaged in moral education" (p. 296), while at the same time saying that "moral education must be defined in terms of justice rather than in terms of majority consensus" (p. 297), Kohlberg is engaging in semantic double-talk. Kohlberg (as well as others) has conveniently defined the morality that he proposes and instruction in religion (that he opposes) such that they supposedly do not overlap. However, make no mistake about it, Kohlberg intends for his philosophy to function as the operative scheme for addressing matters of ultimate concern: "Public education is committed not only to maintenance of the rights of individuals but also to the transmission of the values of respect for individual rights" (p. 37). His own words betray his true position: "Not only can advice about means not be separated from choice of ends, but there is no way for educational consultants to avoid harboring their own criteria for choosing ends. The 'value-neutral' consulting model equates value neutrality with acceptance of value relativity ... but the educator or educational psychologist cannot be neutral in this sense either" (p. 65). Ironically, he *insists* that there is no problem with the legitimacy of moral education in public schools "if the *proper* [emphasis added] content of moral education is recognized to be the values of justice that themselves prohibit the impositions of beliefs of one group on another" (p. 37). While insisting on justice, Kohlberg does not allow for groups to coexist if they disagree that his way is the correct way in public education.

Because public schools cannot be value neutral but, as Kohlberg says, must teach values, the National Catholic Welfare Conference (1961) claimed that such schools are not religiously neutral: "... an 'orthodoxy' is expressed—inescapably so—even in a curriculum from which religious 'orthodoxies' are absent..." (LaNone, 1967, p. 24). From the very same facts, this conference reached the exact opposite conclusion:

> After all, public schools teach students to see nature as purposeless and devoid of sacred qualities. They take no note of the claim basic to all Western religion, that God's hand shapes the structure of history. Psychology and home economics replace the immortal soul with the temporal

self. Economics classes teach students that they are self-interested utility maximizers. Students learn to value the goods of this world, not those of the world to come. (Nord, 1995, p. 44)

Obviously, one's world view does predispose the response given!

The crucial dilemma, as noted at the outset, is in attempting to define for others what is religious for them. In the final analysis, we cannot deny that something is religious in nature if it functions as a religion or if it answers religiously oriented questions for others. The irony of it all is that while public education is declared to be neutral toward religion, it is anything but neutral. For instance, wherever the courts rule that a particular religious perspective cannot be promoted (e.g., biblical creationism), some other belief system substitutes for it. And as the U.S. Supreme Court ruled in *Welsh* v. *United States* (1970), a valid test for something to be considered religious is whether it is "A sincere and meaningful belief which occupies in the life of its possessor a place parallel to that filled by God." In other words, whatever substitutes (e.g., evolution) for what is commonly accepted as a religious belief (e.g., creationism) is a religious belief for its proponents. Matthew's (1971) *Introduction* to Darwin's *The Origin of Species* (1972) says it this way: "Belief in the theory of evolution is thus exactly parallel to belief in special creation—both are concepts which schools know to be true but neither, up to the present, has been capable of proof" (p. xi).

Furthermore, this refusal of the court to officially define religion, leaving it up to the believer instead, equally makes institutions that officially either allow or prohibit religious instruction the determiners of religious orthodoxy. That is, when civil authority prohibits a teaching that is part of a personal religious belief for anyone, it is in fact allowing some substitutionary teaching to prevail. This state judgment over the inappropriateness of certain religious teaching (e.g., Ten Commandments) and the commensurate allowance of some other substitute teaching (e.g., civic morality) effectively establishes a state religion (cf., Montgomery,

1889/1972, p. 80). The state is operating in the realm of deciding what content is appropriate to address and even give answers to, for at least some constituents, what constitutes a religious matter for them. As Neuhaus (1974, p. 74) has observed, the effect of "the 1947 McCollum case banning the teaching of religion in school properly—is to teach religion under another name." Said in a different way,

> if religious exercises are held to be impermissble activity in schools, religion is placed at an artificial and state-created disadvantage. Viewed in this light, permission of such exercises for those who want them is necessary if the schools are truly to be neutral in the matter of religion. And a refusal to permit religious exercises thus is seen, not as the realization of state neutrality, but rather as the establishment of a religion of secularism, or at the least, as government support of the beliefs of those who think that religious exercises should be conducted in private. (Justice Stewart in *Abington School District* v. *Schempp*, 1963)

In a similar way, Judge Hand noted that "some religious beliefs are so fundamental that the act of denying them will completely undermine that religion. In addition, denial of *that* belief will result in the affirmation of a contrary belief and result in the establishment of an opposing religion" (Hand, 1987, p. 54). So, while the courts in some ways claim not to define religion, they do anyway. Again, there is no such thing as neutrality in the matter of religion as it bears on education. To demonstrate, if the courts truly were neutral in this regard then all religious views should be treated equally. But they are not! For example, the following three offenses of religious conscience have received differential rather than similar treatments by the courts (cf., Freund, 1969). That is, since school prayer was religiously offensive to those of a certain religious persuasion, all ceremonial prayers have been eliminated from public schools. Yet the religious offensiveness to a different religious group in forcing their children to salute the flag (considered to be the bowing to an idol) did not at all result in eliminating the practice from any public schools. These children were tolerantly granted permission to not salute, yet they still had to witness its occurrence. In another instance, parents in Tennessee (*Mozart* v. *Hawkins County School District*, 1988) wanted their children excused from reading materials that violated their religious beliefs. In this case, the children were not allowed even to be excused from using the materials nor to be able to use substitute materials instead. Thus the court *did* decide what is and what is not religious in nature, and it did so differently for each of the appellants. Furthermore, such decisions, like removing prayer, affects all children regardless of their religious persuasion. The bottom line to all of this is that even if the decisions were all equitable, they would still be religiously oriented. Neutrality, as should now be obvious, is just not possible. Chief Justice Burger was beginning to see the light when he said (*Lemon* v. *Kurtzman*, 1971), "what would appear to some to be essential to good citizenship might well for others border on or constitute instruction in religion" (Warshaw, 1979, p. 58).

True neutrality means that, for instance, "the public schools cannot teach that all men ought to worship God ... that we ought to tell the truth because God wills it ... equally, they cannot teach anything which implies disagreement with any of these beliefs. They cannot teach that we ought to eat, drink, and be merry because tomorrow we die and are gone forever" (Wolterstorff, 1967, p. 11). Obviously, true neutrality is impossible to achieve!

Departing from the philosophical kind of reasoning above, the same thing has been said more directly in several ways. As admitted by humanist advocate Charles Francis Potter (1930), the United States has established the school in the place of the disestablished church: "This nation thus committed its life to the humanistic position long before such a faith was thought of as a religion" (p. 127). Accordingly, that which goes on in public schools as an alternative to the church has been declared as religious in a number of different court cases. In the Supreme Court 1963 *Abington* v. *Schempp* decision, Justice Clark said "the state may not establish a religion of secularism" (Whitehead, 1982, p. 110). And according to Neuhaus (1987), secular humanism apparently qualifies as a religion whether substantively or functionally defined. In a 1982 Alabama court case, the judge noted that "the religions of atheism, materialism, agnosticism, communism, and socialism have escaped the scrutiny of the courts throughout the years, and make no mistake, these are to the believers religions; they are ardently adhered to and quantitatively advanced in the teachings and literature that is presented to the fertile minds of the students in various school systems" (McCarthy, 1983, p. 92). The judge further noted that "it is time to recognize that the constitutional definition of religion encompasses more than Christianity and prohibits as well the establishment of a secular religion" (p. 92). In the 1961 *Torcaso* v. *Watkins* case, the U.S. Supreme Court footnoted, "Among religions in this country which do not teach what would commonly be considered a belief in the existence of God are Buddhism, Taoism, Ethical Culture, Secular Humanism and others" (Rice, 1978, p. 856). In this case, the court formally included in the sphere of religion those "based on a belief in the existence of God" as well as "those religions founded on different beliefs." Apparently, the humanist churches of secular humanism even qualify for religious tax exemption by the Internal Revenue Service (cf., *The Journal*, 1995, p. 1): "Indeed, the preamble of the American Humanist Association states that the AHA is itself a 'religious organization.' Leaders in the popular movement—from Dewey to Lamont, from Kurtz to Beattie—have repeatedly, or at key stages, identified humanism as a religion... Indeed, this document [Humanist Manifesto I] implies that humanism is the highest realization of man's religious aspirations" (p. 6). Another belief system, that of Transcendental Meditation as practiced in the public schools, was declared an advancement of religion which thus violated the First Amendment (*Malnak* v. *Yogi*, 1979—McCarthy, 1983, p. 78). All of this is to acknowledge that belief systems that are promoted in public schools, even though they are not thought of as stereotypical religions, are religions.

Though this appears to be a phenomenon of only the last several decades in terms of expanding the nature of religion, this is not at all the case. This phenomenon has been documented for at least the last several hundred years. Interestingly, it is incisively spoken to via several different situations of the mid-1800s in the United

States. The first to be discussed occurred in Massachusetts, the state that was for so long the national trend setter in education. Here, Horace Mann promoted what was supposedly a nonoffensive permission of Bible use in the classroom. In his last annual address as school superintendent (Mann, 1849), he said that the charges claiming that he "attempted to exclude religious instruction from the school, or to exclude the Bible from the school, or to impair the force of that volume, arising out of itself, are now, and always have been, without substance or semblance of truth ..." (p.116). He went on to say that the educational "system earnestly inculcates all Christian morals; it founds its morals on the basis of religion; it welcomes the religion of the Bible; and in receiving the Bible, it allows it to do what it is allowed to do in no other system—to speak for itself" (p. 117). The rationale behind Mann's actions was that the Bible was to be used but not explained, allowing it "to speak for itself" so that sectarian instruction would not occur and so that any of various sects would not be offended. Yet his being charged with exactly the opposite of what he claimed to promote points to equivocation on someone's part.

Mann's true position on the Bible seems to be quite the opposite of what he publicly claimed. As Pfeffer (1967) wonders, " ... it is difficult to believe that Mann could accept the practicability of nonsectarian comment—even limited to the exposition of the text" (p. 334). Others who have studied Mann's actions in depth claim that he was actually promoting the religion of Unitarianism in the schools. In denying the opportunity for the Bible to be verbally taught while at the same time promoting the natural and innate capacities of mankind, Mann was surrreptitiously implanting natural religion in the schools. Mann believed in the ideas of natural law and human reason: "[B]ut, for myself, natural religion stands as pre-eminent over revealed religion as the deepest experience ... it gives us a feeling of truth; and however much the lights of revealed religion may have guided the generations of men amid this darkness of mortality, yet I believe that the time is coming when the light of natural religion will be to that of revealed as the rising sun to the daystar that preceded it" (Blumenfeld, 1985, pp. 199-200). In writing to phrenologist Combe, Mann favorably acknowledged "the religious truths contained in your 'Constitution of Man'" (Blumenfeld, 1985, p. 209) and commented that Combe's "system contained all there is of truth in orthodoxy" (p. 210). The insidious nature of substitutionary religion in public schools is revealed in the way Mann promoted it by supposedly endorsing use of the Bible.

It appears that Mann was able to carry out his subterfuge by couching his natural religion in references to God and the Bible— just as long as these terms were defined his way and not the way of mainstream theologians. For instance, in writing to congratulate Combe on the large sales of his book, Mann said, "this fact is most cheering to those who wait for the coming of the intellectual Messiah..." (p. 231). Make no mistake about it, the vision Mann had for public schools was nothing less than sacred. It was "super-iminant over all other institutions" and through it "nine-tenths of the crimes in the penal code would become obsolete; the long cata-logue of human ills would be abridged; men would walk more safely by day; every pillow would be more inviolable by night; property, life, and character held by a stronger tenure; all rational hopes respecting the future brightened" (Blumenfeld, 1985, p. 211). In describing school buildings, Mann called each "a beautiful temple ... dedicated to the noble purpose of improving the rising generation ... fulfilling the sacred object of its erection" (p. 192).

Another situation of approximately this same time period involved a dispute between Protestants and Catholics in New York. While the details of the matter are not of concern, several observa-tions made during the debate are worthy of note. First, in protesting the Protestant claims as to the neutrality of public school instruction, Catholic Bishop Hughes noted that regardless of the supposed neutrality of moral instruction in the public schools, it violated Catholic consciences and therefore did address matters of religion. In what amounted to religious arrogance, the lawyer for the public schools, Hiram Ketchum, claimed that the schools had the "right to declare moral truths" (McCarthy, 1987, p. 65). Second, seeing the wisdom of Bishop Hughes' observation, John C. Spencer, New York Secretary of State, noted that "no books can be found, no reading lessons can be selected, which do not contain more or less some prin-ciples of religious faith, either directly avoided, or indirectly assumed." Accordingly, instruction must always "favor one set of opinions in opposition to another, or others; and it is believed that this always will be the result, in any course of education that the wit of man can devise" (McCarthy, et al., 1981, p. 91). From this position, Spencer argued that to do justice, public funds should be equally distributed to all schools, regardless of their "religious" orientation.

The basic foundation of the above two accounts is found earlier in U.S. history. It was due to the fact that, as Mead said,

> the United States, in effect, had two religions, or at least two different forms of the same religion... The first was the religion of the denominations, which was commonly articulated in the terms of scholastic Protestant ortho- doxy... The second was the religion of the democratic society and nation. This was rooted in the rationalism of the Enlightenment (to go no further back) and was artic- ulated in terms of the destiny of America, Under God, to be fulfilled by perfecting the democratic way of life for the example and betterment of all mankind. (Mead, 1963, p. 135)

W. S. Hudson in his book *The Great Tradition of the American Churches* (1953, p. 161) noted that "the New Theology was essen- tially a culture religion" (see Mead, 1963, p. 154). In this same view, Williams (1969) argues that "a culture is above everything else a faith, a set of shared convictions, a spiritual entity," and thus "systematic and universal indoctrination is essential in the values on which a society is based." According to Mead (1963, p. 69), this is the "first assumption underlying an established church." The second assumption is that "the institution responsible for inculcat- ing the basic beliefs must have behind it the coercive power of the state" (p. 70). According to Williams, this has to be and in fact is the public school system since no other agency "is in as strategic a position to teach democracy and to bring the majority of our people to a religious devotion to the democratic way of life" even though this invariably means "giving the power of wholesale religious indoctrination into the hands of politicians..." (p. 70). Furthermore,

Williams believes that Jefferson was too optimistic in believing that the many sects of the land could instill the necessary virtues for national survival. Thus, for purposes of governmental well-being, civil authority must take over and limit even religious freedom by teaching "the democratic ideal as religion" (p. 71). Mead and Williams both lead us to the proverbial question, "Can the ends ever justify the means?"

As often as Jefferson has been discussed in this text, the above suggests that even more is needed. As McCarthy, et al., note (1982, p. 41), Jefferson thought clergy were tyrants of people's minds and aristocrats were tyrants over the people's bodies and property. His quest was to free people and to do it by way of free public education. He, in fact, was the first American to formalize this doctrine, and it has pervaded American educational philosophy ever since: "If the condition of man is to be progressively ameliorated, as we fondly hope and believe, education is to be the chief instrument in effecting it." As the people become so enlightened, "tyranny and oppression of body and mind will vanish like evil spirits at the dawn of day" (Pfeffer, 1967, p. 327).

For Jefferson, the public school was to promote morality, personal goodness, and a patriotic duty to society. While this may be all well and good, it was Jefferson's religion, and public schools were the vehicle to promote this religion onto all the people. In total, Jefferson held to the Enlightenment view of life wherein reason is higher than faith. That is, reason would not only be the ultimate determiner of truth, but it would also provide even the moral idea of what ought to be, and by it religious truth would be judged. Just as with Mann, Jefferson's meanings of religious terms, like the nature of God, were out of sync with those of mainstream theologians. For instance, he said, "I can never join Calvin in addressing *his* God. He was indeed an atheist, which I can never be; or rather his religion was daemonism. If ever man worshipped a false God, he did. The Being described in his five points, is not the God whom you and I acknowledge and adore..." (McCarthy, et al., 1982, p. 26).

Lest we miss the point, it was not Jefferson's religious differences per se with others more orthodox that is the concern here. No, it is the dangerous and ever so subtle perspective that religion was to be private to each individual without allowance into the public and institutional realm. Jefferson promoted and the majority accepted the notion that life in general operated by rational and naturalistic principles while it was only the private and clearly ecclesiastical institutions (i.e., church) where truly religious (e.g., biblical) teachings were to be practiced. Thus life in general and education in particular followed the natural theology of republicanism. Children were to be taught in public schools according to the dogma of civic morality and virtuous citizenship. The raising of the moral fiber of the citizenry was to be accomplished through education with its emphasis on virtue, tolerance, and the cultivation of rational powers. Just as Jefferson said of the various religions at his University of Virginia, he wanted to "liberalize and neutralize their prejudices, and make the general religion a religion of peace, reason, and morality" (Lee, 1961, p. 79). Religious instruction in the public schools "was to be approached only from the point of view of strict dogmatic rationalism" (Healy, 1961, p. 177). Drawing from McCarthy, et al. (1982), we see that several scholars considered Jefferson to be the promoter of a religion, albeit rationalistic, in the public schools. Conant (1970), for instance, is cited as believing that Jefferson was transferring to America the Scottish idea of developing a Christian nation via the public school system. Namely, Jefferson is viewed as using the monopolistic public education system "to secure religious freedom and personal liberty in the new republic..." (p. 40). The vision of Thomas Jefferson was that "sectarian churches were to be disestablished and replaced by a public school establishment. One of the goals of the new establishment would be the spread of a public (as in *republican*) faith through society ... and Jefferson saw nothing wrong with indoctrinating students into a philosophy of government as long as it corresponded to his understanding of orthodoxy" (McCarthy, et al., 1981, pp. 82, 85). And the reason it was a matter of orthodoxy was because civil and moral order were considered by Jefferson as *the* way to affirm God's plan and destiny for mankind (cf., Little, 1974, p. 195). Jefferson believed that God endowed mankind with a sense of moral right and wrong, and in this sense, education would be the vehicle to make inborn virtue manifest not to mention vindicate his naturalistic position versus the spiritual salvation message of mainstream Christianity against which he was so opposed.

The fact that Jefferson's doctrine has prevailed and even flourished to this day is revealed in the recent statement by education spokesman R. Freeman Butts (1995):

> The historic purpose of families and religious groups is, properly, to instill in their youths the particular personal and moral values that those groups favor. But ever since Jefferson himself led the way in Virginia in 1779, the historic purpose of universal public schooling has become, properly, the study and promotion of the common civic values of constitutional democracy: the public good, freedom of individual rights, justice, equality, diversity, truth, patriotism.

A fitting way to conclude this subsection is to reference the "formula" that is couched in the predominant religious persuasion of this country: "Religion = Christianity + all its competitors" (cf., Nash, 1988, p. 25). There is no neutrality in this regard—the "culture of unbelief" is really what amounts to as "cultures of other-belief" (Marty, 1987, p. 21). Or as was said of the atheist, "He believes in No-God, and he worships him" (James, 1982, p. 35). Obviously, that which answers questions about ultimate matters serves as a religion. For instance, world view answers that address the meaning of the good life are religious in nature. Culture and religion, according to T. S. Eliot, "are different aspects of the same thing—our culture is our *lived* religion" (cf., Adams & Stein, 1989, p. 59).

Without going too deeply into causal reasons for the above, some clarity comes by way of several basic propositions proposed by Goudzwaard (1975). First, "every man is serving god(s) in his life." This is another way to say that there is no neutrality. We make idols out of many different things and worship them. Along this same line, Dostoevsky wrote that we "cannot live without worshipping something" (Tinder, 1989, p. 80). Additionally, Goudzwaard claims that individuals are transformed into images of these gods and also that man makes society into his own image. In other words, we and thus our society take on the nature or characteristics of that which we worship. And this is exactly what we have seen in this last chapter segment. Our educational system has taken on the image of civic virtue which its leaders proclaim as right, proper, and even holy.

All the above is born out by many examples throughout mankind's history. For instance, to be successful, the Nazis knew they had "to substitute their world view for Christianity" (cf., Adams & Stein, 1979, p. 65). Similarly, in order to make U.S. society over into their own image, the Universalists of the early to mid-1800s employed the same strategy. Said Brownson, one of their former members, "The great object was to get rid of Christianity... The plan was to establish a system of state—we said national—schools, from which all religion was to be excluded, in which nothing was to be taught but such knowledge as is verifiable by the senses, and to which all parents were to be compelled by law to send their children... For this purpose a secret society was formed..." (Blumenfeld, 1985, pp. 95, 96). According to the conclusion of the liberal and secularist education writings of Nord (1995), the agenda uncovered by Brownson has been very successful. Nord claims that public school indoctrination "makes religious accounts of the world seem implausible, even inconceivable. It fails to provide students with the intellectual and emotional resources that would enable them to take religion seriously" (p. 36).

Our concluding remarks should not be construed to mean that every educational mandate is devious. But it most certainly is meant to indicate that in the final analysis, those who mandate education onto others make it a sacred rite by deciding what should and should not be taught. Education is in this way a religious activity and a way to bring all of society into a religious image. Interestingly and paradoxically, what the church has been prohibited to do by force of law the public schools are licensed to do. Even those who object to religious instruction in public schools promote the very same thing—they create "a sectarian establishment, consisting of schools, in which the tenets and dogmas of sect are taught" (cf., Glenn, 1988, p. 175).

An example of how the schools have substituted one value system for another is revealed in the very able analysis of public school textbooks by Vitz (1986). The 1983, federally funded analysis by Professor Paul Vitz of ninety currently and widely used elementary readers and social studies and high school history texts is contained in the appropriately titled book, *Censorship: Evidence of Bias in Our Children's Textbooks*. Summarizing briefly, none of the books covering grades one through six contained even one word referring to any religious activity in contemporary American life. No mention was made of praying or of going to church or temple. Further, "not one word or image in any book shows any form of contemporary representative Protestantism." In the fifth grade U.S. history texts, "the treatment of the past 100 or 200 years is so devoid of reference to religion as to give the impression that it has almost ceased to exist in America." The sixth grade books "neglect, often to the point of serious distortion, Jewish and Christian historical contributions." Of all the high school books covering U.S. history, "none came close to adequately presenting the major religious events of the past 100 or 200 years. Most disturbing was the constant omission of reference to the large role that religion has always played in American life. This fact has been seen as a fundamental feature of American society by foreign observers since de Tocqueville" (pp. 2-3). Vitz also claims that this bias against religion is not merely coincidence or insignificant. For example, religion is not mentioned as a part of the Pilgrim's life, and children were led to believe that Thanksgiving was "when the Pilgrims gave thanks to the Indians." In an account of Joan of Arc, "there was no reference to *any* religious aspect of her life. This is an obvious serious misrepresentation of her historical meaning." Similarly in the story of Nobel Laureate and Jewish writer Isaac Singer, words were modified to omit "to God" where the main character prayed to God, and the "Thank God" expression of the man character was changed to "Thank goodness."

The authors of these various biased and substitute-value texts "write in order to produce certain states of mind in the rising generation, if not because they think those states of mind intrinsically just or good, yet certainly because they think them to be the means to some state of society which they regard as desirable" (Lewis, 1947, pp. 39, 40). When books are written from this spirit, "The practical result of education ... must be the destruction of the society which accepts it"

(p. 39). Lewis continued, "A great many of those who 'debunk' traditional or (as they would say) 'sentimental' values have in the background values of their own which they believe to be immune from the debunking process. They claims to be cutting away the parasitic growth of emotion, religious sanction, and inherited taboos, in order that 'real' or 'basic' values may emerge" (pp. 41, 42).

Such authors typically think that they can do away with traditional values and so much for the better:

> We shall probably find that we can get on quite comfortably without them. Let us regard all ideas of what we *ought* to do simply as an interesting psychological survival: let us step right out of all that and start doing what we like. Let us decide for ourselves what man is to be and make him into that; not on any ground of imagined value, but because we want him to be such. Having mastered our environment, let us now master ourselves and choose our own destiny. (pp. 62, 63)

Obviously this is religious world view kind of thinking. Lewis's prophecy is validated more recently through statements like those of the influential Professor Goodlad: "The use of conventional wisdom as a basis for decision-making is a major impediment to educational improvement. The majority of our youth still hold the same values as their parents and, if we don't resocialize, our system will decay" (Schlafly, 1984, p. 145). Lewis goes on:

> if man chooses to treat himself as raw material, raw material he will be; not raw material to be manipulated, as he fondly imagined, by himself, but by mere appetite, that is, mere Nature, in the person of his dehumanized conditions. (p. 84) Nature, untrammeled by values, rules the conditioners and, through them, all humanity. Man's conquest of Nature turns out, in the moment of its consummation, to be Nature's conquest of man ... all nature's apparent reverses have been but tactical withdrawals. We thought we were beating her back when she was luring us on.

What looked to us like hands held up in surrender was really the opening of arms to enfold us forever. (p. 80)

In the final analysis "Each new power won by man is a power *over* man as well... Man's final conquest has proved to be the abolition of man" (pp. 71, 77).

Faith Basis of Education

Whether one agrees or not with the contention that Jefferson's Enlightenment philosophy or any other secular philosophy is a substitute religion in public schools is not important to this next section. Here we present the perspective that all education is rooted in a primary characteristic of religion—that is, faith. It is this matter of faith that brings everything to the same level. Most if not all of what we believe ultimately rests on assumptions or faith statements which are not ultimately provable. Even so, we must stand somewhere and act as though things are true and good else we quickly become befuddled and stagnate.

This matter of believing certain assumptions to be true without ultimate proof clearly applies to the meaning and worth of life—concerns central to the education of youth. Tolstoy said that "faith alone gave man answers as to the questions of life, and consequently the possibility of living." Furthermore, "faith is the knowledge of the meaning of life... Faith is the force of life. If a man lives, he believes in something. If he did not believe that there was something to live for, he would not live" (cf., Creel, 1977, p. 40). Commenting on these passages from Tolstoy, Creel (p. 40) concludes, very apropos to our concern, "the question is not *whether* to be religious, but *how* to be religious."

Specifically, in the education establishment,

We have a kind of faith in the nature of people that we do not have in the botanical processes of nature itself—and I use the word "faith" in its full religious force. We really do believe that all human beings have a natural *telos* toward becoming flowers, not weeds or poison ivy, and that aggregates of human beings have a natural predisposition to arrange themselves into gardens, not jungles or garbage heaps. This sublime and noble faith we may call the religion of liberal humanism. It is the dominant spiritual and intellectual orthodoxy in America today. Indeed, despite all our chatter about the separation of church and state, one can even say it is the official religion of American society today, as against which all other religious can be criticized as divisive and parochial. (cf., Vitz, 1977, p. 107, quoting Kristol)

There are not, as our modern world wants to believe, two separate entities, faith and reason. While it may seem that

the Age of Faith has given way to the Age of Learning, and that education rather than religion is destined to give direction and meaning to modern man and nations ... this conclusion is not tenable, for faith and learning are not mutually exclusive alternatives. On the contrary, they are necessarily inclusive of one another. Faith can have no significant content without learning, and learning can have no direction or motive without faith. (Phenix, 1966, p. 14)

Young (1954) shows us the significance of this proposition in his discussion of Immanuel Kant's attempt to divorce faith and reason. Kant proposed that since knowledge is based on sensory derived information about the natural world, this is the only realm man can know anything about. If a supernatural world does exist, it is unknowable to human knowledge according to Kant. In his critique, which can easily serve as a generalization to the entire question of whether faith and reason are separate entities, Young describes two fallacies in Kant's thinking. First, Kant, as with everyone, has to take it on faith that knowledge or the knowing of something is even possible. Otherwise, Kant could not even speak to knowledge of the natural world. Without this very crucial first step of a faith nature, mankind would never escape from skepticism, born from a lack of certainty, that quickly would deteriorate to nihilism. Secondly, there is a contradiction in the supposed reliance on reason to declare that knowledge is limited to the natural or phenomenal world. It is a contradiction of highest import because this declaration is not logically or reasonably demonstratable. Instead, this highest order premise for Kant is not primarily a function of reason at all but of faith. In other words, Kant believes his proposition not because he has demonstrated its truthfulness but because he accepts it apriori by faith. As alluded to in earlier sections of this chapter and as obvious via Kant, the truth of the matter is that reason is based in faith. The mutually exclusive coexistence of faith and reason is not possible.

In his classic work on education, C. S. Lewis (1947) argues that education taught without a foundation of faith but from reason only will not elevate but instead will lead man to his ultimate downfall—hence the title of his book, *The Abolition Of Man*. Lewis's point is that reason alone cannot arrive at ultimate truths; instead, truths must be taken on faith. Without faith, man must rely either on his instincts or his ratiocination facilities. But instincts, says Lewis, are drives that merely give impulse; they do not provide the all important reason for what *ought* to be. Further, instincts compete against one another and without a standard (which they cannot supply) regarding which one of the oughts should be obeyed at any given time, there can be no order and ultimately no meaningful education. Reason suffers much the same shortcoming. It similarly cannot provide an ultimate standard. Questions of value cannot conclusively be answered by reason. Henry (1995) in commenting on Johnson's examination (1991) of Darwin's theory said, "Much as one may appeal to universal rationality as supplying the content of ethics, universally shared norms cannot be distilled from what Johnson depicts as 'The Unanchored, self-validating human mind'" (p. 60). As a result, Lewis concludes that "neither in any operation with factual propositions nor in any appeal to instinct can [one] find the basis for a system of values" (p. 52). Instead, we must have faith in the great truths within what Lewis calls the "doctrine of objective values" (p. 29) that come to us via major religions and philosophical schools of thought like Platonism, Hinduism, Judaism, and Christianity. It must be taken on faith; it cannot otherwise be invented. Furthermore, any change that would seem necessary to this objective system of values must come from the faith perspective that the system is inherently valid to begin with. Modification from outside the system is meaningless and ultimately self-destructive.

The final point to be made in regard to Lewis's commentary relates to paradoxical consequences of education without faith. Writing in 1947, Lewis described a then-contemporary educational practice of severe prophetic implication. Tragically, the prophetic fulfillment is upon this current generation yet in large part unrecognized. It is unrecognized because it is unaccompanied by faith in the truthfulness of Lewis's observation. Namely, Lewis chronicled that we have removed the basis of morality and virtue yet "continue to clamor for those very qualities we are rendering impossible" (p. 35). His wording at the close of the chapter entitled "Men without chests" says it so poignantly: "In a sort of ghastly simplicity we remove the organ and demand the function. We make men without chests and expect of them virtue and enterprise. We laugh at honor and are shocked to find traitors in our midst. We castrate and bid the geldings be fruitful" (p. 35).

Not at all an aberrant view, Lewis's perspective is echoed by others. Hans Jonas (1966) insightfully observes that for a scientific theory of man to be possible, man has to be conceived of as being determined by casual laws, as being totally a part of nature. The scientist, while maintaining freedom of inquiry and openness to reason, evidence, and truth, assumes and thus comes to know man the subject of study as lower than himself: "Then man-lower-than man explained by the human sciences—man reified—can by the instructions of those sciences be controlled (even 'engineered') and thus used" (p. 196). As Vitz comments (1977, p. 119),

> [T]he price of this growth is considerable. In time it becomes intolerable. If the subject is master and the object is slave, then in true Hegelian fashion there ultimately occurs what can only be described as the object's revenge. The object eventually conquers by reducing the subject to the object's categorical level. The master becomes defined by his slaves, the subject by its objects, the psychologist by his rats or pigeons or cats.

The disastrous and widespread psychological impact of education from this perspective is well documented (cf., Vitz, 1977) and goes well beyond the scope of our present concerns.

In addition to faith being the ground upon which knowledge resides, as demonstrated above, faith is also the key to learning. To learn is to go from the known to the unknown. In this act of becoming vulnerable to the unknown, faith must necessarily be exercised as a prerequisite for learning to occur in any systematic and ongoing way. This exercise of faith seems to involve two components. The one component is abandonment. The security of the known is abandoned in some sense for the unknown. The learner willingly and sometimes even unwillingly abandons stability for an initial and psychologically uncomfortable state of disequilibrium. Italian Renaissance philosopher Pico della Mirendola (cf., Schwehn, 1992, p. 50) claims we are to even welcome such struggles since in academic conflicts "it is a gain to lose." Faith abides in the process by way of allowing the learner to step over the edge into initial chaos without experiencing debilitating fear. The presence of such fear would inhibit learning in no insignificant way. Faith in this sense enables the learner to be receptive rather than resistant to the learning process.

Additionally, faith acts to allow submission to the unknown and/or to the teacher who brings the unknown. Theologians like Emil Brunner (1946, p. 35) speak to this dynamic as a basic human trait. "Faith, therefore, is not only the submission of the self-confident 'I'; it is also the venture of trust in another." Wherein our "distrustful, anxious, self-centered hearts" work against receiving God, according to Brunner, it is likewise the case that our hearts can work against submitting to the authority of the teacher and/or the instructional content. Faith in the learning process according to this second dynamic is the renunciation of independence and of one's own sovereignty; we believe and obey someone else for our betterment when the evidence of this change for the good can come only after the submission and obedience has occurred. This believing before receiving is obviously the essence of faith.

Schwehn (1992, p. 50, quoting Gustafson) applies these ideas on faith very specifically to the educational process: "... we need to acknowledge, each of us as schools, teachers and students, that all our knowing involves 'faith,' human confidence in what we have received." It is an educational truism that thinking and learning are hindered in an atmosphere of distrust (i.e., lack of faith). The acceptance of a teaching from another means that trust in that person and a humility to submit to that person's teachings must be present. All of this equals faith.

We turn now to some specific examples of faith in education. First, we return to the concept of democracy that was discussed in Chapter 9. There we saw that democracy met the qualifications of a religion. Now as further confirmation, we will see that it is taught from a basis of faith. Jefferson, for instance, did not hold onto his notion of republican democracy by way of pure reason no matter how much he "thought" it to be true. He had a conviction about it that could not ultimately be derived from reason. While his assumptions may appear to be "reasonable" (cf., Baer, 1987, p. 11), they could not be proved by reason, Instead, they were faith commitments. Similarly, John Dewey held onto the democratic ideal as a matter of faith. Institutionalizing this idea, the Educational Policies Commission of the National Education Association (1941) cited as its first tenet that "democratic education is devoted to the realization of the democratic faith" (p. 92). Furthermore, the first responsibility of the public school teacher was to "maintain a steadfast loyalty to the democratic faith" (p. 109).

In the twentieth century, democracy came to be conceived as "the super-religion, over and above all religions... America's civil religion, democracy, is the overarching faith, in which the particular religions may find their particular place, provided they don't claim any more" (Herberg, 1974, p. 84).

Another educational content area covered in Chapter 9 which is also faith based is that of science. Dewey's one and one only method for ascertaining truth, the scientific method, was the subject of his book, *A common faith*. His conclusion about this method came not from the laboratory, but from his faith orientation (cf., Young, 1954, p. 40). As Young states, "In practice the man of science is a man of faith just as much as the man of religion. Scientists have faith in their own ability to arrive at cognitive judgments, they have faith in those with whom they work, they have faith in the truth of the discoveries of the past, they have faith in the orderliness of the world with which they work, and so on" (p. 206).

In more specific terms, the issue of evolution nicely illustrates the point about science being rooted in faith. To illustrate how much the belief in evolution is a matter of faith for its adherents, Johnson (1991, p. 130) cites Dobzhansky "the greatest evolutionist of our century and a lifelong Russian Orthodox: "Is evolution a theory, a system, or a hypothesis? It is much more—it is a general postulate to which all theories, all hypotheses, all systems must henceforth bow and which they must satisfy in order to be thinkable and true. Evolution is a light which illuminates all facts, a trajectory which all lines of thought must follow—this is what evolution is."

In discussing evolution, Dobzhansky clearly uses the kind of language reserved for religious activities. In fact, the quoted paragraph would read perfectly well as a passage from any theological document if the name of that theology were substituted for each mention of the name evolution. That believing scientists have faith in this religion of evolution is not even a matter for debate. For instance, the senior paleontologist at the British Natural History Museum and an author on evolution, Colin Patterson, classifies both evolution and creationism as based primarily on faith and not science (Johnson, 1991, p. 9). When Patterson asked evolutionists at the University of Chicago if there was anything true about evolution, all he got was silence. Eventually one person said, "I do know one thing—it ought not to be taught in high school" (p. 10). The renowned science philosopher Michael Ruse calls evolution as much metaphysically based as is creationism (Woodward, 1994, p. 7). Even while continuing to maintain his personal belief in evolution, he says it is to be taken on faith in its philosophical assumptions. Although Ruse no longer believes his former position on the subject, it was his contrast of evolution as science and creationism as religion that in 1982 led a federal judge to abolish Arkansas's "Balanced Treatment Act" (*McLean* v. *Arkansas*). Evolutionist Loren Eiseley wrote, "After having chided the theologian for his reliance on myth and miracle, science found itself in the unenviable position of having to create a mythology of its own: namely, the assumption that what, after long effort, could not be proved to take place today had, in truth, taken place in the primeval past" (Eiseley, 1957, p. 199). The famous Buddhist astronomer Chandra Wickramasinghe stated that "contrary to the popular notion that only creationism relies on the supernatural, evolution must as well, since the probabilities of random formation of life (spontaneous generation) are so tiny as to require a 'miracle' for spontaneous generation 'tantamount to a theological argument'" (Geisler, 1982, p. 151).

Another area in the scientific realm where faith is the pivot point of the matter is that of mathematics. We tend to envision math as being based on anything but faith. Here we see differently. Consider the simple truth that when two numbers are added together they result in an entirely new number. Faith places a major role in the unquestioned belief that the resultant number called the "sum" consistently and reliably describes what happens in nature when the two elements represented by the addends are combined. It truly is an act of faith to believe that the totality of all mathematical formulas, equations, operations, etc., exactly replicate occurrences in nature. These abstract, inherently meaningless, symbols (i.e., numbers), totally disconnected from the quantities they represent, can be combined according to certain rules, not necessarily related to the physical operations they represent, to accurately portray natural phenomenon. So trusting are we in this faith-based system that we do not question, for instance, whether or not our weekly salary can even be represented by such mathematical computations. Similarly, the predictive accuracy of math is so highly trusted that countries launch people into outer space fully believing they will return at a given time and place based only on the results of math calculations and not, say, on a promise from God or a space creature (both of which equally would also have to be faith-based). In his dialogue with Hobbs, the cartoon character Calvin captures the entire matter in only a few sentences (1991):

Calvin: "You know, I don't think math is a science. I think it is a religion."

Hobbs: "A religion?"

Calvin: "Yeah, all these equations are like miracles. You take two numbers and when you add them, they magically become one *new* number! No one can say how it happens. You either believe it or you don't."

Calvin: "This whole book is full of things that have to be accepted on faith! It's a religion."

Hobbs: "And in the public schools no less. Call a lawyer."

Calvin: "As a math atheist, I should be excused from this."

Equally true in other disciplines, our faith is based on the testimony of authority just as alluded to above. History is almost exclusively a record of the past that is believed primarily through faith in the initial witnesses. For instance, no one doubts that Christopher Columbus did exist and that he did travel to the western hemisphere in 1492. While those who are alive to read these words were not alive in 1492 and further were not eyewitnesses to Columbus's voyages, the general accounts of Columbus are believed as a matter of faith. Similarly, the Easter accounts of the resurrection of Christ are believed not because photographs and/or eyewitnesses can be cross-examined in person but because in faith the historical account of eyewitnesses are trusted. Christians believe that the witnesses were able to accurately perceive that the person they saw, communicated with, and touched was Christ and that they could accurately relate the account to others. In other words, the facts of history are not generally examined firsthand. Instead, it is the testimonies about such facts that are accepted or rejected based, for instance, on tests of verification such as corroboration and coherence. History then is ultimately rooted in faith since it cannot be proved but only believed or even not believed in faith. Furthermore, it is the removal of existing values of a religious nature in history that has brought on the "moral crisis" that so many see in the revisionists' versions of, particularly, U.S. history (Cohen, 1995).

The examples could go on, but it seems that the point about faith has been properly established. We hope it is now apparent that faith is basic to knowing of any kind. As Young states, "All men are men of faith... Reason always functions within the framework of faith—that is, in relation to what the individual believes to be of consequence. Faith and reason cannot be separated. Faith is the basic category of all knowing" (Young, 1954, p. 36).

> There is perhaps no better way to conclude this section than to quote from Phenix: It is not possible, then, to deal intelligently with education without reference to the affairs of faith. Education is not a neutral, autonomous, self-justifying enterprise to which modern men may look for salvation as people in former days looked to religion. It is an activity in and through which men seek to discern truth, create beauty, and fulfill goodness—all of which express the faith by which they live. Salvation today, as always, comes through faith informed by learning. The eager peoples now in pursuit of knowledge are still guided by some perhaps unarticulated gospel. The content of what they will learn and the end toward which it will lead them are still determined by their convictions about what is worthy of supreme devotion, that is to say, by their religious orientation... From this standpoint, everybody has a faith, just as he has a psychological or a physical makeup. People differ only in the content of their faiths. (Phenix, 1966, p. 15)

The bottom line issue behind all of this is not that of faith versus reason. The real issue is that in which man puts his faith: "The crucial problem is that some thinkers place their trust in one set of assumptions in their search for truth, while other thinkers place their trust in a quote different set of assumptions" (Young, 1954, p. 37). Yet educators typically "assume one highly controversial set of definitions—those provided by modern science and social science—and then convey them uncritically to their students" (Nord, 1995, p. 44).

Conclusion

There is a bit of folk wisdom which says that if you put a frog in boiling water, it will immediately sense the hotness of the water and jump out of the pot. The "proper way" to cook the frog is to put it in water of room temperature and gradually increase the temperature. Since the frog's body temperature will rise along with that of the water, it will never sense a contrast in temperature and thus will stay in the pot until cooked to death. As documented in the *A Nation at Risk* report of 1983 by the National Commission on Excellence in Education, the same thing is happening in this country in education: "If an unfriendly foreign power had attempted to impose on America the level of educational performance that we have today, we might well have viewed it as an act of war... We have in effect, been committing an act of unthinkable unilateral educational disarmament" (p. 1). We have been immersed in downward achievement without even knowing it. In fact, the report noted that "For the first time in the history of our country, the educational skills of one generation will not surpass, will not equal, will not even approach those of their parents" (p. 11).

As sad as this is, it is eclipsed by a more tragic and far more pervasive "unsuspecting frog" account in education that occurred in this country starting in the early 1800s. In a respectable piece of investigative writing, Blumenfeld (1985) documents the fact that in Boston in 1817,

> an astonishing 96 percent of the town's children were attending school, and the 4 percent who did not, had charity schools to attend if their parents wanted them to. Thus, there was no justification at all for the creation of a system of public primary schools, and Bulfinch [chairman of a subcommittee for The Boston School Committee] reported as much to The School Committee, which accepted the subcommittee's recommendation. (p. 43)

Even so, in 1818 the school committee was ordered by the town officials to implement a new system of public primary schools. According to Blumenfeld, the reason for this forced adoption of public schools centers on religion. It was a question of which religious persuasion was going to prevail in education—Calvinism or Unitarianism. Whereas the initial settlers saw education as a religious activity that was to be under the control of churches and/or parents, the Unitarians wanted to separate children from parents as early as possible and to substitute for Christianity a belief in the natural goodness and limitless potential of mankind to control its own destiny. Additionally, the Unitarians of the day believed that their own salvation hinged on whether or not they promoted the reformation of society, gave to the poor, and engaged in other similar social improvements. As already noted, "The great object was to get rid of Christianity" in the classrooms. (Whatever the incumbent religion was is not the issue. What is important to see is that the replacement or substitute system has successfully but erroneously been promoted as not being a religion.)

Nowadays, the entire matter of religious foundations is considered as inappropriate for public education. Even so, officially endorsed education content regularly answers religious questions. More specifically, the endorsement and teaching by the education system of "absolutism in evolutionary science and relativism (or selective relativism) in morals perfectly reflects the established religious philosophy of late-twentieth-century America" (Johnson, 1995, p. 166).

The problem is that education has not moved from being religiously based in colonial America to being non-religious in contemporary America. No, it is instead a matter of education shifting from a foundation in one religion to that of another (i.e., substitute) religion: "[T]he practice of our schools [was] to force dissenting and nonbelieving children of the poor to behave like Protestants. Eventually the courts said No. That particular tyranny is behind us only to be replaced by another: children of whatever belief now must study the gospel of secular neutrality" (Coons, 1992, p. 18). The early Unitarian substitution for Calvinism is one such example. An example of another type of substitution has been documented by *Newsweek* (June 14, 1993). As many as 6-8 million students in United States public schools have been subjected to the religious teachings of Scientology founder L. Ron Hubbard. His text *The Way to Happiness* (1981) has been used by public schools supposedly to teach values and morality. Teachers who used the text assumed it contained a morals-only perspective. But the president of the Church of Scientology International claims that the book is a "part of Hubbard's extensive, philosophical and religious writings, which for Scientologists are the same as the Bible is for Christians and the Koran is for Muslims" (p. 76). Most troubling, critics and former Scientology officials alike claim that the morals text "is primarily a recruiting tool for the church" (p. 77). Obviously, what substitutes for a religion is still a religion. The four defining characteristics of religion (i.e., declaration of education as religion, world view based, non-neutrality, and faith based) as discussed in this chapter are all satisfied in this regard. Further, whether or not the substitute beliefs fit our stereotype of religion, if they substitute for a recognized religion or functionally act as a religion, they are religious, objections from nonbelievers in the substitute notwithstanding. After all, no one can decree what is or is not religious for some other person.

The failure to see that educational practices are religiously based because they have over some period of time been definitionally excluded as such is explained by an observation from C. S. Lewis (1947, p. 17). The well-established declaration that education is not religious is an example of "an assumption, which ten years hence, its origin forgotten and its presence unconscious, will condition him [the deceived] to take one side in a controversy which he has never recognized as a controversy at all." The removal of formal religious doctrines from schooling through promoting some substitute beliefs instead, declaring the substitute as non-religious, is self-deceiving. In fact, humanists no longer call humanism a religion because of the attacks from fundamentalists brought on by the humanists in saying that they are a religion (cf., *The Journal*, 1995, p. 6). Vested interest positions of this type should be immediately suspect if not totally disregarded. A story attributed to Abraham Lincoln helps us see the point that the mere relabeling of something does not change it: "Abraham Lincoln once asked a critic, 'How many legs does a cow have?' "Four' was the reply. 'If you call her tail a leg, how many does she have?' asked Lincoln. 'Five' was the answer. "No' declared Lincoln. 'Just *calling* a tail a leg does not *make* it a leg.' " (Gabler, Gabler, & Hefley, 1985, p. 42). In other words, declaring that something is not a religion when it fully serves a religion does not make it any less a religion.

The frog-in-the-pot analogy demonstrates that we have been saturated for so long in a particular narrowly-defined perspective of religion that we accept it as the norm. Yet as this chapter has shown, religion is not confined to formally organized doctrines found within the typically deceived church. Religion guides all of life's activities such that there really is no distinction between the secular and the sacred for the vast majority of people. Our religion is what we act out regardless of what we may say to the contrary.

Obviously, the implications for the proposition that education is a religious activity are enormous. For one, education should formally be recognized as subject to the religious provisions of the First Amendment to the Constitution. This already is the case in the sense that courts rule on what aspects of religion are to be allowed in education. So even without this chapter's revolutionary perspective, education needs to be recognized as being under the jurisdiction of the First Amendment because of the way it is interpreted. It is not a matter of whether education is religious but of which religious perspective informs education.

When the more enlightened conceptualization of religion in this chapter is coupled with the original-intent interpretation of the First Amendment as covered in Chapter 5, many new implications arise. This will be discussed in detail in Chapter 11.

Another implication regarding the religious nature of education addresses not the federal but instead the role of each state in education. For instance, state provisions regarding religion must by definition incorporate educational matters. Conversely, state statutes regarding education mandates now need to be viewed as potential infringements on religious matters. Obviously worthy of detailed consideration, this matter is discussed in Chapter 12.

Our last statement for the present chapter comes from the 1889 writing of United States Assistant Attorney General Zach Montgomery. The very fact that his quote is equally applicable now as it was one hundred years ago gives regretful validity to Santayana's statement that (1905/1980) "those who cannot remember the past are condemned to repeat it." These words from Montgomery will hopefully be heeded this time:

Our conclusions, then, are these, namely: First, that Washington was right when he said: 'Let us with caution indulge the supposition that morality can be maintained without religion.' Second; that the State cannot teach morality without teaching religion as its foundation. Third; that the state cannot teach either morality or religion without either establishing a new religious denomination, or else teaching it as it is taught by some one of the existing denominations. Fourth; that the state can neither teach religion as it is now taught by any existing denomination, nor as it might be taught by a State-begotten denomination, without a fatal infringement upon the doctrine of religious liberty; and that, therefore the true and proper business of the state is not to teach nor to pay for teaching either morality or religion, but to foster and encourage the teaching of both, by carefully and scrupulously guarding and protecting the equal rights of all citizens to worship God and to educate their children according to the dictates of their own consciousness. (p. 70)

References

A Nation at Risk. (1983). Washington, D.C.: U.S. National Commission on Excellence in Education.

Abraham, Henry J. (1982). *Freedom and the court.* (4th ed.) New York: Oxford Univ. Press.

Adams, Blair & Stein, Joel (1989). *Wisdom's children.* Austin, TX: Truth Forum.

Adams, Blair (1991). *Who owns the children?* Waco, TX: Truth Forum.

Arons, Stephen (1976). The separation of school and state: Pierce reconsidered. *Harvard Educational Review, 46* (1), 76-104.

Baer, Richard A., Jr. (1983). Focus the education debate not just on quality, but on control. *Wall Street Journal*, Aug. 2.

Baer, Richard A., Jr. (1987). American public education and the myth of value neutrality. In Neuhaus, Richard John, (Ed.) *Democracy and the renewal of public education.* Grand Rapids, MI: Wm. B. Eerdmans.

Baer, Richard A. (no date). Character education and public schools: The question of context. (unpublished manuscript)

Barton, David (1989). *The myth of separation.* Aledo, TX: Wallbuilder Press.

Beard, Charles A. & Beard, Mary R. (1927). *Rise of American Civilization. Vol. I*, p. 177 (cited in Pfeffer, pg. 321).

Berger, Peter L. (1967). *The secret canopy.* Garden City, NY: Doubleday.

Blum, Virgil C. (1987), Secularism in public schools. *Crisis*, March, 22-24.

Blumenfeld, Samuel L. (1985). *Is public education necessary?* Boise, ID: The Paradigm Co.

Brunner, Emil (1946). *Revelation and reason.* Philadelphia: The Westminster Press.

Butts, R. Freeman (1995). Antidote for antipolitics: A new "Text of civic instruction!" *Education Week.* Jan. 18, Commentary page.

Coe, George Albert (1916). *The psychology of religion.* Chicago, IL: The University of Chicago Press.

Cohen, Philip (Winter, 1995). Challenging history: The past

remains a battleground for schools. *Curriculum update.*

Coles, Robert (1994). Point of view. *The Chronicle of Higher Education*, Oct. 26, A64.

Conant, James (1970). *Thomas Jefferson and the development of American public education.* Los Angeles, Univ. of Calif. Press.

Coons, John E. (1992). School choice as simple justice. *Network News & Views.* May 17-24.

Creel, Richard E. (1977). *Religion and doubt: Toward a faith of your own.* Englewood Cliffs, NJ: Prentice-Hall.

Dewey, John (Sept. 13, 1922). Education as a religion. *The New Republic,* 63-65.

Dreisbach, Daniel L. (1987). *Real threat and mere shadow.* Westchester, IL: Crossway Books.

Duffield, D. Bethune (1857). Education—A state duty. *American Journal of Education,* March, 81-100.

Dunphy, John (1983). A religion for a new age. *The Humanist.* Jan/Feb, 23-26.

Educational Policies Commission (1941). *The education of free men in American democracy.* Washington, DC: National Education Association of the United States.

Education Week (1986). Excerpts from testimony in mobile secular humanism suit. Nov. 5.

Eiseley, Loren (1957). *The immense journey.* New York: Vintage Books.

Freeman, Derek (1983). *Margaret Mead and Samoa.* Cambridge, MA: Harvard University Press.

Freund, Paul A. (1969). Public aid to parochial schools. *Harvard Law Review,* 8\\82, 1680-1692.

Fugate, J. Richard (1980). *What the Bible says about child training.* Garland, TX: Aletheia Publ.

Gabler, Mel, Gabler, Norma, & Hefley, James C. (1985). *What are they teaching our children?* Wheaton, IL: Victor Books.

Geisler, Norman L. (1982). *The creator in the courtroom.* Milford, MI: Mott Media.

Glenn, Charles L., Jr. (1988). *The myth of the common school.* Amherst, MA: The Univ. of Mass. Press.

Goudzwaard, Bob (1975). *Aid for the overdeveloped west.* Toronto,

Ontario: Wedge Publ. Foundation.

Greeley, Andrew M. (1985). *Unsecular man.* New York: Schocken Books.

Hand, W. Brevard (1987). *American education on trial.* Cumberland, VA; Center for Judicial Studies.

Healy, Robert (1962). *Jefferson on religion and public education.* New Haven: Yale Univ. Press.

Henry, Carl F.H. (1995). Natural law and a nihilistic culture. *First things*, January, 49, 54-60.

Herberg, Will (1974). America's Civil religion: What it is and whence it comes. In Richey, Russell E. & Jones, Donald G. (Eds.) *American Civil religion.* New York: Harper & Row.

Holmes, Arthur F. (1983). *Contours of a world view.* Grand Rapids, MI: Eerdmans.

Holy Bible. NIV. (1985). Grand Rapids, MI: Zondervan.

James, William (1982). *The varieties of religious experience.* New York: The Penguin American Liberty.

Jefferson, Thomas (1984). *Writings.* New York: Literacy classics of the U.S., Inc.

Jellema, Wm. Henry (1951). Calvinism and higher education. In *God-centered living: A symposium.* Grand Rapids, MI: Baker Book House.

Johnson, Phillip E. (1991). *Darwin on trial.* Washington, D.C.: Regnery Gateway.

Johnson, Phillip E. (1995). *Reason in the balance.* Downers Grove, IL: InterVarsity Press.

Johnston, Lucile (1987). *Celebrations of a nation.* Willmar, MN: Biword Publications.

Jonas, Hans (1966). *The phenomenon of life.* Westport, CT: Greenwood Press.

Jorgenson, Lloyd P. (1987). *The state and the non-public school 1825-1925.* Columbia, MO: University of Missouri Press.

Kallen, Horace M. (1951). Democracy's true religion. *Saturday Review of Literature.* July 28, 6-30.

Katz, Michael B. (1968). *The irony of early school reform.* Cambridge, MA: Harvard Univ. Press.

Kennedy, Gail (1952) (Ed.) *Education for democracy.* Boston, MA:

D.C. Heath & Co.

Kohlberg, Lawrence (1981). *The philosophy of moral development.* San Francisco, CA: Harper & Row.

Kuhn, Thomas S. (1970). *The structure of scientific revolutions.* Chicago, IL: University of Chicago Press.

LaNoue, George R. (1967). The conditions of public school neutrality. In Sizer, T.R. (Ed.) *Religion and public education.* Wash. D.C.: University Press of America.

Lee, Gordon C. (1961). *Crusade against ignorance.* New York: Teachers College.

Lewis, Clive S. (1947). *The abolition of man.* New York: Macmillan.

Little, David (1974). The origins of perplexity: Civil religion and moral belief in the thought of Thomas Jefferson. In Richey, R.E. & Jones, D.G. *American civil religion.* New York: Harper & Row.

Luckmann, Thomas (1967). *The invisible religion.* NY: Macmillan.

Mann, Horace (1849). *Twelfth annual report of the secretary of the board of education.* Boston, MA: Dutton & Wentworth.

Marsden, George M. (1994). *The soul of the American university.* New York: Oxford University Press.

Marty, Martin (1987). *Religion and republic.* Boston: Beacon Press.

Matthews, L. Harrison (1971). *Introduction.* In Darwin, C. (1972). *The origin of species.* London, England: J.M. Dent & Sons, Ltd.

McCarthy, Martha M. (1983). *A delicate balance: Church, state, and the schools.* Bloomington, IN: Phi Delta Kappan Educational Foundation.

McCarthy, Rockne M., Oppewal, Donald, Peterson, Wilfred, & Spykman, Gordon. (1981). *Society, state, and schools.* Grand Rapids, MI: Eerdmans.

McCarthy, Rockne M., Skillen, James W. & Harper, William A. (1982). *Disestablishment a second time.* Grand Rapids, MI: Christianity University Press.

McCarthy, Rockne M. (1987). Public schools and public justice: The past, the present, and the future. In Neuhaus, Richard John (Ed.) *Democracy and the renewal of public education.* Grand Rapids, MI: Wm. B. Eerdmans Publ. Co.

McMillan, Richard C. (1984). *Religion in the public schools: An introduction.* Mercer University Press.

Mead, Margaret (1961). *Coming of age in Samoa.* New York: Morrow.

Mead, Sidney E. (1963). *The lively experiment.* New York: Harper & Row.

Midgley, Mary (1985). *Evolution as religion.* London: Methuen.

Montgomery, Zach. (1889/1972). *The school question.* New York: Armo Press & The New York Times.

Moynihan, Daniel P. (April 1978). Government and the ruin of private education. *Harpers,* 28-38.

Nash, Ronald H. (1988). *Faith & reason.* Grand Rapids, MI: Academie Books.

Neuhaus, Richard J. (1974). No more bootleg religion. In Allen, D.W., *Controversies in education.* Philadelphia, PA: W.B. Saunders Co.

Neuhaus, Richard J. (1987). Introduction. In Hand, W.B., *American education on trial. Is secular humanism a religion?* Cumberland, VA: Center for Judicial Studies.

Newsweek (12/21/92). If he could make it here. Education section. p. 57.

Nord, Warren A. (1995). Rethinking indoctrination. *Education Week,* May 24, p. 44.

Oates, Wayne E. (1973). *The psychology of religion.* Waco, TX: Word Books.

Perry, Richard L. (Ed.) (1978). *Sources of our liberties.* Buffalo, NY: William S. Hein & Co. Inc.

Pfeffer, Leo (1967). *Church, state and freedom* (Rev. ed.). Boston, MA: Beacon Press.

Phenix, Philip H. (1959). *Religious concerns in contemporary education.* New York: Teachers College, Columbia University.

Phenix, Philip H. (1966). *Education and the worship of God.* Philadelphia, PA: The Westminster Press.

Potter, Charles F. (1930). *Humanism: A new religion.* New York: Simon & Schuster.

Pratt, James B. (1926). *The religious consciousness.* New York: MacMillan.

Profile (1990). Psychologist unloads on 'Religious Trash in

Nation's schools. *World*, Oct. 27, 10-11.

Purpel, David E. (1989). *The moral and spiritual crises in education*. Granby, MA: Bergin & Garvey Publ. Inc.

Rice, Charles E. (1978). Conscientious objection to public education: The grievance and the remedies. *Brigham Young University Law Review*, 847-888.

Robertson, Pat (1984). *Answers*. Nashville, TN: Thomas Nelson.

Rushdoony, Rousas J. (1963). *The messianic character of American education*. Nutley, NJ: The Craig Press.

Rushdoony, Rousas J. (1981). *The philosophy of the Christian curriculum*. Vallecito, CA: Ross House Books.

Santayana, George (1905/1980). *The life of reason*. New York: Dover Publ.

Schlafly, Phyllis (Ed.) (1984). *Child abuse in the classroom*. Alton, IL: Pere Marquette Press.

Schwehn, Mark (1992). Knowledge character,...In Hauerwas, Stanley & Westerhoff, John H. (Eds.) *Schooling Christians*. Grand Rapids, MI: Eerdmans.

Smith, Elwyn A. (1972). *Religious liberty in the United States*. Philadelphia, PA: Fortress Press.

Spilka, Bernard, Hood, Ralph W., Jr., & Gorsuch, Richard L. (1985). *The psychology of religion*. Englewood Cliffs, NJ: Prentice-Hall.

Stormer, John A. (1984). *Growing up God's way*. Florissant, MO: Liberty Bell Press.

The Journal (Feb. 1995). The religion of secular humanism, Manitou Springs, CO: Summit Ministries.

Tillich, Paul (1951). *Systematic theology*. Chicago, IL: Univ. of Chicago Press.

Tinder, Glenn (1989). Can we be good without God? *The Atlantic Monthly*, December, 69-85.

Titus, Herbert W. (1982). Education—Caesar's or God's: A Constitutional question of jurisdiction. *Journal of Christian Jurisprudence*, 101-180.

Tyler, Ralph W. (1949). *Basic principles of curriculum and instruction*. Chicago, IL: Univ. of Chicago Press.

Vitz, Paul C. (1977). *Psychology as religion*. Grand Rapids, MI:

Eerdmans.

Vitz, Paul C. (1986). *Censorship: Evidence of bias in our children's textbooks*. Ann Arbor, MI: Servant Books.

Walsh, Brian J. & Middleton, J.Richard (1984). *The transforming vision*. Downers Grove, IL: InterVarsity Press.

Warshaw, Thayer S. (1979). *Religion, education, and the supreme court*. Nashville, TN: Abingdon.

Whitehead, Alfred N. (1957). *The aims of education*. NY: Macmillan.

Whitehead, John W. (1982). *The second American revolution*. Westchester, IL: Crossway Books.

Williams, John Paul (1969). *What Americans believe and how they worship*. (3rd ed.) New York: Harper & Row.

Wolterstorff, Nicholas (1967). Neutrality and impartiality. In Sizer, Theodore R. (Ed.). *Religion and public education*. Washington, D.C.: University Press of America.

Wolterstorff, Nicholas (1992). The schools we deserve. In Hauerwas, Stanley & Westerhoff, John H. (Eds.) *Schooling Christians*. Grand Rapids, MI: Eerdmans.

Woodward, Kenneth, L. & Fleming, Charles (June 14, 1993). Scientology in the schools: Is L. Ron Hubbard's morals text harmless? *Newsweek*, pp. 76-77.

Woodward, Tom (1994). Ruse "gives away the store," admits evolution a philosophy. *The Real Issue*, November/December 13 (4), 7.

Young, Warren C. (1954). *A Christian approach to philosophy*. Grand Rapids, MI: Baker Book-House.

Chapter 11

Federal Powers Gained By Usurpation

The powers not delegated to the United States by the Constitution, nor prohibited by it to the states, are reserved to the states respectively, or to the people. (Tenth Amendment to the Constitution, ratified as part of the Bill of Rights, December 15, 1791)

If Congress can apply money indefinitely to the general welfare, and are the sole and supreme judges of the general welfare, they may take the care of religion into their own hands; they may establish teachers in every state, county or parish, and pay them out of the public treasury; they may take into their own hands the education of children, establishing in like manner schools through the Union... (James Madison, February 6, 1792)

If in the opinion of the people the distribution or modification of the Constitutional powers be in any particular wrong, let it be corrected by an amendment in the way which the Constitution designates. But let there be no change by usurpation; for though in this one instance may be the instrument of good, it is the customary weapon by which free governments are destroyed. (President Washington's Farewell Address, 1796)

The theme of this present chapter is that the Federal Government has overstepped its Constitutional authority by being involved in education. It will be demonstrated that there is no provision in the original Constitution nor in any of its amendments for the Congress of the United States to collect taxes for or to control any portion of education in the states. Congressional oversight of education within the District of Columbia is the notable exception as specifically authorized by provision number 17 of Article I, Section 8, of the U.S. Constitution.

Our first introductory quote indicates that the powers contained within the U.S. Constitution are of a delegated nature only. The commonly accepted phrase is that the powers of the federal government are "limited and enumerated." In other words, the federal government has power or authority only as specified in the Constitution or as necessary and proper for executing these specified powers. Madison said it this way: "...this is not an indefinite Government, deriving its powers from the general terms prefixed to the specific powers, but a limited Government tied down to the specific powers, which explain and define the general terms..." (Hyneman & Carey, 19967, p. 116). Thus, as Senator John Henderson said in 1866, no matter how beneficial, merciful, and "welling up from a good and pure fountain" (Avins, 1974, p. 146) a proposed federal act may appear, it cannot be executed without the benefit of an enumerated Constitutional provision.

The second introductory quote, that of James Madison, speaks to the wrongful consequence of misreading the Constitution and particularly the general welfare phrases. Only by misreading the provisions of the Constitution can it be said that the federal government can tax for or otherwise control the education of children in the various states. It needs to be emphasized that, as is obvious in the quote, Madison made federal control of education as equally wrong as federal control of religion. To the latter, we as citizens have consensually objected, but we have endorsed the former.

The conundrum to be discussed in this chapter should now be apparent. If it is true, as suggested above, that the federal government has no authority over education, how can it be that a cabinet-level U.S. Office of Education exists and further that it manages a budget in the billions of dollars of taxpayer monies? At a deeper level, why is it that for the two Constitutionally-excluded areas of religion and education, one is jealously guarded from federal encroachment and the other is actively welcomed?

Our final introductory quote combines two ideas for consideration. President Washington proposed, first, that any change deemed necessary to the Constitution, such as educational involvement, be obtained by the only acceptable method—a Constitutional amendment. But as we will see, no such amendment exists now or ever did, yet federal educational involvement at the very least is an expensive reality. Continuing, Washington urged that any needed Constitutional amendment not be neglected in favor of obtaining power by usurpation. Yet, as we shall see, this chapter argues that this is precisely the method by which the federal government has acquired educational powers, good intentions notwithstanding.

Federal Involvement

In spite of the many cautions like those mentioned above by President Washington or Madison's "first duty" assertion in his "Memorial and Remonstrance" to take "alarm at the first experiment of our liberties," the federal government has taken control of education policy, decision-making, and taxation. As we shall soon see, rights reserved either to the states and, most importantly, to the people are not respectively enjoyed, but are wrongfully preempted by governmental authority.

For instance, in the year 1995, the Federal Department of Education controlled a budget of $31 billion, and overall the federal government spent about $70 billion for education (Robinson, 1995). It all started with the passage of the Morrill Land Grant Act of 1862. Then giving it all an administrative umbrella, a Federal Department of Education was authorized in 1867. One year after its origination as a federal department, the status of the department was changed to a bureau and it was placed under the Department of the Interior for the next seventy years. In 1939 the office was transferred to the newly created Federal Security Agency under President Franklin Roosevelt. Then in 1953, under President Eisenhower, the office was transferred to the newly created Department of Health, Education, and Welfare (HEW). Although there were as many as fifty legislative efforts from 1908 to 1951 and eighty more after 1953 to give the office a separate, Cabinet level identity, this did not occur until 1979 under President Carter (U.S. Code, 1979, Vol. II, p. 1534).

When initially founded in 1867, the budget for the Federal Department of Education was less than $15,000. By 1914, the Smith-Lever Act followed by the Smith-Hughes Act of 1917 authorized millions of dollars of direct federal aid to education. In the 1930s and 40s, the Public Works Administration, the Works Project Administration, and other relief efforts allocated approximately one billion dollars for public school construction and hundreds of millions for the improvement of educational facilities and financial aid to both teachers and students alike. The Lanham Act of 1940 channeled almost a billion dollars into school construction projects. Since WWII, the "GI Bill" (i.e., Servicemen's Readjustment Act) has provided millions of dollars in educational payments (Kursh, 1965, pp. 27-28). In 1953, as part of HEW, the federal education budget was $400 million, and at the time of the education office's separate identity in 1979, the budget was more than $10 billion (*United States Code*, 1979, p. 1535).

While federal government involvement in education seems to grow without constraint, the truth of the matter is that, as Kursh notes in his history of the U.S. Office of Education (1965), "the word 'education' appears nowhere in the United States Constitution" (p. 27). All the early Presidents functioned totally within this clearly understood constraint. President Washington, for instance, while urging the legislature to consider how to be involved, constrained his zeal to providing support for education to the only geographic region possible according to the Constitution, that being Washington, DC. President Jefferson specifically declared that public education and the funding of it was not a power "enumerated in the Constitution, and to which it permits the public moneys to be applied" (Richardson, Vol. I, 1897, p. 398). For Jefferson, the only route for federal involvement was by way of a Constitutional amendment. President Madison, known as the "Father of the Constitution," followed Washington's example to propose educational intervention in Washington, DC, the only Constitutionally permissible area possible. Earlier, while yet a congressman, Madison stated that education in the states could come under federal authority only by way of a wrongful interpretation of the Constitution.

Most problematic in this regard is the dialogue that led up to passage of "the first real Federal role in education, the first divergence from Constitutional intent" (Kursh, 1965, p. 27). This "divergence," known as the Morrill Land Grant Act (1862), was preceded by a bill, just three years earlier, to donate public lands to the states for the purpose of building colleges. President Buchanan, in signal significance, vetoed this direct precursor to the present federal role in education because neither the granting of financial support, even if via marketed land grants, nor the subsequent enforcement of fund applications are within the powers granted to Congress by the U.S. Constitution (Richardson, 1897, Vol. VII, pp. 3077-3078).

In spite of uniform interpretations of the gentlemen of the Constitutional era to the contrary, the federal government is obviously very much involved in educational matters, including funding of the same. A closer look follows.

Constitutional Philosophy

To understand the U.S. as well as state constitutions, it is essential to first understand the general theory of government that undergirds these written documents. Almost without exception, the men who fashioned the U.S. and the state constitutions believed that the state was a dependent creation of its own members. As such, its basis is a political compact by which members agree with one another to surrender some of their sovereign powers for their mutual benefit. Most importantly, the only parties to the compact are the people themselves, either as individuals or as communities; government is not a party to the compact but only a dependent creation of it. Moreover, the qualities of limited and enumerated powers by definition exclude any supposed inherent right or power of these derived institutions for self-preservation no matter how needful it may seem.

It is because the people as individuals first possess natural rights such as life, liberty, and property that the government has any power at all. In his pre-political condition, man is believed to have absolute authority over his person and property and the right to protect the same. When natural rights such as protection are surrendered by each individual to the government, the government is thereby empowered to enforce these rights. In the surrendering, however, each individual surrenders nothing other than that which is clearly specified. All other natural rights of original sovereignty each individual retains to himself. This is in essence the message of the Ninth Amendment to the U.S. Constitution. That is, the declaration in the Constitution of certain rights of citizens is not meant to be exhaustive nor even a prioritizing of such rights. (As stated in Amendment IX, "The enumeration in the Constitution, of certain rights, shall not be construed to deny or disparage others retained by the people.")

Government is thus one of limited, even only enumerated powers. The creature of political compact, government is not a party to it and has no rights under it. The right of change and even revolution is specifically retained by the people should the government transgress its delegated authority, just as the Declaration of Independence eloquently expressed (cf., Padover, 1953, p. 48).

It was from this widely accepted foundation of derived powers (cf., Burns, 1938, Chapters 2 & 6) that the federal and state constitutions were developed. It is also by way of this foundation that Constitutional interpretations have their fealty to proper meaning.

Constitutional Provisions

General Welfare

A provision of the U.S. Constitution that has potential implications for education and that is informed by the above Constitutional philosophy relates to providing for the general welfare of the United States.

This concern for the general welfare is articulated twice in the U.S. Constitution. The Constitution's Preamble lists among the reasons for establishing the Constitution to "promote the general welfare." Similarly, Article I, Section 8, grants power to Congress to lay and collect taxes, etc., to "provide for the common Defense and general welfare of the United States..." Both these provisions for the "general welfare" are wont by some to justify the federal government's intrusion into education. Yet this is merely wishful thinking not at all consistent with either the language or the philosophy of the Constitution.

First, mention of the general welfare in the Preamble gives no right over education to the federal government. Those who say otherwise base their argument on the proposition that education directly relates to the general welfare. However, the Preamble grants no right at all in any area including education precisely because it is only the Preamble. As Constitutional experts acknowledge, "The general welfare clause is only an introductory expression and was never intended to be a grant of power of any sort" (Burns, 1938, p. 169). The Preamble in whole or part delegates no new or additional powers to Congress (Hutchison, 1975, p. 15). In fact, if the Preamble is construed to grant powers, there would be no limit to such powers. The Constitution would not then be a document of limited and enumerated powers, as discussed earlier, but of unlimited and unenumerated powers. Obviously, this cannot be.

A more substantive yet equally invalid argument is that the authority of federal government over education is granted by the general welfare wording of Article I, Section 8. According to Madison, the phrase "common defense and general welfare" was inserted into the clause by a "freak of history" (Burns, 1938, p.

111). Arguing against an expansive interpretation, Madison noted,

> It is to be recollected that the terms 'common defense and general welfare,' as used here, are not novel terms, first introduced into this Constitution. They are terms familiar in their construction and well known to the people of America. They are repeatedly found in the old Articles of Confederation where, although they are susceptible of as great latitude as can be given by the context here, it was never supposed or pretended that they conveyed any such power [beyond that enumerated] as it now assigned to them. On the contrary, it was always considered as clear and certain that the old Congress was limited to the enumerated powers, and that the enumeration limited and explained the general terms... (Hyneman & Carey, 1967, p. 115)

According to Madison, except for the one tangential yet defeated proposal to Congress to provide payment for public debts "and for defraying the expenses that shall be incurred for the common defense and general welfare," no reference was ever made in the Constitutional Convention to the general welfare clause as a grant of Congressional power. Furthermore, at no time among all the amendments proposed by the states to safeguard their own rights did any of them refer to the term "general welfare" which, if truly understood to be a federal grant of power, would have stirred widespread resistance among the states.

The Article I general welfare clause was never intended to be a grant of power. Hutchison (1975, p. 98) rightly notes that the power that is given in this clause is limited to levying taxes for the general welfare responsibilities that are specifically given to Congress rather than the power to do anything whatever for the general welfare. And those responsibilities which are specifically given to Congress are found in the list that follows the general welfare introduction: "If Congress as the supreme and sole judge of that subject can apply money to the general welfare, then it may assume control over religion, or education or any other object of state legislation down to the most trivial police measure" (Burns, 1938, p. 113). But, as we have previously noted, Madison made it clear that "the general government does not have the slightest right to intermeddle with religion" (Cord, 1982, p. 8). In fact, with any amount of thought at all on the matter, Madison said it would be patently obvious that practically everything relates to either the common defense or general welfare and the exercise of practically every power involves an expenditure of monies.

To think that the general welfare clause applies beyond those enumerated duties violates the specific and limited powers philosophy behind the U.S. Constitution, the generally understood meaning of the wording at the time of discussion and adoption, as well as the literal wording of the total clause itself. Accordingly, no power is given to Congress to either directly dictate educational matters nor even to levy taxes for the cause of education.

Madison addressed the point very soundly in his speech to the House of Representatives on February 6, 1792 (Hyneman & Carey, 1967, pp. 114-117):

> It is supposed by some gentleman that Congress have authority ... [to] do anything which they may think conducive to the 'general welfare.'
>
> This, sir, in my mind raises the important and fundamental question, whether the general terms which have been cited are to be considered as a sort of caption or general description of the specified powers and as having no further meaning and giving no further power than what is found in that specification; or as an abstract and indefinite delegation of power extending all cases whatever; to all such, at least, as will admit the application of money, which is giving as much latitude as any Government could well desire.
>
> I, Sir, have always conceived—I believe those who proposed the Constitution conceived, and it is still more fully known and more material to observe that those who ratified the Constitution conceived—that this is not an indefinite Government, deriving its powers from the

general terms prefixed to the specified powers, but a limited Government tied down to the specified powers, which explain and define the general terms... It will follow, in the first place, that if the terms be taken in the broad sense they maintain, the particular powers afterwards so carefully and distinctly enumerated would be without meaning and must go for nothing... In fact, the meaning of the general terms in question must either be sought in the subsequent enumeration which limits and details them, or they convert the Government from one limited, as hitherto supposed, to the enumerated powers, unto a Government without any limits at all... The novel idea now annexed to these terms, and never before entertained by the friends or enemies of the Government, will have a further consequence which cannot have been taken into the view of the gentlemen... There are consequences, sir, still more extensive, which, as they follow clearly from the doctrine combated, must either be admitted or the doctrine must be given up. If Congress can apply money indefinitely to the general welfare, and are the sole and supreme judges of the general welfare, they must take the care of religion into their own hands; they may establishes teachers in Every State, county, or parish, and pay them out of the public Treasury; they may take into their own hands the education of children, establishing in like manner schools throughout the Union ... for every object I have mentioned would admit the application of money, and might be called, if Congress pleased, provisions for the general welfare.

This absence of any provision for and hence a clear prohibition against Federal authority over educational policy, practice, and taxation is documented, as we shall now see, in both pre and post Constitutional accounts of early America.

According to Madison's minutes of the Constitutional Convention, when the Committee of detail presented its proposed U.S. Constitution on August 6, 1787, it contained no reference to

Congressional authority over education. Precisely because of this omission, Madison requested, on August 18th, that the Committee of Detail add, among certain additional powers to the General Legislature, "To establish an University." Then specifically, on September 14th, James Madison and William Pinkney motioned "to insert in the list of powers vested in Congress a power— 'to establish an University, in which no preferences or distinctions should be allowed on account of religion'" (*Documents Illustrative*, 1984, p. 725). The notes of Maryland delegate Dr. James McHenry further indicate that the motion by Madison and Pinkney on September 14th would also enable Congress to erect the institution "in the place of general government" and that Congress was "to possess exclusive jurisdiction" (p. 950). In agreeing with the defeat of this motion, Gouverneur Morris noted, "It is not necessary. The exclusive power at the Seat of Government, will reach the object." In other words, the outcome will naturally be reached at the level of government where the exclusive power to do so resides, i.e., at the state level.

The interpretation given here to Morris' comment regarding the preexisting, exclusive power of the separate states in educational matters is obviously supported by McHenry's notes where the motion wanted Congress instead (of the states) to have "exclusive jurisdiction." Further support comes from the recollection of Roger Sherman, who was present at the Federal Constitutional Convention as a representative of Connecticut. Speaking on May 3, 1790, regarding the topic of President Washington's request to encourage science and literature, Sherman, by then a Congressman, noted that when a similar proposition was made in General Convention "to vest Congress with power to establish a National University ... it was negatived. It was thought sufficient that this power be exercised by the States in their separate capacity" (Gales, 1834, #21604, pp. 1550-1551).

Finally in speaking to the House of Representatives on February 6, 1792, Madison specifically acknowledges that an undesirable consequence of Congress wrongfully interpreting the U.S. Constitution would be the belief that "they may take the care of religion into their own hands; they may establish teachers in every

State, country, or parish, and pay them out of the public Treasury; they may take into their own hands the education of children, establishing in like manner schools throughout the Union..." (Hyneman & Carey, 1967, p. 117).

The fact, well established here, is that at its ratification, the clear and certain understanding of the Constitution was that it contained no power of Congress over education. Furthermore, even when efforts were made by such greats as James Madison, the "Father of the Constitution," to include such powers within the Federal Constitution, these efforts were all denied.

Evidence from Congressional debates after, yet still close to ratification of the Constitution, yield the same conclusion. Namely, the Constitution grants no power over education to Congress.

Evidently, the first effort at incorporating education under Federal jurisdiction occurred soon after the 1789 ratification of the Constitution. Believing that "the security of a free constitution" comes from activities such as "teaching the people themselves to know and to value their own rights," George Washington suggested to Congress that "there is nothing which can better deserve your patronage than the promotion of science and literature" (Richardson, 1897, Vol. I, p. 58). To this end, President Washington in his First Annual address (January 8, 1790) asked Congress to take under deliberation the possibility of giving "aids to seminaries of learning already established, by the institution of a national university, or by other expedients..." (p. 58).

On May 3 of this same year, when Congressman William Smith of South Carolina motioned to refer Washington's "encouragement of science and literature" to a select committee, Mr. Stone of Maryland objected by asking, "[W]hat part of the Constitution authorized Congress to take any steps in a business of this kind?" (Gales, 1834, 21604, p. 1551). He noted further, "We have already done as much as we can with propriety; we have encouraged learning, by giving to authors and exclusive privilege of vending their works; this is going as far as we have the power to go by the Constitution" (Gales, 1834, 21604, p. 1551). Congressman Sherman agreed, as discussed earlier, that at the time of its conception the Constitution did not give Congress any power over education. The House never did take action on the matter.

With no Congressional action on the matter, George Washington similarly proposed in his Eighth Annual address (December 7, 1796) that Congress establish "a national University and also a military academy" (Richardson, 1897, Vol. I, p. 194). On December 21st of this same year (4th Congress, 2nd Session), Madison presented a resolution to the House of Representatives that they establish a university as urged by the President. Part of Madison's argument for doing so was that those who

> ceded a large territory for the purpose of a federal city ... by their deeds of cession authorized the President of the United States for the time being to appropriate such portions thereof as he should judge necessary for public use. In virtue of this power the President has appropriated nineteen acres one rood and twenty-one perches, part of the land so ceded, for the site of a national university. (Lowrie & Clarke, 1832 # 037, misc. 91)

As Madison further explained in the House discussion on December 26, the management of the newly created District of Columbia, to include a national university, was solely under the jurisdiction of Congress, as the 17th enumerated power of Article I, Section 8. When the vote was taken of the House as a Committee of the Whole on December 27th, it was "negatived by a great majority." This was in spite of the fact that the motion asked for no federal money but only an encouragement for a "Seminary of Learning" in the District of Columbia and an authorization for a "number of gentlemen into a corporate capacity to enable them to receive donations..." (Gales, 1849, 21608, p. 1704). In the protracted discussion on the issue that covered many concerns including potential future financial liabilities, Mr. Brent voiced objections on Constitutional grounds: "he was of the opinion that imposing a revenue for such a purpose would be unconstitutional and arrogating a right they did not possess" (Gales, 1849, 21608, p. 1710). Ultimately the matter was postponed apparently not to be reconsidered by this session of Congress.

No less an advocate for public education, Thomas Jefferson declared, as President of the United States, that education was outside the realm of authority of the federal government. In fact, as the following quote from his Sixth Annual Message (to Congress on December 2, 1806) reveals, the Constitution does not permit Congress either the right of involvement in or the use of public funds for education:

> The question therefore now comes forward, to what other objects shall these surpluses be appropriated, and the whole surplus of import, after the entire discharge of the public debt, and during those intervals when the purposes of war shall not call for them... Their patriotism would certainly prefer its continuance and application to the great purposes of the public education, roads, rivers, canals, and such other objects of public improvement as it may be thought proper to *add* [emphasis added] to the Constitutional enumeration of Federal powers... Education is here placed among the articles of public care, not that it would be proposed to take its ordinary branches out of the hands of private enterprise, which manages so much better all the concerns to which it is equal, but a public institution can alone supply those sciences which though rarely called for are yet necessary to complete the circle, all the parts of which contribute to the improvement of the country and some of them to its preservation... I suppose an amendment to the Constitution, by consent of the States, necessary, because the objects now recommended are not among those enumerated in the Constitution, and to which it permits the public moneys to be applied. (Richardson, Vol. I, 1897, pp. 397-398)

The third president, James Madison, was equally a participant of the Constitutional debates. In his Second Annual Message to Congress (December 5, 1810), Madison said, "I can not presume it to be unreasonable to invite your attention to the advantages of superadding to the means of education provided by the several states a seminary of learning instituted by the National Legislature within the limits of their exclusive jurisdiction... But alone all, a well-constituted seminary in the center of the nation is recommended..." (Richardson, 1897, Vol. I, p. 470).

President Madison's recommendation regarding a national university was referred to a select committee of the House of Representatives on Monday, December 10th, 1810, as part of the 11th Congress, 3rd Session (Gales, 1834, 21624, p. 388). The report of Samuel Mitchell, the committee chairman, on February 18, 1811 (Gales, 1834, 977, p. 976), was totally consistent with prior actions as reported thus far. In fact, the committee briefly recounted the history of this effort as follows:

> ... the patriot spirit of Washington led him more than once to recommend, in his speeches to Congress, an attention to such an undertaking. He even bequeathed a legacy to the national university, which he persuaded himself would, at some day, be brought into being. Two other Presidents have subsequently presented the subject to the Legislature as worthy of special consideration... Authorities so respectable, in favor of a project so desirable, carry with them great weight.

While the educational benefit of such an establishment was applauded, the Constitutional restriction against such an establishment was cited as a major hindrance to approval:

> To a free people it would seem that a seminary, in which the culture of the heart and of the understanding should be the chief objects, would be one of the best guards of their privileges, and a leading object of their care... On weighing these and other advantages, it was necessary to consider whether Congress possessed the power to found and endow a national university.
>
> It is argued from the total silence of the Constitution, that such a power has not been granted to Congress, inasmuch as the only means by which it is

therein contemplated to promote the progress of science and the useful arts, is by securing to authors and inventors the exclusive right to their respective writings and discoveries for limited times. The Constitution, therefore, does not warrant the creation of such a corporation by any express provision.

But it immediately occurred that, under the right to legislate exclusively over the district wherein the United States have fixed their seat of Government. Congress may erect a university at any place within the ten miles square ceded by Maryland and Virginia. This cannot be doubted.

Here, however, other considerations arise. Although there is no Constitutional impediment of the incorporation of trustees for such a purpose, at the City of Washington, serious doubts are entertained as to the right to appropriate the public property for its support. The endorsement of a university is not ranked among the objects for which drafts ought to be made upon the Treasury. The money of the nation seems to be reserved for other uses...

The matter then stands thus: The creation of a university, upon the enlarged and magnificent plan which would become the nation is not within the powers confided by the Constitution of Congress...

The conclusion obviously was not to adopt any of this part of Madison's message.

True to the pattern, the next president, James Monroe, likewise addressed the same issue. This time however, Monroe spoke the conclusion of the matter himself. In his First Annual Message to Congress (December 2, 1817) he addressed the issue of federal intervention in education in the larger context of the legitimate right of Congress to establish "a system of improvement" (e.g., "good roads and canals") (Richardson, 1897, Vol. II, p. 587). He concluded on this matter,

the result is a settled conviction in my mind that Congress

does not possess the right. It is not contained in any of the specified powers granted to Congress, or can I consider it incidental to or a necessary means, viewed on the most liberal scale, for carrying into effect any of the powers which are specifically granted. In communicating this result I cannot resist the obligation which I feel to suggest to Congress the propriety of recommending to the states the adoption of an amendment to the Constitution which shall give to Congress the right in question. ...I think proper to suggested also, in case this measure is adopted, that it be recommended to the states to include in the Amendment sought a right in Congress to institute likewise seminaries of learning, for the all important purpose of diffusing knowledge among our fellow-citizens throughout the United States.

While more evidence from early America could be cited, the point is that Congress is not empowered by the U.S. Constitution to involve itself in educational matters. Further, it has no authority to collect or spend public money for education even when an educational object is received gratis by the federal government as with President Washington's bequeath of land for a national university. It is not that education was of no concern to Congress—quite the contrary as we have seen even by the frequency of attempts to promote Congressional involvement. However the statements of those closest to the actual writing of the Constitution and the philosophy foundational to the writing argues forcefully against interpreting the Constitution any other way.

Implied versus Inherent Powers

A route not covered thus far to possibly permitting Congressional involvement in education relates to the final enumerated power of Article I, Section 8. That provision reads, "To make all Laws which shall be necessary and proper for carrying into Execution the foregoing Powers, and all other Powers vested by this Constitution in the Government of the United States, or in any

Department or Officer thereof."

This potential entree is easily eliminated however by its very own wording. That is, "necessary and proper" laws can be made by Congress to facilitate the execution of enumerated powers of the Constitution. Since educational matters are not contained in any of those enumerated powers, no laws in this regard are authorized. Additionally, it should be recalled that none of the cited efforts to involve Congress in education ever appealed to this final Section 8 provision. In fact, President Monroe commented, apparently without opposition, that even the most liberal reading of this last provision would not encompass educational authority.

Implied powers were not at all unknown in English legal theory. "No axiom is more clearly established in law or in reason," said Madison, "than that where the end is required, the means are authorized" (Hutchison, 1975, p. 127). Accordingly, a member of the Committee of Detail, James Wilson, said the provision (which appears in the Constitution exactly as they proposed) was intended to give Congress "the power of carrying into effect the laws which they shall make under the powers vested in them by this Constitution" (Hutchison, 1975, p. 127).

Inherent powers, however, are a different matter altogether. Madison emphasized, in fact, that the doctrine of inherent powers is one not to be tolerated. This doctrine proposes that the power of government is inherent in the basic sovereignty of government. However, as discussed earlier, if Congress was meant by the founders to have powers of this inherent nature, the entire process of defining powers would be superfluous. Instead, the federal government gets its power from what is granted or *necessarily implied* in the Constitution. Madison noted, for instance, that had the power of making treaties been omitted, "the defect could only have been lamented, or supplied by an amendment of the Constitution" (Burns, 1938, pp. 106, 107).

Contrariwise, powers that come by way of implication must be admitted; otherwise, many of the granted powers would be without the necessary and proper means to carry them into execution. For instance, the enumerated power of regulating foreign commerce must necessarily carry with it the implied power to address trade restrictions of other countries.

In this regard, Madison spoke against the proposal to add the word "expressly" to the Tenth Amendment to have it read "The powers not *expressly* delegated to the United States by the Constitution, nor prohibited by it to the States, are reserved to the States respectively, or to the people." Addition of the word "expressly" would, he contended, deny operation of the desirable concept of implied powers and thus be inappropriate. Conversely, retention of "powers delegated" (as it reads today) rightly prohibits the inherent powers interpretation while allowing for implied powers.

Yet at the same time, implied powers cannot be construed beyond what is really necessary no matter how convenient, conducive to, or even highly effective in the business of government. And those powers considered legitimate for federal jurisdiction are clearly enumerated. For instance, as central as providing for armies and naval forces are to the prior enumerated power of "To declare war..." (number 11), these provisions are not left to discovery by deduction as being "necessary and proper." Rather, they are expressly provided for in the enumerated powers (number 12 and 13, respectively). Madison took strong exception to Chief Justice Marshall's interpretation that all means not specifically prohibited toward Constitutionally legitimate ends are thus Constitutionally appropriate. Madison cogently noted that the permitting of anything and everything not prohibited would ultimately expand federal powers such that reserved powers of the states would be so minimized that Constitutional ratification by the states would have been considered an act of suicide and thus not accomplished.

<u>Property Disposal</u>

Another potential way that Congress could involve itself in educational efforts would be by way of Article IV, Section 3, of the Constitution. The second paragraph of this provision reads, "The Congress shall have power to dispose of and make all needful Rules and Regulations respecting the Territory or other property belonging to the United States..."

This provision was, in fact, the basis of a bill that proposed the sale of federal property donated to each state for "the endowment, support, and maintenance of at least one college [in each state]..." (Richardson, 1897, Vol. VII, p. 3074). The advocates of this effort thought that "by a fair interpretation of the words 'dispose of' in this clause, Congress possesses the power to make this gift of public lands to the States for the purposes of education" (Richardson, 1897, Vol. VII, p. 3079).

> President Buchanan disarmed this rationale, however, in his veto of the 1859 bill: It would require clear and strong evidence to induce the belief that the framers of the Constitution, after having limited the powers of Congress to certain precise and specific objects, intended by employing the words 'dispose of' to give that body unlimited power over the vast public domain. It would be a strange anomaly, indeed, to have created two funds—the one by taxation, confined to the execution of the enumerated powers delegated to Congress, and the other from the public lands, applicable to all subjects, foreign and domestic, which Congress might designate... This would be to confer upon Congress a vast and irresponsible authority, utterly at war with the well-known jealousy of Federal power which prevailed at the formation of the Constitution. The natural intendment would be that as the Constitution confined Congress to well-defined specific powers, the funds placed at their command, whether in land or money, should be appropriated to the performance of the duties corresponding with these powers. If not, a Government has been created with all its other powers carefully limited, but without any limitation in respect to the public lands. (p. 3079)

Buchanan was clear, as will be discussed later, to differentiate the outright and unencumbered giving of land for educational purposes from the mandating of how to use that land after relinquishment including requiring its sale and prescribing proper use of the profits. What is apparently the only historical effort to use Article IV, Section 3, to involve the federal government in education was, for the time being, disallowed.

Constitutional Amendments

With the inescapable conclusion that the main body of the Constitution does not authorize educational powers nor commensurate taxation authority of Congress over the peoples, there is only one other possible source of such empowerment. Before moving forward into new material, however, a review of certain pertinencies already covered points to a tentative response in this regard. Specifically, certain observations were made by the gentlemen of the Constitutional era that discount in advance the possibility that the Bill of Rights grants educational access for the federal government.

To the point, since the Bill of Rights became effective on December 15, 1791, any comments made after yet close to that time regarding Constitutional powers and provisions would logically be tempered by a proper understanding of the contents of these ten amendments. Interestingly, the bulk of the comments presented thus far postdate the 1791 ratification. And most importantly, these subsequent comments, which would logically be inclusive of the Bill of Rights provisions, deny educational authority to Congress.

Taken in chronological order, Madison's House speech of February 1792 (recall that Madison himself proposed the Bill of Rights in 1789) declares that congressional intrusion into education, including Treasury support, would be an unauthorized consequence of wrongfully interpreting the Constitution's general welfare provisions. Additionally, Madison's support of President Washington's call for a national university was carefully crafted within the isolated enumerated right of Congress to manage the District of Columbia only.

Even more telling, Jefferson directly declared, in 1806, that a Constitutional amendment was needed (beyond the Bill of Rights amendment) to authorize congressional care of education. Madison, as President, proposed congressional involvement in education but, again, *only* within the enumerated provision of managing Washington, DC. But even then it was denied by Congress for fear of a future financial liability that would automatically be without

Constitutional authorization.

Equally telling are the arguments in Congress that specifically address the inappropriateness of the amendments to federal educational involvement. Consider the Fourteenth Amendment, which was adopted in 1868, as it has been used to force educational involvement. The educationally relevant part of Section I reads as follows: "No State shall make or enforce any law which shall abridge the privileges or immunities of citizens of the United States; nor shall any State deprive any person of life, liberty, or property, without due process of law; nor deny to any person within its jurisdiction the equal protection of the laws."

Representative William Read of Kentucky, in speaking against the proposed Civil Rights Bill (Civil War Reconstruction efforts) of 1874 had this to say about the applicability of the Fourteenth Amendment: "By what right does Congress assume to impose this bill upon the country? They cannot find any warrant for it in the Constitution or its amendments. The friends of the bill contend that the right is found in the fourteenth amendment. I deny it. It is not warranted by that instrument either in the thirteenth, four-teenth, or fifteenth amendments to the constitution." One of the fears of Read was that the bill in question would "break up the common-school system in all the Southern States..." (Avins, 1974, p. 708). Some, however, in noting that Read was from a southern state (Kentucky), would argue that he may have had ulterior motives in opposing the bill, and thus his argument particularly regarding the 14th may be flawed.

But the inapplicability of the 14th was also cited by others. Notably, Representative William Finck of Ohio was especially artic-ulate in discounting educational intrusion via the Fourteenth Amendment: "Now, sir, I deny that there is any grant of power contained in this article of amendment [14th] which confers upon the Federal Government the power to pass a law to regulate ... what class of children shall go into the common schools of the states" (Avins, 1974, p. 716). He further explained, "I was insisting that the fourteenth amendment to the Constitution, for the reasons I have already suggested, did not confer upon the General Government any power to go into the States and regulate ... the admission of scholars into the public schools... It is a commandment to the State. But it does not confer upon Congress any affirmative power to go into the States and regulate..." (Avins, 1974, p. 716).

Finck further supported his position by reference to state and U.S. supreme court decisions: "We have a decision made by the Supreme Court of Ohio in regard to the common schools of that State, in which this clause of the fourteenth amendment was fully considered and discussed by the court... In that decision they held that this clause of the amendment did not authorize the Government of the United States to control the schools within the State" (Avins, 1974, p. 716). Similarly, Finck cited what were known as the 1872 "Slaughter-house cases" of the U.S. Supreme Court. Claiming that the Court "has decided that the rights, privileges, and immunities of citizens of the States as such, are left to the protection of the States; and not to the protection of the Federal Government; and it has decided that the rights and immunities belonging to citizens of the States cannot be controlled by the Federal Government." Then the federal government cannot, among other things,

> go into the State and say how its school system shall be conducted... If the Federal Government may do this, there is no limitation which can be set to the power it may exercise within the States. I say, therefore, at the very threshold, that the provisions of this bill are without authority; there is no power conferred upon the Federal Government to pass the proposed measure. The Supreme Court of the United States has already decided in the case adverted to, that no such powers have been conferred upon the Federal Government by the fourteenth amendment. (Avins, 1974, p. 717)

As late as 1817 (26 years after the Bill of Rights ratification) the observation was again made by a U.S. President (i.e., Monroe) that a Constitutional amendment was necessary in order to permit educational involvement by the federal government. Even more recently, President Buchanan, in 1859, denied that Congress had Constitutional authority in education.

Can there be any doubt that there is no right of Congress—even of the federal government overall—to involve itself in education or educational financing? This is so even including the existence of the Bill of Rights provisions that are sometimes interpreted to install the federal government as the provider of diverse and innumerable citizen rights and liberties.

Overwhelming and conclusive evidence notwithstanding, the federal government is heavily invested, via policy and finances, in education across all the states.

Federal Rationale

Just as the constant pounding of the seas eventually erode the sea wall, so too does the constant pounding of well-meaning educational intentions impair prohibitory Constitutional walls. The key to understanding the rationale behind the current massive involvement of the federal government in educational matters resides in understanding both the nature of government and the people who run it. This understanding is not a new revelation at all, but as Jefferson said in a different context, "it was at the time, a common understanding of the matter." In the brief rehearsal of this understanding that follows, it is important to see the basic and pivotal tension inherent in promoting liberty, especially when the liberty may be misused.

George Washington in his First Inaugural Address (April 30, 1789) articulated the crux of the matter as follows: "... the preservation of the sacred fire of liberty, and the destiny of the republican model of government are just considered, perhaps, as *deeply*, as *finally*, staked on the experiment intrusted to the hands of the American people" (Richardson, 1897, Vol. I, p. 45). In other words, the future of this new government was trusted to the peoples themselves. Is it any wonder, then, that Washington, like so many of his successors, placed a high premium on education? As he said shortly afterwards in his First Annual Address (January 8, 1790) to Congress,

Nor am I less persuaded that you will agree with me in opinion that there is nothing which can better deserve your patronage than the promotion of science and literature. Knowledge is in every country the surest basis of public happiness. ...To the security of a free constitution it contributes in various ways—by convincing those who are intrusted with the public administration that every valuable end of government is best answered by the enlightened confidence of the people, and by teaching the people themselves to know and to value their own rights... Whether this desirable object will be best promoted by affording aids to seminaries of learning already established, by the institution of a national university, or by any other expedients will be well worthy of a place in the deliberations of the Legislature. (Richardson, 1897, Vol. I, p. 58)

As should be obvious, *the ultimate success of this newly instituted government is perceived to lay in an area where the government was never granted any control.* Is there any wonder that the pressure was inevitably too great to resist?

Moreover, the potential of this pressure to become a reality rather than remain just an intellectual irritant is eventuated by human nature itself. Madison spoke in *The Federalist Papers*, No. 51 (Hamilton, Madison & Jay, 1961), of the need for governmental structures to guard against selfish human tendencies, as did many other founders in their various writings. Staying with our first President as we finish this point, Washington spoke thusly in his Farewell Address of September 17, 1796:

Toward the preservation of your Government and the permanency of your present happy state, it is requisite not only that you steadily discountenance irregular oppositions to its acknowledged authority, but also that you resist with care the spirit of innovation upon its principles, however specious the pretexts... It is important, likewise, that the habits of thinking in a free country should inspire caution in those intrusted with its administration to confine themselves within their respective Constitutional spheres, avoiding in the exercise of the powers of one department to encroach upon another... *A just esti-mate of that love of power and proneness to abuse it which predominates in the human heart is sufficient to satisfy us of the truth of this position* [emphasis added] ... (Richardson, 1897, Vol. I, pp. 210-211)

To the fact that the federal government is heavily invested in education, Washington's Farewell Address speaks prophetically: "But let there be no change by *usurpation* [emphasis added]; for though this in one instance may be the instrument of good, it is the customary weapon by which free governments are destroyed. The precedent must always greatly overbalance in permanent evil any partial or transient benefit which the use can at any time yield" (Richardson, 1897, Vol. I, p. 212).

Federal Usurpation

Washington's insights, and particularly the observation that usurpations of authority typically emanate from beneficial (temporar-ily, anyway) but unauthorized actions, are keenly pertinent to under-standing how the federal government moved from a position of prohibited to permitted and even promoted involvement in education. The very first instance of this involvement came in the federal decree of 1785 that state townships sell Lot No. 16 and use the profits thereof for education. This action, however, was under the authority of the Continental Congress and thus is not relevant to our concerns vis a vis the authority of the U.S. Constitution. Even so, this provi-sion did not place the federal government in a position of state educa-tional involvement. As stated earlier, official federal involvement in education under our existent Constitution started with the Morrill Land Grant Act of 1862. Impetus for this Act centers around the Civil War Reconstruction activities of the U.S. Congress.

The poignancy of Washington's observations are revealed in the contrast of two opposing positions of the mid-1800s that are spaced no more than three years apart. In 1859, a bill was autho-rized by Congress to donate land to the states and territories to be sold and the profits used solely to "provide colleges for the benefit of agriculture and mechanical arts." More specifically, the purpose of the gift was "the endowment, support and maintenance of at least one college [in each state]..." (Richardson, 1897, Vol. VII, p. 3074). In his veto of this bill, President Buchanan expressed two concerns relevant to our study. First, Buchanan concluded that the absence of Constitutionally-based power for Congress to appropriate public money "for the purpose of educating the people of the respective states" (Richardson, 1897, Vol. VII, p. 3078) similarly disbarred the use of land profits for the same ends: "I presume the general proposition is undeniable that Congress does not possess the power to appropriate money in the Treasury, raised by taxes on the people of the United States, for the purpose of educating the people of the respective States" (Richardson, 1897, Vol. VII, p. 3078). Land granted specifically to generate capital through its sale for educational purposes was in effect equally prohibited by the Constitution, said Buchanan, since it served the same disallowed object. Buchanan's discriminating understanding of the Constitution allowed him to agree however with earlier congressional land grants that contained no other stipulations than that the land be used for educational purposes. These latter grants were apparently within the disposal provisions of Article IV, Section 3, were good stewardship actions of this provision, and did not presume upon the Article I, Section 8 nonenumeration of educational powers, or use public funds for the same.

It is interesting to note that Representative Justin Morrill's call for an override vote of the President's veto (after the veto message was read and Morrill voiced his veto objections) failed to attain the necessary two-thirds majority (Rives, 1859, p. 1414). Even so, Vermont Representative Justin Morrill (and Senator Benjamin Wade of Ohio) was able to achieve the objective under a different president. When the land grant bill was again approved by the House on June 17, 1862, Morrill noted that "It has been five years before the country, and is essentially the same bill that has repeatedly been before the House" (Rives, 1862, 37th Congress, 2nd Session, p. 2769). In terms of specifics, it granted land to each state and territory to then be sold and invested in stocks to become a perpetual fund. Each state could then access the interest from its

respective fund to apply "to the endowment, support and maintenance of at least one college..." Among the several stipulations was
the requirement that the governors of the respective states report to
Congress annually how the monies were apportioned.

President Lincoln's different interpretation from Buchanan's that
allowed him to sign the Morrill Land Grant Act on July 2, 1862 (cf.,
James, 1910, 16019, p. 8) is not a matter for quibbling. What appears
to be a different interpretation regarding the use of public monies
versus public lands is trivial compared to the total disregard of the
Constitutional silence on education in the years closely following.

The eloquent articulation of principled Constitutional reasoning
by President Buchanan stands in direct contrast to the reasoning of
the same era that accomplished the exact opposite ends. George
Washington's astute observations on so-called beneficial usurpations of governmental authority explain the motivational basis of
this obverse reasoning.

Two Causes

The event that highlights the poignancy of Washington's insights
was that of establishing a federal department of education. And the
issue that totally bypassed Constitutional prohibitions against educational involvement, particularly the funding of it, was that of
national well-being. The setting for this concern for the health of the
country was the aftermath of the Civil War. Subordinate to this
concern was the highly articulated rationale of providing educational
opportunities for a long-deprived race of people.

For a number of early lawmakers, education should have been a
responsibility of the federal government. It was promoted by some
before adoption of our Constitution, and then President Washington
himself promoted it in general philosophical terms and specifically
in the government's constitutionally legitimate governance of the
nation's capital. Further, it was addressed during the tenure of practically every president until Lincoln finally made it official in 1862.
Even when various presidents vetoed unconstitutional efforts in this
regard, they nonetheless urged the legitimizing of it, typically by
way of an amendment to the Constitution.

The motivational vehicle that gave legitimacy to federal involvement in education was the Civil War reconstruction efforts. Compassion for the slaves, but even beyond that, the overall concern for national survival quickly made the unconstitutional nature of federal involvement in education a moot or irrelevant point. Washington's observation that the most dangerous of usurpations start from truly good intentions was being played out less than a century after he so warned.

The usurping yet nonetheless successful effort at creating a national Bureau of Education serves as the focal point for our discussion. On June 5, 1866, Representative James Garfield proposed, as chairman of the select committee on education, a bill (the revision of an earlier one) to establish a national Bureau of Education. The bill provided, among other things,

> that there should be established in the city of Washington, a Department of Education for the purpose of collecting such statistics and facts as shall show the condition and progress of education in the several States and Territories, and of diffusing such information respecting the organization and management of schools and school systems and the methods of teaching as shall aid the people of the United States in the establishment and maintenance of efficient school systems, and otherwise promote the cause of education throughout the country. (Avins, 1974, p. 232)

Additionally, a Commissioner of Education was to be appointed at an annual salary of $5,000.

The very first response to Garfield's proposal confirms the present hypothesis regarding the two-pronged motivation to officially install the federal government in the educational arena. Representative Ignatius Donnelly spoke directly to these matters saying, "Two great conclusions have been reached." The first conclusion regarded national security just as hypothesized:

> We have found that the hitherto governing populations of those States could not be trusted to uphold the national

Government. Nay, more than that they have sought, through unparalleled sacrifices to overthrow it... The people have been rendered unfit to wisely govern themselves, much less to participate in the government of others. They strove to drag down the entire temple of our liberties; they have succeeded at least in burying their own prosperity in ruins. (Rives, 1866, pp. 2966-2967)

Following quickly, Donnelly addressed the second motivation: "Another great fact presents itself: four million human beings have been lifted from a condition as low as that of the brute to manhood... We have taken the shackles... We have thrown open all doors to the black man and cried God speed to him as he moves forward into the future" (Rives, 1866, pp. 2966-2967).

Summarizing these two orientations, Donnelly said, "What pressing necessity results from these two great facts? Education." In wanting education for both the white man and the black man, he desired that, as a country, "we may become the most enlightened people upon the face of the earth..." (Rives, 1866, pp. 2966-2967).

In anticipating the protest that such a bill would be unconstitutional, Donnelly responded by actually begging the question: "We will be told that we have left all that to the States. *Yes* [emphasis added]; and we have had the rebellion as a consequence... We cannot build a republic without intelligence" (Rives, 1866, p. 2967).

Pressing his point, Donnelly said, "Can we doubt for one instant the great and pressing necessity for the General Government to interest itself in this question of education?" (p. 2967). And then speaking in contradictions, he urged passage of the bill as the very least remedy in that "We carry the world upon our shoulders"; yet naively, as we see in hindsight, he declared the bill "will have no power to enter into the States and interfere with their systems" (Rives, 1866, p. 2968).

Representative Andrew Rogers of New Jersey had a different perspective regarding Garfield's proposed department of education. Rogers had good reason, as we have already seen, to state that the attempt to have the federal government determine how "the children of the State shall be educated would be something never before attempted in the history of this nation." His objection was as follows:

> I say, sir, in the first place, there is no authority under the Constitution of the United States to authorize Congress to interfere with the education of the children of the different States in any manner, directly or indirectly... I am content, sir, to leave this matter of education where our fathers left it, where the history of the country has left it, to the school systems of the different towns, cities, and States. Let them carry out and regulate the system of education without interference, directly or indirectly, on the part of any bureau established as an agent of the Federal Government... Although the bill does not propose to go into the States and interfere with the regulation of the school systems there; yet it proposes to collect such statistics which will give controlling power over the school systems of the States... No man can find anywhere in the letter or spirit of the Constitution one word that will authorize the Congress of the United States to establish an Educational Bureau. (Rives, 1866, p. 2969).

Rogers went on to predict the future consequences of passage of the bill in question:

> If Congress has the right to establish an Educational Bureau here in this city for the purpose of collecting statistics and controlling the schools of the country, then, by the same parity of reason, a' fortiori, Congress has a right to establish a bureau to supervise the education of all children that are to be found in the thirty millions of the population of this country ... there are to be public buildings put up here in Washington, and new bureaus to be established here, and the head of this bureau must hold a seat in the Cabinet of the President of the United States; for it will not do to have a great educational bureau here, one to diffuse so much knowledge, such a grand scheme for

concentrating the intelligence and enlightenment of the whole world in the United States, without making it a part of the executive government of the country. (Rives, 1866, p. 2969)

When we later discuss President Carter's action of 1979, we will see how insightful Rogers' comments were.

Even with the passage of the bureau of education bill by the House on June 19, 1866, (Rives, 1866, p. 3270) and its subsequent signing into law in 1867, the collection of statistics could have been instead only a census type function just as Representative Samuel Randall of Pennsylvania proposed (Rives, 1866, p. 3047) by way of an amendment:

But I conceive at this time, and under present circumstances, that there is no necessity whatever for the establishment of a Bureau of Education, to be controlled by the central power here. The systems of education throughout the country have been left to State authority... Now, my amendment proposes to leave this question of statistics in reference to the State educational systems to the Secretary of the Interior, where it properly belongs, if it belongs to any Department of the Government. It is, as has been said by the gentleman from Massachusetts, (Mr. [Nathaniel] Banks) a part of the system, or should be part of the system, of taking the census. (Rives, 1866, p. 3047)

But census taking was not the main purpose behind Garfield's motion. As he explained on June 8th, prior to the bill being rejected before its successful recall on the 19th,

The question is not whether our people will be educated or not. If they are not educated in the school of virtue and integrity they will be educated in the school of vice and iniquity. We are, therefore, afloat as the sweeping current; if we make no effort we go down with it to the saddest of destinies... We must pour upon them all the light of the public schools. We must make them intelligent, industrious, patriotic citizens or they [immigrants, freed slaves and other illiterates] will drag us and our children down to their level. (Rives, 1866, p. 3049)

Yet in the midst of this emotionally-charged statement of purpose, Garfield insisted that it was not to institute "a compulsory system of education" but to allow instead "the power of letting in light on subjects and holding them up to the verdict of public opinion... If their [the States] records could be placed beside the records of such States as ... the very light shining upon them would rouse up their energies and compel them to educate their children. It would shame out of their delinquency all the delinquent States of this country" (Rives, 1866, p. 3050).

Donnelly's outspoken acclaim of the bill was not some lone voice crying in the wilderness. It instead was manifestly typical, as our hypothesis suggests, of the prevailing mood of the time. The great compassionate dual causes of preserving the union and uplifting the condition of the black man became the license to disregard Constitutional constraints and enter the education realm. Beyond violating the written document itself, the lawless act of treading into education violated the spirit of the Constitution. As noted earlier, the philosophy behind it excluded the right or power of governmental self-preservation. Yet the authorization of a national department of education was founded on the desire gone awry to save, or more accurately, as Donnelly proposed, to make this the greatest nation in the world.

The larger perspective to which Donnelly and Garfield resonated is revealed in the following statements from the reconstruction amendments debates. On the matter of freedom for the slaves, Donnelly earlier noted (Feb. 1, 1866) that "suffrage without education is an edged tool in the hands of a child—dangerous to others and destructive to himself... The number of ignorant is indicated by the proportion unable to read and write... I repeat, the condition of the South in this respect would be shameful to any semi-civilized people..." (Avins, 1974, p. 135). General Howard, head of the Freedman's Bureau claimed, "Education is absolutely essential to the freedmen to fit them for their new duties and responsibilities" (p. 142). Charles Sumner of Massachusetts summed up the attitude with this question in 1870: "How can you organize reconstruction except on the everlasting foundation of education?" (p. 421). Senator Oliver Morton, of Indiana, on this same matter, noted, "Now, there is one other provision in the constitution of Virginia which I regard as important to the colored people as the right to hold office, and that is the establishment of a common-school system and the creation of a school fund" (p. 421). In speaking on the civil rights bill in 1874, Representative Richard Cain of South Carolina said, "Sir, if you look over the reports of superintendents of schools in several States, you will find, I think, evidences sufficient to warrant Congress in passing the civil-rights bill as it now stands." After reviewing the laws of several states regarding education, Cain closed with this statement, generalizable to all states reviewed, about Illinois:

> While the law guarantees education to every child, yet such are the operations among the school trustees that they almost ignore, in some places, the education of colored children... Some think it would be better to modify it [the civil-rights bill], to strike out the school clause, or to modify it that some of the *State constitutions should not be infringed* [emphasis added]. I regard it essential to us and the people of this country that we should be secured in this if in nothing else. I cannot regard that our rights will be secured until the jury-box and the school-room, those great palladiums of our liberty, shall have been opened to us. (Avins, 1974, p. 670)

Apparently, for Cain, correcting one injustice (i.e., lack of education for colored children) justified committing a different injustice (i.e., infringing upon certain state constitutions). As we have already seen and will continue to see, when it comes to federal involvement in education there is no shortage of this kind of rationalized thinking.

Senator Sumner, in 1867, quoted in agreement from a constituent's letter in favor of a resolution that would mandate that "public schools must be established for the equal good of all." The letter stated, "Shall the southern States still be controlled by the men and the policy that have already brought them ruin and disgrace ... or shall we take a new departure from the old course, and secure universal education and free schools..." (Avins, 1974, p. 269).

While there was genuine compassion for the educational plight of the freed black man, the more inclusive concern was tied to the intelligent use of newly granted suffrage for the black person. As Senator John Henderson of Missouri stated in 1866, "In the judgment of many, an education, moral and intellectual, is as necessary to freedom as the ballot itself; but when this is given it may be found that freedom is an empty name without competency" (Avins, 1974, p. 146). Senator Henry Wilson of Indiana, in speaking on education for the blacks in the District of Columbia in 1866, chastised,

> These thousands that went into the ballot-box last year and voted with so much unanimity against extending the right of suffrage to the colored people of this District, finding that we will only allow the colored men who can read and write to vote, will see to it that as few colored men shall be qualified as possible. They kept the colored man in ignorance to keep him in slavery; they will continue to keep him in ignorance to prevent his becoming a voter. (Avins, 1974, p. 255)

Senator Lane captured the essence of this orientation in his words of 1866: "I think the ballot itself is worth all the schools and all the schoolmasters to educate voters to enable them to vote intelligently" (Avins, 1974, p. 255).

As proper and noble as was the concern for intelligence in the ballot-box, this also was not the highest priority reason for overstepping the Constitutional exclusion on education. After all, blacks were denied education and suffrage for a greater and historically earlier time period than just the decade of the 1860s—more like 200 years. The prosperity and welfare of the black race was not the ultimate, highest-priority reason to gain educational control—it was instead the prosperity and welfare of the nation. Again, we draw upon statements from the reconstruction amendments debates to demonstrate this point. Senator Morton said, in 1867, "The education of the people is essential to the execution of the guarantee that we shall secure to each State a republican form of government; it is indispensable to the success of republican government; and we cannot hope for successful reconstruction except upon the basis of making provision for the speedy education of all the people of the South" (Avins, 1974, p. 269). Similarly, Senator Timothy Howe of Wisconsin, at the same time, noted, "... you cannot maintain republican principles and republican forms of government over a people where education is not, and is not universal" (p. 269). Giving the right to vote was not enough for those interested in the national welfare. Senator Sumner claimed, in 1867, "As the education of the people is essential to the national welfare ... public schools must be established for the good of all" (p. 269). Representative Donnelly noted in 1866, "Having voted to give the negro liberty, I shall vote to give him all the things essential to liberty" (Avins, 1974, p. 135).

Support for the highest priority of national welfare rather than suffrage and/or education for the blacks per se also comes in those statements calling for universal education for all citizens. Senator Morton noted, in 1867, that the South deprived not only blacks of education, but whites also:

> Why, sir, it has always been to the interest of the people of the South that they should educate the poor whites, but they have not done it. The leading classes kept them in ignorance because they could thereby the more readily control them, and the educated classes of the South will now refuse to establish voluntarily a system of common schools... They will never do it unless they are coerced to it by the terms of reconstruction.

Accordingly, Morton called for "a system of common schools established open and free to all, without distinction of race or color" (Avins, 1974, p. 269). Senator Lane properly saw, in 1866, that the concern for the blacks' freedom was not the larger concern. He rejected Morton's rationale by observing that the uneducated white (as described above) voting in ignorance has never been an issue to force the necessity of universal education: "White men ... are to be permitted to vote in ignorance" (Avins, 1974, p. 255).

Principled Opposition

The unconstitutional motive to guarantee the success of the reconstruction, and more importantly, of the nation overall, through federally-mandated universal education was not without its correct discerners. Senator Henderson early (1866) saw the illogic of such arguments. From the belief that the negro "cannot maintain his freedom without the suffrage..." it was thought that "Congress may adopt any measures necessary to enforce his freedom." He continued, "This argument makes the discretion of Congress the only limit of its power in the employment of means to maintain and perpetuate his freedom. Were this true, Congress might deem it necessary to educate him... The argument, though on the side of mercy, and welling up from a good and pure fountain, I think is untenable..." (Avins, 1974, p. 146).

Representative Rogers also exposed the illogic of these arguments when contesting Garfield's bill to establish a national department of education. For one, the educational level of the U.S. compared favorably with "the most glorious days of Rome and Greece or of English history" (Rives, 1866, p. 2968). But more germane to our hypothesis, Rogers claims that the foundational rationale of "educating the people of the South, as though they ... had no education, learning, or intelligence" consisted of a false argument: "I am here to say that they have intelligence in the South, and that the intelligent classes there are those who are responsible for bringing this rebellion upon the country, and not the uneducated classes who were dragged into the movement" (Rives, 1866, p. 2969). Apparently Rogers was alluding to a different quality in humans other than education per se to account for slave-holding and insurrection against the government. These perceived acts of a rebellious nature of the Southerners were paradoxically also reflected in the behavior of those who proposed to correct the problem via federal legislation. After all, usurpations of the Constitution via federal intervention in education, even if to correct rebellious-ness, are likewise acts of rebellion only of a different form.

Henderson thought it untenable, i.e., wrong, to give Congress authority to do whatever necessary to guarantee the freedom of former slaves, and thereby making Congress itself the only limit to its power. He proposed instead that the states be prohibited only in discriminating on the basis of race or color. Anything beyond that would violate the rights of the states which would be unconstitu-tional at the federal level no matter how wrongful the states in their exercise of these rights. And educational incursions would be, he claimed, one of those Congress-ordained but untenable, i.e., unconstitutional, actions.

Senator William Fessenden of Maine was of a similar opin-ion—namely, the power of state suffrage resides with the individual states and not the federal government. The only power Congress should have is that of telling the states "most distinctly, if you exer-cise that power wrongfully, such and such consequences will follow" (Avins, 1974, p. 143). The attempt to make education one of the functions of the federal government was openly rebutted by Senator John Sherman of Ohio. As he plainly but succinctly noted in 1867, "That has never been attempted before as one of the func-tions of this government" (p. 269).

More graphic speech to the same effect comes from Congress-man John Storm of Wisconsin. Speaking in 1872 against a bill to establish an educational fund and apply the proceeds of the public lands to the education of the people, he said of this familiar effort, "I believe this measure has been substantially here before, and it has received its quietus in the former Congress. It is not new here. It is only the old cat disguised in the mealbag." More specifically Storm charged that the bill's attempt "to take charge of the public school system of the country ... attempts to do indirectly what we are not allowed to do directly" (Avins, 1974, p. 604). Representative Henry McHenry of Kentucky believed that Congress had "no power to pass this bill." McHenry's speech against the bill well summarizes much of what has been said in this chapter to this point:

The preamble does not pretend to define the power of any branch of Government; nor can Congress look to it for any power whatever. It has been so determined by the courts, and is a principle admitted by all Constitutional lawyers. The powers of Congress are all expressly defined and limited by the eighth section of the first article of the Constitution, and the tenth article expressly reserved to the States or the people all powers not delegated to the United States, and gentlemen have failed to show and cannot show any express power delegated to Congress to establish a system of schools in the States, and consequently that power is reserved to and belongs only to the States. (Avins, 1974, p. 604)

Furthermore, McHenry voiced the same opinion on the matter of sale of public lands as did President Buchanan, as discussed earlier. McHenry said,

The public lands belong to the people, and I do not question the power of Congress to dispose of them, and I would cheerfully vote for the ... substitute, distributing the proceeds of the sale of public lands among the States for educational purposes, without any conditions or restrictions, and without any Federal management or interference with the Funds after they shall go to the States ... but it prescribes certain conditions and limitations which are objectionable, and which render it amenable to the Constitutional objections urged against the former bills. (Avins, 1974, p. 604)

The arguments against reconstruction-driven federal control of or even involvement in education eventually prevailed. On February 3, 1875, Representative Stephen Kellogg of Connecticut motioned that all references to public school be stricken from the Civil Rights Bill. His motion was passed on February 4th.

Usurpation Achieved

Yet as noted earlier, the Morrill Land Grant Bill did pass and thus became the way the federal government came into education. Rogers, as also noted earlier, rightly predicted the eventual outcome of enactment of this grant. The prediction of Representative Storm is worthy of reviewing because although the education section of the Civil Rights Bill did not pass, the outcome he predicted was realized anyway via the Land Grant Act. The very fact that Storm's prediction came true in spite of the bill's failure does provide more support to the motivational hypothesis expressed earlier. That is, a systematic effort at molding national character and preserving the union was truly operative in our country to justify educational intrusion. Most crucial, the effort to fulfill the educational agenda operates even if Constitutional provisions and/or restrictions have to be violated.

Storm predicted that "If this bill becomes law you will see an amendment to it compelling the States to educate the races in the same schools, and the State that refuses to make provision for the education of the races together will lose its share of the appropriation under this bill" (Avins, 1974, p. 604).

Obviously, from all that has been said to this point, Mr. Rogers must have indeed been a very disappointed statesman. His wish, as stated on February 26, 1866, not only did not come true, but its opposite did. Rogers said, "I had hoped ... that the time had come when the Constitution of the United States would be secure from invasion by Congress" (Avins, 1974, p. 150). The final low point of Rogers' wish appeared in 1979 with the creation of a cabinet-level Department of Education, just the outgrowth he had predicted of the so-called non-intrusive act to establish a federal bureau of education in 1866.

It is indeed a paradoxical twist of fate that James Garfield, a man who promoted federal intervention in education with its consequent deprivation of individual self-governance, admirably favored the following quote on self-governance from John Stuart Mill: "That the ballot is put into the hands of men, not so much to enable them to govern others as that he may not be misgoverned by others" (Avins, 1974, p. 213).

The ultimate capstone to federal involvement in education came with passage of the U.S. Department of Education Organization Act of October 17, 1979, otherwise known as Public Law 96-88. Signed into being by President Carter, this Act removed education as a component of the Department of Health, Education, and Welfare, where it had been since its inception in 1953, and made it a specific Cabinet-level department within the federal government. Section 102 of the Act declares that the Department "is in the public interest, will *promote the general welfare* [emphasis added] of the United States, will help ensure that education issues receive proper treatment at the Federal level, and will enable the Federal Government to coordinate its education activities more effectively."

The seven purposes of the Act are, in brief form,

(1) to strengthen the Federal commitment ...
(2) to supplement and complement the efforts of States, the local school systems ...
(3) to encourage the increased involvement ... in Federal education programs ...
(4) to promote improvements ... through federally supported ...
(5) to improve the coordination of Federal education programs ...
(6) to improve ... Federal education activities ... and
(7) to increase the accountability of Federal education programs ...

In passing the Act, Congress was clear to specify its intention "to protect the rights of State and local governments and public and private institutions in the areas of educational policies ... [nor] diminish the responsibility for education which is reserved to the States and the local school systems and other instrumentalities of the States" (*United States Code*, 1979, Vol. I, p. 670).

Our incomplete but nonetheless mundane accounting of purposes has a purpose. The contradictions in all of these purposes with the message of this chapter should be obvious. That is, while the Federal Government is not authorized by the U.S. Constitution to have educational involvement, this Act legitimizes just the opposite. For instance, it has clearly been shown that the general welfare clauses of the Constitution are without authority of power, yet one of the reasons given for establishing the Department of Education was to "promote the general welfare." Furthermore, it has clearly been shown that use of public funds for education is not authorized in Article I, Section 8, nor anywhere else in the Constitution, yet expenditures of such funds are explicitly involved or implicitly necessary to each of the seven stated purposes of the Department.

The ultimate contradiction of the Act is found in the wording of Section 103—Federal-State Relationships. Namely, "the establishment of the Department of Education shall not increase the authority of the Federal Government over education..." (p. 670). *The literal truth of this statement actually nullifies the entire Act since no such authority exists in the first place and thus cannot be increased.*

The contradictions are even further exaggerated with two general understandings stated at the introduction of this law. First it is noted that "parents have the primary responsibility for education of their children, and States, localities, and private institutions have the primary responsibility for supporting that parental role..." (p. 669). With any experience at all in relating to State, local, and even private institutions, it is uniformly observed that such agencies have supportive responsibility. Instead, the agencies operate in quite the opposite manner. Secondly, Congress notes in the Act that "in our Federal system, the primary public responsibility for education is reserved respectively to the States and the local school systems and other instrumentalities of the States..." Here we see a contradiction in that, according to the "Federal system," parents to not have public responsibility but by deduction only private responsibility, contrary to what the just prior provision states about parental responsibility being the primary one.

We look to the Senate bill (96-49), since it and not the House bill was the one enacted into law, to perhaps obtain a clearer understanding of the *legitimate* basis of the Education Act. Three major reasons are given, but as we shall again see, they are all without Constitutional legitimacy.

The first rationale is that of public support. The Senate bill acknowledges support of private citizens as well as that of "More than 100 major national organizations and associations..." (p.

1514). Yet, public support is not synonymous with the passage of a Constitutional amendment that President Jefferson and others said was absolutely necessary to authorize federal involvement in education.

Second, the Senate bill claimed as a rationale the fact that at that time (1979) the $25 billion expenditure on education by the federal government "was severely hampered" by bureaucratic problems (p. 1515) as well as by "tremendous problems in American education" (p. 1529). It was thought, obviously, without concern for Constitutional legitimacy, that "the establishment of a Cabinet-level Department of Education will go far towards remedying these problems..." This so-called "strong and persuasive need" apparently was sufficient in and of itself regardless of Constitutional constraints to the contrary.

Last, and most important, the Senate bill claimed it was based on "the Constitutionally-backed principle that the Federal role is limited to supplementing, not supplanting. State and local prerogatives and rights in determining their individual educational program" (p. 1529). In so many words, "The Federal role in education ... is a legitimate ... one" because "The Federal government has been involved in education for more than a century" (p. 1529). Obviously, the authority derives via fiat and precedent rather than by Constitutional permission.

Representative Rogers was quite insightful in protesting the authorization of a Federal Bureau of Education in 1866: "You will not stop at simply establishing a bureau for the purpose of paying officers to collect and diffuse statistics in reference to education" (Rives, 1866, p. 2969). In fact, Rogers cannily predicted the full impact of this creeping federal intrusion by contesting the argument of proponents of a federal department of education who claim "that this country is groveling in low ignorance." Rogers responded to this accusation with an analysis of the mental qualities of the men in the Civil War. He said,

> ... there are many men who have only been educated in
> common schools, who ... have shown themselves as much
> fitted for their duties by their intelligence... They have

shown by their acts that they were men of understanding and judgment and discretion. And why should we now undertake to interfere with the education of their children, and compel them to pay their share of the tax for that purpose? It is a step toward taking away from them rights to which they alone are entitled. (Rives, 1866, p. 2969)

Conclusion

Except for the Constitutionally permitted right of Congress to be involved in education in the District of Columbia, no other provision exists for the federal government to govern or to collect taxes for education. As central as an educated populous would appear to be toward promoting the general welfare of the United States, this is not at all a sufficient nor empowering rationale for federal involvement.

The gentlemen of the Constitutional era were all in agreement that education was not an authorized activity for Congress. This fact was acknowledged both before the Constitution was adopted as well as after, being both ratified and amended in later years.

A powerful and in actuality a consuming tension for law and policy makers resides in the fact that Congress was specifically not given any authority in the very area where the success or failure of the United States so pivotally seemed to reside—in education. Yet the U.S. Constitution was not some hastily thrown together document that would naturally admit many untried ideas. No, history reveals that the framers of the governing document were well aware, both historically and practically, of Constitutional strengths and shortcomings. The writers, like Madison, Washington, and Franklin, had a solid intellectual grasp of mankind's legacy in civil governance as well as the practical experience of the positive and negative attributes of the prior Articles of Confederation. In fact, the prevailing philosophy of the time that the Constitution and thus the federal government were inventions of the people not to be self-promoting but citizen-serving meant that the Constitution was not even conceived of as something to control the people to guarantee its enduring existence. In testimony, the elegant creativity of the authors of the Constitution did not arise from federal mandates over the education of the people, including their leaders, but from the conspicuous absence of educational mandates.

As suggested by the early statesmen and as verified in early American dilemmas, most notably the Civil War reconstruction efforts, perceived good causes can make sufficient rationale for unauthorized actions. In fact, the perceived need by the reconstructionists for federal involvement in education was so powerful they were unable to see that their consequential violations of the Constitution were no less rebellious than actions of the southern states they were trying to remediate. Both groups self-deceptively promoted Constitutionally unauthorized actions as legitimized means to assumed higher ends. With the benefit of the very first two terms of the U.S. presidency, George Washington, upon leaving office, sagaciously observed, prophetically relevant to our education issue, that usurpations of power are the modis operandi for such initially good but ultimately destructive causes.

In this regard, we have debunked every potential Constitutional way that the federal government can involve itself in education— save in Washington, DC. The general welfare phrases of the Preamble and of Article I, Section 8, are not empowering but only introductory-type expressions. The entirety of Article I, Section 8, which defines taxation provisions, makes absolutely no reference to education. The power to make all laws necessary and proper for executing the enumerated powers of the subsuming Section 8 (provision 18) are thereby equally inapplicable to education since education, as just explained, is not an enumerated power of the Constitution. Admittedly, it does seem that Article IV, Section 3, does allow Congress to designate U.S. property for educational purposes, but still no tax money can be used and no power to control education is authorized in this regard. Any First Amendment application to education has already been qualified in Chapter 4. And finally, the Fourteenth Amendment, as discussed earlier, has been disqualified in intent by the U.S. Supreme Court as being applicable to education in the States.

In spite of exhaustively prohibited access of the federal government into education, approximately 75 billion federal dollars were spent on education as recently as 1998 (U.S. Census Bureau, 1999, p. 165). Furthermore, what has to be rightly labeled as an outlaw organization enjoys Cabinet level status in the federal government. And it has occurred without the Constitutional authority that Presidents like Jefferson, Monroe, and Buchanan claimed essential to permit federal involvement in education.

George Washington's caution about usurpation through federal power has gone unheeded, and the dire predictions by various Constitutional guardians have come true. For instance, the 1875 prediction of Representative Storm that states can lose appropriations if they make no provision for "the education of the races together" has become a real threat in spite of the wording of the 1979 Education Act that claims no right of the federal government to interfere with state-directed education. Further, the prediction of Representative Rogers that the creation of the so-called nonintrusive Bureau of Education in 1867 would result in a Cabinet level office has obviously occurred. Rogers' appeal is even more urgent today than it was in 1866: "I had ... hoped that the time had come when the Constitution of the United States would be secure from invasions by Congress." Instead, as Senator Henderson warned in 1866, the discretion of Congress has apparently become the only limit of its own power in the off-limits field of education.

References

Avins, Alfred (1974). *The Reconstruction amendments debate.* Richmond, VA: Virginia Commission on Constitutional Government.

Burns, Edward M. (1938). *James Madison: Philosopher of the Constitution.* New Brunswick, NJ: Rutgers University Press.

Cord, Robert L. (1982). *Separation of church and state.* New York: Lambeth Press.

Documents illustrative of the formation of the Union of the American states. (1984). Sewanee, TN: Spencer Judd Publ.

Gales, Joseph (Ed.) (1834). *Debates and proceedings of the Congress of the United States.* Library of American Civilization. Washington, DC: Gales and Seaton.

Hamilton, Alexander, Madison, James & Jay, John (1961). *The Federalist papers.* New York: New American Library.

Hutchison, David (1975). *The foundations of the Constitution.* Secaucus, NJ: University Books, Inc.

Hyneman, C. S. & Carey, G. W. (1967). *A second Federalist.* Columbia, SC: University of South Carolina Press.

James, Edmund J. (1910). *The Origin of the Land Grant Act of 1862.* Library of American Civilization. Urbana-Champaign, IL: University Press.

Kursh, Harry (1965). *The United States Office of Education.* Westport, CT: Greenwood Press.

Lowrie, Walter & Clark, Matthew, St. C. (1832). *American state papers: Documents, legislative and executive, of the Congress of the United States.* Washington, DC: Gales & Seaton.

Padover, Saul K. (1953). *The complete Madison.* New York: Harper & Brothers.

Richardson, James D. (1897). *A compilation of the messages and papers of the Presidents.* New York: Bureau of National Literature.

Rives, John C. (1859). *The Congressional Globe.* Washington, DC: Rives Publ. (microfiche)

Rives, John C. (1862). *The Congressional Globe.* Washington, DC: Rives Publ. (microfiche)

Rives, John C. (1866). *The Congressional Globe.* Washington, DC: Rives Publ. (microfiche)

Robinson, Matthew (1995). The federalization of education? *Investor's Business Daily*, Nov. 21, p. A1.

United States Code, 96th Congress-1st Session (1979) Vol. I. St. Paul, MN: West Publ. Co.

United States Census Bureau. (1999). *Statistical abstract of the United States* (199th ed.). Washington, DC.

Chapter 12

The State Versus The People—
An Unfinished Revolution

The powers not delegated to the United States by the Constitution, nor prohibited by it to the States, are reserved to the States respectively, or to the people. (Tenth Amendment to the Constitution, ratified as part of the Bill of Rights, Dec. 15, 1791)

As Americans, we understand that there is a line, dividing the jurisdictions of the State Governments from the jurisdiction of the Federal Government ... religious rights embrace the relations between the creature and the Creator... Rights, therefore, which are strictly religious, lie out of, and beyond the jurisdiction of civil governments. They belong, exclusively, to the jurisdiction of the Divine government... The jurisdiction which God exercises over the religious obligation which his rational and accountable offspring owe to Him, excludes human jurisdiction. And, hence it is, that religious rights are inalienable rights. Hence, also, it is, that it is an infinitely greater offense to invade the special and exclusive jurisdiction which any foreign nation rightfully possesses over its own subjects or citizens. The latter would only be an offense against international law; the former is treason against the majesty of Heaven. The one violates secular and temporal rights only; the other violates sacred and external ones... For any human government, then, to attempt to coerce and predetermine the religious opinions of children, by law, and contrary to the will of their parents, is unspeakably more criminal than the usurpation of such control over the opinions of men. The latter is treason against truth; but the former is sacrilege. (Mann, 1849, pp. 119-120, 125)

... to compel a man to furnish contributions of money for the propagation of opinions which he disbelieves, is sinful and tyrannical; that even the forcing him to support this or that teacher of his own religious persuasions, is depriving him of the comfortable liberty... (Jefferson's Act for Religious Freedom, 1779)

[H]aving taken into serious consideration, a Bill printed by order of the last session of General Assembly, entitled 'A Bill establishing a provision for Teachers of ...' and conceiving that the same if finally armed with the sanctions of a law, will be a dangerous abuse of power ... we remonstrate against the said Bill... Who does not see that the same authority which can establish Christianity, in exclusion of all other Religions, may establish with the same ease any particular sect of Christians, in exclusion of all other sects? that the same authority which can force a citizen to contribute three pence only of his property for the support of anyone establishment, may force him to conform to any other establishment in all cases whatsoever? (James Madison's Memorial & Remonstrance, 1785)

The dilemma of this chapter concerns the location and potential overlap of state, in fact, of all civil government, and citizen jurisdictions in education. As our first quote indicates, there is a division of powers among these entities. As noted in the just prior chapter, U.S. federal powers specifically exist by way of being delegated and thus must be so articulated, but in education there are none. Further, the Tenth Amendment declares that the federal government, as an instrument of the people themselves, has the power to prohibit, where specifically articulated, powers of each of the states. Beyond this, those powers not specifically delegated to the federal government reside either with the individual states or the people themselves. And typically, state and local governments claim vast powers over education.

Our second introductory quote goes beyond expressions of rights as literally recognized in legal documents to, instead, pre-existing inalienable rights. Horace Mann's quote places religious rights in this category. Violations against such rights, as perhaps occur in written Constitutions, are offenses of the highest order. A particularly offensive violation in this regard, says Mann, occurs when human governments try to influence the religious opinions of children, even if by law, and when such attempts are contrary to the will of the parents.

The third quote, authored by Thomas Jefferson in 1779 and enacted into law in Virginia in 1786, is as relevant to public education as to religion, as originally intended. Just as people should not be required to pay for the teaching of a religion, even if they are of that persuasion, they should not have to pay for the teaching of any other opinion as regularly occurs in education whether it be aligned with a formal sect/religion or not. And certainly to be forced to pay for the teaching of opinions one does not believe is all the more tyrannical, if there is such a thing as varying degrees of tyranny. In either case, the forcing of payments for the teaching of opinions is a violation of citizen liberties. In the words of Jefferson's Act, this mandate "is depriving him injuriously of those privileges and advantages to which in common with his fellow-citizens he has a natural right..." (Alley, 1985, pp. 60-61). Continuing, the act forbids the compulsory attendance or support of any "religious worship, place, or ministry," which by logical deduction would again have to include education.

In this regard, the last quote, from Madison, similarly argues against governmental control and funding of teachers of any particular religious persuasion. It establishes, he argues, the precedent and right of government to subsequently use the sanctions of law to force citizens to conform to any doctrinal orientation whatever at the whim and will of the state. In the full text of his "Memorial and Remonstrance," Madison declared this jealous and rightful "alarm at the first experiment of our liberties" to be "the first duty of citizens." Those readers who protest the use of Mann's, Jefferson's, and Madison's quote about teachers of religion as a generalization for all teachers, particularly those in public school, are reminded of the message in Chapter 10. More importantly, these quotes relate to a pivotal underlying principle regarding individual rights and Constitutional limitations. Thus, this chapter goes beyond the education-as-religion position of Chapter 10.

In Chapter 11 we saw that religion and education are exempt from federal control. Education was typically considered to be in the hands of the state governments and thus not within the jurisdiction of the federal government. In times past, religion was equally considered a matter of exclusive state jurisdiction, but more recently it is viewed as being beyond the restrictions of all civil government: "To God and God alone does man answer for his religious beliefs." In both cases (i.e., education and religion) the issue is one of rightful jurisdiction.

Regarding the role of federal government in education, the main consideration for both constructing and amending the Constitution was that the states had the antecedent claim making federal involvement an infringement on states' rights. (Parenthetically, there were those, e.g., Representative Rogers, who had the more enlightened insight that the parents had final educational authority. The U.S. Department of Education Organization Act of 1979 even acknowledged the truthfulness of ultimate parental responsibility.) From this preeminent states' rights doctrine, subsequent constitutional interpretation must necessarily acknowledge the fact that the U.S. Constitution is silent on the matter of federal involvement in education. So the task for Chapter 11 was to demonstrate that extant federal involvement in education is, in principle, constitutionally impermissible.

The task for this present chapter is quite different. Whereas state governments typically have had jurisdiction over education, the present chapter demonstrates the wrongfulness of this jurisdictional claim. It will be shown that education must, by virtue of inalienable human rights, be disestablished at the state level just as religion was during 18th century America. In fact, as demonstrated in our chapter (five) on the First Amendment, because education has not been disestablished, full religious disestablishment has consequently not occurred in practice despite claims to the contrary. The truth of the matter is that when the various branches of civil government tell schools what they can and cannot do in matters such as the teaching of creationism and evolution, the authorizing of prayers at commencement activities, and so on, religious freedom and religious disestablishment are not operative. In this sense, the *American Revolution is not yet complete.*

On this note, a good starting point for our discussion is the occasion and circumstances of the Revolutionary War. To know the reasons behind the War of Independence and thus the guiding philosophy of the U.S. Constitution, as well as of state constitutions, will be to know the reason why education should be freed from civil government (local, state, and federal) control, just as with religion. Only when freedom of education is realized will the American Revolution be complete.

<u>Rightful Revolution</u>

Before entering into this presentation, a brief explanation of certain relevant terms will help understand this chapter. The pivotal phrase, "American Revolution," is in truth a misnomer. In the first place, it was not a revolution as we are currently wont to define it. *Webster's 9th New Collegiate Dictionary* (1986) defines revolution as "a fundamental change in political organization; especially the overthrow or renunciation of one government ruler and the substitution of another by the governed." According to this same dictionary, a revolution is the successful outcome of a rebellion. And this is exactly how the British government labeled it at the time—a rebellion. But it can be and is argued that it was not a revolution at all (cf., Fisher & Chambers, 1981, p. 90).

When the colonists referred to their resistance to the British government, they were using the term revolution to describe the rightful defense against authoritarian and unconstitutional power. A dictionary much closer to that time (Webster, 1828) defines revolution as a material or entire change in the constitution of government. This dictionary cites the 1688 revolution in England as the restoration of the constitution to its primitive (i.e., original) state. Revolution in this sense does not connote at all something negative, unlike the word rebellion. Rebellion, according to Webster's 1828 dictionary, is the open and avowed renunciation of the authority of the government to which one owes allegiance—it is a traitorous act.

From these latter definitions appropriate to the era, the real picture is that the colonists were in legitimate *revolution* to regain their rights first as Englishmen and then as freemen. Moreover, these rights had been taken away by an English government acting in *rebellion* to its legitimate authority.

The second reason why the phrase "American Revolution" is a misnomer is that it was in fact an English revolution. It initially started as an effort to maintain the rights, privileges, and immunities due all English citizens and not as an attempt to either overthrow and replace the existing government (as did the French Revolution of the same era) nor even, at least at the outset, to be independent of that government. Bailyn (1967) suggests that the colonists were reacting to "nothing less than a deliberate assault launched surreptitiously by plotters against liberty both in England and in America ... whose ultimate manifestation would be the destruction of the English constitution with all the rights and privileges embedded in it" (p. 95). He quotes George Washington, who, along with George Mason, saw, in 1774, the English government "endeavoring by every piece of art and despotism to fix the shackles of slavery upon us." Washington believed there was "a regular systematic plan to enforce them" (p. 120). This perception was not held just on the colonists' side of the Atlantic, nor was it some fabricated rationale to break from Great Britain. As Bailyn (1967) amply documents, "Again and again reports from the home country [England] proclaimed that the English nation had departed, once and for all and completely, from the true principles of liberty..." (p. 132).

The plan of this present chapter, then, is to describe the rights inherent to the colonists and how the deprivation of these rights ultimately led to a revolution to restore all the rights and privileges of a citizenry. From this, it will be shown how state (at any governmental level) control of education is a reemerging deprivation of human rights from the pre-Revolutionary period and must also be abolished for the Revolution to be complete. In fact, the expanding loss of this right will result in the eventual loss of most other rights. Following the advice of French historian Guizot, "In order to understand a revolution, it is necessary to consider it at its origin and at its termination" (Frothingham, 1910, p. 165).

Theory of Government and Man

The origin of the American Revolution resides in ancient cultural ideas about the nature of mankind. These ideas were in full influence when Rome was at its peak. In essence, the social order assumed a natural inequality of humanity and its subservience to the state. The Roman idea was that each person was a thing and not an individual. The individual had value only as he contributed to the welfare of the state. While some were favored, it was only because of their pragmatic value to the state. The vast majority, however, lived a life of impersonal servitude. It was as Plato said (Frothingham, 1910, p. 6): "that men are to be considered, not as men, but as elements of the state—a perfect subject, differing from a slave only in this, that he has the state for his master." Naturally those in control considered themselves exempt from such subservience. In fact, they often considered it to be their divine right to be in control of others.

The termination or end-point of this revolution is the full realization of the exact opposite of the above ideas. It is where the state exists for the proper benefit of the individual and where government acknowledges the source of its power as the people themselves. Rights such as liberty and equality are inalienable and inherent to each individual and can never be delegated. Governments are constituted by way of powers delegated by the individuals to be served who always retain the inalienable right to change or in other ways reconstitute their delegated governments. It was to this end that the "American Revolution" was directed. The voices of this inherent rights message include those of both the Reformation and the Enlightenment such as Locke, Sidney, Milton, Buchanan (Frothingham, 1910, pp. 7-8), Voltaire, Rousseau, Montesquieu, Delolme, Beccaria, Grotius, Pufendorf, Burlamaqui, Seabury, and Vattel (Bailyn, 1967, p. 27). Guiding documents to this end are also many, but foundational is the Magna Carta of 1215. It is to that document we now turn.

Source of Rights

> The history of the Magna Carta is the history not only
> of a document but also of an argument ... it sought to estab-
> lish the rights of the subjects against authority and main-
> tained the principle that authority was subject to law. If the
> matter is left in broad terms of sovereign authority on the
> one hand and the subjects' rights on the other, this was the
> legal issue at stake in the fight against John ... and in the
> resistance of the American colonists to George III. (J. C.
> Holt, 1965, p. 16, as reported in Howard, 1968, pp. 2-3)

This document of English liberties, wrestled out of King John on the grounds of Runnymede in England, is the foundation of common law in America. The commemorative plaque, presented in 1959 at the Jamestown, Virginia celebration of the introduction of common law into America speaks explicitly to the role of the Magna Carta in American history. The plaque cites the First Charter granted by James I which declared that the inhabitants of the Virginia colony "shall have and enjoy all liberties, franchises and immunities ... as if they had been abiding and borne within this our realm of England..." "[S]ince Magna Carta the common law has been the cornerstone of individual liberties, even as against the Crown. Summarized later in the Bill of Rights, its principles have inspired the development of our system of freedom under law, which is at once our dearest possession and proudest achievement"

(Howard, 1968, p. 46). This commemorative statement actually confirmed the prediction of colonist Ezra Stiles in 1774: "If oppression proceeds, despotism may force an annual congress; and a public spirit of enterprise may originate an American Magna Carta and Bill of Rights... There will be a Runnymede in America" (quoted in Frothingham, 1910, p. 343).

The influence of the Magna Carta, as great as it was, must nonetheless be kept in proper perspective. Some commentators suggest that certain political leaders have constructively read into it every reform they wished to introduce (cf., Wright, 1976, p. 42). Beyond that, early spokesmen for liberty in America, such as colonists John Dickinson and James Otis, spoke succinctly to a deeper perspective: "Written laws—even the great declarations like Magna Carta—do not create liberties; they 'must be considered as only declaratory of our rights, and in affirmance of them'" (Bailyn, 1967, p. 187). The beginning words of the Magna Carta serve to confirm this perspective. To wit, "KNOW THAT BEFORE GOD, for the health of our soul and those of our ancestors and heirs, to the honour of God, the exaltation of the holy Church, and the better ordering of our kingdom..." After this introduction, the first chapter (i.e., provision) addressed the liberty of the English Church, which served as the initial point from which all other liberties apparently flowed:

> (1) FIRST, THAT WE HAVE GRANTED TO GOD, and by this present charter have confirmed for us and our heirs in perpetuity, that the English Church shall be free, and shall have its rights undiminished, and its liberties unimpaired ... we have also granted, for us and our heirs for ever, all the liberties written out below, to have and to keep for them and their heirs, of us and our heirs... (Wright, 1976, p. 54)

There was, then, two major sources from which all arguments for liberty were drawn: natural rights and constitutional law (cf., Howard, 1968, p. 36). The influence of these two orientations will be seen over and over again as we examine the influences that practically made the revolution a foregone conclusion.

Magna Carta

The 1215 document established the precedent of rule according to law as opposed to imposition by arbitrary will and discretionary power. The sixty-three chapters of rights and liberties included provisions of only local relevance such as no taking of wood without the owner's consent (Chapter 31) to universal and timeless guarantees such as equal justice to all (Chapter 40). By the time of the Middle Ages the charter was thoroughly embedded in the laws of England; it became the standard by which the legality of new laws were measured, and it was the seed-bed of many governing documents to come. For instance, documents of English liberties like the 1628 Petition of Rights, the 1679 Habeas Corpus Act, and the 1689 Bill of Rights all germinated from the Magna Carta. So ingrained into English law were the rights of the Magna Carta that both Parliament and the kings appealed to them in their battles against each other. For instance, Parliament invoked the rights of the Charter against Charles I and the Stuarts when they withheld legitimate rights. After the defeat of Charles I, the Charter was invoked against Parliament in its withholding of legal guarantees.

The signing by King John of the Magna Carta ushered in a new era of liberty. Limiting the king's control, the document established a Great Council composed of the king and lesser rulers such as barons, earls, and bishops. Together they became a Parliament.

Not at all happy with the charter of rights being forcefully wrestled from him by the lesser rulers, King John enlisted the aid of Pope Innocent III. The pope had John excused from the charter and all the "revolutionary" barons excommunicated.

The battle between the kings and "holy men" on the other side and the common people on the other side raged for centuries. Leaders were killed, and citizens and in many ways were tortured for desiring liberties rightfully due them. Atrocities of unbelievable magnitude claimed thousands upon thousands of lives. The process of leaders claiming absolute authority to determine truth and control the lives and thoughts others and people resisting against this tyrannical arrogance cycled back and forth endlessly. "[T]he intellects and consciences of men were in slavery" (Coffin, 1897/1987, p. 40) for a long time.

But a new cycle began with the opening of America. Particularly, it was in the year 1620 that the cyclical tug-of-war between leaders and the people was broken. Now instead of citizens wrenching their rights from a reluctant leader, government was, perhaps for the first time ever, formed by the people and only the people. It was only one party and not two opposing parties who formed the governing structure. On board the Mayflower in 1620, the Pilgrims "covenant and combine ourselves together into a civil Body Politick" (Perry, 1978, p. 60). Because they landed far north (Cape Cod) of their commissioned area (Virginia) via the Virginia patent, they were outside of English jurisdiction. Thus they were able to base their Mayflower Compact on the natural right of self-governance. In this action, liberty found a home. While the contest between civil authority and the rights of men continues, the seemingly endless cycle of leaders against citizen rights had been broken.

By the time of the "American Revolution," the birthright of liberties was well established in the minds and practices of all English citizens and therefore of the majority of colonists in America. The Magna Carta was acknowledged by all the English colonies as the primary source of these liberties (Wright, 1976, p. 43). At first, the colonists, as deserving Englishmen, appealed to its provisions in the development of their own charters and also during the initial stages of the conflict with Great Britain. As independence from England and a separate American identity became more and more a reality, specific transfer of Magna Carta provisions waned. Instead, the inalienable, natural rights of all men formed the basis of their appeal. Uniquely American charters still however embodied the Magna Carta's spirit of citizen liberties, ruler restrictions, and constitutional enumerations.

As mentioned, documents authorizing the settlement of America explicitly incorporated Magna Carta provisions. For instance, the 1606 First Charter of the Virginia Company said,

> that all and everie the parsons being our subjects which
> shall dwell and inhabit within everie or anie of the said

severall Colonies and plantacions ... shall have and enjoy all liberties, franchises and immunities within anie of our other dominions to all intents and purposes as if they had been abiding and borne within this our realme of Englande or anie other of our saide dominions. (Howard, 1968, p. 15)

The words "liberties, franchises, and immunities" appear many times over in one form or another in early charters of America, including the Declaration of Independence, which was written more than 150 years after these initial acknowledgments. This guarantee of Englishmen rights, as rooted in the Magna Carta, similarly appeared in the charters of Maryland (1652), Maine (1639), Connecticut (1662), Carolina (1663), Rhode Island (1663), Carolina (1665), Massachusetts (1691), and Georgia even as late as 1732 (cf., Howard, 1968, p. 19).

When the colony of Massachusetts wanted written laws to replace rule by personalities, they looked to the Magna Carta and the Word of God. As Governor Winthrop wrote, "it was agreed that some men should be appointed to frame a body of laws, in resemblance to a Magna Carta..." (Howard, 1968, p. 36). The wording of the subsequent Body of Liberties of 1641 resembled the Magna Carta in a number of its provisions. That is, the protections of life and property resembled the wording of Chapters 28 and 39 of the Magna Carta, the just punishment provision resembled Chapter 20, and the right of free fishing resembled Chapter 33. Commenting on these 1641 provisions two hundred years later (1851), the Supreme Court of Massachusetts said the use of the word liberty in the Body of Liberties drew directly on the Magna Carta (Howard, 1968, pp. 36-40).

Even so, by 1646 various citizens of Massachusetts petitioned that they were not enjoying the full rights of Englishmen. To this the General Court claimed the liberties guaranteed by the Magna Carta were being enjoyed and demonstrated this by comparing the provisions of the laws of England, beginning with the Magna Carta, to the laws of Massachusetts. Specifically, the guarantee of church liberty paralleled Chapter 1 of the Magna Carta, town and city liberties and customs paralleled Chapter 13, a uniform measure for agriculture products paralleled Chapter 55, that courts be in specific locations paralleled Chapter 17, the amount and method of fines paralleled Chapter 20, the requirement for witnesses to a crime paralleled Chapter 38, and safe conduct for merchants paralleled Chapter 41. As this investigation proceeded, a more comprehensive drafting of laws, known as Lawes and Liberties of Massachusetts, occurred in 1648. It has been referred to as "the first modern code of the Western world" (Howard, 1968, p. 47). Again, the parallels to the Magna Carta were obvious and intentional.

The Magna Carta and the Word of God were the benchmark standards for liberty throughout the colonies. References to Magna Carta protections were regularly replicated throughout the early colonies. Provisions for rights either paraphrased specific chapter provisions of the Magna Carta or referenced Magna Carta inspired liberties for all Englishmen. Regarding paraphrased chapters, Maryland captured the essence of the chapter one provision for church liberties beginning with its 1639 statement of Laws; New Jersey restated, in 1682, Chapters 39 and 40 regarding justice and jury trials; the 1663 Carolinas charter paralleled Chapters 28, 30, and 31 protecting property; and New York in its 1684 charter based its right of taxation directly on the Magna Carta.

Regarding the guarantee of English rights for all the colonists, as inspired by the Magna Carta, Maryland's 1776 Declaration of Rights entitled its inhabitants to "the common law of England" (Howard, 1968, p. 65), and the North Carolina Assembly voted in 1715 that the common law should be in force there just as England. In fact, within 10 years of its founding, Maryland tried on four different occasions to write the specific guarantees of the Magna Carta into its statutes (Wright, 1976, p. 43).

Perhaps more important than the official pronouncements of charters, documents, and assemblies regarding citizen rights was the orientation of the colonists when addressing grievances. The presence in these appeals to Magna Carta provisions reveals the pervasiveness of their influence. The influence truly was substantial. For instance, when a matter of legislation was submitted in 1658 to the Governor and Council in Virginia, they based their decision on whether it was agreeable or not with the provisions of the Magna

Carta. Similarly, the 1682 judicial defense of habeas corpus of a colonial troublemaker was not based on the directly relevant Habeas Corpus Act of 1679 but instead on Chapters 36 and 39 of the Magna Carta. In Maryland, a 1670 lawsuit regarding a deceased's estate was adjudicated with specific reference to the provisions of the Magna Carta. In 1727 charges against the governor of North Carolina accused him of acting contrary to the Magna Carta, as did charges in 1731 against a court judge. In New Jersey a similar action occurred when the citizens accused its new governor in 1702 of acting in ways "repugnant to the Magna Carta" (Howard, 1968, p. 75). In Massachusetts an attempt to levy taxes without consent of an assembly was rejected by the citizens as a violation of the Magna Carta.

Pennsylvania presents a unique picture of dependence on Englishmen's rights as initiated by the Magna Carta. When the founder of Pennsylvania, William Penn, was on trial in London in 1670 for holding a "tumultuous assembly" by preaching Quaker beliefs, he relied heavily on the Magna Carta for his defense. As a result, the right of jury trial became firmly established in England. When Penn developed his frame of government for Pennsylvania, he drew heavily on the provisions of the Magna Carta. He considered the document so sacred that he had a copy of it placed in the archives of his colony. In defending the codification of rights of Pennsylvanians, Penn claimed, "In this act nothing more is contained than what every Englishman enjoys by Magna Carta" (cited in Howard, 1968, p. 94).

The rights secured by the Magna Carta, as summarized by the Supreme Court of Illinois in 1845, are listed below. The Court noted that limitations placed on King John's improper exercise of authority protected six classes of citizen rights:

1. To secure the personal liberty of the subjects;
2. To preserve his landed property from forfeiture;
3. To defend him against unjust outlawry;
4. To prevent unjust banishment;
5. To secure him against all manner of destruction; and
6. To restrict and regulate criminal prosecutions at the suit of the king ... (cited in Howard, 1968, p. 348)

As much as the above guarantees of the Magna Carta are a part of America's constitutional history, the document itself is not specifically referenced by the U.S. Declaration of Independence, the U.S. Constitution, or individual State Constitutions. Among the specific reasons for its absence, four stand out as preeminent. First, the document was not inherently amenable to the American scene since it was a grant from the king to the people. As such, it did not cohere with the prevailing philosophy in America that any power in the hands of the king or government is basically a grant from the people themselves and not vice versa. Second, because it was a restriction on only the executive power of government, as embodied in the king, then Parliament, as the legislative body, was independent from its restrictions and could modify it in whole or part at any time. Obviously, its protections were therefore not very secure for the colonists (Howard, 1968, p. 237).

Third, as revealed in the U.S. Declaration of Independence, rights of citizens as founded in natural rights or natural law both transcended and were foundational to granted rights. This we see in the next section (Howard, 1968, p. 371). Fourth, as Madison declared to Congress in promoting the U.S. Bill of Rights,

> Although I know whenever the great rights ... come in question in that body, the invasion of them is resisted by able advocates, yet their Magna Charta does not contain any one provision for the security of those rights, respecting which the people of America are most alarmed, the freedom of the press and the rights of conscience, those choisest privileges of the people, are unguarded in the British Constitution. (cited in Howard, 1968, p. 234)

Natural Law

It bears repeating that the Magna Carta was not considered the originator of the rights of Englishmen but a compilation of them. These rights were seen as being inherent to being human (cf., Howard, 1968, p. 110). Jefferson's response, in 1812, to the issue of English common law versus natural law states this fact very succinctly: "I deride with you the ordinary doctrine, that we brought with us from England the *common law rights*. This narrow notion was a favorite in the first moment of rallying to our rights against Great Britain... The truth is, that we brought with us the *rights* of men..." (cited in Howard, 1968, p. 259). From this perspective it is easy to see why James Otis could appeal to the standard of "natural equity" [i.e., equality] in his 1761 argument against tĥe issuance of writs of assistance [i.e., broad based and generalized search warrants]; additionally, he spoke of "the law of nature ... and to the divine dictates of natural and revealed religion" (Howard, 1968, pp. 136, 138) in his 1764 statement about "The Rights of the British Colonies..." (p. 138).

Otis's 1761 speech, which some consider as influential as Patrick Henry's "Liberty or Death" speech, set the tone for much that followed (Howard, 1968, p. 133). For instance, England's attempt to tax the colonies to help pay for their defense during England's involvement in the Seven Years' War (1756-1763) was resisted by the colonies on similar grounds. Rights such as no taxation without representation and trial by jury were considered as inherent rights and, as such, were confirmed by the Magna Carta (p. 143). The official protest of the Stamp Act Congress noted that the subjects of Great Britain had inherent rights and liberties that were confirmed in the "Great Charter of English Liberty" (Howard, 1968, p. 145).

More specifically, Otis's 1764 highly influential pamphlet "The Rights of the British Colonies Asserted and Proved" declared that the colonists' rights did not originate in their charters nor even in the Magna Carta. Instead, their rights were inalienable and inherent, coming from natural law, common law, and acts of Parliament. Similarly, the Virginian Richard Bland in his "Inquiry into the Rights of the British Colonies" argued that their rights came from several written documents plus natural rights. A Connecticut contingent of The Sons of Liberty claimed that the colonists had the right of authority from nature, and though delegated, it could equally be reclaimed.

The essential injustice of the Stamp Act, according to its opponents, was twofold: taxation without representation and lack of a trial by jury. Both of these injustices directly violated the Magna

Carta, claimed John Adams, and particularly Chapters 20 and 39. But as Samuel Adams wrote in protesting the Stamp Act, the rights of Englishmen are "founded in the law of God and nature, and are the common rights of mankind" (cited in Howard, 1968, p. 166) and are confirmed in the Magna Carta. From this kind of thinking it was easy to argue, as he and others did, the precedent for American constitutional theory that Parliament was under and not above the great charter. Parliament, and thus the legislature, cannot change the Constitution since it guarantees to citizens rights that precede it and that inherently belong to the people themselves.

Although the Stamp Act was repealed by Parliament, the tension between the colonists and the mother country continued. The infamous Boston Tea Party of 1773 in many ways epitomized this tense relationship. The punishment that England placed on Boston for this act was met by many constitutionally-based complaints including that of the right to a fair trial. The citizens of Fairfax, Virginia, under the leadership of George Washington, were among many defending the colonists saying they were "by the laws of nature and Nations entitled to all its privileges, immunities, and advantages" as if they were still in England proper (Howard, 1968, p. 175).

When the Continental Congress submitted, in 1774, their list of grievances, it was still within the desire to be one with the British and under the leadership of the king. Their appeal thus continued to be based in the rights of free-born Englishmen. Foundational to these rights were four major sources of differing proportional value depending on personal interpretation. These four basic sources were natural rights, charter provisions, the British Constitution, and immemorial usage. As the colonists continued to generate expressions of indignation, their expressions increasingly began to build off rights and documents subsequent to the Magna Carta. These later documents included the Petition of Rights, the Revolution of 1688, state charters (Howard, 1968, p. 206), the Bill of Rights, and the Act of Settlement (p. 182). This synthesizing activity also laid the foundations for the federal and state constitutions. The nature of these root foundations is demonstrated by these words from a Massachusetts sermon of that time: "Thanks be to God that he has given us, as men, natural rights independent on all human laws whatever, and that these rights are recognized by the grand charter of British liberties" (cited in Howard, 1968, p. 185). Connecticut lawyer, Jesse Root, in arguing the basis of his state's laws, said that while less abundantly documented than the common law, the law of nature "is near us, it is within us, written upon the table of our hearts, in lively and indelible characters" and that it is "the Magna Carta of all our natural and religious rights and liberties" (cited in Howard, 168, p. 262).

In fact, for all the evidences that the Magna Carta and other written documents were the foundation pieces of British colonial rights, natural law and natural rights were ultimately more momentous in their influence. John Dickinson was of this persuasion, claiming that the colonists' rights came "from a higher source— from the King of kings, and Lord of all the earth... They are born with us; exist with us; and cannot be taken from us by any human power, without taking our lives. In short, they are founded on the immutable maxims of reason and justice" (cited in Howard, 1968, p. 190). The "Magna Carta itself is in substance but a constrained declaration, or proclamation and promulgation in the name of Kings, Lords, and Commons of the sense the latter had of their original, inherent, indefeasible, natural rights" (cited in Bailyn, 1967, p. 78). John Cartwright, an Englishman, also placed the Magna Carta within a more basic context:

> It is indeed a glorious member of the super structure, but of itself would never have existed had not the constitution already had a basis, and a firm one, too... I have elsewhere observed, that the original and only real foundations of liberty were, by the Almighty architect, laid together with the foundations of the world, when this right was ingrafted into the nature of man at his creation... (cited in Howard, 1968, p. 192)

In the colonies themselves, Alexander Hamilton echoed similar sentiments:

> That Americans are entitled to freedom, is incon-

testible upon every rational principle. All men have one common original; they participate in one common nature, and consequently have one common right. No reason can be assigned why one man should exercise any power, or pre iminence over his fellow creatures more than another; unless they have voluntarily vested him with it. (cited in Howard, 1968, p. 195)

More specifically, Hamilton wrote, in 1775, that "the sacred rights of mankind are not to be rummaged for among old parchments or musty records. They are written, as with a sunbeam, in the whole *volume* of human nature, by the hand of divinity itself, and can never be erased or obscured by mortal power" (cited in Bailyn, 1967, p. 188).

The logic of rights as written was that they came out of preexisting ideals and not vice versa. For instance, the 1765 resolutions from Massachusetts against the Stamp Act treated natural law as the foundation and the Constitution of Britain as the superstructure. But the colonists were not interested in the philosophical issue of which came first; instead, they focused on the pragmatic issue of guaranteeing the rights they had. Plus, their appeal would logically stress the specific rights of the colonists as Englishmen rather than rights of men in general because it was to Englishmen that the appeals were written and from whom the charters were issued. In the overall scheme of things, the colonists cited several sources in their defense, and these sources often merged into a coherent whole. In the final analysis, it was a legal rather than a philosophical issue, and all the evidence relevant to winning their case was naturally used in their appeals.

By the time the colonists seriously considered seeking independence, their writings actually specified more rights than the English documents explicitly guaranteed. With a clear understanding of the natural and written sources of colonialist rights now established, we look closer at the nature of these rights.

Contested Rights

The entire matter of the revolution can be summarized as a battle between the natural or legitimate rights of man and the limited authority of governing institutions (cf., Frothingham, 1910, p. 79).

At the start, it was the King, the Crown, who granted to the colonists the authority to settle and to govern themselves. And it was the Crown to whom appeals were made upon injustices committed either directly by the Crown or indirectly by not correcting those committed by Parliament. The injustices were not something of very limited duration but extended over an appreciable period of time. The Declaration of Independence claims that they were not merely "light and transient causes" but consisted of a "long Train of Abuses and Usurpations." Preceding the culminating injustices of George III were those of George II and George I, Queen Anne, William and Mary, James I and II, and Charles I and II. Overall, the rulers exercised an arbitrariness of power that befitted aliens and rivals rather than natural children of the mother country.

Up until the closing days, the colonists worked diligently at preserving both their liberties and their union with Great Britain. This attitude is expressed in 1763 by James Otis in celebration of England's victory in the Peace of Paris announcement: "We in America have abundant reason to rejoice. The heathen are driven out and the Canadians conquered. The British dominion now extends from sea to sea, and from the great rivers to the end of the earth. Liberty and knowledge, civil and religious, will be co-extended, improved and preserved to the latest posterity" (cited in Frothingham, 1910, p. 160). Even when finally declaring independence, Jefferson lamented in his original draft of the Declaration, "We might have been a free and a great people together" (cf., Harrison & Gilbert, 1993, p. 44). But the rights and freedoms granted by the Crown which led to a very real experiencing of individual and institutional freedoms eventually conflicted irreconcilably with the persistent feudal and paternal attitudes of the Crown.

There is a difficulty encountered at this point in the chapter in attempting to enumerate all the various freedoms that were violated. For instance, the final listing of injustices in the Declaration of Independence are not always mirror images of the chapter provisions in the Magna Carta. Two very obvious mismatches in this regard are the injustices of inciting the Indians against the colonists and the taking of colonists as prisoners on the high seas. These infractions are however mirrored in principle by Magna Carta chapters that address the general provisions of liberty and justice. In this same way, the lofty and reverential tones of the Declaration's philosophical introduction regarding inalienable rights bestowed by a Creator are seemingly mismatched with the more practical matters addressed in the Declaration's enumerated injustices. Not even one injustice addresses the purely religious aspects of life that would logically be expected from a preamble that stresses Creator endowed inalienable rights. For instance, the right to be free of standing armies and the restrictions on naturalization processes are not high in the perceptions of what constitute Creator-given rights.

But the apparent difficulty in enumerating guaranteed rights is in reality a foundational strength. This is a key point in understanding the preeminence of natural rights over contractual rights. To underscore this point, what currently seems like a difficulty in aligning rights and injustices was obviously not a difficulty for the colonists. That for which they staked their lives, their fortunes and their honor, that for which they went to war, was crucially clear and real to them: "A revolution centered upon truths declared to be self-evident, truths written by the hand of divinity itself, never to be erased or obscured by mortal power, hardly seems like a revolution beset by doubt, introspection, or skepticism as to its *meaning*" (Jaffa, 1978, p. 59). Inalienable rights such as life, liberty, property, pursuit of happiness, as well as perhaps the consent of the governed are the final foundations against which specific, practical, and even mundane injustices were measured.

The wording of the Declaration of Independence tells us that mankind's basic inalienable rights are not finitely enumerated. They are, after all, "self-evident" or non-provable and not exhaustively listed, i.e., "that *among these* [emphasis added] are Life, Liberty and the Pursuit of Happiness..." Furthermore, natural or inalienable rights are not the product of covenants, compacts, and charter but the reason for such agreements (cf., Conkin, 1974, p. 124). Since natural rights cannot be surrendered in any morally valid way, but only the means of protecting them, there is no compelling reason for itemizing them in governmental agreements. Also, any attempt at listing them all would not succeed since they often are not consciously acknowledged until violated in one way or another. Thus it is to be expected that rights and liberties truly can be violated even when these very rights are not literally enumerated but when, instead, they are self-evident rights like equality, right of revolution, liberty, and property.

The uniquely American reliance on natural rights is expressed very clearly in George Mason's Virginia Bill of Rights of 1776. Serving as a model for many other states and for the federal Bill of Rights, it grounds all the Magna Carta type provisions (e.g., trial by jury) in natural rights. In declaring the rights that serve as "the basis and foundation of government," the Bill first specifies:

1. That all men are by nature equally free and independent, and have certain inherent rights of which, when they enter into a state of society, they cannot by any compact deprive or divest their posterity; namely, the enjoyment of life and liberty, with the means of acquiring and possessing property, and pursuing and obtaining happiness and safety.

2. That all power is vested in, and consequently derived from, the people; that magistrates are their trustees and servants, and at all times amenable to them.

3. That government is, or ought to be instituted for the common benefit, protection, and security of the people, nation or community; of all the various modes and forms of government, that is best which is capable of producing the greatest degree of happiness and safety, and is most effectually secured against the danger of maladministration; and that when any government shall be found inadequate or contrary to these purposes, a majority of the community hath an indubitable, unalienable and indefeasible right to reform, alter or abolish it, in such manner as shall be

judged most conducive to the public weal. (Morison, 1979, p. 149)

Similarly, but earlier in time, James Otis wrote in his 1764 "The rights of the British colonies asserted and proved" that even if deprived of their charter privileges, "there are, thank God, natural, inherent and inseparable rights as men, and as citizens, that would remain..." (Jensen, 1977, p. 24). In fact Otis declared that "unlimited passive obedience and non-resistance" to tyrants is to "rebel against common sense, as well as the laws of God, of Nature, and his Country" (p. 22).

Jefferson, in contesting the nature and limits of the English constitution in his "A Summary View of the Rights of British America" established himself as the frontrunner of America's patriot leaders (cf., Peterson, 1987, p. 69). The document carried to logical conclusion convictions expressed by others, as in Richard Bland's "Inquiry into the Rights of the British Colonies" (1766) and the Boston Town Meeting's "Rights of the Colonists" (1772) (cf., Jensen, 1977, p. lii). In this 1774 document, Jefferson claimed that the King had made "many unwarranted encroachments and usurpations ... upon those rights which God and the laws have given equally and independently to all" (Jensen, 1977, p. 258). He listed the grievances as "a free people claiming their rights, as derived from the laws of nature, and not as the gift of their chief magistrate..." (p. 275). "The same God "who gave us life," he said, "gave us liberty at the same time..." (p. 276).

Jefferson's final word on the matter and this country's official statement on the reason for its independence rests exclusively on natural, God-given inalienable rights. In the Declaration, Jefferson was able, according to Jeffersonian scholar Merrill Peterson (1987, p. 90), "to compress a cosmology, a political philosophy, [and] a national creed" into a triumphant document heralding this nation's birthright. As revolutionary as it was, this creed contained no new ideas or principles but encapsulated the majority sense of the matter for the colonists: "[I]t was intended to be an expression of the American mind... All its authority rests then on the harmonizing sentiments of the day..." (cf., Commager & Morris, 1967, pp.

315-316). This common sense of the matter is seen in related documents like Mason's Virginia Declaration of Rights, the Virginia Constitution, and Jefferson's Summary Views.

The commonly acknowledged principles that Jefferson crystallized in his Declaration are fourfold in expression. First, there is the concept of equality: "all men are created equal." All were alike in possession of reasoning ability, biological needs, and an innate moral sense. Second, natural rights are acknowledged in the phrase: "They are endowed by their Creator with certain inalienable rights." The representative rights of life, liberty, and pursuit of happiness were not an exhaustive listing and, as noted by Peterson (1987, p. 94), were not meant to belittle the popular right of property. In fact, property most likely was seen by Jefferson as instrumental in nature to achieving the more basic rights. Without the enjoyment of property and the commensurate enjoyment of the fruit of one's labor, other rights are not likely to be attained at all. Third, the right of sovereignty of the people makes government subordinate to the people. Governments were not sovereign, the people were; and governments were to serve the people. In fact, as Thomas Paine articulated in "Common Sense," government is a necessary evil to make secure and protect wherever man operates from less than truly pure motives (Jensen, 1977). Whereas society promotes happiness in a positive way, government works in a negative way to restrain vices. Finally, the right of revolution ensures that government stays submitted to the sovereignty of the people. Just as the people established government to guarantee the security of their inalienable rights, they could change government. The people always retained their sovereignty over government, which was to serve them in meeting their inalienable rights and not vice versa.

With the separation from Great Britain came the full recognition and emplacement of man's inalienable rights. Now they needed to be worked out in very practical ways.

America's Internal Liberty

The next step in attaining full liberty after attaining independent national status was to break the pattern of religious intolerance imported from the Old World. As documented earlier, the various colonies and then states often had official religious establishments. Injustices imposed on unbelievers were similar in severity to those administered on the European continent.

The notable writing against this spiritual tyranny was Jefferson's Act for Establishing Religious Freedom. Written in 1779, it did not become a statute in Virginia until 1786. The struggle to gain religious freedom was said by Jefferson to be "the severest contest in which I had ever been engaged" (cited in Peterson, 1987, p. 133). But he could do no less to remain true to the natural rights principles that led to America's independence. His goal in all such efforts was: "I have sworn upon the altar of God eternal hostility against every form of tyranny over the mind of man" (cf., Lippman, 1928, p. 15).

For Jefferson, the established church of any state was a form of tyranny and a deprivation of natural liberty. In Virginia for instance, over one-half of its inhabitants were dissenters from the Anglican establishment, yet they were taxed to support it. The key issue was "what right has the state to adopt an opinion in matters of religion?" Jefferson's two-part reply was (cf., Peterson, 1987, p. 137) that men are answerable solely to God regarding the rights of conscience, and since the exercise of these rights does not injury to others, they are beyond the scope of governmental jurisdiction. While government admittedly was instituted by the consent of the governed, inalienable rights could not be surrendered. Where lesser rights were surrendered, they could always be reclaimed. A maxim stated in the Act was that error along needs the support of government—truth can stand by itself.

Jefferson's Act for Religious Freedom, the U.S. Bill of Rights (1792), and especially the First Amendment, set in place all that was necessary for freedom, liberty, and all other natural rights to have unhindered expression. Jefferson's Bill "has been called the first law ever passed by a popular assembly giving perfect freedom of conscience, and by common consent it is regarded as one of the great charters of human liberty" (Lippman, 1928, p. 11).

The point of this chapter is that man's natural rights have not flourished in the United States but have subtly taken a reversal or a 180 degree turn from their intended direction. Specifically, the path along which the loss of our targeted liberty, i.e., education, has taken is the same as that of the loss of religious liberty. Rulers have decreed, contrary to the servant-role of government, what children of citizens should and should not learn and citizens have no choice but to pay taxes to support this decree.

Tragically, the person who stands as a most stalwart defencer of religious liberty equally stands as an epitome capitulator of educational liberty.

Education Establishment

In a nutshell, "Jefferson's Bill for the More General Diffusion of Knowledge was a landmark in the history of American education ... the plan broke sharply with the essentially religious idea of New England education, *substituting* [emphasis added] for it the citizen-republicanism of the new nation" (Peterson, 1987, p. 151).

Jefferson's viewpoint in disestablishing the church and establishing education in its place is insightfully revealed in Lippmann's simulated Socratic dialogue (Lippmann, 1928, pp. 17-22) as follows:

> SOCRATES: I should like to ask Mr. Jefferson some more questions. For example: the Church which you disestablished had a creed as to how the world originated, how it is governed, and what men must do to be saved? Had it not?

> JEFFERSON: It had ... I argued that the validity of this creed was a matter for each individual to determine in accordance with his own conscience.

> SOCRATES: But all these individuals acting as citizens of the state were to assume, I take it, that God had not revealed the nature of the universe to man.

JEFFERSON: They were free as private individuals to believe what they liked to believe about that.

SOCRATES: But as citizens they could not believe what they liked?

JEFFERSON: They could not make their private beliefs the official beliefs of the state.

SOCRATES: What then were the official beliefs of the state?

JEFFERSON: There were none. We believed in free inquiry and letting reason prevail.

SOCRATES: I don't understand you. You say there were many people in your day who believed that God had revealed the truth about the universe. You then tell me that officially your citizens had to believe that human reason and not divine revelation was the source of truth, and yet you say your state had no official beliefs. It seems to me it had a very definite belief, a belief which contradicts utterly the belief of my friend St. Augustine for example. Let us be frank. Did you not overthrow a state religion based on revelation and establish in its place the religion of rationalism?

JEFFERSON: I'll begin by pointing out to you that there was no coercion of opinion. We had no inquisition.

SOCRATES: I understand. But you established public schools and a university?

JEFFERSON: Yes.
SOCRATES: And taxed the people to support them?

JEFFERSON: Yes.

SOCRATES: What was taught in these schools?

JEFFERSON: The best knowledge of the time.

SOCRATES: The knowledge revealed by God?

JEFFERSON: No, the best knowledge acquired by the free use of the human reason.

SOCRATES: And did your taxpayers believe that the best knowledge could be acquired by the human reason?

JEFFERSON: Some believed it. Some preferred revelation.

SOCRATES: And which prevailed?

JEFFERSON: Those who believed in the human religion.

SOCRATES: Were they the majority of the citizens?

JEFFERSON: They must have been. The legislature accepted my plans.

SOCRATES: You believe, Mr. Jefferson, that the majority should rule?

JEFFERSON: Yes, providing it does not infringe the natural rights of man.

SOCRATES: And among the natural rights of man, if I am not mistaken, is, as you once wrote, the right not to be compelled to furnish contributions of money for the propagation of opinions which he disbelieves, and abhors.

SOCRATES: Is freedom of thought a fundamental principle, Mr. Jefferson?

JEFFERSON: It is.

SOCRATES: Well, how would you ... compose your principles, if a majority, exercising its fundamental right to rule, ordained that only Buddhism should be taught in the public schools?

JEFFERSON: I'd exercise the sacred right of revolution. What would you do, Socrates?

SOCRATES: I'd re-examine my fundamental principles.

The essence of the entire matter is revealed in Socrates' hypothetical dialogue with Jefferson. The church had been disestablished because it violated natural rights like liberty and freedom of conscience by dictating what citizens should and should not believe and by requiring payment for the support of these teachings. But in its place education has been established with all the same violations of natural rights that existed in previous religious establishments. That is, children are required by the state to learn what the state declares to be valid opinions, and parents, but more, all citizens, are required to financially support these opinions. It is crucial to note that the mere fact of mandatory financial support of opinions, even when they are agreeable to the citizen taxpayer, are a violation of the natural right of conscience (cf., Jefferson's Act for Religious Freedom of 1779). This entire matter is obviously worthy of further discussion. First, we look at state laws in terms of mandatory education.

State Laws

Each of our fifty states has either mandatory attendance (seven states) or mandatory education (forty-three states) laws. While exemptions are possible from these laws, the point is that the civil government has presumed upon itself to dictate to citizens what their own children should do regarding education. In and of itself this is an offense against the rights of parents. As noted in Chapter 11, the 1979 federal law that established the U.S. Department of

Education acknowledged that parents have the primary responsibility for the education of their children and that civil government has the primary responsibility to support the parents in that role.

Courts have equally recognized this right of parents. In 1983, a South Carolina court declared that the parents' right to teach their children in a home school "is a basic constitutional 'liberty' guaranteed by the U.S. Constitution and the Fourteenth Amendment of the Constitution" (Family Court, Calhoun County, June 18, 1983—cited in Whitehead & Bird, 1984, p. 31). Similarly, in 1972 the U.S. Supreme Court ruled in *Wisconsin* v. *Yoder* that

> the history and culture of Western civilization reflect a strong tradition of parental concern for the nurture and upbringing of their children. This primary role of the parents in the upbringing of their children is now established beyond debate as an enduring American tradition. If not the first, perhaps the most significant statements of the Court in this area are found in *Pierce* v. *Society of Sisters*.

In this latter case, a state law requiring public school education was overturned by the U.S. Supreme Court. It said,

> [T]he act of 1922 unreasonably interferes with the liberty of parents and guardians to direct the upbringing and education of children under their control... The fundamental theory of liberty upon which all governments in this Union repose excludes any general power of the state to standardize its children by forcing them to accept instruction from public teachers only. The child is not the mere creature of the State; those, who nurture him and direct his destiny have the right, coupled with the high duty, to recognize and prepare him for additional obligations.

The ultimate statement on this matter comes from a 1976 Ohio Supreme Court decision (*State of Ohio* v. *Whisner*): "Thus, it has long been recognized that the right of a parent to guide the education, including the religious education, of his or her children is indeed a 'fundamental right.'"

From this sampling of decisions, it would seem that mandatory education and/or attendance laws should all be recognized as in violation of inalienable parental rights. Certainly, the presumptiveness of states to interfere with citizen liberties by mandating educational requirements onto their children violates liberties founded in both natural law as well as constitutional law. The distinction between a legitimate and an illegitimate liberty "rests *solely* [emphasis added] on whether the parallel liberties and rights of others are invaded" (Zuckert, 1992, p. 161). And as acknowledged at the founding of this country, governments are instituted to serve the governed, not to dictate to them. Surely citizens do not surrender or commission to civil government the right to take away liberties and particularly the right to obstruct inalienable rights like those of parents over children. Jefferson in his *Notes on Virginia* (1781) explained the principle this way: "The legitimate powers of government extend to such acts only as are injurious to others. But it does me no injury for my neighbor to say there are twenty gods or no god. It neither picks my pocket, nor breaks my leg" (Koch & Peden, 1972, p. 275). Thus it can be said that the upbringing of one's child is a natural or fundamental right that cannot be interfered with by civil government. Using Jefferson's standard, parental insistence to be in charge of a child's education does not invade the rights of others. But the dictating of educational requirements to parents is an invasion of their rights by others. Educational freedom can, in fact, be enjoyed by all citizens at no cost in rights to any other citizen.

The contrary argument that is based on assumed damage to the good of the country that results from the loss of civil governmental control of education is flaws on at least two counts. First, to assume that parental rather than governmental control of education will result in a decline in educational attainment begs the question. In fact, the evidence indicates that home schoolers as a group are much better educated, more mature, and better disciplined than their public school counterparts (Mayberry, 1992; Texas Home School Coalition, 1986). Similarly, private high school students generally fare at least equally with and certain religious schools outperform their public school counterparts on most measures of attainment (Coleman & Hoffer, 1987).

The second flaw is seen by way of analogy. That is, many in this country would argue that without a moral or religious upbringing for children, our country will deteriorate to lawlessness and immorality. Even so, it is clearly an established principle in all of America that civil government has no right to interfere in this crucial matter. The right of religious conscience overshadows any supposed right of government or the citizenry at large to ensure the well-being of the country by way of religious mandates. The end, that of national well-being, whether real or only imagined, never justifies the means of violating the natural right of freedom of religious conscience. Since government is the creature of liberty, that is, it is called into being to guarantee liberty, it becomes organized against itself when it deprives men of liberty in pursuing other ends, no matter how desirable these other ends may be (cf., Herbert, 1978, p. 63).

From this perspective all laws that mandate educational matters violate inherent inalienable rights of citizens and also violate America's philosophy of the role of government.

But civil government and its officers, while saying that parents have the final responsibility in education, nonetheless argue for and in fact have established the "right" to intervene. That argument is typically expressed in terms of either compelling state interests or balancing parental and state obligations. Court decisions expressive of these rationalizations include the following. In 1981 *Thomas* v. *Review Board*, the U.S. Supreme Court said, "The state may justify an inroad on religious liberty by showing that it is the least restrictive means of achieving some compelling state interest." Or as said in 1972 *Wisconsin* v. *Yoder*, "The essence of all that has been said or written on the subject is that only those interests of the highest order and those not otherwise served can overbalance legitimate claims to the free exercise of religion" (406 U.S. 215).

As noted above, all of these compelling interests or balancing rationalizations are based on a wrong understanding of the role of government and an erroneous belief that there are exceptions to inalienable rights. These presumptions on the part of the state are eerily similar to those offered by King George III and so many others who wanted the state supreme over the people. Even in those instances where the outcome would basically be good, as in the Reconstruction efforts after the Civil War, constitutional limitations and the inalienable rights of the citizens must not be violated. The above argument in favor of educational freedom, truly worthy to stand on its own is, even so, complemented by the acknowledgment that education is a religious function.

Education as a Religious Function

From the earlier chapter on this topic, we must conclude that all of the rights, immunities, and privileges applicable to religion are equally applicable to education. Probably the best way to make this point is to quote from Jefferson's Act for Religious Freedom:

> ...The impious presumption of legislators and rulers, civil as well as ecclesiastical, who being themselves but fallible and uninspired men, have assumed dominion over the faith of others, setting up their own opinions and modes of thinking as the only true and infallible, and as such endeavoring to impose them on others ... that to compel a man to furnish contributions of money for the propagation of opinions which he disbelieves, is sinful and tyrannical; that even the forcing him to support this or that teacher of his own religious persuasion, is to deprive him of the comfortable liberty ... to restrain the profession or propagation of principles on supposition of their ill tendency, is a dangerous fallacy ... because he being of course judge of that tendency will make his opinions the rule of judgment, and approve or condemn the sentiments of others only as they shall square with or differ from his own... (Morison, 1979, pp. 706-707).

In other words, if it is wrong for the civil government to require people to go to church, it is wrong to require them to attend school; if it is wrong to mandate religious tithing, then it is wrong to mandate taxes for education; if it is wrong to prescribe what is orthodoxy in religion, then it is equally wrong to prescribe what children shall and shall not learn or believe. Herbert notes, "Whoever fairly faces the question must admit that the same set of arguments which condemns a national religion also condemns a national system of education" (Herbert, 1978, p. 73). As Jefferson said in closing his Act, "the rights hereby asserted are of the natural rights of mankind and if any Act shall hereafter be passed to repeal the present, or to narrow its operation, such Act will be an infringement of natural right." Accordingly all the infringements in education spoken to in the former part of this paragraph that are parallel to religious infringements are infringements of natural rights.

The matter is made all the more indisputable for those who by way of religious conviction hold children's education as a divine command from their Creator. There certainly can be no argument in such cases. As an inalienable right, freedom of religious conscience must allow them to educate their children as they wish. Horace Mann in his Twelfth Annual Report said,

> But if a man is taxed to support a school, where religious doctrines are inculcated which he believes to be false, and which he believes that God condemns; then he is excluded from the school by the Divine law, at the same time that he is compelled to support it by the human law. This is a double wrong. It is politically wrong, because, if such a man educates his children at all, he must educate them elsewhere, and thus pay two taxes ... and it is religiously wrong, because he is constrained, by human power, to promote what he believes the Divine Power forbids. The principle involved in such a course is pregnant with all tyrannical consequences. (Mann, 1849, p. 118)

Again, the inalienable right of education does not withhold commensurate rights from others, and so it must not only be allowed, but it must also be promoted to all.

One final point is worthy of special note. Since education is a religiously based activity, the civil requirement to support it by taxes is, without question, a forced tithe. So when the civil government considers itself tolerant enough, in this counterfeit of intolerance, to permit parents to educate children in places other than the public school (e.g., home, religious or otherwise private), it is no great favor, so to speak. These parents are still under the wrongful but legal obligation to tithe to a system and a belief content (i.e., public education) which they do not believe. From this it should even make more sense that public education has become the religion of the U.S. just as discussed in Chapter 10.

Property Rights

The final major argument against civil government interference in education addresses a natural right that, at first glance, may even appear as irrelevant to the issue.

The property to which we refer to here is not the physical external world of which we may own by way of title or deed. It is not even the typically conceived results of one's labor as when the land is cultivated and brings forth fruit that the landowner has a right to sell as his legitimately affirmed property. It is not even that thing that Madison calls man's most sacred property, that is, his conscience (Alley, 1985, p. 77).

The property referred to here is that into which parents expend tremendous amounts of time, energy, resources, and emotions. It is that property that parents cultivate—hopefully diligently—to be able to some day enjoy the fruit of their labors. Obviously this property is their children. Just as with physical property, children are not absolute possessions of their parents. After all, neither properties depart with their owner at death.

As Madison said (1792), property is "that dominion which one man claims and exercises over the external things of the world, in exclusion of every other individual ... it embraces every thing to which a man may attach a valid and have a right; and *which leaves to everyone else the like advantage.*" For Madison, property included not only land, merchandise, and money, but also man's own opinions. He felt that man had the right to the free communication of his opinions, the safety and liberty of his person, the free use of his faculties, and free choice of the objects on which to employ them (like children). According to Madison, "In a word, as a man is said to have a right to his property, he may be equally said to have a property in his rights" (Alley, 1985, p. 76).

In the healthy, positive sense of the word, children are the property of their parents. And just as the civil government cannot demand that a property owner cultivate his land toward any certain goal, neither can it demand an educational goal for the property he has in his offspring. That would deprive the parent of his natural liberty and his natural right to his property.

By extension, if the human mind is expected to be fruitful, then it has to be properly cultivated in its development. Parents, having natural rights of property over the child, have then the right, exclusively, to guide the cultivation of the child's mind. The fruit of the child's mind eventually becomes his own, but until that time, the development of the child's mind is the rightful responsibility of the child's parent. Government has no right to develop opinion but only to serve the rightful opinions of its citizens.

So again, but now from a different natural right, civil government has no right of education over the children of its citizens. As the colonists' philosophy of government would propose, government is actually to protect the inalienable right of parents to educate their children as they consider best according to their own consciences.

In fact, reflecting on Madison's belief that conscience is the most important or sacred of all our property, this particular right of property must be honored by civil government. Parents are to be able to manage their property of conscience in educating their children. According to Madison, "that is not a just government ... where the property which a man has in his ... personal liberty, is violated by arbitrary seizures of one class of citizens for the service of the rest" (cf., Alley, 1985, p. 77). But this is exactly the state of education in our country. The personal liberty and "property rights" of parents over the education of their children is seized by the government for the supposed good of all. Instead, "a *just* government ... impartially secures to every man, whatever is his *own*" (p. 76).

Conclusion

Civil establishment of education, as symbolized by Thomas Jefferson, must be rejected as contrary to natural rights.

The contradiction in substituting an education establishment for a religious establishment was apparently not seen by Jefferson. It is no wonder—education was considered to be the prime if not the only vehicle by which the liberty of the people and thus the republican form of government could be preserved. Thus it was considered highly appropriate for government to control it. Jefferson called his education bill "the most important bill in our whole code" (Peterson, 1987, p. 151). If Jefferson did see the contradiction, he must have rationalized it as a proper means to a "sacred" end. For Jefferson, a government-endorsed and government-provided education was the only way "to guard the sacred deposit of the rights and liberties" of the citizens (cited in Peterson, 1987, p. 146). Jefferson in fact called for (in 1781) an amendment to the Virginia Constitution to ensure that the people would be equipped by way of public education to be the "safe depositors" of liberty: "An amendment to our constitution must here come to the aid of public education" (Koch & Peden, 1972, p. 265).

The contradiction is made all the more ill-founded in that for Jefferson and the other statesmen of his era, their education, which contributed so greatly to the development of republicanism, was not of this nature at all. For many of these great visionaries, their education was determined by their parents and guardians rather than by any state-controlled institution. But apparently the perceived personal responsibility of guaranteeing the success of the republican system left Jefferson with this fatal blind spot. He could not see that it was not his nor the government's responsibility to convince and to accordingly equip the people for liberty any more than it was the government's responsibility, a priori, to equip him as a young student to help usher in this grand experiment in liberty. But the experiment happened anyway and obviously not at all by chance, even without benefit of public education.

Even more sadly, the apparent contradiction is lost on many subsequent generations. For instance, the "father of public schools,"

Horace Mann, was also oblivious to this contradiction. As his chapter-opening quote indicates, he considered the legally enforced coercion of the religious opinions of children to be a sacrilege against Creator-granted inalienable rights of religious conscience. Yet, as we have documented elsewhere, Horace Mann led the way, with full civil statute backing, in proscribing applications of the Bible to school children for the so-called good of society. In our present generation, many leaders and citizens likewise believe these great myths about education (cf., Blumenfeld, 1985). In spite of opinions to the contrary, public education is not "a great democratic institution fundamental to America's prosperity and well-being," nor is it true that "society cannot survive without it" (pp. 1-2). It is instead, as already documented, a mandated religion (quite contrary to the spirit of the First Amendment), which offends the religious consciences of many parents, and which is supported by a system of forced tithes. It is an infringement of natural liberties, yet in many states it appears as a constitutional mandate.

The constitutional establishment of education is the ultimate contradiction. That is, every state of the union, without exception, guarantees freedom of religious conscience in their constitutions. The guarantee is so fundamental that a number of states (eight) closely replicate in their religious provisions the wording of the First Amendment. The guarantee is so foundationally consistent that at least 50% specifically reference God, a Supreme Being, or Creator. Yet these guarantees of freedom of religion and religious conscience are contradicted, and thus patently undone, by either constitutional or statutory provisions that provide for an alternative albeit mandated religion, i.e., education. Compulsory, state-directed education and/or educational attendance laws effect an establishment of religion contrary to the state's own constitutional guarantees for religious freedom. As absurd as it may sound, this deception has operated for too long, either by blindness or by purposeful will of at least some of the people of the states.

It is woefully all too clear why Madison considered his defeated amendment to the U.S. Constitution—"no state shall violate the equal rights of conscience"—"the most valuable on the whole list" (Koch, 1966, p. 31). It is as equally necessary, as we now see, to restrain the state as it is the federal government from violating inalienable rights, particularly in the area of education. The tyranny that King George III epitomizes has to be checked at every level of government but by the people themselves and not another governmental level.

The eloquent rallying cry of Patrick Henry—"Give me liberty or give me death"— literally did foretell the fate of many Americans. This fight to the death for full liberty has not been against just Great Britain but against all tyrants since then. Dare we betray the spirit of this mighty struggle and much sacrifice and purchase peace at "the price of chains and slavery" or instead shall the American Revolution be carried to full fruition to include educational freedom?

References

Alley, Robert S. (1985). *James Madison on religious liberty.* Buffalo, NY: Prometheus Books.

Bailyn, Bernard (1967). *The ideological origins of the American Revolution.* Cambridge, MA: The Belknap Press.

Blumenfeld, Samuel L. (1985). *Is public education necessary?* Boise, ID: The Paradigm Co.

Coffin, Charles C. (1879/1987). *The story of liberty.* Gainesville, FL: Maranatha Publ.

Coleman, James S. & Hoffer, Thomas (1987). *Public and private high schools: The impact of communities.* New York: Basic Books.

Commager, Henry Steele & Morris, Richard B. (Eds.) (1967). *The spirit of 'Seventy-Six'.* New York: Harper & Row.

Conkin, Paul K. (1974). *Self-evident truths.* Bloomington, IN: Indiana Univ. Press.

Fisher, Gene & Chambers, Glen (1981). *The Revolution myth.* Greenville, SC: Bob Jones Univ. Press, Inc.

Frothingham, Richard (1910). *The rise of the republic of the United States.* Boston, MA: Little, Brown & Co.

Gales, Joseph (Ed.) (1834). *The debates and proceedings in the Congress of the United States.* Washington, DC: Gales and Seaton.

Harrison, Maureen & Gilbert, Steve (Eds.) (1993). *Thomas Jefferson: Word for word.* LaJolla, CA: Excellent Books.

Herbert, Auberon (1978). *The right and wrong of compulsion by the state, and other essays.* Indianapolis, IN: Liberty Classics.

Howard, A.E. Dick (1968). *The road from Runnymede: Magna Carta and Constitutionalism in America.* Charlottesville, VA: The University Press of Virginia.

Jaffa, Harry V. (1978). *How to think about the American Revolution.* Durham, NC: Carolina Academic Press.

Jensen, Merrill (Ed.) (1977). *Tracts of the American Revolution 1763-1776.* Indianapolis, IN: Bobbs-Merrill Co.

Koch, Adrienne (1966). *Madison's "Advice to My Country."* Princeton, NJ: Princeton University Press.

Koch, Adrienne & Peden, William (1972). *The life and selected writings of Thomas Jefferson.* New York: Random House.

Lippmann, Walter (1928). *American inquisitors.* New York: The Macmillan Co.

Mann, Horace (1849). *Twelfth annual report of the secretary of the board of education.* Boston, MA: Dutton & Wentworth.

Mayberry, Maralee (1992). Home-based education: Parents as teachers. *Continuing Higher Education Review* 56 (1&2), 48-58.

Morison, Samuel E. (Ed.) (1979). *Sources & documents illustrating the American Revolution* (2nd Ed.). New York: Oxford Univ. Press.

Perry, Richard L. (Ed.) (1978). *Sources of our liberties.* Chicago, IL: American Bar Foundation.

Peterson, Merrill D. (1987). *Thomas Jefferson and the new nation.* Norwalk, CT: The Easton Press.

Texas Home School Coalition (1986). *Home education: Is it working?* Richardson, TX.

Webster's Ninth New Collegiate Dictionary (1986). Springfield, MA: Merriam-Webster, Inc.

Webster, Noah (1828/1967). *American dictionary of the English language.* San Francisco, CA: Foundation for American Christian Education.

Whitehead, John W. & Bird, Wendell R. (1984). *Home education and constitutional liberties.* Westchester, IL: Crossway Books.

Wright, Louis B. (1976). *Magna Carta and the tradition of liberty.* Washington, DC: United States Capitol Historical Society and the Supreme Court Historical Society.

Zukert, Michael P. (1992). *Thomas Jefferson on nature and natural rights.* In Licht, Robert A. (Ed.) *The framers and fundamental rights.* Washington, DC: The AEI Press.

Chapter 13

The Illogic Of It All!!

A general State education is a mere contrivance for molding people to be exactly like one another, and as the mould in which it casts them is that which pleases the predominant power in the government—whether this be a monarch, a priesthood, an aristocracy, or the majority of the existing generation—in proportion as it is efficient and successful, it establishes a despotism over the mind, leading by natural tendency to one over the body. (John Stuart Mill, *On liberty*, 1859/1978, pp. 104-105)

[S]o long as the State undertakes to force upon the children of any class of parents a system of education which they cannot accept without a violation of conscience and of Nature's laws, it is nothing less than the most cruel tyranny on the part of the State to make such a system compulsory. (Montgomery, 1889/1972, p. 55)

At the close of the preceding chapter, Patrick Henry's rallying cry for war rejected "chains and slavery" for either one of two options— "liberty or death." A state of slavery or despotism over mind and/or body (see quote no. 1 above) was not even considered as an option for the colonists. Yet look where we are approximately 200 years later. According to the *A Nation at Risk* report of 1983, we have allowed what Mill called "that contrivance for molding people" to reduce us to the condition where "for the first time in the history of our country, the educational skills of one generation will not surpass, will not equal, will not even approach, those of their parents." The report noted, quite unlike Patrick Henry's position, "If an unfriendly foreign power had attempted to impose on America the mediocre educational performance that exists today, we might well have viewed it as an act of war. As it stands, we have allowed this to happen to ourselves... We have, in effect, been committing an act of unthinking, unilateral educational disarmament" (p. 5).

The matter is made all the more traitorous in nature when viewed from the perspective, as explained by Horace Mann (1849, p. 117), that the public "is taxed to support schools, on the same principle that he would be taxed to defend the nation against foreign invasion, or against rapine committed by a foreign foe..." Quite contrary to the second introductory quote of Chapter 7, American society via its public school system is using its own hands to destroy itself just as an unfriendly foreign power would do.

This tyrannical act of our own government (see quote no. 2), that which we have done to ourselves, has been so successful that the American people by and large obediently take no offense at having sacrificed liberty to purchase peace at the price of chains and slavery. In fact, the prevailing mind-set is more like gratitude to our government and unending pride in the American public school system as we live oblivious to the chains of ignorance and bondage. The end result is dangerously similar to the governmental technique in Orwell's *1984*, where mind-controlled citizens were taught, successfully, to gratefully love Big Brother government even as it robbed them of their rights, liberties, and even personalities.

Given this injustice against inalienable rights, if not also the abysmal quality of educational attainments, it is indeed a mystery why Americans love and take pride in their public school system. As indicated in what has been presented thus far and as will be concluded here, the system is the embodiment of tyranny not unlike that which ultimately propelled the colonists to separate from Great Britain. A question that would be good for the reader to answer while reading this concluding chapter is, "Why do Americans hold in such high esteem a system of tyranny that keeps them in chains while promising just the opposite?"

Two tentative answers are given by Montgomery (1889/1972, p. 53). Both are equally condemning not just of our educational system but of the fruit produced by the system:

> [T]he first and most important reason we shall assign, is *ignorance*; ignorance of the true and Heaven-ordained relations between parent and child... Another reason why no remedy has been applied to this fearful malady is a long-standing, deep-seated, and constantly fomented prejudice in favor of the public-school system, which makes the politicians afraid to attack the monster lest they hurt their popularity.

According to Finn (1989, p. 19), the major obstacle is denial: "Most Americans appear to agree that the nation as a whole is experiencing some sort of educational meltdown, but simultaneously persist in believing that they and their children are doing satisfactorily." The truthfulness of any of these answers serves to reinforce the charge, stated in Chapters 3 and 12, that a government sponsored school system is not likely to teach that which threatens its own existence no matter how valid the teaching (cf., Spring, 1982).

The illogic of it all is on par with the biblical account of the Israelite worship of Moloch. The Israelites, even when commanded to the contrary, would actually sacrifice their children in fire as an offering to the Ammonite god Moloch, supposedly for their own selfish needs (cf., Leviticus 18:21). The difference now is that Americans are sacrificing their children to a different god, i.e., the public school system. The wasting of a future generation for supposed immediate benefits was just as illogical in the worship of Moloch as it is in the worship of the institution of public education. Is this an overly dramatized and unreasonable comparison? Let the reader decide as the facts are summarized below!

<u>False Promises</u>

While the nature of the arguments in this book have been primarily from a principled perspective, and rightly so, a certain but limited amount of empirical evidence is now cited to reinforce these arguments. (Even so, it needs to be said that principled living is not necessarily productive of nor primarily justified by empirical data.) A problem with yet another rehearsal of U.S. educational shortcomings is in its numbing effect and the resultant psychological denial in not wanting to hear more bad news. It does not help that this evidence appears to be contradicted by the high standard of living that so many citizens enjoy (just as Finn noted).

<u>Literacy</u>

The evidence regarding illiteracy is so disturbing that it must be acknowledged regardless of the potential to elicit denial and defensiveness. The acknowledged base-line standard for most recent improvement efforts, the *A Nation at Risk* report of 1983, prefaces its list of educational shortcomings with the shortcoming, in principle, that this country's guiding educational promise to its citizens is itself at risk:

> Part of what is at risk is the promise first made on this continent. All, regardless of race or class or economic status, are entitled to a fair chance and to the tools for developing their individual powers of mind and spirit to the utmost. This promise means that all children by virtue of their own efforts, competently guided, can hope to attain the mature and informed judgment needed to secure gainful employment and to manage their own lives, thereby serving not only their own interests but also the progress of society itself. (p. 8)
>
> Evidence cited in the report as indicators of this risk includes (pp. 8-9):

1. Some 23 million American adults are functionally illiterate...
2. Average achievement of high school students on most standardized tests is now lower than 26 years ago when Sputnik was launched.
3. The College Board's Scholastic Aptitude Tests demonstrate a virtually unbroken decline from 1963 to 1980.
4. Business and military leaders complain that they are required to spend millions of dollars on costly remedial education and training programs in such basic skills as reading, writing, spelling, and computation.
5. International comparisons of student achievement, completed a decade ago, reveal that on 19 academic tests American students were never first or second and, in comparison with other industrialized nations, were last seven times.

Ten years later (practically, one educational generation), after much purposefully concentrated effort to improve educational attainments in this country, educational evaluations continue to report bad news. In 1993, the most comprehensive study of literacy ever done on Americans (cf., *Newsweek*, 1993) revealed that nearly half of the 191 million adults in the United States are functionally illiterate. "Since 1983, more than 10 million Americans have reached the 12th grade without having learned to read at a basic level. More than 20 million have reached their senior year unable to do basic math. Almost 25 million have reached 12th grade not knowing the essentials of U.S. history" (*Policy Review*), 1998, p. 23). Study after study confirms that educational achievements are not rising. (cf., Walberg, 2001). In comparison with other countries, U.S. educational attainments are consistently low and are not getting better (cf., *Newsweek*, 1992).

The tragedy inherent to these disheartening statistics goes beyond that of a failed or unfulfilled promise. Bad as it is, the findings reflect not just a failure to attain to a promise, they are the deplorable evidence of a national betrayal, of a traitorous act.

Recall from Chapter 6 that estimates of literacy (not illiteracy) in colonial America were very high. More than one source claimed that adult male literacy was not only high (approximately 70-100%) but also better than that of most European countries. While admittedly the segment of the population sampled was more restrictive (adult males) than now (all adults) and standards of literacy may not have been as comprehensive as now, the point still remains. That is, the goal of literacy attempted back then was high, and it was attained (cf., Jacoby, 2000). Such is not the case now—standards are not attained, nor are they all that high. Currently the U.S. Department of Education reports that only 25% of America's public school children know enough to write a competent term paper (*World*, 1999). The drastic decline in performance that resulted from mandated education represents a betrayal of the American citizens by its own educational establishment. Prototypically, the mandated public education system in early Boston that illogically resulted from a mere 4% illiteracy rate (see Chapter 10) did not bring better or even comparable results but attainments far worse.

Increased Funding Benefits

The general promise or expectation repeated ad infinitum by the educational establishment is that the results will turn positive if only more funds are designated for education. Given the findings reported immediately above, suspicions should be aroused immediately upon hearing this monetary appeal. After all, the increase in and purposeful targeting of funding over the years has *not* been accompanied by increased educational attainments.

More specifically, recent studies describe a relationship between funding and achievement that argues against the granting of even more money. For instance, in 1993 the nation's largest private, bipartisan membership association of state legislators, the American Legislative Exchange Council, described the following in its state-by-state analysis of education. Over the twenty-year period of 1972-73 to 1992-93, school spending increased by 390% (47% in constant 1992 dollars), while school enrollment decreased over this same time period by 7%; over this same time period Scholastic Achievement Test (SAT) scores declined by thirty-five points. Interestingly, teacher salaries rose substantially, and pupil-teacher ratios declined in all fifty states. Regarding teacher salaries, none of five highest salaried states was among the fifteen top SAT scoring states. Conversely, four of the ten states with lowest per pupil spending were among the states with the highest SAT scores (cf., *Business/Education Insider*, October 1993, pp. 3-4). These findings regarding the lack of a positive relationship between educational funding and educational attainments in this country are evident in many similar studies. (cf. Hanushek, 2001).

Competence

The certification in the vast majority of states to the effect that the high school graduate is competent to function effectively in society is contradicted by at least two types of information. The first type is found in what external sources like business and military spokesmen are saying they must do to prepare high school graduates for entry level employment. Corporations complain of the millions of dollars they must spend to bring such graduates up to minimal competence in calculating, communicating, and even basic responsibility-taking (cf., *Business/Education Insider*, March 1990). As tragic as this information is regarding lack of preparedness, it is actually eclipsed in a negative way by the various states' own messages.

The states by and large tell the very same individuals they have certified as competent after twelve years of education that they are nonetheless assumed to lack competence to personally replicate their own preparation onto their children. And in spite of the abundance of evidence about the fruitfulness of parent-directed education, the states have their own graduates so convinced of the superiority and efficacy of governmental control of education that these graduates typically do not even see the contradiction. The logic of it all is perplexing to say the least.

On balance, it is quite reasonable that an educated person's competence may not extend to content areas not included in his or her education. For instance, an educated person is not thought of as being competent in something like airplane mechanics or quantum mechanics unless of course that person was instructed in the same, which is not usually the case in K-12 programs. But it is quite another thing to tell people who have been recipients of twelve years of teaching across general competence and citizenship areas by a goodly number and variety of teachers that they have failed to learn enough to teach their own children. Moreover, when these children are at the lower grade levels, prohibitions based on supposed lack of parental knowledge truly defies logical understanding. After twelve years of observing and receiving education, a person with enough intelligence to graduate surely has to possess at least the necessary minimum ingredients to start teaching their own children, especially where no special group management skills are needed.

This is not to argue that high school graduates are fully qualified to teach, but that they do have enough acquired understanding after twelve years of exposure to begin the activity themselves. As with most endeavors in which the high school graduate may be newly engaged, refinement naturally comes with continued application and interest.

A strong argument can even be made that the teaching of one's own children can be done short of having a high school diploma. The maturity commensurate with adulthood and the acknowledged responsibility that typically comes with being a parent—even a young parent—usually combine to offset the disadvantage of missing the final few years of schooling needed to begin teaching one's own. Again, those years that were spent in school, even without completing twelfth grade, can provide a reasonable basis from which to start teaching, particularly at the lower grade levels.

The illogic of it all is made even more obvious by the fact that parents are not excluded from teaching their children on a case-by-case basis, but all are typically denied that right as the starting position on the matter. This suggests that the central matter is not one of parental incompetence but of state sovereignty instead. It would be more reasonable for the state to identify those who somehow have graduated from high school but are still lacking, academically, than to deny the inalienable right of parenting to all graduates as a matter of policy. Furthermore, if the state really was desirous of facilitating rather than denying parental inalienable rights, there would be a proliferation of public school courses designed to aid parents-to-be in this regard.

Even so, any and all facilitative efforts such as course offerings cannot be the prerequisite for granting the inalienable right of parenting and educating one's own. In fact, by definition, an inalienable right cannot either be granted or taken away. Courses to enhance this right should never be turned into vehicles of permission, selective or universal, granted to the parent by the state. To do so would be to deny the very inalienability of this right. The issue is not at all one of competence but of a parent's inalienable right. The point here is to reveal the logical inconsistency of government policies on this matter and not at all to argue for a different way for government to stay in control.

Freedom of Religion

Government also tries to stay in control by the way it guarantees religious freedom. The federal government primarily by way of the First and Fourteenth Amendments, and the state and local governments by way of their public school statutes deny exactly what religious freedom is all about. In this way they are guilty of promoting false promises.

As documented in Chapters 5 and 8, the First Amendment was intended to prevent the federal government from either establishing a national religion or from encroaching on state establishments of religion. Now, however, this amendment is wrongly interpreted to allow the federal government to rule on matters that were supposed to be reserved exclusively to religious institutions and establishments. Instead of protecting religious interests, current interpretations of the amendment allow the federal government to discriminate against religious concerns. The U.S. Supreme Court is even guilty of using a double standard in the way it defines religion. Specifically, for conscientious objectors to war, the Court defines religion in terms of sincerely held beliefs about matters of ultimate concern. Yet in matters of education, sincerely held nonsectarian beliefs of ultimate concern are not treated as religious in nature and thus are granted privileged access into the school system. Conversely, sincerely held formal religious teachings about matters of ultimate concern are discriminatorily denied public school exposure. This blatant piece of illogic is compounded by the inescapable fact that no one can decree what qualifies as a religious belief for someone else. Yet the courts in particular continue to decide for others what is and what is not religious in nature. On top of all this is the misreading of the Fourteenth Amendment such that the federal government can supersede state practices in this matter giving the federal government a religious sovereignty that was to be prohibited (see also Chapter 11).

Even more, since education is ultimately a religious endeavor, it should be protected from encroachments at all governmental levels. Education should enjoy all the freedoms and protections promised to religions by the various federal, state, and local constitutions and statutes. Yet exactly the opposite is the norm. A promise cannot be any more unbroken, so to speak, than in this area of religious hence educational freedom. The bottom line of it all is that education should have the same relationship to government that formal religions typically enjoy. That is, just as government is to have no say over religious matters, neither should it over educational matters. Appropriateness of educational content, teacher preparation, taxation, curriculum standards, and so on should be the sole prerogative of the professionals and immediate participants (i.e., parents of children) to the process just as with religions.

Freedom of Speech

The First Amendment to the U.S. Constitution also guarantees freedom of speech to each U.S. citizen. Yet as reviewed in earlier chapters, the freedom of speech that parents should have in teaching their children is too often directly subverted by teachings of the public school system. Coons (1992) makes a cogent case that the freedom of speech that parents have regarding their children manifests itself in two different ways. The most obvious, as already alluded to above, is the right of each parent to teach, without subversive governmentally sponsored efforts to the contrary, values and morals to their children consistent with their own consciences. Yet instances abound where taxpayer-supported public schools indoctrinate children into beliefs quite the contrary to those of their parents and even deny parental teachings any voice at all.

The second and less obvious but perhaps more impactful way freedom of speech works in education is the fact that parents can have a voice in society overall by way of their children. For some, and particularly for the poor, education provides a very real if not the only way that parents can speak in the public square. Education has always been viewed as the primary ladder to success in many countries including the United States. This hope that parents have in public schools enabling their children to positively impact society for them is, because of current illiteracy rates and oppositional value systems, a broken promise.

Education for Liberty

Chapter 3 made the point that even if against his own will, the young child must be protected while in his dependent, immature state. The parent is the one to supervise this restriction of liberty to eventually make the child autonomous in the best sense of the word.

But as we have seen, the school system claims a right to subjugate the child even against the wishes of the parent. The end product of this usurpation of parental rights is a citizen who is not at liberty—even though this was the articulated and intended outcome all along. For instance, the child is told by the government what constitutes educationally legitimate religious teachings. When graduated and then a parent, this former student repetitively authorizes the government to similarly indoctrinate the next generation. Perhaps even more insidious, students as parents-to-be are also indoctrinated to believe, even if by default, that the public education system is *the* way. The student has not been set at liberty upon graduation—quite the opposite. Liberty is further deprived in that the parent must continue to pay taxes (i.e., forced tithes) to support a religious perspective officially authorized by the government. To proclaim that religious liberty exists while mandating both the educational tithe and the ultimate-concern educational content is similar to the "doubtthink" described in Orwell's *1984*—two contradictory beliefs are held and believed simultaneously.

Education as a Mature Discipline

The final broken promise to be discussed concerns the basic capability of education to even deliver on its promises. Education expert Frank Murray (1989), for instance, questions whether the discipline of education is sufficiently well developed to be able to prescribe answers to educational questions. He argues (p. 11) "that the discipline of education still is in its earliest period of development." He claims that "available theories, while useful in guiding research, are inconclusive on most vital points. No one, for example, is sure what educational mechanism moves the pupil along from one stage to another, or why schools have taken, in various times and places, one form and not another" (p. 7). According to this former college of education dean, "On the whole, few educational theories are sufficiently well-formulated to permit ... unambiguous classroom practices to be drawn from them" (p. 12).

To the degree that this representative finding (Murray is far from being alone on this perspective) truly reflects the general inability of theory to influence educational practice, that is the degree to which the American public is being deceived.

Education professionals speak as if they really do know how to successfully prescribe and therefore solve learning problems. For instance, students, especially those diagnosed as having certain disabilities, are treated with prescribed educational practices on the assumption that there is a verified and productive rationale for so doing. The public is led to believe that the professionals know, by way of research, theory, and informed-practice, that implemented educational techniques are the research-verified best choice. Yet, such is apparently not generally the case. Reflective of this problem, the National Longitudinal Transition Study (cf., Yesseldyke, Thurlow & Shriner, 1992) reported that two-thirds of the people with disabilities have not transitioned successfully to the workplace even in spite of outcomes specifically constructed to that end.

Similarly, for all the push toward Outcomes Based Education, Evans & King (1994, p. 12) report that the research that could document "its effects are fairly rare. An earlier literature review noted that existing evidence was largely perceptual, anecdotal, and small scale." Murray's admonition "to adopt a skeptical view toward the claims of educational theorists and researchers..." (1989, p. 11) is apparently well-founded. If this truly is the case, then school children would seem to be nothing more than human guinea pigs for an ongoing massive experiment in education. It is another false promise.

The truth of the matter is that the educational process in schools is more like an ongoing experiment than any systematic implementation of well-documented and research-proven techniques (cf., Joyce & Calhoun, 1996, p. 180). True, there are practices that have positive, research substantiated results (see *What Works*, 1987), but the vast majority of educational practices are not founded in prior verifications.

> "Owing to the emerging nature of the knowledge base, teacher educators cannot give their students firm prescriptions about such general administrative questions as social promotion, tracking, grouping, skipping grades, early entrance, year-round schooling, family groupings, nongraded schooling, optimal class size, school uniforms, corporal punishment, or pull-out lessons. Teacher educators cannot even give firm guidance on more fundamental educational issues such as the nonnegotiable core curriculum, the role of memorization, the dependability of specific and nonspecific transfer, bilingual instruction, portfolio assessment, and the value of IQ tests in the school and classroom" (Murray, 2001).

Overall the knowledge base for teaching teachers is unable to convert knowledge about teaching into predictable student outcomes (Donmoyer, 1996). Yet practices from these theories continue to be promoted in education. Worse, even when research data clearly shows an educational practice to be flawed or counterproductive, the practice has been promoted anyway by the education establishment (cf., Hirsch, 1996, p. 42). For instance, when a number of independent studies showed a strong correlation between sex education in schools and increased teenage pregnancies (cf., *Education Reporter*, 1986), school systems continued to adopt and implement such programs, sometimes even the exact programs linked to the problem behavior.

As stated earlier, the first line of proof for principled arguments should not be empirical evidence but logic and common sense instead. However, from the limited but highly representative data that has just been presented, it seems that the undergirding principles of public education are flawed. Methodological problems invariably point to problems in foundational assumptions and ideologies. Accordingly, we now turn to an examination of the premises that inform current educational policies, practices, and promises. They are in fact false premises.

False Premises

Public School Is the Answer

Blumenfeld (1985) claims that this belief is based on five myths or untruths. The first myth is that public education is a great democratic institution that is necessary for America's well-being. But we have already seen that for the immediate past it is not working positively for America academically, and in terms of setting people at liberty, it has worked ill for a much longer time period (cf., Klicka, 1995). Also, it is not seen as an activity in which the democratic way has or should prevail. As it is, school superintendents and boards often do not decide either by way of a majority position of the respective citizens or consistent with individual parental desires for the child, even while claiming to be democratic. Thus, while educational authority should be autocratic, it is wrongly autocratic. Parents, not other people, should be sovereign over their children.

Second, public education is seen as the great equalizer for a homogeneous America. But this is in itself a bad premise. For the good of the country and the individual, the gifted should be maximally challenged rather than equalized as is currently happening (*Business/Education Insider*, November 1993). This failure to challenge America's brightest students is recognized as a quiet but major crisis in education. The U.S. Department of Education says that "The U.S. shortage of graduate students in mathematics and science forces many large companies—such as Texas Instruments, Bell Laboratories, and IBM—to fill jobs, particularly in research, with people educated outside the United States." Conversely, the disadvantaged are supposed to be brought up to some median level. Yet report after report documents that the poor and the disadvantaged are the ones most handicapped by the system (cf., Kozol, 1991).

Third, the next myth assumes that because the U.S. spends the most money, we have the best system. As already discussed, this is obviously not the case (cf., *Business/Education Insider*, April 1990).

The fourth myth is that the neighborhood school belongs to the local community. Yet our review of court and administrative decisions tell us that government and the education establishment own the schools instead (cf., Arons, 1983).

The fifth myth is that society cannot survive without public education. Evidence presented thus far shows clearly however that achievement levels were higher in pre-public school America than now. In fact, the foundational governing documents of America were developed by those who were educated before public education as we now know it came into being. Furthermore, over just the last thirty years (1960-1990), our social well-being has declined drastically (Bennett, 1993). For instance, the percentage of illegitimate births has risen from 5.3% to 26.2%; children with single mothers increased from 8% to 22%; the teen suicide rate changed from 3.6% to 11.3%; and the violent crime rate (per 10,000) went from 16.1 to 75.8. If public schooling has anything at all to do with these tragic figures, society will not survive *with* public schools. And if public schools truly are the answer, the figures above suggest that we are asking the wrong question or believing in wrong premises or both. As organizational principles go, the system is perfectly designed to give the results we are getting.

Public Schools Are Public

It is a wrong premise to think that public schools are public. They are not. (cf. Hill, 2001) That is, a public institution is typically available to all. A public park, for instance, is where all people can freely gather even without an admission fee (although tax dollars usually support it). A public movie theater is where all people can be entertained with no other qualifications than merely the price of admission. Yet public schools tax citizens and do not permit them to freely select from among the schools in that taxing locale. In fact, with school busing arrangements designed to achieve various social, not education agendas, children are not even permitted to attend their local, neighborhood school. Furthermore, these "public" schools are antipublic when private school or home school parents may want their children to selectively attend only certain courses in their own tax-supported local schools (see Chapter 8).

Educational Content Neutrality

To assume that curriculum content is neutral or can be neutral is a false and impossible-to-achieve assumption. The dictum "There are no absolutes" actually explains it all. The dictum's denial of absolutes is itself an absolute, non-neutral statement. Its obverse, "Everything is absolute," is equally a non-neutral, absolute statement. In other words, as explained in Chapter 10, all educational content always comes from some value system which invariably has absolutes. And when this content is proclaimed as life-guiding truth (e.g., evolution, the good life, sex before marriage, the role of citizens vis a vis government) over competing ideas, it actually constitutes religious content for both the adherents and the opponents. Thus, education cannot help but be a religiously oriented activity.

Separation of Church and State

This phrase from Thomas Jefferson's letter to an oppressed religious group was his way of telling them that he could not, as chief executive of the federal government, interfere with the religious, i.e., church, establishment in Connecticut no matter how unjust because of the restrictions of the First Amendment religious provision. The "separation" phrase is similarly used now to indicate that the government must be separate from the church and thus cannot promote any religious view. While this position of neutrality is impossible to achieve, ass noted immediately above, civil government, while verbally claiming to uphold the separation, behaves in exactly contrary ways. That is, our official coins, governing documents, anthems, institutional prayers and the like do not at all separate church and state, yet schools are expressly prohibited by government, educational establishments, and court systems from engaging in the same general type of expression. The premise of our early forefathers, as reflected in their magnificent founding documents, was to protect religion from governmental hierarchy. The contemporary view, particularly in the educational arena, is that nonbelievers need to be protected from believers through direct governmental restrictive impositions on believers. This is not separation of church and state; it is an official state hierarchy over religion supported by bogus First Amendment interpretations.

First Amendment Establishment

For too long now, the Establishment Clause of the First Amendment to the U.S. Constitution has been presumed to mean that government cannot do anything to help or, in other words, to establish religion. This is a false presumption. The amendment debates, and even the grammatical structure of the clause, "Congress shall make no law respecting an establishment of religion," demonstrates it has to mean something else.

Specifically, the Establishment Clause means that Congress shall not do anything to legalize an establishment of religion, that is, a religious monopoly. It does not at all mean that religions cannot be aided or protected. The tax exempt status enjoyed by religions attests to this as just one of many such examples. And actions of early presidents and legislatures in support of various religious causes also attest to this interpretation. These are the very kinds of so-called "entanglements" that the U.S. Supreme Court erroneously claims are prohibited by the First Amendment. This so-called entanglement prohibition actually entangles the court in making decisions such that, for instance, public money can be used for busing private school children to and from school but not to and from field trip sites or that public funds can be used to buy books but not maps for private schools (see Chapter 8).

Because religion is ultimately determined by each individual, government invariably addresses and entangles itself in religion whenever it involves itself in education. But allowing or promoting religion in education is not at all the same thing as establishing a national religion. In fact, whenever any religious view is systematically excluded, its opposite is promoted; and its opposite, as the alternative, is equally a religious view. Thus, the condition of nonentanglement is not only impossible, it is not even a First Amendment prohibition. The First Amendment Establishment Clause simply prohibits one religion from being exclusively favored by the federal government.

First Amendment Free Exercise

Whether or not the free exercise of religious conscience occurs within the various states is not even an issue of the First Amendment religious provision. The free exercise clause, "nor prohibit the free exercise thereof," simply and plainly prohibits the federal government from limiting the free exercise of whatever religion, religious views, and religious establishments are authorized at the state level. In religion in general and education in particular, the federal legislature has no jurisdiction over matters of religious conscience at the state level. Religious conscience is not even mentioned in the First Amendment; what is stated is that Congress cannot interfere with the free exercise of establishments of religion. It is thus a false premise to think that the federal government, by way of the First Amendment, can decide on educational matters because of charges of unconscionable religious practices in education. No such jurisdiction is granted by the First Amendment.

Fourteenth Amendment Protection

Whatever protection of liberties the Fourteenth Amendment provides, it does not include any First Amendment provisions. The First grants no liberties; it only restricts Congress. Literally applying the First Amendment to the states would be contradictory. States would be prohibited from establishing a state religion and, at the same time, from interfering with the free exercise of these same establishments it was not supposed to establish in the first place. So when the courts rule that the First Amendment applies to the states, they are operating from a false premise.

Complaints about any and all religious practices such as prayer in public schools and the violation of the consciences of parents and/or children are not even addressable by way of the Fourteenth Amendment combined with the First Amendment's free exercise clause. The wisdom of the original intent of these amendments is seen by way of the futility of trying to depart from the original intent to satisfy everyone's religious conscience. Not only is there no such thing as religious neutrality, but religious beliefs also differ among people, even people of the same denomination. To expect that an outside authority can, by mandate, satisfy all brands and types of religious conscience is truly an impossibility. The only satisfactory option is, just as originally intended, for the federal government to respect whatever state and religious authorities claim as their prerogative in this matter of education and religion, and to not compel education hence religious beliefs for anyone. Any other position will lead to federal court judges and justices becoming priests over education as they declare what is and is not appropriate religious content.

Religious Content Defined

The U.S. Supreme Court, in the matter of conscientious objection to war-time service, officially and rightfully declared that any belief system that addresses ultimate concerns for any particular person is for that person a religious belief (see Chapter 9). In refusing to define what specific content would and would not qualify as religious, the courts in effect are properly indicating that each person must do that for themselves—no one else can do that.

Yet for all the proper liberty the court recognizes for conscientious objectors, it does just the opposite in the area of education. In education, the courts fallaciously believe they can define for parents and their children not only what is religious but what is permittedly religious for the schools. With this practice, the courts and the educational establishment have propelled America back to the era of religious persecution that in large part motivated the settlers to come to America. Then, as now, an elite group audaciously defined what religious content others should and should not believe or even be exposed to. With no new relatively unsettled land to which to migrate, Americans must now stand and insist on their Creator-given rights for true religious and hence educational freedom to prevail.

Federal Constitutional Provisions

It is a false premise of major consequence to assume the right of the federal government to be involved in education. No such constitutional provision exists (see Chapter 11)!

George Washington spoke very prophetically about the strategy of usurpation to gain federal power. While seemingly for the good of the nation, as during the Civil War Reconstruction era, unauthorized use of power will be, just as Washington said, only a short-run benefit and a long-term failure in more ways than imaginable. And until a Constitutional amendment is passed to allow federal involvement in and taxation for public education, it remains as a Constitutionally impermitted action. In this sense the U.S. Office of Education, even though a cabinet-level office, is an outlaw organization. Plainly said, there is no authority in the U.S. Constitution for education taxation or control.

Government Granted Rights

Federal, state, and local governments typically perceive themselves as granters of human rights. The First Amendment right to religious freedom at the federal level and its spawned state provisions of the same nature are generally construed to mean that these rights are granted by government. Governments are not, however, the granter but the protector of such rights that are inalienably and inherently the natural property of each adult person.

Governments are created to serve citizens and their rights, not to grant them. Thus, it is not within the provision of government to mandate education or to insist that parents educate their children a certain way. Government is instead dependent on the will of the people and has their permission to exist only as long as it works to protect their rights. The Declaration of Independence tells us it is not just the right but it is the duty of citizens to abolish governments that do not protect these inalienable rights.

Citizens Serve the State

The assumption that the civil government needs to educate its citizens so that they may become productive and law-abiding citizens, while appealing, is a falsehood. This line of reasoning by extension has citizens exist for the benefit of the state, which obviously is counter to the philosophical creed of the United States (e.g., as written in the Declaration of Independence).

The truth of the matter is that civil government is to serve its citizens and not primarily vice versa. From this perspective, there can be no validity to the argument that government should do everything it can, like educate its citizens, to perpetuate itself. The hard truth is that government is the slave of the citizens to do their bidding, not to either direct their lives or promote itself beyond the will of the people. Commissioned to guarantee to citizens their inalienable rights, the state cannot take away these rights even if it means the demise of that form of government.

Religion and Education Are Rightfully State, Not Federal, Prerogatives

One of the arguments typically voiced in the 1700s and 1800s to keep the federal government out of education (and religion) was that it was properly a state concern. It was, and is, faulty reasoning to think that inalienable rights exist at one governmental level (i.e., federal) but not at other levels (i.e., state and local). Inalienable rights such as freedom of religion and education and parental control of children are inalienable at all levels, without exception. With the growing awareness that doctrinal purity in matters of conscience could not be maintained via legal mandates, governmental control of the transmission of orthodoxy slowly diminished in fuller realization of the liberty initially sought in the settling of America. Yet the process was truncated in that the relaxing of religious mandates was purposely accompanied by a tightening of education mandates. One form of orthodoxy and the means for controlling it was substituted for another, all supposedly for the good of the country. What religion was prohibited from doing, education was fully authorized and encouraged to do.

The revolution toward full liberty needs to be reignited. That precious experiment in liberty and self-governance launched in colonial America needs to reach full expression. One of the acknowledged strengths of this country is its religious freedom. Mandated religion did not achieve this strength—quite the contrary, even at the original misgivings of those who wanted to insure religious strength via government control. This same phenomenon of freedom from governmental intermeddling is pregnantly awaited in education. It must not be aborted but allowed to come to full-term delivery. Government control is the fallacy that will abort the process.

Government Has the Right to Tax for Education

Madison's Memorial and Remonstrance" is a landmark argument for preventing government from taxing citizens to support the predominant religion no matter how "good" the religion is for the community or how much that religion is in the majority. In other words, government cannot extract a forced tithe from its citizens.

Chapter 10 documents the fact that education is ultimately a religious activity. Yet citizens are taxed at federal, state, and local levels to support these religious teachings even when parents send their children to other educational institutions, when parents sincerely object to these teachings, or when various citizens do not even have children to attend public schools. The taxing is ultimately nothing more or less than a government-mandated tithe and thus totally against federal and state guarantees of religious freedom.

Government Has the Right to Mandate Education

It was indeed a dream come true for early Americans to be able to freely attend or not attend the worship place of their choice. Mandated church attendance is thus a thing of the past—or is it?

Civil governments in America still do require a form of church attendance and support. That is, the public education system, in its teaching of government/education establishment-censored materials of ultimate issues, is, in many ways, America's church. If true religious freedom is to be a reality rather than a false belief, government mandates (at all levels) in education (at all levels) must cease. Government has no more right to mandate that children attend public schools, with its state-sanctioned teachings, than it has the right to force citizens to worship at any church, synagogue, mosque, or temple. Both education and religion provide sanctioned answers to religiously-oriented questions, i.e., questions about ultimate issues. Neither institution should be under government control.

Free Enterprise is Bad for Education

Suggestions to the educational establishment that free enterprise in education could be healthy are quickly dismissed as heretical. While public schools typically teach the many benefits of the free enterprise system in America, the establishment a priori dismisses the possibility in education. It is an assumption the system believes without proof. In fact, initial reports on the results of choice point to promising results (cf., Peterson, 2001). The anti-free enterprise stance is more like a protective reaction to the possibility of losing control than a reasoned and researched answer to an empirical question. (cf. Merrifield, 2002). For instance, in their annual meeting in 1994, the National Education Association (the nation's largest teachers' union) adamantly declared private management of public schools to be a threat to the existence of public schools and voted to boycott companies that support private education interests (*Business/Education Insider*, August/September 1994). This is in conflict with the fact that the general public wants competition in school choice and school management for the purpose of breaking the public school monopoly (*Business/Education Insider*, October 1992). It is also in conflict with the conclusion of researcher Andrew Coulson (1999, p. 193) who claims that throughout recorded educational history, a free market in education is the key to effective schools. Parenthetically, if the education establishment itself reasons in such a closed-minded fashion, how can it reasonably be expect to teach children any other way?

Religious Schools, Because They are Religious, Cannot Receive Public Tax Support

The separation of church and state concept is often used to keep public funds from going to religious schools. Yet public funds do support chapels and chaplains in the armed forces academies (places of learning), and the U.S. Supreme Court has allowed public monies to fund many causes in private religious schools (e.g., transportation to and from religious schools, purchase of textbooks and standardized tests, diagnostic services, and therapeutic and remedial services). Furthermore, private, religious, and public schools equally claim to be educating children to positive and not negative social ends. And as documented earlier, both are promoting their own presanctioned answers to religious questions. Thus, the various arguments used to deny public funds to private, religious schools are flawed. In fact, from this perspective, religion is not even the issue— it is a false premise. What does uniquely distinguish the two systems are the sources of control. Officially, the government does not control these private schools like it does the public schools; however, practically speaking, the government often does control private schools by way of curriculum, health codes, and other regulations. Could it be that the religious issue is really a smoke screen for the more power-oriented issue of who has control?

Schools Are a Marketplace of Ideas

It is not uncommon to hear the claim that public schools are a melting pot or a marketplace of ideas. It is even bragged that public schools are places where all ideas can be fully articulated and examined without prejudice and preconceived answers. The history of public school indoctrination in Chapters, 6, 7, and 8 tell a far different story. Public schools and, in fact, all schools ultimately are mechanisms of some level of indoctrination in belief. Make no mistake about it; ultimately all institutions of education provide what they consider to be right and wrong answers. Even the values-free or values-clarification approach in public schools of approximately twenty years ago provided an answer in telling students they could decide values for themselves. They were telling students the value-laded belief that overarching, transcendent values were relative and personally chosen and not absolute and external to each person's preference.

As Coons (1992) claims, the curriculum of the public schools is whatever survives its comprehensive censorship process. Worse, it is typically the case that the curriculum that survives is not determined on the basis of pedagogical needs but more a result of a political tug-of-war. What survives the public school censorship process is often that which is acceptable to special interest groups (e.g., feminists, revisionists, seniors) than that which is academically best.

Education Decisions Are Pedagogically Driven

Far too many decisions about education are made for reasons other than pedagogical appropriateness and effectiveness. The massive transfer and busing of students out of their neighborhood schools is not based primarily on creating an effective learning environment (usually just the opposite happens) but on satisfying some sociological agenda. The recently developed history curriculum that was supposed to set the standard for history competencies (cf., *Newsweek*, 1994) was wisely rejected by Congress because it was too obviously motivated by politically correct rather than educationally-based ideas. Also, a number of curriculum as already reviewed in Chapter 10 have, as their primary goal, orientations such as a socially motivated tolerance for diversity, as opposed to the learning of academic skills. The building of self-esteem independent of content competence, which is a psychological rather than educational agenda, has been a major decision orientation of the last decade. The push behind outcomes-based-education, as revealed by its guru William Spady (Spady & Marshall, 1991), has been a futuristic, reconstructionist agenda, not primarily an education skills agenda. Similarly, even the recent cry for more quality in education is at least partially motivated by the politically oriented international rank ordering of educational attainments. What should be driving educational concerns is the question of how well our students are performing in regard to the competencies needed in this country, and perhaps secondarily how other countries are doing. Lastly, as explained in Chapter 7, religiously oriented prohibitions far too often divert decision-making from education issues. Without going into more examples, the point is that far too many decisions in education are not focused on satisfying education needs but on religious, sociological, political, and psychologically based agendas.

All Students Can Learn

In its literal sense, this assumption is absolutely true. But this statement, when typically made in conjunction with educational innovations such as outcomes-based-education and mastery learning, conveys a different message. When public school superintendents and other education spokesmen make this statement, they are implying that they somehow have the magic key to unlocking the ability to learn. This also infers that up to this point, in spite of what other education spokesmen have said, they key has not been possessed.

The delusion in this statement is the implication that the public education system can cause learning to occur. The truth oft matter, however, is that learning is always occurring. The surprising amount that even newborn infants learn is typically the proud boast of every new parent. Not only that, but by age three most children have mastered the structure of their language system, worldwide, no matter how difficult, without benefit of any systematic instructional interventions.

Since learning is always occurring, the real issue for educators is in discovering how to guide learning toward the desired outcome. Yet when spokesmen proclaim that all children can learn (implying that the educators themselves cause it), announcements regarding how to pedagogically accomplish it are typically omitted. Thus the message deceptively implies a newfound level of educational intervention that somehow is rarely ever submitted to public scrutiny.

Liberty Withheld Prepares for the Exercise of Liberty

One of the acknowledged goals of K-12 education is to prepare students to be self-governed. This liberty from external governance for which students are supposedly being prepared will never fully be realized, however, because parents are not allowed full exercise of their rights over their children. Parents are told by civil authorities what content and what schools are and are not appropriate. The liberties enjoyed, even inalienable liberties, are only those that the civil authorities permit high school graduates as they become parents over their own school-aged children. Obviously, the public schools not only do not prepare for full liberty, but they are instruments of liberty deprived.

Liberty deprived rests on this nonsequitur: "We will ensure freedom to 'the people' by denying freedom to them in education, for if their education is entrusted to freedom they will remain uneducated and thus, will not be able to enjoy the blessings of freedom" (Read, 1964, p. 206).

A major outcome of the public school system is the practical manifestation of an underlying assumption that is believed by the establishment but never openly declared. That assumption is that the dignity of inalienable rights is conditioned by the views of the apostles for public education.

Dignity Denied

One of the major attributes of humans, as discussed in our early chapters, is the inborn need for dignity. Each human desires to be treated with the full respect and dignity inherent to the highest created being on earth. Included in the various dimensions of dignity are the motivations to learn, to be competent, to be responsible, and to have a proper dominion over one's environment. No one has to force-feed these desires to others—they are naturally part of what it means to be human.

The government mandate that forces children to be educated, while well intentioned, carries the underlying negative assumption that people by and large must be prodded or in other ways forced to submit to the learning process. This is a dignity-robbing assumption. Worse, it becomes a self-fulfilling prophecy.

By way of a rough analogy, mandated education is like telling the infant that he must learn the language spoken in his family. The mandate is absolutely unnecessary. The child wants to learn and learns very well with no more sophisticated parental instructional techniques than modeling, repetition, and reinforcement. While learning our first language is likely the most difficult learning task we encounter, with the exception of people with disabilities, all learn it well, without trained language teachers, quickly, and without possession of extensive content prerequisites or systematic learning experiences. In fact, to somehow structure the child's environment as if learning could not otherwise occur is to communicate the expectation of inability that will forever plague the child and feed on itself like an unrealistic fear or paranoia. This dignity-robbing phenomenon surfaces in several different ways.

Demeaned Parents

It is a general truth to say that America wants parents to be honored in the eyes of their children. In fact, it is known that the absence of such respect co-occurs with the breakdown of the family and then, in turn, of the society. Yet at about the age of six, and every year thereafter, those in governmental authority communicate to children that parents are not to be trusted. Even when certified as competent to function in society, parents are still branded as suspiciously unable to rear their own children. The message to children from those who self-promote that they best know how to teach children, is that strangers are better teachers and better judges of what is right for the children than the parents themselves (cf., Coons, 1992).

It is not uncommon, for instance, for the education establishment to demand more of home schooling parents, in terms of qualifications and student performance, than it expects of public schools in general.

Parents Incapable of Learning

With the establishment's message that strangers are better able to raise children than are parents, children also learn that parents are incapable of being taught how to raise and teach their children. Children learn that the school can teach math, science, automobile driving, sex, and so on to those who are not yet respectively competent but that somehow the teaching of parenting is not worth the effort. Instead, someone else is taught how to teach children. Yet these certified teachers, if parents themselves, often must, in turn, request permission to teach their own child at home.

Obviously, the issue is not one of competence but of control and permission. At any rate, parental dignity is not the goal sought and most certainly not the goal achieved.

Dependence Developer

Messages heard often enough become part of our cognitive framework—even messages heard by implication rather than by explicit articulation.

The unspoken message constantly communicated to the American public is that without government intervention, the people would not be either literate or responsible. But, thank goodness, government is kind enough to force us to do what we either do not want to do or cannot do so that we can be saved from ourselves. Eventually this message is believed—that is, government has been successful in teaching the citizenry that they are otherwise educationally helpless. Naturally, government becomes, in the eyes of its citizens, the benevolent parent it wants to be. Citizens, then, are happy to receive what liberties government allows and likewise consent when liberties, like freedom of education, are withheld supposedly for their own good.

Tragically, these tyrannical outcomes, symbolized in our opening allegory (i.e., The Setting) and described throughout, were anticipated much earlier (mid-1800s) by social commentator Alexis de Tocqueville (Mayer, 1969). While positively disposed to the democratic nature of American society, he feared the possibility of internal threat far different "from anything there has ever been in the world before" (p. 691). His prophetic fear was that individuals would increasingly be robbed of free will choices by a government intent on keeping them in perpetual childhood as opposed to allowing them to mature into self-governing citizens. By making the exercise of free choice less and less useful and increasingly rare, this paternalistic government would predispose citizens "to endure it and often even regard it as beneficial" (p. 692), which is in large part exactly the public's reaction to the lack of both choice and parental authority in education today. By not breaking but by softening and bending the will, "this brand of orderly, gentle, peaceful slavery" would reduce citizens to "no more than a flock of timid and hardworking animals with the government as its shepherd" (p. 692).

While loss of dignity is definitely a negative consequence, it is only one manifestation of the more inclusive principle described next.

Sowing and Reaping

The larger principle called into action through government control of education is that which we will call sowing and reaping. Whatever is sown in this regard is reaped. For instance, where the government sows distrust, it breeds distrust. When the ruling hierarchy distrusts certain people, like the poor, by closing out their educational options while other economic classes are not so restricted from alternative schools, the distrusted class soon distrusts both the other classes and the education establishment itself. The various divisions of people that are treated differentially soon distrust each other. Additionally, these varying groups then battle each other to gain influence and even control of the establishment to work it to their own parochial interests, and so the cycle continues.

The examples could go on. But most importantly, the frustration on the part of the education establishment about citizens' dependence predictably is brought about by treating the citizens as if they are necessarily dependent. With this foreordination by the education establishment that it cannot remediate all of society's shortcomings, it in turn invites frustrations of the citizens with the establishment. Similarly, the government does not deal with the supposed problem of parental incompetence but treats the symptoms and consequences of parental dysfunction, i.e., the child's lack of education, by teaching the child instead of the parent practically everything except how to parent. The model is thus set for citizens to follow. That is, citizens by and large focus only on the symptomatic shortcomings of the educational system instead of dealing with the underlying problem of usurpation of parental rights.

Beyond a principled objection to deprived parental rights, the phenomenon that might be labeled "family paradox" speaks to a subtle pragmatic injustice in this regard. The basis of this paradox is the durable finding that family environment is correlated far more significantly with student academic achievement than the child's school (cf. Hoxby, 2001). The consistency and magnitude of these findings lead rather easily to the conclusion that family environment rather than the school is the predominant influence on a student's academic performance. The paradox is in the typical way that the educational establishment acknowledges the high importance of family influence. That is, one would suppose that the establishment would try to fit itself to the already potent family dynamic hoping to compliment, supplement, or in other ways support an obviously highly significant influence. Yet, in an attempt to make the influence of the family its own, the establishment tries to induce at least a minimal level of parental involvement as if the unique parent/family dynamic is directly transportable into an entirely different human relationship environment. This co-opting of the obviously superior influence of the family over the school certainly seems self-serving of the institution of formal education. Enhancing and undergirding rather than manipulating the family dynamic would seemingly be the highest goal of an educational system sponsored by a government intent on preserving a nation's freedom. Planting and sowing rather than uprooting seeds of family sovereignty in education would undoubtedly bear fruit in families, education, and the nation.

Finally, it is good to be reminded of George Washington's warning about the fruits of usurpation. Specifically, while the effect of usurpation for the supposed good of the country will likely bring short-term benefits, the long-term results will be in the form of an evil that has the power to destroy a free government. Could the fruit we see about us regarding both education and social failures be the consequence of which Washington warned?

Conclusion

The tyranny against inalienable rights through government involvement in education is summarized chapter by chapter as follows.

By their nature, the basic rights of equality and liberty, as discussed in Chapter 1, prohibit the deprivation of equal rights of others. In fact, the only real way to safeguard one's own rights is to help defeat the first attempt at robbing others of their rights. No one, elected official or otherwise, thus has the right to deprive others of what he would claim for himself or what is by right an inalienable possession. Among those rights that are inalienable is the right to educate or to govern the education of one's own children.

Furthermore, inalienable rights are not to be construed as a license to do whatever one wishes. The Creator who bestowed these rights on mankind holds mankind responsible for their faithful usage. And it is the conscience that serves as the internal agent of accountability in this regard. True happiness and dignity comes from following the conscience-led urgings of the Creator, as Chapter 2 revealed.

Educational policy based on these principles of equality, liberty, and godly conscience would protect inalienable rights and would by design result in optimum realization of both dignity and competence. As affirmed by the principles embodied in the Declaration of Independence, official education policies that violate inalienable rights are sufficient cause to change government. Government, after all, is created by the citizens for the protection of their inalienable rights. Governmental deprivation of inalienable rights, including that of parental sovereignty, are sufficient cause and, in fact, provoke the necessary duty (also an inalienable right) of citizens to alter the government for the purpose of restoring these rights.

Chapter 3 made explicit the inalienable right of parents, not government, over children. Included in the right or duty to raise children is the equipping of them with both the knowledge of their inalienable rights and the skills to know when they are being deprived and how to remedy their deprivation.

The examination in Chapter 4 of America's governing documents, and particularly the First Amendment to the U.S. Constitution, confirms that this country had a decidedly religious foundation. Thankfully, the progress of U.S. history places religious liberty in a good perspective. As religion and morality were perceived necessary to the future success of this country, each person was to be free to follow the religious conviction of personal conscience. In that chapter, the foundation was laid for fully understanding how the First Amendment is now wrongly interpreted and, also, the pattern was set for conceptualizing how the other activity crucial to America's future, i.e., education, should similarly be governed.

The evidence of Chapter 5 speaks strongly against the prevailing contemporary interpretation of the First (and the Fourteenth) Amendment and proves that Congress interferes with religion when it interacts with education. The original intent of the First Amendment was to prohibit the federal government from establishing a national religion and from adversely interfering with religion. With these restrictions, religion was to be protected, not inhibited. Further, since the First Amendment is not specifically a grant of religions freedom but more properly a restriction on Congress, it addresses no liberty as mentioned in the Fourteenth Amendment and hence does not transfer to the states. Religion, and more specifically religious influences in education, are entirely out of the reach of First Amendment provisions. Federal courts accordingly have no First or Fourteenth Amendment jurisdiction in these matters of religion in education.

Chapters 6, 7 and 8 examined the history in the United States of three different thrusts in education. That is, education has been seen both as and as not a religious activity but invariably treated as religious by governmental mandates.

After Chapter 9 clarifies that religious beliefs are best thought of as functional and personal in nature, Chapter 10 proposes that education is invariably a religious activity. The coupling of two primary truisms—that religious beliefs are those that address issues of ultimate concern and that they can only be defined by each person for him/herself and by no other—when considered with the fact that education ultimately addresses ultimate matters, makes education inescapably a religious activity. Thus education must enjoy the same status vis a vis government as religion—that is, no mandating of it and no taxing to support it.

Since education is a religious activity, it must, by federal, state, and local statutes, be separated from governmental control. Accordingly, Chapter 11 confirms the unity of this principle by documenting the fact that there is purposely and absolutely no constitutional authority for the federal government to be involved in education. The federal government is currently involved only by way of usurped power, and thus its involvement is illegal and must be disempowered.

State and local involvement in education, seen in Chapter 12 as parallel to early official government establishments of religion, awaits a similar disestablishment. Whereas federal involvement violates constitutional provisions, state and local involvement likewise violates natural rights and must be disallowed.

The conclusion is that with the disbarment of governmental powers in education, parental sovereignty can be rightly restored to its proper role in educational matters.

Recommendations

Recommendations past this point from the author are minimal. It would be presumptuous to tell parents and citizens at large how to reorganize education in their exercise of freedom of education. Surely the United States with all its notable accomplishments can similarly effect an education revolution without another expressed mandate.

The best guidance would seem to be to follow the initial lead to Roger Williams. He unreservedly saw education as a religious activity that deserved to be out from under governmental control. "The *Civil State* and *Magistrate* are merely and *essentially civil*, and therefore can not reach (without transgressing the bounds of civility) to judge in matters *spiritual*, which are of another *sphere* and *nature* than *civility* is" (Cobb, 1968, p. 426). The ideal, not always the practice, in this country of keeping government out of the control of religion while at the same time protecting religious freedom is the same way that government should relate to education matters. Accordingly, the current trend towards vouchers, charter schools, and the like are not the answer. These various mechanisms all continue government in the business of collecting tithes and determining religious practices in education. Instead, tax dollars spent on each public school child should never be collected in the first place. This would mean in 1999, for instance, that the approximately 393 billion dollar expenditure for elementary and secondary public education that averages approximately $6,548 per student could be retained by the citizens (*Statistical Abstract of the United States*, 1999, pp. 166 & 182). This would amount to approximately $3,386 annually per individual taxpayer (p. 347). Even where citizens may want the government to educate their children, attendance should never be mandated, and funding for the same should never be asked of non-attending families. After all, if the law takes from some what they own and gives to others to whom it does not belong, it has committed what Bastiat (1950/1850) calls 'legal plunder.'

To those who raise the objection that there will be some parents who do not take their educational responsibilities seriously, this is really a straw-man objection. The vast majority of parents do want better for their children than they had. In the words of Marva Collins (1979), the founder, principal, and teacher in her own inner-city, ghetto-based school, "I have not seen a parent yet who wants their children to fail." But even where the objection may be true, it is no reason to deprive all parents of their inalienable rights. The problem, not the symptom, should be the focus of action (cf., Morgan, 1997).

In closing, reference is made once again to the two pronouncements that guided a lot of thinking in this book and that were pivotal in the American Revolution—the U.S. Declaration of Independence and the First Amendment to the U.S. Constitution. On close analysis, both expressions are seen as incomplete in their official form. That is, the Declaration of Independence declares all men (generically referenced) to be equal and deserving of liberty, yet, for political expediency, Jefferson's original inclusion of liberty for the black man was omitted from the final official document (see Chapter 2). Similarly, the incompleteness of another liberty, i.e., religious liberty, is reflected in the free exercise clause of the First Amendment. This clause specifically allows for whatever religious practices and hence religious injustices to exist at the state level, again for political expediency. In both cases, the only way these measures would have most likely passed a vote of the states was to not attack what was prevalent in many of the states. As declared in Chapter 12, the American Revolution is thus not complete.

Regarding the deficiency of the Declaration of Independence, four score and seven years later Lincoln completed the American Revolution in human liberty by declaring the black man to be free by way of the Emancipation Proclamation. Yet the revolution in full religious and, by extension, full educational freedom awaits its own proclamation. May this book be a humble step in that direction.

Madison's statement about the injustice of religious persecution in his own home state appropriate closes our account of tyranny in education: "... I have squabbled and scolded, abused and ridiculed so long about it ... that I am without common patience ... praying for Liberty of Conscience..."

THE END

References

A Nation at Risk (1983). Washington, DC: National Commission on Excellence in Education.

Arons, Stephen (1983). *Compelling belief.* New York: McGraw-Hill Book Co.

Bastiat, Frederic (1850/1950). *The law.* Irvington-on-Hudson, NY: Foundation for Economic Education, Inc.

Bennett, William J. (1993). *The Index of Leading Cultural Indicators.* Washington, DC: The Heritage Foundation and Empower America.

Blumenfeld, Samuel L. (1985). *Is public education necessary?* Boise, ID: The Paradigm Co.

Business/Education Insider (March 1990). Help wanted: Employees with basic skills. Washington, DC: The Heritage Foundation, p. 2.

Business/Education Insider (April 1990). The U.S. *does* spend more internationally. Washington, DC: The Heritage Foundation, p. 2.

Business/Education Insider (October 1992). Public backs competition in education. Washington, DC: The Heritage Foundation, p. 4.

Business/Education Insider (October 1993). Once again, spending isn't everything. Washington, DC: The Heritage Foundation, p. 3.

Business/Education Insider (November 1993). The quiet crisis: Schools fail America's brightest. Washington, DC: The Heritage Foundation, p. 3.

Business/Education Insider (August/September 1994). National Education Association holds annual convention. Washington, DC: The Heritage Foundation, p. 3.

Cobb, Sanford H. (1968). *The rise of religious liberty in America.* New York: Cooper Square Publishers, Inc.

Collins, Marva. *Marva* (16mm film). (1979). Carousel Films, Inc.

Coons, John E. (April 1992). School choice as simple justice. *First Things,* 15-22.

Coulson, Andrew J. (1999). *Market education: An unknown history.* New Brunswick: Transaction Publishers.

Donmoyer, Robert (1996). The concept of a knowledge base. In Murray, Frank B. (Ed.), *The teacher educator's handbook.* San

Francisco, CA: Jossey-Bass.

Education Reporter (1986). New study: Government-funded birth control, sex ed lead to increase in teenage pregnancies, August, p. 2.

Evans, Karen M. & King, Jean A. (1994). Research on OBE: what we know and don't know. *Educational Leadership,* 12-17.

Finn, Chester E., Jr. (1989). A nation still at risk. *Commentary,* May, pp. 17-23.

Hanushek, Eric A. (2001). Spending on schools. In Moe, Terry M. (Ed.), *A primer on America's schools.* Stanford, CA: Hoover Institution Press.

Hill, Paul T. (2001). What is public school education? In Moe, Terry M. (Ed.), *A primer on America's schools.* Stanford, CA: Hoover Institution Press.

Hirsch, E. Donald, Jr. (1996). Reality's revenge: Research and ideology. *American Education,* 4-46.

Hoxby, Caroline M. (2001). If families matter most, where do schools come in? In Moe, Terry M. (Ed.), *A primer on America's schools.* Stanford, CA: Hoover Institution Press.

Jacoby, Jeff (2000). Testing the limits. *Virginian Pilot,* July 2, pp. J1, J2.

Joyce, Bruce & Calhoun, Emily (Eds.) (1996). *Learning experiences in school renewal.* Eugene, OR: Clearinghouse on Educational Management, University of Oregon.

Klicka, Christopher J. (1995). *Home schooling: The right choice.* Sisters, OR: Loyal Publishing.

Kozol, Jonathan (1991). *Savage inequalities.* New York: Crown Publishers.

Lippmann, Walter (1973). *An inquiry into the principles of the Good Society.* Westport, CT: Greenwood Press.

Mann, Horace (1849). *Twelfth annual report of the Secretary of the Board.* Boston, MA: Dutton & Wentworth.

Mayer, Jacob P. (Ed.) (1969). Alexis de Tocqueville—*Democracy in America.* Garden City, NY: Doubleday & Co.

Merrifield, John (2002). *School choices: True and false.* Oakland, CA: The Independent Institute.

Montgomery, Zach. (1889/1972). *The school question.* New York:

Arno Press & The New York Times.

Morgan, Kerry L. (1997). *Real choice real freedom.* Lanham, MD: University Press of America.

Murray, Frank B. (1989). Explanations in education. In Reynolds, Maynard (Ed.) *Knowledge base for the beginning teacher.* New York: Pergamon Press.

Murray, Frank B. (2001). The overreliance of accreditors on consensus standards. *Journal of Teacher Education, 52* (3), 211-222.

Newsweek (1994). Red, white—and blue. November 7, p. 54.

Newsweek (February 17, 1992). An 'F' in world competition, p. 57.

Newsweek (September 29, 1993). Dumber than we thought, pp. 44-45.

Orwell, George (1949). *1984.* New York: New American Library.

Peterson, Paul E. (2001). Choice in American education. In Moe, Terry M. (Ed.), *A primer on America's schools.* Stanford, CA: Hoover Institution Press.

Policy Review (1998). *A nation still at risk..* July-August, 23-29.

Rapaport, Elizabeth (Ed.) (1978). John Stuart Mill: *On liberty.* Indianapolis, IN: Hackett Publ.

Read, Leonard E. (1964). *Anything that's peaceful.* Irvington-on-Hudson, NY: The Foundation for Economic Education, Inc.

Spady, William G. & Marshall, Kit J. (1991). Beyond traditional outcome-based education. *Educational Leadership*, October, 67-72.

Spring, Joel (1982). The evolving political structure of American schooling. In Everhart, Robert B. (Ed.) *The public school monopoly.* Cambridge, MA: Ballinger Publ. Co.

Statistical Abstract of the United States (1994). Washington, DC: U.S. Bureau of the Census.

The Holy Bible, NIV (1985). Grand Rapids, MI: Zondervan Bible Publishers.

Walberg, Herbert J. (2001). Achievement in American schools. In Moe, Terry M. (Ed.), *A primer on America's schools.* Stanford, CA: Hoover Institution Press.

What works: Research about teaching and learning (1987). Washington, DC: U.S. Department of Education.

World (1999). A 25 percent shame. October 16, p. 12.

Yesseldyke, James E., Thurlow, Martha L. & Shriner, James G. (1992). Outcomes are for special educators too. *Teaching Exceptional Children*, 25(1) 36-50.

Printed in the United States
30137LVS00001B/118-123

9 781594 675430